Anthony C. Thiselton is Emeritus Professor of Christian Theology in the University of Nottingham, and Emeritus Canon Theologian of Leicester and Southwell & Nottingham. He has written 22 books, and is a Fellow of the British Academy. His commentaries include the Greek text of 1 Corinthians (2000); an English commentary on 1 Corinthians (2006); 1 and 2 Thessalonians (2011); and Hebrews (2003). His theological works include *The SPCK Dictionary of Theology and Hermeneutics* (2015 with a different American title); *The Holy Spirit* (2013); *The Hermeneutics of Doctrine* (2007); *Thiselton on Hermeneutics* (2006); *Hermeneutics* (2009); *The Last Things* (2012); and *The Living Paul* (2009). He has received four doctorates.

T0341760

Discovering Biblical Texts

Content, interpretation, reception

Comprehensive, up-to-date and student-friendly introductions to the books of the Bible: their structure, content, theological concerns, key interpretative debates and historical reception.

Also available:

Ian Boxall, *Discovering Matthew* (2014)
Ruth B. Edwards, *Discovering John* (second edition, 2014)
Iain Provan, *Discovering Genesis* (2015)

'Thiselton has provided perhaps the easiest and quickest access to the issues in the letter to Romans and to the relevant scholarship and trends concerning the letter. Few people have the ability to demonstrate the contribution and relevance of the tradition of Romans interpreters throughout the Church's history in the way Thiselton can.'

Klyne Snodgrass, Emeritus Professor of New Testament
North Park Theological Seminary, Illinois

'The grand British commentary tradition is alive and well with this commentary on Romans by Anthony Thiselton. But this commentary is more than just another one on the book of Romans. Thiselton brings his unique perspectives and interests to this central Pauline book. HIs several introductory chapters provide useful insights into various strategies for interpreting Romans and how this has affected its reception history. These chapters set the stage well for a commentary full of provocative exegetical and theological insights.'

Stanley E. Porter, President and Dean, Professor of New Testament
and Roy A. Hope Chair in Christian Worldview, McMaster
Divinity College, Ontario, Canada

'*Discovering Romans* is a highly accessible guide to both the biblical book itself and a wealth of secondary literature about it. The introduction is particularly notable for the ways in which Thiselton applies some of his other areas of expertise to the task of exploring Romans: we find a distillation of years of hermeneutical scholarship, as well as particular insight into the ways in which this letter – written from Corinth – relates to the Corinthian correspondence. The commentary section displays exegetical finesse, theological insight and pastoral warmth. One of the distinctive strengths of this volume is Thiselton's careful engagement with a variety of historical and recent interpreters, providing a senior scholar's reliable guidance amid a host of influential views. This is an enjoyable and rewarding work for all those who wish to explore the apostle Paul's most influential letter.'

Matthew Malcolm, editor of *Horizons in Hermeneutics* and
The Future of Biblical Interpretation

'Demonstrating once more the erudition, the clarity of expression and the rich insight that have characterized the whole of his academic career, Anthony Thiselton here provides an accessible and engaging guide to Paul's great epistle to the Romans and to the ways it has been read through the course of Christian history. We are left in no doubt of the profound contribution Paul has made to Christian reflection upon our relationships with one another and with God.'

Murray Rae, Professor of Theology and Religion
University of Otago, New Zealand

'If only more biblical commentary would bring together, as Thiselton does, good scholarship, deep theology, wisdom drawn from the way the text has been read down the centuries, and alertness to the issues that occupy us today! It is a major achievement to do this with Romans, and Thiselton's rich, multifaceted engagement with Paul's most influential letter is a tour de force.'

David F. Ford, Regius Professor of Divinity
Selwyn College, University of Cambridge

'To those puzzled by terms like reception history and arguments about "the new Paul", *Discovering Romans* is – to quote Maimonides – a "Guide for the Perplexed". To those who want to understand what Paul was driving at and why he wrote in the way that he did, Anthony Thiselton's book is without equal.'

Colin Brown, Senior Professor of Systematic Theology
Fuller Theological Seminary, California

DISCOVERING ROMANS

Content, interpretation, reception

ANTHONY C. THISELTON

First published in Great Britain in 2016

Society for Promoting Christian Knowledge
36 Causton Street
London SW1P 4ST
www.spck.org.uk

British Library Cataloguing-in-Publication Data
A catalogue record for this book is available from the British Library

ISBN 978–0–281–07376–4
eBook ISBN 978–0–281–07377–1

Typeset by Graphicraft Limited, Hong Kong
First printed in Great Britain by Ashford Colour Press
Subsequently digitally printed in Great Britain

eBook by Graphicraft Limited, Hong Kong

Produced on paper from sustainable forests

To Rosemary, fellow worker for the gospel

Contents

Contents

Preface

Having published with SPCK and Eerdmans before, I was delighted and honoured to receive an invitation from Mr Philip Law of SPCK to write on Romans. In earlier years I had lectured on Romans as a set text, and the opportunity to update my work with reference to the half-dozen major commentaries which had appeared since then was more than appealing. I had produced commentaries on 1 Corinthians, 1 and 2 Thessalonians and Hebrews, but Romans presented an outstanding challenge to appreciate anew God's purposes for world history, and for the daily life of the Christian.

The series, Discovering Biblical Texts: Content, Interpretation, Reception, spoke at once to my immediate interests. In addition to discussing the content of Romans with students and writing on Paul, I had written twice on reception history, and produced six books on hermeneutics or interpretation. In Chapters 2 and 3 of the present book, I have set out 12 such methods. Three of them remain essential, and nine remain useful for limited purposes. Although this series is not designed for Greek specialists, some reference to Greek is indispensable for Romans. I have transliterated all Greek words into English letters, and carefully explained the meaning of those Greek words and occasionally syntax which are absolutely necessary for non-Greek readers.

I have tried not to use a bewildering variety of names, but since this series requires an account of diverse views, I have included references to the most influential commentators. I have referred mainly, but not exclusively, to English-speaking writers. The names of Dunn, Cranfield, Fitzmyer, Wright and Jewett crop up so frequently that it would be pointless to index every reference. On the other hand many more, including Barrett, Nygren, Käsemann and Ziesler, are listed in the Index, together with others.

Of all those to whom I owe a debt of gratitude, my wife, Rosemary, must come top of the list. She has typed virtually all of my handwriting, advised me when my style became obscure, and helped with the compiling of the index of modern authors. I am also grateful to Mr Philip Law of SPCK and Mr Jon Pott of Eerdmans for their encouragement.

Anthony C. Thiselton, FBA
Emeritus Professor of Christian Theology, University of Nottingham

Abbreviations

AB	Anchor Bible
ANF	*The Ante-Nicene Fathers: Translation of the Writings of the Fathers Down to A.D. 325* (Grand Rapids: Eerdmans, 1956–62 [1885–96])
ANRW	*Aufstieg und Niedergang der römischen Welt: Geschichte und Kultur Roms im Spiegel der neueren Forschung*, ed. H. Temporini and W. Haase (Berlin, 1972–)
AV/KGB	Authorized Version/King James Bible
BDAG	W. Bauer, F. W. Danker, W. F. Arndt and F. W. Gingrich, *A Greek-English Lexicon of the New Testament and Other Early Christian Literature* (Chicago: University of Chicago Press, 3rd edn, 2000)
BDB	F. Brown, S. R. Driver and C. A. Briggs, *Hebrew and English Lexicon of the Old Testament* (Lafayette, IN: Associated Publishers, 1980)
BI	*Biblical Interpretation*
BZNW	Beihefte zur Zeitschrift für die neutestamentliche Wissenschaft
CBQ	*Catholic Biblical Quarterly*
EKKNT	Evangelisch-katholischer Kommentar zum Neuen Testament
EQ	*Evangelical Quarterly*
ExGrT	*Expositor's Greek Testament*
FRLANT	Forschungen zur Religion und Literatur des Alten und Neuen Testaments
HTR	*Harvard Theological Review*
IB	*Interpreter's Bible*
ICC	International Critical Commentary
Int	*Interpretation*
JAC	Jahrbuch für Antike und Christentum
JB	Jerusalem Bible
JBL	*Journal of Biblical Literature*
JCE	*Journal of Christian Education*
JPT	*Journal of Pentecostal Theology*
JRH	*Journal of Religious History*
JSNT	*Journal for the Study of the New Testament*

JSNTMS	Journal for the Study of the New Testament Monograph Series
JSNTSup	Journal for the Study of the New Testament: Supplement Series
JSOT	*Journal for the Study of the Old Testament*
JTS	*Journal of Theological Studies*
LCC	Library of Christian Classics
LCL	Loeb Classical Library
LXX	Septuagint
NCB	New Century Bible
NEB	New English Bible
NIB	*New Interpreter's Bible*
NICNT	New International Commentary on the New Testament
NIGTC	New International Greek Testament Commentary
NIV	New International Version
NJB	New Jerusalem Bible
NovTSup	Novum Testamentum: Supplement Series
NPNF	*Library of Nicene and Post-Nicene Fathers of the Christian Church*, ed. Philip Schaff (ser. i, 14 vols); ed. Philip Schaff with Henry Wace (ser. ii, 14 vols, Edinburgh: T & T Clark; repr. Grand Rapids: Eerdmans, 1991–)
NRSV	New Revised Standard Version
NTS	*New Testament Studies*
PG	Patrologiae cursus completus: Series Graeca, ed. Jacques-Paul Migne (Paris: Garnier, 1844–65) (known as Patrologia Graeca)
PL	Patrologiae cursus completus: Series Latina, ed. Jacques-Paul Migne (Paris: Garnier, 1844–65) (known as Patrologia Latina)
REB	Revised English Bible
RSV	Revised Standard Version
RV	Revised Version
SBLDS	Society of Biblical Literature Dissertation Series
SBT	Studies in Biblical Theology
SJT	*Scottish Journal of Theology*
SNTSMS	Society for New Testament Studies Monograph Series
TDNT	*Theological Dictionary of the New Testament*, ed. G. Kittel and G. Friedrich (10 vols, Grand Rapids, Eerdmans, 1964–76)
TDOT	*Theological Dictionary of the Old Testament*, ed. G. J. Botterweck and H. Ringgren (15 vols, Grand Rapids: Eerdmans, 1974–)
UBS	United Bible Societies
WBC	Word Biblical Commentary
WUNT	Wissenschaftliche Untersuchungen zum Neuen Testament

1

Why read Romans? Eight brief reasons

Why is it important to read and even to reread Romans today? We suggest eight reasons. To understand these reasons also helps us to appreciate the sequence of Paul's argument in Romans, which we shall later trace chapter by chapter.

(1) In Romans 1.15 Paul writes of his 'eagerness to proclaim the gospel to you'. After his demanding travels, and his earlier letters to the churches of Thessalonica, Galatia and Corinth, he has for the first time the opportunity for *mature reflection*, and longs to present a rounded, more balanced picture of the gospel. It is common knowledge that in this epistle Paul elaborates some of his central themes with more balance and careful reflection than in Galatians. Two distinctive marks of this commentary are also to show (i) how closely Paul articulates in Romans the problems which he expounded in 1 Corinthians, and (ii) how he relates them to wider theological issues, many of which feature in theology today. In Romans he does this more widely and universally, even relating the gospel to the whole of humankind, as is clear from the fifth chapter.

(2) Paul's ultimate aim is also a *missionary* one. In Romans 15.19–24 Paul explains that this proclamation of the gospel of Jesus Christ serves a special purpose. He wants to proclaim the gospel 'not where Christ has *already* been named' (v. 20). He states that he has in effect completed his mission to the eastern regions of the Roman Empire, and now looks in eagerness and expectancy to the lands of the west, especially 'when I go to Spain' (v. 24), and 'set out by way of you to Spain' (v. 28). Robert Jewett argues convincingly that since most people in Spain were Latin-speakers, who did not speak Greek, Paul wants the church at Rome to constitute a missionary group themselves, under the leadership of Phoebe, the deacon from Cenchreae. He hopes for confidence that the Imperial City will provide a network of Latin-speaking friends and sympathizers, who will constitute a base of not only prayer and friendship, but also administrative capacities, knowledge of provincial government, and financial resources, to make possible this mission to the western Mediterranean.[1] We discuss this reconstruction in due course.

---

[1] Jewett, Robert, *Romans: A Commentary* (Minneapolis: Fortress, 2007; Hermeneia), pp. 87–91.

It is an added bonus that virtually no serious scholar doubts that Paul the apostle wrote Romans. The authorship of Romans is authentic. Robinson declared, 'The author, occasion, and date of the Epistle are fortunately all beyond serious dispute. There is general agreement that it was written by the apostle Paul to Rome, almost certainly from Corinth.'[2] The date would have probably been between the winter of AD 56 and very early in AD 57, at most some three years after the writing of 1 Corinthians. Gaius (1 Cor. 1.14) was his host (Rom. 16.23). Any possible doubts apply only to the authorship of chapters 15 and 16, which we discuss later.

(3) The particular focus of Paul's gospel lies on the *grace, or free generosity, of God*, and thereby mirrors precisely the teaching of Jesus. What usually stays in the mind from the Gospels is the teaching of Jesus, often through parables, concerning the love and forgiveness of God, especially, for example, in the Parable of the Prodigal Son (Luke 15.11–32). This son 'was lost and has been found' (15.32), just as earlier in the chapter the Lost Coin and the Lost Sheep were restored 'home', or to where they belonged, from their condition of being lost. Jesus no less taught God's 'free of charge' grace, or freely given grace, in the Parable of the Labourers in the Vineyard (where grace in the end trumps supposed justice, Matt. 20.1–16), and the Parable of the Tax-collector and the Pharisee, in which the tax-collector finds God's welcome, and elsewhere (Luke 18.9–14). *Paul's gospel in Romans exactly fits this focus of Jesus*: God's love in Christ is free of charge. This theme, too, looks back to Paul's question in 1 Corinthians 4.7: 'Who sees anything different in you? What do you have that you did not receive?' This gospel of reassurance for any who may doubt their salvation has brought assurance throughout Christian history. That is why from Romans 1.18 to the end of chapter 3 he carefully shows that all of humanity alike stands in need of this generous grace.

(4) The Epistle to the Romans has a unique and privileged place in constituting a *transforming agent in many Christian lives over the centuries*. Probably Augustine, Martin Luther and John Wesley stand among the most famous of all of these. We shall trace what is called the 'reception' of this epistle in Chapter 4. But here we cite only one example, which is probably the most famous. In 1514 Martin Luther was already a doctor of theology and professor of biblical studies. Yet he recalled life until then: 'I hated Paul with all my heart.' Nevertheless he wrestled with Romans day and night, examining the context of its words. He writes, 'I began to understand that the righteousness of God is that by which the righteous

---

[2] Robinson, J. A. T., *Wrestling with Romans* (London: SCM, 1979), p. 1.

lives by a gift of God.' Focusing on Romans 1.17, 'The one who is righteous will live by faith' (New Revised Standard Version (NRSV)), Luther wrote: 'I felt that I was altogether born again, and had entered paradise itself through open gates. There a totally other face of the entire Scripture showed itself to me.'[3] In his *Preface to the Epistle to the Romans* (1522) Luther called this epistle 'the chief part of the New Testament . . . the purest gospel', and proposed that every Christian should know it 'word for word by heart . . . as daily bread for the soul', adding, 'We can never read it or ponder it too much.'[4] We give a fuller account of Luther's experience in Chapter 4.

In our chapter on reception history we give a fuller account of Augustine and Luther, but not John Wesley. Wesley's account is well known. In May 1738, he recalls,

> I went very unwillingly to a society in Aldersgate Street, where one was reading Luther's Preface to the Epistle to the Romans. About a quarter before nine . . . I felt my heart strangely warmed. I felt I did trust in Christ, in Christ alone, for my salvation; and an assurance was given to me that he had taken *my* sins away, even *mine*; and saved me from the law of sin and death.[5]

(5) We discuss the text and integrity of Romans in our Chapter 5. To understand arguments about its integrity, we are obliged first to offer a basic introduction to textual criticism. On the other hand, if, as we believe, the whole of Romans is authentic to Paul, chapter 16 reminds us that Paul was a *gregarious person*, and *certainly not a misogynist*. This chapter is not merely a list of names or greetings. It reveals Paul as an eminently social apostle, a man of warm and affectionate friendships with both men and women. It is worth quoting F. F. Bruce on this point in full. Paul, he writes,

> was eminently 'clubbable', sociable, and gregarious. He delighted in the company of his fellows, both men and women. The most incredible feature in the Paul of popular mythology is his alleged misogyny. He treated women as persons . . . The range of his friendship and the warmth of his affection are qualities which no attentive reader of his letters can miss . . . Priscilla and Aquila risked their lives for him in a dangerous situation.[6]

---

[3] Luther, Martin, *Luther's Works* (St Louis and Philadelphia: Concordia and Fortress, 1955–2015), vol. 34, pp. 336–7.

[4] Luther, *Luther's Works*, vol. 35, p. 365.

[5] Wesley, John, *The Works of John Wesley* (Jackson edition, 14 vols, 3rd edn, 1831; reprinted by the Wesleyan Conference Office, London, 1872), vol. 6, p. 103.

[6] Bruce, F. F., *Paul: Apostle of the Free Spirit* (Exeter: Paternoster, 1977), p. 457.

Would Priscilla, Bruce asks, have willingly risked her neck for Paul if he had been the misogynist that he is often made out to be? Romans 16 gives us a good idea of Paul's network of friends in the churches.

(6) With the global explosion of Pentecostalism and the Charismatic Renewal Movement, much is often claimed about 'prophecy' and 'immediate revelation'. Paul does not shrink from calling himself a prophet. Yet the Epistle to the Romans is one of the most carefully *considered, reflective, logically ordered, and even argumentative* of all Paul's writings. Ever since the very earliest work of Rudolf Bultmann, many have debated whether it constituted a 'diatribe' after the fashion of many Graeco-Roman orators.

Stowers and Jewett have provided excellent treatments of this issue. We can acknowledge the contrary view of Judge that a diatribe style might seem sometimes to signify a lack of engagement with actual people, circumstances and issues.[7] Nevertheless Stowers and Jewett convincingly trace many examples of argumentative dialogue in Paul, especially Romans 3.27—4.2. We examine these arguments further below. Pannenberg writes, 'Argumentation and the operation of the Spirit are not in competition with each other. In trusting in the Spirit, Paul in no way spared himself thinking and arguing.'[8] Bornkamm takes the same view. At very least the point has been seen as worthy of debate, and this shows that for Paul there is no exclusive alternative between being inspired to reveal God's truth by the Holy Spirit and to use reflection, logical argument and reasoned persuasion.

(7) *Reconciliation, mutual respect and tolerance* characterize chapters 14 and 15. We examine further later the exact historical circumstances in which friction between Jewish Christians and Gentile Christians arose in Rome. In outline terms, Jewish Christians had lived in Rome from earliest possible times. Jews from Rome had been present to hear Peter's sermon (Acts 2.10). Further, Jewish Christians had a long-standing knowledge of the Scriptures from their earliest years, and thought of themselves as the chosen people of God. Then, on at least one occasion in AD 49, the emperor Claudius expelled a number of Jews from Rome. Until the death of the emperor, Gentile believers may well have constituted the majority of the Christians or even of the whole Church, and found themselves in positions of leadership.

When Claudius died, and Nero succeeded him in AD 54, only one or two years before Paul probably wrote Romans, many Jews would have returned to Rome in considerable numbers. Would they expect to become

---

[7] Stowers, Stanley K., *The Diatribe and Paul's Letter to the Romans* (Chico: Scholars Press, 1981; SBLDS 57), p. 42.

[8] Pannenberg, Wolfhart, *Basic Questions in Theology*, vol. 2 (London: SCM, 1971), p. 35.

leaders again? How would they fare in a predominantly Gentile Christian Church? Some degree of friction or misunderstanding was almost inevitable. Doubtless some Jewish Christians might have pointed to their greater understanding of Scripture, and to their status as God's chosen people. Gentile Christians might have responded by pointing out that God had rejected physical Israel. Paul addresses both aspects of this in Romans 9—15. Chapters 9—11 concern the 'true' Israel. Gentile Christians who had grown accustomed to leadership perhaps saw themselves *alone* as the true Israel. Many Jewish Christians, for their part, were accustomed to observing the customs of the Jewish law. The stage was thus set for mutual recrimination and misunderstanding. Paul urgently saw the need to appeal for mutual tolerance, mutual respect and unity.

At the beginning of chapter 14, Paul writes,

> Welcome those who are weak in the faith . . . Some believe in eating anything, while the weak eat only vegetables. Those who eat must not despise those who abstain, and those who abstain must not pass judgement on those who eat; for God has welcomed them. Who are you to pass judgement on servants of another? (Rom. 14.1–4)

This is the section that gives rise to an acknowledgement that all, whether Jewish or Gentile by birth, belong to Jesus as Lord: 'We do not live to ourselves . . . If we live, we live to the Lord . . . We are the Lord's' (14.7–8). Paul continues in this vein into chapter 15: 'Welcome one another, therefore, just as Christ has welcomed you' (Rom. 15.7). The basis of this mutual acceptance by the one of the other is, once again, that God's grace alone has made everyone what they are (cf. 1 Cor. 4.7).

This is fully in line with 1 Corinthians 8.1—10.32. Similarities become unmistakable. Admittedly in 1 Corinthians the 'weak' and the 'strong' cannot simply be equated with Jew and Gentile, as they usually can in Romans. Some identify 'the strong' in Corinth with socially privileged believers. Theissen argues for this.[9] Horsley, Gardner and Gooch rightly argue that 'the strong' can be identified with Christians who have an under-sensitive conscience, and 'the weak' as believers with an over-sensitive conscience.[10] The passage in 1 Corinthians anticipates the thrust of Romans

---

[9] Theissen, Gerd, *The Social Setting of Pauline Christianity: Essays on Corinth* (Philadelphia: Fortress, 1982), pp. 121–44.

[10] Horsley, R. A., 'Consciousness and Freedom among the Corinthians: 1 Corinthians 8—10', *CBQ* 40 (1978), pp. 574–89; Gardner, Paul D., *The Gifts of God and the Authentication of a Christian* (Lanham, MD: University Press of America, 1994), pp. 48–54; Gooch, Peter D., '"Conscience" in 1 Corinthians 8 and 10', *NTS* 33 (1987), pp. 244–54; and *Dangerous Food: 1 Corinthians 8—10 in Its Context* (Waterloo, ON: Wilfred Laurier University Press, 1993).

14—15: food is not the determining element in the Christian's relationship to God. Hence, Paul argues to the strong: 'Take care that this liberty of yours does not somehow become a stumbling-block to the weak' (1 Cor. 8.9). But to both the weak and the strong he argues: 'Whether you eat or drink . . . Give no offence to Jews or Greeks or to the church of God' (1 Cor. 10.31– 32). As in the case of many other problems in Corinth, Paul has had time to reflect further on his earlier writing, and has become aware that the difficulty which he has already addressed to Corinth can be a serious source of divisions in any church.

This issue has become a decisive reason to appreciate Romans. Robert Jewett even calls this 'The Epistle of Tolerance', because, he argues, each new generation of Christians needs to learn this tolerance and mutual respect for the other. This transcends barriers of class, race, culture and background, and speaks to every age.[11]

(8) Romans 9—11 forms an integral part of Paul's argument in Romans. This is not only because Paul stresses the sovereignty of God in election. It also provides a magnificent panorama of *God's sovereign purposes in world history*. This forms part of his concern for the relation between Jews and Gentiles, especially Christian Jews and Gentiles. These chapters are far from constituting a digression, still less any kind of embarrassment. To grasp the message of these chapters is an enriching and illuminating experience. Most significantly of all, Romans presents a picture of the sheer wonder, love and sovereign purposes of God, which is, after all, the ultimate purpose of all Bible-reading and faithful preaching.

[11] Jewett, Robert, *Christian Tolerance: Paul's Message to the Modern Church* (Louisville: Westminster/ John Knox, 1982; Biblical Perspectives on Modern Issues).

2

Strategies of interpretation: three essential strategies for Romans

From among varied strategies of interpretation, three are essential for understanding Paul's argument: historical-critical methods, rhetorical criticism and socio-scientific criticism. Seven others, which include reader-response theory, liberation hermeneutics, structuralism and existential interpretation, vary in importance from one section of the epistle to another, but all nevertheless remain very useful. It is therefore appropriate to divide what was a single chapter on strategies of interpretation into two, especially since including the first three would create a chapter of more than normal length.

Historical-critical methods

In spite of the fact that so many speak of *the* historical-critical method, in practice *many* such methods abound. To use *the singular 'method'* is a misleading mistake. There is no such thing as 'the' critical method, even if Karl Donfried in *The Romans Debate* speaks of 'the' historical-critical method.[1] Initially the term denoted an approach mainly through historical reconstruction *alone*, together with what many regard as 'the assured results of biblical criticism'. The initial method carried a strongly anti-theological dimension, as if theology came only from church tradition.

Further, it is also misleading to speak of these methods as a 'modern' phenomenon. Historical-critical approaches emerged not only in the seventeenth century, but also in anticipatory and fragmented traces in Origen, Luther and other pre-modern figures. The eighteenth and nineteenth centuries (though with strong exceptions) are more indebted to a 'history versus theology' mentality than approaches during the post-war years of the later twentieth century, and even more so today. We must therefore outline how historical-critical methods have developed and been modified.

---

[1] Donfried, Karl P., 'Introduction' to Donfried, Karl P. (ed.), *The Romans Debate* (Grand Rapids: Baker Academic, 2nd edn, 1991), p. xlvii.

Some trace proto-critical methods back to Benedict Spinoza the Jewish philosopher (1632–77), to Richard Simon the Catholic Jesuit (1638–1712), to Jean Astruc (1684–1766) and to the Deists. But these were only partial anticipations of a more systematically critical approach. Spinoza identified and criticized biblical 'contradictions'. Simon challenged the assumption that Moses wrote the Pentateuch, in a quest to undermine Protestant appeals to the biblical writings. Astruc postulated that two sources lay behind Genesis and Exodus, largely on the basis of their use of two different divine names, Jahweh or Yahweh (the 'J' sources), and Elohim, God (the 'E' sources). This occurred long before Wellhausen popularized the same idea.

A more systematic approach came with the work of J. S. Semler, who published his *Treatise on the Free Investigation of the Canon* (1771–5), in which he argued that reason or rational enquiry should not be 'hindered' by any appeal to faith or to Christian theology. The tragic separation between theology and strictly historical versions of biblical criticism can be traced to his originally positive motives for separating rational and historical study from faith and theology.

During the eighteenth century this approach became institutionalized through the work of J. D. Michaelis (1788), J. J. Griesbach (1776), G. E. Lessing (1777) and W. M. L. de Wette (1788–1849). De Wette, for example, stressed different outlooks in Kings and Chronicles, arguing that Chronicles was a secondary historical source. In the nineteenth century, David Strauss (1808–74) extended such historical criticism to the Gospels. Others began to include the epistles, including F. C. Baur (1792–1860), whom we discuss under our Chapter 4, 'The reception history of Romans'.

In the early years of the twentieth century Paul Wendland (1907) and Rudolf Bultmann (1910) proposed analogies between Greek literature and Paul's style in Romans (see below under 'Rhetorical criticism'). Wilhelm Wrede (1904) and Albert Schweitzer (1930) denied the centrality in Romans of justification by grace through faith. They were building largely on H. Lüdemann's earlier theory (1872) that Paul held two quite different doctrines of redemption. One centred on the juridical theme of Romans 1—4; and the other on the 'mystical' theme of dying-and-rising with Christ, found in Romans 5—8. The former derived largely from Judaism; the latter was allegedly borrowed from Greek thought or Hellenism.

This seemed to cohere with advocates of the history-of-religions school of W. Bousset, R. Reitzenstein and P. Wendland. Bousset's *Kyrios Christos* (German 1913, English 1970) was endorsed by Bultmann. Like Harnack, the classical liberal, Bousset contrasted the simple ethical demands of Jesus with Paul's more complex theology, which allegedly draws on the

Hellenistic mystery religions. Reitzenstein (1861–1931) was primarily a classical philologist, who sought to understand what he called 'the Redeemer-myth' of Gnosticism. He argued that Paul derived some aspects from the Gnostic myth of a saviour figure, who came down from heaven to rescue spirits imprisoned on earth.

The sheer range of historical-critical methods can be illustrated further by selecting two reactions to the theories of Reitzenstein. Günther Wagner carefully examines Paul's view, not least in Romans 6.1–11, and compares the myths or 'mysteries' of Isis, Mithras and other ancient deities.[2] His arguments were that, first, if there is any parallel with Paul, this does not at all mean that Paul borrowed from them. Second, the dating of such sources indicates that they often post-date Paul, so could not have influenced him. Third, supposed 'parallels' do not turn out to be parallels at all. Similarly Munck convincingly demolishes the hypotheses of Baur. We discuss his work under 'Reception history', our Chapter 4, below.

T. W. Manson was Professor of Biblical Criticism and Exegesis at Manchester University for some 20 years from 1936, and again represents a different type of critical approach. We discuss his theory about Romans in our Chapter 5 on the text and integrity of Romans.

After the Second World War, historical-critical studies often provided a deeper understanding of Judaism. In the post-war era W. D. Davies argued that Paul's thought was best understood against the background of 'Palestinian' Judaism and the new exodus. He rescued Paul from a one-sided emphasis on the Greek background. In Romans the apostle illustrates affinities with, rather than opposition to, Jewish rabbis. For example, in his chapter on 'the flesh and sin', Davies examined not only these terms in Romans, but also the rabbinic notion of *he-yêtzer hâ-ra'*, or evil impulse.[3] This may well stand behind Paul's language about the ineffectiveness of the law alone. There are also links, he adds, with the fall of Adam in Romans 5.12–21.[4] He comments on Romans 5.12: 'Paul accepted the traditional rabbinic doctrine of the unity of mankind in Adam.'[5]

Further Jewish approaches to Paul were then discussed and represented by H. J. Schoeps. Stendahl also offered a new approach, and we discuss his work under 'Reception history'. In 1977 E. P. Sanders published his

---

[2] Wagner, Günther, *Pauline Baptism and the Pagan Mysteries: The Problem of the Pauline Doctrine of Baptism in Romans VI:1–11, in the Light of Its Religio-Historical 'Parallels'* (Edinburgh: Oliver & Boyd, 1967).

[3] Davies, W. D., *Paul and Rabbinic Judaism* (London: SPCK, 2nd edn, 1955), pp. 20–31.

[4] Davies, *Paul*, pp. 31–5.

[5] Davies, *Paul*, p. 57.

monumental book, *Paul and Palestinian Judaism*, which aimed to draw a more careful comparison between Paul and Judaism than had yet appeared. For many, but not for all, this constituted a watershed in the study of Paul, introducing what came to be called 'The New Perspective'. We discuss Sanders, again, under our Chapter 4, on reception history.

James Dunn (b. 1939) contributed a positive but modified assessment of Sanders' 'New Perspective' in 1991. He conceded that Sanders built on earlier approaches of Stendahl and N. A. Dahl and confirmed their general point: 'Pauline exegesis has far too long allowed a typically Lutheran emphasis on justification by faith to impose a hermeneutical grid on the text of Romans.'[6] This suggested that first-century Judaism presented a system in which salvation is 'earned' through the merit of good works. Dunn explains: 'The role of the law ... provides a crucial hinge in the argument (Rom. 3:19–21; 8:2–4; 9:31 – 10.5).'[7] He criticized Sanders, however, for understanding the justification theme and that of Christ-Union as *contradictory* lines of thought, as Schweitzer did.

Dunn insists, 'The law ... became a basic expression of Israel's distinctiveness as the people specially chosen by (the one) God to be his people.' In sociological terms the law became an 'identity-marker' and 'boundary', reinforcing Israel's sense of distinctiveness.[8] Thus Israel's revelling in the law as a badge of God's favour ran counter to Christian Jews welcoming the Gentiles as their equals. The law, Dunn concludes, was what divided Jew from non-Jew. He adds, 'Paul regularly warns against "the works of the law" not as "good works" ... but rather as that pattern of obedience by which "the righteous" maintain their status within the people of the covenant.'[9]

N. T. Wright (b. 1948) developed a further modification of the New Perspective in 2005.[10] He regards Romans as entailing 'the redefinition of God's people around the Messiah'.[11] On Romans he insists: 'Rom. 2:17–25 examines the Jewish claim to special status, based on election and the covenant.'[12] Wright, like Dunn, regards this as corporate and national, not as individual. The presence of sin, and boasting in the Torah, deceives Israel into thinking that God will achieve his purposes through that nation,

---

[6] Dunn, James D. G., 'The New Perspective on Paul: Paul and the Law' in Donfried, Karl P. (ed.), *The Romans Debate* (Grand Rapids: Baker Academic, 2nd edn, 1991), p. 299; cf. pp. 299–308.

[7] Dunn, 'New Perspective', p. 301.

[8] Dunn, 'New Perspective', p. 304.

[9] Dunn, 'New Perspective', p. 307.

[10] Wright, N. T., *The Messiah and the People of God* (Oxford: OUP, 1980), esp. ch. 2.

[11] Wright, N. T., *Paul: Fresh Perspectives* (London: SPCK, 2005), p. 117.

[12] Wright, *Fresh Perspectives*, p. 117.

rather than through Christ. It is more accurate to say that the 'alternative' to law is not 'abandoning good works', but *Christ*. Wright also notes elsewhere that Alister McGrath recognized that the doctrine of justification 'has come to develop a meaning quite independent of its biblical origins, and concerns the means by which men's relationship to God is established . . . thereby giving the concept an emphasis quite absent from the New Testament'.[13]

Meanwhile C. E. B. Cranfield, Seyoon Kim and many others firmly *resist* the New Perspective. In an oral interview with Ben Blackwell Cranfield told him that he remained unconvinced by the New Perspective, and thought that Dunn's commentary was 'off target' in this area.[14] As we have noted, Seyoon Kim refuses to 'elevate it into a dogma'. On the other hand many allow for its broad recasting of Jewish–Gentile relations in Romans, without following its claims in detail. Notably the two most recent major and classic commentaries on Romans, those by Fitzmyer and Jewett, appear to pay relatively little attention to the New Perspective as such.

In conclusion it is clear that 'the historical-critical method' is *no single approach*, but embraces many methods, and no longer carries the 'history versus theology' slogan of earlier years. Its more positive attitude to *theology* can be seen from the last five or six major commentaries on Romans. Barrett (1957), Dunn (1988), Ziesler (1989) and Jewett (2007) are Methodists; Fitzmyer (1992) and Byrne (1996) remain convinced Catholics; Cranfield (1977) is a committed member of the Reformed Church; Nygren and Käsemann (1973) are Lutherans; Wright (2002) is an Anglican, and became Bishop of Durham (like Westcott and Lightfoot); while Bruce belonged to the Christian Brethren. Jewett states concerning his magisterial commentary:

> This commentary employs all the standard methods of historical-critical exegesis. This includes historical analysis, text-criticism, form criticism and redaction criticism; rhetorical analysis, social scientific reconstruction of the audience situation; an historical and cultural analysis of the honour-shame, and imperial systems in the Graeco-Roman world, and a *theological interpretation that takes these details into account*, rather than following paths formed by church traditions.[15]

---

[13] Wright, Tom, *What St. Paul Really Said* (Oxford: Lion, 1997), p. 115; quotation from McGrath, Alister E., *Iustitia Dei: A History of the Christian Doctrine of Justification* (2 vols, Cambridge: CUP, 1986), vol. 1, pp. 2–3.

[14] Blackwell, Ben C., and others (eds), *Reading Romans in Context: Paul and Second Temple Judaism* (Grand Rapids: Zondervan, 2015).

[15] Jewett, Robert, *Romans: A Commentary* (Minneapolis: Fortress, 2007; Hermeneia), p. 1 (my italics).

His commentary powerfully and convincingly deploys all the different methods which he has cited under the heading 'historical-critical exegesis'.

Rhetorical criticism

In one sense rhetorical criticism is as old as the analysis of the literary artistry of the Old Testament (OT), and as handbooks of rhetoric in ancient Greece and Rome. Duane Watson cites the rhetorical style of Amos 1—2 and the Song of Deborah in Judges 5.[16] He also cites such literary studies as Michael Fishbane's *Text and Texture*, Robert Alter's *The Art of Biblical Narrative* and Northrop Fry's *The Great Code*.

We are concerned, however, with Romans and Paul. In this respect one of the earliest modern studies to draw heavily on Greek and Roman rhetoric was Rudolf Bultmann's thesis in 1910.[17] He refers to G. F. G. Heinrici's work of 1908 on the literary character of the New Testament (NT) writings, and to some earlier works, including those of Wilke (1843) and Paul Wendland (1895). But here he scrutinizes specifically the diatribe in Graeco-Roman authors. These include Bion, Teles, Horace, Musonius Rufus, Dion, and above all Epictetus and Plutarch.[18] Plutarch (*c.*46–120) and Epictetus (*c.*50–*c.*130) were almost contemporary with Paul. Lucius Annaeus Seneca (*c.*1–65) overlapped with Paul. These provided examples of Stoic diatribe and of the popular ethical preaching of the Cynics.[19]

Bultmann examined especially the dialogical character of the Stoics' diatribe, their rhetorical style, their groupings and style, and their distinctive manner of argumentation. He argued that Paul includes all these features. In Paul he selects several examples of the diatribe style. These include rhetorical questions (Rom. 6.16, 'Do you not know that ... ?', and similarly Rom. 11.2; 7.1; cf. 1 Cor. 3.18; 5.6; 6.15; 9.15).[20] Paul addresses both single people and groups as rhetorical opponents or dialogue-partners. Often he addresses questions about consequences.

Epictetus practises exactly the same style. He addresses single identities, e.g. *anthrōpe*, 'O human person' (cf. Rom. 1.13). Often Paul presses hypothetical arguments which he rejects with such emphatic negatives as 'By

---

[16] Watson, Duane F., and Hauser, Alan J., *Rhetorical Criticism and the Bible* (Leiden: Brill, 1994; BI 4), pp. 9–12.

[17] Bultmann, Rudolf, *Der Stil der paulinischen Predigt und die kynisch-stoische Diatribe* (Göttingen: Vandenhoeck & Ruprecht, 1910; FRLANT 13).

[18] Bultmann, *Der Stil*, p. 109 and throughout.

[19] Bultmann, *Der Stil*, pp. 9–10.

[20] Bultmann, *Der Stil*, p. 65.

no means!' (NRSV); Greek *mē genoito* (Rom. 3.4; 3.31).[21] In Romans 9.19
Paul declares, 'You will say to me then . . .' Romans 2.21 borrows Diaspora
Jewish rhetoric, to which Paul replies: 'You, then, that teach others, will
you not teach yourself?'[22] Bultmann also includes as evidence the 'catalogue
of vices' which we find in Romans 1.24–31. With these lists we may compare Epictetus, *Discourses* 1.18, 22 and 1.11, 33.[23] Opposition on the part
of a fictitious opponent is sharpened not only in Paul, but also in Teles
15.14; 26.8; Epictetus, *Dis.* 1.2, 22; 14.11; Plutarch, *De Tranqu. Animae*
469E; Seneca, *De Const. Sap.* 1.2. Fictitious conversations are prominent
(Epictetus, *Dis.* 1.4, 5; 18.17; 19.2; 24.9).

Bultmann also includes in this rhetorical diatribe style word-play,
antithesis, parallelism, paradox, reversal of values, and exclamations.[24]
Word-play is difficult to illustrate in English, but we refer to examples in
Greek in our commentary (Rom. 1.25, 27, 28; 2.8; 5.16, 19). Bultmann
concludes, for example, 'A certain similarity between Paul and the diatribe
comes to light.'[25]

For many years Bultmann had established Paul's use of the diatribe. But
his approach undermined A. Deissmann's later claims about spontaneous,
artless, 'letters'. He established that Paul deliberately involved and engaged
his audience, relying especially on conversational style. He concluded:
'The cloak of the Greek orator does indeed hang on Paul's shoulders, but
Paul has no sense for skilful drapery.'[26] But the most decisive work came
from Stanley Stowers in 1981.[27] He pointed out that Ernst von Dobschütz
had identified question-and-answer methods and styles in the *Jewish
rabbis*, in the Midrash and in the Talmud.[28] Similarly in 1972 Edwin Judge
had argued that NT scholars had worked on the Cynic–Stoic diatribe with
insufficient critical awareness.[29]

Stowers recognizes that 'there is a strong dialogue element' in Teles,
Epictetus and Paul.[30] Bultmann's conclusions, he argues, remain ambiguous,
but do underline the role of rhetoric. In this respect he agrees that 'The

---

[21] Bultmann, *Der Stil*, pp. 67–8.
[22] Bultmann, *Der Stil*, p. 70.
[23] Bultmann, *Der Stil*, pp. 71–4.
[24] Bultmann, *Der Stil*, pp. 74–88.
[25] Bultmann, *Der Stil*, p. 96.
[26] Bultmann, *Der Stil*, p. 108.
[27] Stowers, Stanley K., *The Diatribe and Paul's Letter to the Romans* (Chico: Scholars Press, 1981; SBLDS 57).
[28] Dobschütz, E. von, *Der Apostel Paulus* (Halle: Waisenhaus, 1926), pp. 122–3; and Stowers, *The Diatribe and Romans*, p. 40.
[29] Judge, Edwin, A., 'St Paul and Classical Society', JAC 15 (1972), p. 33.
[30] Stowers, *The Diatribe and Romans*, p. 55.

function of Rom. 2:1–5 is to bring home, to concretize and to sharpen the indictment in 1:18–32.[31] In particular Paul uses rhetoric to characterize those who are 'arrogant' or 'pretentious'. Stowers compares Romans 2.17–24 with the Stoic indictment of the arrogant.[32] Passages with similar traits are Romans 9.19–21 and 11.17–24. In 11.13 he says, 'Now I am speaking to you Gentiles.' Even in the ethical section (Rom. 14.4 and 10), Paul asks, 'Who are you to pass judgments on servants of another?' (v. 4).

The crowning study of Paul's rhetoric in Romans, however, comes in Jewett's *Romans* (2007). His section covers 23 quarto pages. Rhetoric, he argues, aims to persuade, as Paul did. He refers to the ancient epistolary handbooks which provided a distinctive rhetorical analysis. He first discusses 'invention' (Latin *inventio*), which seeks the most appropriate means of persuasion. These usually provide an *exordium* or prologue, a *narrative* which provides the background, an *argument*, and a *peroration* or epilogue.[33] The argument often draws on pre-Pauline creeds, hymns, and citations from Scripture. All these feature in Romans. Romans 1.3–4, for example, reflects a pre-Pauline christological creed. Romans 3.30 uses the pre-Pauline formula 'God is one'. Romans 4.24 employs a pre-Pauline formula concerning the resurrection of Christ; while 4.25 borrows the Suffering Servant language from Isaiah 53.

Jewett selects Romans 2.1–16 as 'a diatribe that sustains Paul's doctrine of impartial judgment' that overturns much group exceptionalism in the Graeco-Roman world.[34] Paul introduces an imaginary interlocutor who is a self-congratulatory bigot, to evoke contempt for him from his audience. Two diatribes follow in 3.1–8 and in 3.9–21, with questions and answers. Another follows in 4.1–12, and Paul introduces three rhetorical questions in 5.15–16. In 6.1–14 'the diatribal form is clearer'. Paul resumes the diatribe form in 9.30—10.4 and 11.1–10; 'God did not cast off his people for ever, did he?' A final diatribe appears in 13.3b. This list constitutes ten or more examples of this rhetorical form, which consistently serves Paul's argument.

Jewett finally argues that Paul uses the formal argument of an *enthymeme* (Greek *enthumēma*), with special reference to Moores.[35] Both Jewett and Moores highlight Paul's emphasis on persuasion. Moores argues,

---

[31] Stowers, *The Diatribe and Romans*, p. 110.

[32] Stowers, *The Diatribe and Romans*, p. 112.

[33] Jewett, *Romans*, p. 24.

[34] Jewett, *Romans*, p. 26.

[35] Moores, John D., *Wrestling with Rationality in Paul: Romans 1—8 in a New Perspective* (Cambridge: CUP, 1995; SNTSMS 82).

'Reader-response theories turn Paul's ideas upside down.'[36] Stressing Paul's use of indirect communication, Moores writes, 'It is in the nature of enthymematic argument that it creates puzzles.'[37] Some of Moores' arguments may verge on the speculative, but he argues convincingly that the superimposition of one 'code' onto another is 'a pervasive feature of sign-production'.[38] He moves beyond the classical rhetoric cited by H. D. Betz and the 'New Rhetoric' advocated by W. Wuellner.

A number of recent books and research articles on rhetoric in Paul relate to epistles other than Romans. Especially well known is Margaret Mitchell and L. L. Welborn (1997) on 1 Corinthians.[39] Hans Dieter Betz on Galatians (1979) remains a classic.[40] Several articles address the rhetoric of Romans, including especially those by Wuellner and Dunn.[41]

Sociological or socio-scientific reading

This strategy of interpretation has essential relevance to Romans. The method has been growing in influence since at least the 1960s and 1970s. Edwin Judge, an ancient historian of Macquarie University, Australia, has been writing articles on this since 1960 and 1980.[42] The social groupings and social composition of the ancient church in Rome are deeply relevant to understanding Romans. A first question concerns the economic status of believers in Rome. Were they desperately poor, or reasonably well off and educated? Answers may largely depend on whether different groups of Christians represented both ends of the spectrum. A second question asks what light can be shed on the Jewish and Gentile constituency of the church. Which group predominated, if both were present? Paul was writing, among other aims, to argue that both Jewish Christians and Gentile Christians stood on an equal footing before God. They were to welcome each other in mutual respect (Rom. 15.7).

---

[36] Moores, *Wrestling with Rationality*, pp. 133–4.

[37] Moores, *Wrestling with Rationality*, p. 60.

[38] Moores, *Wrestling with Rationality*, p. 26.

[39] Welborn, L. L., *Politics and Rhetoric in the Corinthian Epistles* (Macon, GA: Mercer University Press, 1997).

[40] Betz, H. D., *Galatians* (Philadelphia: Fortress, 1979; Hermeneia).

[41] Dunn, J. D. G., 'The Formal and Theological Coherence of Romans' in Donfried, Karl P. (ed.), *The Romans Debate* (Grand Rapids: Baker Academic, 2nd edn, 1991), pp. 245–50; and Wuellner, W., 'Paul's Rhetoric of Argumentation in Romans' in Donfried (ed.), *Romans Debate*, pp. 128–46.

[42] Judge, Edwin A., *The Social Pattern of the Christian Groups in the First Century* (London: Tyndale, 1960); and 'The Social Identity of the First Christians: A Question of Method in Religious History', *JRH* 11.2 (1980), pp. 201–17.

First, on *economic status* there is no clear consensus about the intellectual and cultural constituency of the Roman church. This is hardly surprising, since there may have been some five or more groups within the church. Arguing for the higher end of the social scale, Robinson offers the common-sense answer: 'Certainly some intelligence would have been needed to cope with the Epistle to the Romans.'[43] Similarly, Bruce observes, 'Christianity may already have begun to make some impact in the higher reaches of Roman society.'[44] He cites, for example, the involvement with Christians and probably the Christian faith of Pomponia Graecina, the wife of Aulus Plautius, who commanded the military expedition to Britain in AD 43. Following J. B. Lightfoot, Robinson accepts that the congregation was probably largely made up of freedmen and slaves, but probably 'the better sort of Greek and some oriental slaves', who would be more highly educated than their masters.

Sanday and Headlam cite Prisca and Aquila as business people. In Romans 16.10–11, Paul mentions 'those of the family of Aristobulus' and 'my relative Herodian'. This seems to point to members or the staff of the best families. In Romans 16, ten of the names mentioned are Latin names; 18 are Greek names; and two are arguably Hebrew names. The Roman historian Tacitus described Pomponia Graecina as an eminent or notable woman (Latin *insignis femina*).[45] Although the later years of Nero's reign witnessed numerous crimes, his earlier reign from 54 to 59 was known as Nero's prosperous and peaceful quinquennium.

On the other side Peter Lampe contributed a landmark study of Christians in ancient Rome, in which he states that in the first century: 'Poverty was such that some Roman Christians sold themselves into slavery to raise money for the poor in the church.'[46] Only after the 90s do we hear of 'wealthy' Christians. Lampe argues that in early years lower social strata predominated. Most Christians, he concluded, lived outside Rome on the western edge in the Valley of the Appian Way and the Tiber, or in Trastevere.[47] A number of writers, including Jewett, speak of tenements in these areas. As in Corinth, the general picture may be 'not many . . . powerful' (NRSV), namely 'influential people' (1 Cor. 1.26), although there were also clearly specific exceptions to this.

[43] Robinson, J. A. T., *Wrestling with Romans* (London: SCM, 1979), p. 7.

[44] Bruce, F. F., *The Epistle of Paul to the Romans* (London: Tyndale, 1963), p. 16.

[45] Tacitus, *Annals*, 13.32.

[46] Lampe, Peter, *Die stadtrömischen Christen in den ersten beiden Jahrhunderten* (Tübingen: Mohr, 1987; WUNT II.18), esp. pp. 68–9; Eng., *From Paul to Valentinus: Christians at Rome in the First Two Centuries* (Minneapolis: Fortress, 2003).

[47] Lampe, *Die stadtrömischen Christen*, pp. 41–9.

Jewett argues,

> Most of the population in Rome lived in the upper levels of 'multi-story tenement houses' or in the rears of shops, while the nobility and the wealthy citizens of Rome occupied the lower floors of these buildings or in mansions in the better parts of the city.[48]

Crowding was intense for slaves or poorer people. Many tenements had four or five storeys, and consisted of apartment blocks. Jewett argues that most rooms were small (about 10 square metres), and the population density was 'almost two and a half times higher than modern Calcutta and three times higher than Manhattan Island'.[49] Spaces were often rented out by landlords or managers, and long-term tenure and rights of privacy were rare.

While Roman citizens and the reasonably wealthy were greatly concerned with 'honour and shame', which Paul often calls 'boasting', slaves and the poor were generally beneath such considerations. Jewett comments, 'Largely exempt from the system of public honour were slaves and barbarians.'[50] Slaves were more numerous than we might imagine. Jeffers reports that slaves constituted 'something like 2 to 3 million of the 7.5 million inhabitants of Italy'.[51] Slaves originated from those captured in war, the children of slaves, those who chose to sell themselves into slavery for financial reasons, and those criminals for whom the penalty of their crime was slavery. As we shall note, some slaves were seen as mere 'possessions' or 'things', with neither freedom nor power, while others might achieve high-status work as managers of estates, secretaries and so forth. Martin has done much to show the range and complexity of the social status of slaves, which depended on the character of their 'lord'.[52]

Jewett and Dunn, however, argue convincingly that there was more than one Christian community in Rome, and probably a very wide mix of social status. Jewett argues that Paul needed to rely on well-educated, Latin-speaking Romans to spearhead his hoped-for mission to Spain. Jewett works out a fascinating and convincing reconstruction, which we discuss below. The deacon Phoebe was eminent, he argues, and she would probably oversee this mission.

---

[48] Jewett, *Romans*, p. 53; and Jeffers, James S., 'Jewish and Christian Families in First-Century Rome' in Donfried, K. P., and Richardson, P., *Judaism and Christianity in First-Century Rome* (Grand Rapids: Eerdmans, 1998), pp. 128–50.

[49] Jewett, *Romans*, p. 54.

[50] Jewett, *Romans*, p. 51.

[51] Jeffers, 'Jewish and Christian Families', p. 221.

[52] Martin, Dale B., *Slavery as Salvation* (New Haven: Yale University Press, 1990).

Our second question is about the church's composition of *Jews and Christian Gentiles*. Every key theme or section in Romans reflects the composition of the church in Rome in this respect. Romans 9—11 and 12—15 speak as much to the church in Rome as the more classic chapters 1—8. Some have suggested that the Christians in Rome formed five separate groups of Christian believers, whom Paul sought to bring together as *one united church*. As James Dunn comments, 'the letter seems to be . . . dominated by the issue of Jew/Gentile relationships'; signalled by such an example as, 'To the Jew first and also to the Greek' (1.16).[53]

Although some scholars, including Lietzmann and O'Neill, have argued that the readers of the epistle were *all* Jewish Christians, the majority of writers rightly reject this conclusion. But Fitzmyer observes that Paul deliberately calls himself 'Apostle to the Gentiles' (Rom. 11.13) and even addresses his readers as one with other Gentiles (Rom. 1.13). By the 50s the Christians in Rome would have been well established. Paul had hoped to visit them 'for many years' (Rom. 1.10; 15.23). But, as Dunn observes, 'Paul never speaks of the Christians in Rome as a church'.[54] This is in marked contrast to his usual practice (1 Cor. 1.2; 2 Cor. 1.1; Phil. 4.15; 1 Thess. 1.2). Almost certainly they were too numerous to meet in a single house, and shared, in Dunn's words, 'the same sort of fragmented existence as the wider Jewish community . . . The Christians functioned as several "churches" in Rome, but were not seen as a single entity.'[55]

Fragmentation would have been further complicated when Jews returned to Rome after the death of Claudius. Fitzmyer rightly distinguishes controversies between Jewish Christians and Gentile Christians in Rome from that of Judaizers in Galatia.[56] He concludes,

> When Paul writes to the Romans about justification by grace through faith, he is reflecting on his missionary endeavours of an earlier time . . . It is far from certain that charges levelled against Paul in Asia Minor and Greece made their way to Rome . . . [He] sounds . . . different from the tone in which he wrote Galatians.[57]

Cranfield expresses the same thought differently. He writes,

---

[53] Dunn, James D. G., *Romans 1—8* (Dallas: Word, 1988; WBC 38), p. xlv.

[54] Dunn, *Romans 1—8*, p. lii.

[55] Dunn, *Romans 1—8*, p. lii.

[56] Fitzmyer, Joseph A., *Romans: A New Translation with Introduction and Commentary* (New York: Doubleday, 1992; AB 33), p. 34.

[57] Fitzmyer, *Romans*, p. 34.

It would appear that there were a number of different groups. Did these groups meet on their own when they met for worship? Did they ever meet together as a single 'church of God' ... *ekklēsia* is never used in Romans ... We ought to reckon with the fact that there may have been little, if any, central organisation.[58]

Cranfield urges caution about this conclusion. Nevertheless it would explain further the clear theological links with 1 Corinthians, and Paul's deep concern for mutual welcome and mutual tolerance between different Christians.

Jews constituted a massive population in Rome. Some have calculated a number between 15,000 and 60,000 in the city in the 50s. Some occupied poorer quarters such as Trastevere, at least according to Philo.[59] Others, including those captured by Pompey in 63 BC, became Roman citizens. Leon cites evidence for the poverty of some from their graves.[60] The result of this quantity and variety emerged in the shape of several synagogues in Rome. One group was probably located in Trastevere; another in a district of labourers and small shopkeepers to the east of the Forum.

It is generally agreed that initially the church in Rome was composed largely of converted Jews, and that these grew alongside Gentile adherents until the expulsion of many Jews from Rome by Claudius. Then, when Paul wrote, there was a problematic relation between a Gentile majority and a Jewish minority. Many, if not most, identify these two groups with the 'weak' and the 'strong' in Romans 14.1—15.13, although many scholars are reluctant to define these too closely. Jewett argues that Paul's characterization of each group is rhetorically exaggerated. Thus the strong 'eat everything', while the weak eat only 'leafy vegetables' (Rom. 14.2).[61] Kosher regulations would not in practice be so sweeping. But the general point is clear. The 'weak' would judge the 'strong' for not living up to kosher standards of the law; the 'strong' would judge the 'weak' for lacking Christian freedom from the law. Paul constantly strives to show that in God's eyes Jewish Christians and Gentile Christians are equal. Each should welcome and respect the other (Rom. 15.1–13, especially v. 7).

---

[58] Cranfield, C. E. B., *A Critical and Exegetical Commentary on the Epistle to the Romans*, vol. 1 (Edinburgh: T & T Clark, 1975; ICC), p. 22.
[59] Philo, *Legatio*, 155–6.
[60] Leon, H. J., *The Jews of Ancient Rome* (Peabody: Hendrickson, 1995), pp. 122–4.
[61] Jewett, *Romans*, p. 71.

3

Nine further strategies often useful for parts of Romans

Our first three strategies of interpretation remain essential tools for understanding Romans. However, since the late 1960s and early 1970s a variety of further strategies have emerged, especially from literary theory. These may be useful for certain purposes, even if they are of more limited value as general models. To our first three we may add the most relevant strategies to Romans: (1) reader-response theory; (2) structuralist exegesis; (3) methods used in liberation hermeneutics; (4) existentialist interpretation; (5) pre-critical exegesis; (6) Barthian exegesis; (7) lexical and grammatical exegesis, and the fruit of textual-critical research; (8) a more explicit emphasis on such social factors as the shame–honour system in the ancient world, and the relevance of the imperial cult; and (9) some form-critical techniques, although these fall largely under rhetorical strategies in Paul. We have endeavoured to subsume the first four within our exegesis below, and they are more usually part of a thorough historical-critical approach. Yet for the sake of demonstrating the variety of strategies of interpretation possible, we have included a total of 12 such strategies in these two chapters.

(1) Reader-response strategies of interpretation

An initial impetus to this approach came from literary theory, when theorists had long reacted against seeking the historical intention of the author by largely historical enquiry. Literary critics sometimes expressed scorn about supposedly locking the text into a dead past, and some critics of the 1950s had also criticized what they called 'the intentional fallacy'. Indeed in 1954 Wimsatt and Beardsley published their essay 'The Intentional Fallacy'.[1] The contrast with historical exegesis was not as sharp as many had believed, because Wimsatt and Beardsley had as their primary target poetry, not sacred texts.

---

[1] Wimsatt, W. K., and Beardsley, M., 'The Intentional Fallacy' in Wimsatt, William K., *The Verbal Icon: Studies in the Meaning of Poetry* (New York: Noonday Press, 1966 [1954]).

Nevertheless at the time many biblical scholars were seduced by their idea. One eminent Cambridge NT scholar promoted 'The Intentional Fallacy' as if it were gospel truth. I was initially excited by a seminar in the USA called 'The Text, and Only the Text'. But in fact this approach was not anchored in the real world. It neglected the author of the text, its readers, its directedness and its historical situation, as if it were an abstract, context-free, poem. More careful reflection soon showed that we cannot simply extract the text from its historical setting. As the philosopher Ludwig Wittgenstein conclusively demonstrated, the meaning of words and sentences usually depends on the form of life from which they arise. Poetry may provide one exception. In the Bible, poetic psalms may not necessarily depend on our knowledge of the author. Some literary theorists, however, found 'the text alone' a plausible and fashionable model of reading. But other literary theorists found the need to anchor the text in the real world, although they suggested a different route from the historical one. They explored the relation of the text *to its readers*. A concern for the original readers had been developed by Manson and Baird in biblical studies, usually called *audience criticism*. Reader-response theories could include this, but mostly concerned *today's modern readers*. Thus was born the reader-response theory of the later 1970s and 1980s.

Baird published his work on audience criticism in 1969.[2] But it seems to have been largely neglected. He builds partly on Manson's work of 1931, in which Manson distinguished between passages of the Sayings of Jesus which were addressed to four different audiences. This was to be 'a tool for . . . hermeneutic, as well as historical questions'.[3] But this was not immediately utilized for the Pauline epistles.

The founder of reader-response theory was arguably Wolfgang Iser, a literary theorist. The advantage of Iser's theory was that it was based on an understanding of *perception*, which he drew mainly from Roman Ingarden and ultimately from Edmund Husserl. Ingarden adopted the model of '*filling out a schema*', in which from the visual perspective of the onlooker not every aspect was fully visible. For example, if we view a table or chair, we may be able only to observe three legs; and yet the mind construes a fourth leg on the basis of what regularly occurs in life. When this is applied to literature and to biblical texts, it entails the readers becoming *involved* in constructing what is 'there' in the text. In Iser's words, it involves their 'filling in the blanks'. Literary theorists welcomed this

---

[2] Baird, J. A., *Audience Criticism and the Historical Jesus* (Philadelphia: Westminster, 1969).
[3] Baird, *Audience Criticism*, p. 18.

model because it gave more attention than before to *the active role of the reader* as someone who *participated actively* in the act of reading.[4]

It is not surprising that many biblical scholars warmed to this idea, since it emphasized the need for *activity and engagement* on the part of the reader. The reader was *not now a passive spectator*, but an *active participant*. In NT studies a long list could be made of those scholars who followed this route, including Wittig, Bassler, Resseguie, Fowler and others. Admittedly some literary theorists take this approach to its extreme, as arguably Stanley Fish does. Whereas Iser had spoken of actualizing what was in the text, Fish concluded that there was nothing 'there' or 'in' the text to actualize or to construe. The reader saw, he claimed, as 'there' only what he or she had already *decided* was there. Stanley Fish's theory led to a radically postmodern stance, which most moderate biblical scholars regarded as undermining the authority of the biblical text, and substituting for it the authority of the interpretative community.[5]

In the case of Romans, reader-response theory may be illustrated by our discussion of reception history, which notes the different ways in which readers through the centuries have read and understood Romans. In Luther's case the epistle speaks largely of a new understanding of 'the righteousness of God'. In Augustine's case, the epistle above all speaks of renouncing the old life, and transformatively embracing new creation in Christ. Marcion and Sanders–Dunn–Wright have opposite ways of understanding Paul and the Jewish law. Jewett sees the epistle's major contribution as the call for tolerance and mutual respect. We should not dismiss most of these views as wrong, and reader-response theory enables us to understand each in turn with some contextual insight. Its weakness is perhaps that it does not provide clear criteria whereby we may regard some interpretations as doing better justice to Paul's text than others.

(2) Structuralist strategies of interpretation

Structuralism did not arise originally as part of biblical studies. It drew on three distinct routes: (a) the *general linguistics* of Saussure, Trier, and others; (b) the *social anthropology* of Lévi-Strauss and his systems of kinship;

---

[4] Iser, Wolfgang, *The Act of Reading: A Theory of Aesthetic Response* (Baltimore and London: Johns Hopkins University Press, 1978).

[5] Fish, Stanley, 'Going Down the Anti-Formalist Road' in Fish, *Doing What Comes Naturally* (Oxford: Clarendon, 1989), pp. 1–33; 'Why No One's Afraid of Wolfgang Iser' in Fish, *Doing What Comes Naturally*, pp. 68–86; and *Is There a Text in This Class? The Authority of Interpretative Communities* (Cambridge, MA: Harvard University Press, 1980).

and (c) the *structural analysis of narrative* suggested by Propp, Greimas and others. Yet in biblical studies François Bovon introduced this subject by stating that its goal was to understand the biblical text 'for itself, apart from all reference to an author, to a history, or to a reader', as 'a way of understanding the biblical material better'.[6] Bovon wrote in an era when biblical interpreters sought to escape the subjectivity of existentialist hermeneutics.

(a) Ferdinand de Saussure's *General Linguistics* was published as long ago as 1913. He distinguished between the actual *event of speech* or writing (*la parole*) and an abstract *system of language* from which speech or written words were selected (*la langue*). In this abstract system or reservoir of language it is clear that every word has meaning only in relation to that with which it stands in contrast (called its 'paradigmatic' relation) and to that to which it is adjacent (called its 'syntagmatic' relation). Thus, to select an example, the scope of the word *red* depends on whether it operates with *orange* or simply with *yellow* as its contrasting term. Trier developed this principle further by asserting that *only within a field* can words have meaning (German *nur im Feld gibt es Bedeutung*). Similarly Nida writes, 'Critical studies of meaning must be based primarily upon the analysis of related meanings of different words, not upon the different meanings of single words.'[7]

(b) Claude Lévi-Strauss applied this structural principle to kinship systems in anthropology (1958). Here he argued that a marriage system, for example, operates as a network, in which 'kinship rules' emerge as determinants of permissible and impermissible marriage-relationships. The terms *brother*, *sister* and *wife*, he argued, derive their significance *from similarities and differences within a kinship system or structure*.

(c) Vladimir Propp (1895–1970) and A. J. Greimas (1917–92) produced a 'narrative grammar', in which the roles of different characters in a narrative depended on their place *within a binary system or structure*. Thus a *hero* and a *villain* stand in opposition to each other; and related roles are assigned to a *helper*, a *task*, a *sender*, a *reward* and so on. Propp proposed 31 such related roles or events, and Greimas reduced these to about 20 'actantial models' in 1966. In many traditional folk-tales it is not difficult to see how these categories work out in stories about princes or knights as heroes, kings as senders, tasks such as slaying a dragon, and marriage to a princess as the reward.

---

[6] Bovon, François, 'Introduction' to *Exegesis: Problems of Method* (Pittsburgh: Pickwick, 1956), pp. 1 and 6.

[7] Nida, E. A., 'The Implications of Contemporary Linguistics for Biblical Scholarship', *JBL* 91 (1972), p. 86 from pp. 73–89.

In the 1960s and increasingly during the 1970s these types of models began to play an increasing part in biblical studies. An experimental journal, entitled *Semeia*, was largely devoted to structuralism, semiotics and narrative theory. Roland Barthes in France showed both the distinctive characteristics and differences in biblical narratives from features in many common narrative or mythological forms. In 1976 Patte edited *Semiology and Parables*, which concerned 'the possibilities offered by structuralism for exegesis'.

But how do Paul's epistles feature in this? One of the few structuralist approaches to the Pauline epistles came from Patte.[8] It is necessarily less indebted to narrative grammar. But it appeals to structure in that it calls Paul's faith 'a system of convictions'.[9] Patte writes, 'A specific *system of convictions* . . . can be termed a semantic universe . . . [It] establishes a realm of reality of other elements'.[10] In Romans and Galatians, Patte writes, 'The negative counterpart of "being in the right relationship with God" is "being under a curse" or "being a slave" to Torah, idols, or . . . spirits of the universe.'[11] Patte argues, 'Paul's Letter to the Romans is the most systematic presentation of his faith.'[12] He also sees Paul's concern for the 'weak' as not undermining his balancing concern for the 'strong' (Rom. 12.3; 14.3, 10; 15). The Jewish and Gentile believers have 'equal status'.[13] The responsibility of Gentiles and Jews as being 'without excuse' is equal (Rom. 1.18–32; 2.1—3.20; 7.2–25).[14]

Patte's approach to Romans remains a broader or 'softer' application of 'structuralism' in its original sense. But it probably has greater relevance to meaning and exegesis. Many regard the earlier numbers of *Semeia* as severely disappointing, while the journal often seems to ask *how*, rather than *what*, meaning has been generated by the texts. Often, later numbers of *Semeia* were given over more to post-structuralist concerns. Increasingly the voices of postmodernists such as Jacques Derrida and Michel Foucault have been influential, and polysemous or *indeterminate meaning* and fragmentation often dominate their work. Crossan was one of the earliest to pursue this trajectory towards the postmodern. Nowadays some regard structuralism as passé. Sturrock convincingly comments:

---

[8] Patte, Daniel, *Paul's Faith and the Power of the Gospel: A Structural Introduction to the Pauline Letters* (Philadelphia: Fortress, 1983).

[9] Patte, *Paul's Faith*, p. xviii.

[10] Patte, *Paul's Faith*, p. 21.

[11] Patte, *Paul's Faith*, p. 242.

[12] Patte, *Paul's Faith*, p. 244.

[13] Patte, *Paul's Faith*, p. 249.

[14] Patte, *Paul's Faith*, pp. 252–3 and 63–77.

Structuralism was taken up, and found to be exciting; an intellectual fashion was created, and for a time all sense of proportion was lost . . . Some found structuralism a genuine revelation . . . others have found structuralism [merely] a heady catchword.[15]

(3) Strategies derived from liberation hermeneutics

An affinity exists between social-critical readings which draw on Marx and some traditions of Latin-American liberation theology. In 1971 Gustavo Gutiérrez (b. 1928) outlined the programme of liberation theology. He demanded an understanding of the socio-economic situation of the poor in Latin America; faith as commitment to change, with the early Marx as a paradigm; a recovery of the exodus theme of 'going out'; and compassion for the oppressed, and eschatological hope. He appealed to Romans 8.24: 'We are saved by hope.'[16] Juan Luis Segundo and others share his emphasis on hermeneutics.

The most relevant to a distinctive reading of Romans is José Porfirio Miranda (1924–2001), who seeks to build 'a classless society'.[17] He wrote out of his context in Mexico, where he sees 'violence . . . that is institutional, legal, [and] juristical'.[18] He is less concerned about supposed parallels between Marx and the Bible than about justice and philosophies of power. As we might expect, he draws especially on Exodus, Amos and the Psalms. But he also makes distinctive use of Romans. He argues that 'the true meaning of Romans' is *not that of the justification of the individual, but a 'putting right' as a corporate, social, structural transformation.*[19] In Romans 1.15—3.20, he argues, Paul attacks all *adikia* (*injustice*). He approves of Otto Michel's comment, '[The] justice of God is at the same time judicial sentence and eschatological salvation'.[20] He rejects any individualistic or autobiographical interpretation of Romans 7, as Kümmel and others have done. Paul, he notes, shows that the law failed 'to put things right'.[21] Miranda then engages with other world-views of the modern era, including

---

[15] Sturrock, John (ed.), *Structuralism and Since: From Lévi-Strauss to Derrida* (Oxford: OUP, 1979), pp. 2–3.

[16] Gutiérrez, Gustavo, *A Theology of Liberation* (Eng., New York: Orbis, 1973), pp. 27–33, 82–4 and 216–25.

[17] Miranda, José Porfirio, *Marx and the Bible: A Critique of the Philosophy of Oppression* (Maryknoll, NY: Orbis, 1974, and London: SCM, 1977), p. xiii.

[18] Miranda, *Marx and the Bible*, p. 11.

[19] Miranda, *Marx and the Bible*, pp. 169–99.

[20] Miranda, *Marx and the Bible*, p. 173.

[21] Miranda, *Marx and the Bible*, pp. 187–92.

those of Heidegger and Sartre. These represent the wisdom of the world, which stands under judgement. Faith, in Romans, is not a special kind of 'work', but is directed to Christ and his resurrection (Rom. 4.17).[22] 'Putting on Christ' brings about *a new order for the world.*

(4) Existentialist interpretation

Bultmann is probably most closely identified with existential interpretation of the NT. In the UK Macquarrie has been a sympathetic but also critical writer on the subject. Bultmann remains indebted to Heidegger with whom he shared seminars in the 1920s. In his 'Reply to John Macquarrie', Bultmann declares: 'Heidegger's analysis of existence has become for me fruitful for hermeneutics, that is, for the interpretation of the New Testament.'[23] He writes, 'I learned from him [Heidegger] not *what* theology has to say, but *how* it has to say it, in order to speak to the thinking man of today in a way that he can understand.'[24]

Bultmann claims, 'The problem of comprehension has been brought into decisive clarity by Heidegger's demonstration of understanding as something existential.'[25] In practice this means distancing oneself from a purely 'objective' or merely *descriptive* mode of historical reconstruction, and having '*interest in history as the sphere of life in which human existence moves*'.[26] Bultmann endorses Heidegger's maxim, 'Nor is interpretation the acquiring of information . . . It is rather the working out of *possibilities projected in understanding.*'[27]

Heidegger has sought to break away from the traditional subject–object relation that has dominated theories of knowledge from Descartes onwards. *Dasein,* or the concrete human person, does not have abstract properties, but *possibilities, modes of being,* or *existentialia.* In his Germanic terminology, the ready-to-hand (*zuhanden*) is 'closer' to Dasein than the present-at-hand (*vorhanden*). In Anglo-American language, *self-involvement takes precedence over abstract description.* Descriptive language may speak of a person's weight, height and gender. 'Objective knowledge' belongs supposedly to

---

[22] Miranda, *Marx and the Bible*, pp. 201–10.

[23] Bultmann, Rudolf, 'Reply to Critics' in Kegley, Charles W. (ed.), *The Theology of Rudolf Bultmann* (London: SCM, 1966), p. 275.

[24] Bultmann, 'Reply', p. 276.

[25] Bultmann, Rudolf, 'The Problem of Hermeneutics' in his *Essays Philosophical and Theological* (London: SCM 1955), pp. 251–2.

[26] Bultmann, 'Hermeneutics', p. 253 (his italics).

[27] Heidegger, Martin, *Being and Time* (Oxford: Blackwell, 1973 [1962]), pp. 188–9 (my italics).

the realm of science. Understanding, Heidegger stressed, involves 'state of mind' (*Befindlichkeit*), which includes more than intellect; sometimes even emotion.[28]

At once Bultmann sees the utmost relevance of this to *Paul's view of humankind under sin* and of *humankind under grace*. The former faces nothing but bondage, dissolution and death. The latter faces infinite possibilities of life. In this sense, Bultmann writes, 'Man-under-the law has been made to see his situation under it as that of the "miserable wretch" groaning for deliverance from the "body of death"' (Rom. 7.7—8.11).[29] On the other hand, he declares, 'Spirit may be called the power of futurity', and under grace humankind is 'open for the genuine future, letting oneself be determined by the future'.[30]

Macquarrie, in spite of his severe criticisms of Bultmann's programme of demythologizing, maintains that Bultmann rightly borrows from Heidegger a way of putting questions (*Fragestellung*) and an improved *conceptual scheme* (*Begrifflichkeit*).[31] Here this becomes convincing. Paul never thought of the human person primarily in terms of 'parts', such as body and soul, but in terms of *modes of being*, and each with possibilities. In terms of humankind's being trapped in the cause–effect nexus of history, people face only condemnation for their past deeds and self-sufficiency. In terms of grace, eschatology, the Holy Spirit and the work of Christ, humankind faces increasing possibilities, and comes to live in accordance with these possibilities. Bultmann writes, 'The *imperative* "walk according to the Spirit" not only does not contradict the indicative of justification (the believer is "rightwised") but results from it ... The indicative is the foundation for the imperative.'[32]

These themes are acutely relevant to interpreting Romans, especially chapters 7 and 8. The existential interpretation of Christ as Lord is that the *Christian believer belongs to the Lord* as his property and care. It is ontologically the case that God made and declared Christ Lord (Rom. 1.3, 4). But in existential terms, Bultmann writes,

> *The believer*, as one 'ransomed', *no longer 'belongs to himself'* (1 Cor. 6:19). He no longer bears the care for himself, for his own life, but lets this care

---

[28] Heidegger, *Being and Time*, pp. 172–82 (sects 29 and 30).

[29] Bultmann, Rudolf, *Theology of the New Testament*, vol. 1 (London: SCM, 1952), p. 301.

[30] Bultmann, *Theology of the NT*, vol. 1, p. 335.

[31] Macquarrie, John, *An Existentialist Theology: A Comparison of Heidegger and Bultmann* (London: SCM, 1955), pp. 13–14, and broadly pp. 3–26.

[32] Bultmann, *Theology of the NT*, vol. 1, pp. 332–3 (his italics).

go, yielding himself entirely to the grace of God; he recognizes himself to
be the property of God . . . and lives for Him: 'None of us lives to himself . . .'
(Rom. 14:7–8).[33]

All of these themes stress the practical dimension of Pauline theology in
Romans and elsewhere.

Nevertheless Pannenberg and others call attention to the severe limitations of an existential approach. It carries the risk of devaluing both
ontology and propositions. Believers 'belong to' Jesus as Lord only because
God has made and declared him to be Lord through the resurrection
(Rom. 1.3). This approach equally risks transforming a biblical and Pauline
emphasis upon *God* into a modern-day emphasis on humankind and
'experience', as Barth has pointed out. I recall Pannenberg observing in
a one-to-one conversation about Heidegger, 'That one man should have
such a huge influence on so many people has been a disaster.' This does
not at all condemn *any* use of Heidegger and existentialist modes of
interpretation, but does condemn an insufficiently *critical* and *wholistic*
dependence on his thought.

(5) Pre-critical exegesis

This is best seen in our reception history from Marcion to Calvin. 'Pre-
critical' exegesis overlaps with reception history, but is not identical with
it. Cranfield strongly advocated delving into the commentaries of patristic
writers, including John Chrysostom, together with the classic commentaries
of Calvin, Bengel and others. This often provides a perspective which has
not been predetermined by what some *not altogether accurately* call 'the
assured results of biblical criticism'. Many gems lie hidden among the
commentators and theologians of earlier years.

(6) Karl Barth's approach

It is virtually unique to Romans that Barth (1886–1968) produced a classic
commentary on Romans (1st edn 1919, 2nd edn 1921). It constituted a
landmark and turning point in Christian theology. As in his small commentary on 1 Corinthians, *The Resurrection of the Dead*, the emphasis is
on the transcendence or otherness of God, on God's sovereignty as Creator,
and on his generous, free grace as Redeemer. From about 1915 Barth had
begun to disown the liberalism in which he was trained, and by 1919 was

---

[33] Bultmann, *Theology of the NT*, vol. 1, p. 331 (his italics).

writing on God's free grace. By 1921 he wrote on God's utter transcendence, which was partly inspired by Kierkegaard. He wrote concerning other commentaries of the era that they '[seem] to me to be not commentaries at all, but merely the first step towards a commentary'.[34] Calvin, he comments, 'sets himself to re-think the whole material and wrestles with it, till the walls which separate the sixteenth century from the first become transparent'.[35] The same cannot be said of Jülicher or Lietzmann, who attack 'practical theology' with 'intolerable and old-fashioned assurance'.[36] Barth, for his part, stresses what Kierkegaard called '"the infinite qualitative distinction" between time and eternity . . . "God is in heaven and those are on earth"'.[37]

On the beginning of Romans, Barth comments that the theme of Paul's mission 'is not within him but *above* him – unapproachably distant and *unutterably strange*. His call to apostleship is not a familiar episode in his own personal history [but] beyond his personal self-identity (Kierkegaard).'[38] In his relation to God, he is unique. On Romans 1.16, 17, he comments,

> The Gospel is not a truth among other truths. Rather, *it sets a question-mark against all truths* . . . The Gospel is the victory by which the world is overcome. By the Gospel the whole concrete world is dissolved and established . . . The Gospel of the Resurrection is . . . the supreme miracle, by which God, the unknown God dwelling in light unapproachable . . . makes himself known.[39]

He later comments on Romans 3.19, 20, 'What men account righteous and valuable . . . in God's sight is unrighteous and valueless.'[40]

This is the period of 'dialectical' theology: a 'no' upon the old life and a 'yes' upon the new life. All humans are relativized before the transcendent and gracious God. As in Bultmann and Kierkegaard, James Robinson comments, human 'subjectivity provides an access to the subject matter', not the pseudo-objectivity of most historical-critical methods.[41] He adds, 'The flow of the traditional relation between subject and object . . . has been significantly reversed. For it is now the object . . . the subject matter – that puts the subject in question.'[42] In this sense, Barth's work on Romans

---

[34] Barth, Karl, *The Epistle to the Romans* (Eng., Oxford: OUP, 1933), p. 6.
[35] Barth, *Romans*, p. 7.
[36] Barth, *Romans*, p. 9.
[37] Barth, *Romans*, p. 10.
[38] Barth, *Romans*, p. 27.
[39] Barth, *Romans*, p. 35.
[40] Barth, *Romans*, p. 89.
[41] Robinson, J. M., 'Hermeneutic since Barth' in Robinson, J. M., and Cobb, J. B. (eds), *New Frontiers in Theology, vol. 2: The New Hermeneutic* (New York: Harper & Row, 1964), p. 23.
[42] Robinson, 'Hermeneutic since Barth', pp. 23–4.

provides a decisive step towards 'The New Hermeneutic' of Fuchs and Ebeling in the late 1950s and 1960s, and indirectly to Gadamer. Barth's aim is that the sovereign God of grace should address the reader through Paul, not that the reader should simply discover Paul's thoughts *about* God.

(7) Lexical and grammatical exegesis and textual-critical research

The final three approaches have already been partly subsumed under other strategies of interpretation and in our exegesis below. Most thorough historical-critical approaches embody both lexical studies of the uses and meanings of words and phrases, and textual criticism. It is inconceivable that exegetes who use historical-critical methods might not work from secure texts, and that any could ignore significant word-studies in lexicons and articles in journals. Chapter 5 introduces textual criticism and the question of the integrity of Romans.

(8) Issues about shame and honour, and the imperial cult

This may constitute a special sub-category within the socio-scientific approach to biblical texts. It certainly applies to Romans. Jewett argues that the Roman Empire was 'held together' by 'the workings of honour and pride'. This 'provided the underpinnings of loyalty and gratitude for benefactors' that made the empire functional.[43] The combination of force, propaganda and patronage supplemented this. Jewett adds, 'This background is essential for understanding the argument of Romans, which employs honour categories from beginning to end.'[44] Shame and honour was, he claims, what Paul called *boasting*.[45] Judge makes a similar point, arguing: 'Self-magnification thus became a feature of Hellenic higher education.'[46] He alludes to an aristocracy of esteem. It is also easy to see how this theme runs throughout 1 Corinthians.

Slaves and barbarians were usually outside this system of honour and shame. But for Roman citizens and educated or literate Greeks this system formed a world of self-identity and status. Paul's proclamation of the

[43] Jewett, Robert, *Romans: A Commentary* (Minneapolis: Fortress, 2007; Hermeneia), p. 49, quoting Lendon, J. E., *Empire of Honour: The Art of Government in the Roman World* (Oxford: Clarendon, 1997), p. 13.

[44] Jewett, *Romans*, p. 49.

[45] Malina, B. J., *The New Testament World: Insights from Cultural Anthropology* (Atlanta: John Knox, 1981), pp. 51–70.

[46] Judge, E. A., 'The Conflict of Educational Aims in New Testament Thought', *JCE* 9 (1966), p. 39; also pp. 32–45.

gospel undermines such a working system, together with self-generated pride. At Corinth it is clear from archaeology and observation that monuments and benefactions very often constituted sources of pride and self-esteem which the gospel could undermine or sometimes reverse.

(9) The claims of form criticism

In the study of the Gospels, this approach becomes more prominent than it is for Pauline studies. Nevertheless fundamental formulae, such as thanksgiving forms, blessings and so on, all presuppose a setting in life. Whereas, however, a *Sitz im Leben* often removes material from Jesus to the setting in the life of the church, in Pauline studies the same approach may anchor the use of certain forms in the pre-Pauline church; we see them handed down in common apostolic tradition. The drawback of much form criticism is that too large a proportion of it may remain speculative and indemonstrable. On the other hand it may rightly help us to see Paul not as an isolated loner, but as sharing common traditions and forms with other apostles. In Pauline studies it is perhaps more helpful to regard the identification of literary forms and their usual settings in life as part of Paul's rhetorical or literary resources.

We have outlined 12 different 'strategies of interpretation' altogether. Three remain indispensable. The remaining nine are useful to a limited extent for passages in Romans. Our outline, however, is neither exhaustive nor exclusive, and includes overlappings and blurred edges.

4

The reception history of Romans

We first outline the origins and development of reception history. Second, we trace characteristics among prominent commentators or communities from each era of the Church, mainly before the modern era. Third, we select Romans 13.1–7 as an example of the varied reception of Romans over the centuries and today.

The origins and growth of reception history

Reception history in the fullest sense began as an aspect of literary theory in Hans Robert Jauss (1921–97). In the traditional sense of how the epistle has been received and understood, this has long been an interest during the centuries.[1] Jauss sees the purpose of reception history as to escape from 'a closed past', and to free the readers from 'prejudices and predicaments of a lived praxis . . . to a new perception of things'.[2] Questions and answers 'can provide access to the otherness of the past'.[3] All of these features are valuable in biblical studies, especially what Jauss calls the 'socially formative function' of the reception of texts.[4] Jauss was initially influenced by Heidegger and Gadamer, and later set out a programmatic agenda in his inaugural lecture in the University of Constance, under the title 'Literary Theory as a Challenge to Literary History'.[5]

Parallels with concerns in biblical studies proliferate. To summarize: (i) Jauss *rejects value-neutral positivism* or historicism, and this is now a growing trend among many NT scholars, notably in Francis Watson and N. T. Wright. (ii) Jauss explores *the horizon of expectation* with which readers come initially to the text. This is a more sophisticated version of what many scholars in hermeneutics call preliminary understanding, or 'pre-understanding'. What do we expect in advance that a text will say,

---

[1] Jauss, Hans Robert, *Toward an Aesthetic of Reception* (Minneapolis: University of Minnesota Press, 1982); and 'Question and Answer: Forms of Dialogic Understanding' in *Theory and History of Literature* 68 (1989), pp. 51–94.

[2] Jauss, *Toward an Aesthetic of Reception*, pp. 5 and 41.

[3] Jauss, 'Question and Answer', p. 63.

[4] Jauss, *Toward an Aesthetic of Reception*, p. 45.

[5] Jauss, *Toward an Aesthetic of Reception*, reprinted as pp. 3–45.

and why would it say it? (iii) All readers live and read within a *historically given situation*, which Jauss interprets as having pre-existing horizons. These can subsequently move, grow, change and expand. A number of philosophers and theologians stress this, especially Gadamer and Pannenberg. Often this is called our 'historical finitude' or 'historicality' (German *Geschichtlichkeit*). (iv) When horizons change, such changes may be profoundly *formative*. We begin to understand the text in a new way. (v) Like Gadamer, Jauss stresses the importance of *questions*, and their potential for unfolding potential meanings, and also *levels of meanings*.[6] This leads to our having new horizons. The readers then need to *appropriate* the reading anew.

It is not surprising that biblical specialists and theologians have paid close attention to reception history. Several survey the whole field, including Parris, Thiselton, Evans and Rush.[7] Some have explored the reception of particular books, for example, Luz on Matthew; the Blackwell series of biblical books 'through the centuries'; volumes in the Ancient Christian Commentary series; and *Reading Romans through the Centuries*, edited by Greenman and Larsen.[8] More general works also relate to reception theory.[9]

Particular eras of reception history

The patristic period

Marcion (c.150)

We know Marcion's work only through those apologists and Church Fathers who opposed him and attacked his theology, most notably Justin, Irenaeus, Tertullian, Clement and Origen. According to them, he excised parts of Romans, including Romans 1.3, 7, 15; 1.19—2.1; 3.31—4.25; 9; 10.5–11; 12.1; and chapters 15—16. In other words he regarded as non-Pauline

---

[6] Jauss, *Toward an Aesthetic of Reception*, p. 30; Gadamer, Hans-Georg, *Truth and Method* (London: Sheed & Ward, 2nd edn, 1989), pp. 369–79.

[7] Parris, David P., *Reception Theory and Biblical Hermeneutics* (Eugene, OR: Pickwick, 2009); Thiselton, Anthony C., 'Reception Theory, Jauss and the Formative Power of Scripture', *SJT* 65 (2012), pp. 289–308; Evans, Robert, *Reception History, Tradition, and Biblical Interpretation: Gadamer and Jauss in Current Practice* (London: Bloomsbury/T & T Clark, 2014); and Rush, Ormond, *The Reception of Doctrine* (Rome: Pontifical Gregorian University, 1996).

[8] Luz, Ulrich, *Studies in Matthew* (Grand Rapids: Eerdmans, 2005), pp. 254–79; Edwards, Mark, *John* (Oxford: Blackwell, 1988); Thiselton, Anthony C., *1 & 2 Thessalonians through the Centuries* (Oxford: Wiley-Blackwell, 2011); Rowland, Christopher, and Kovacs, Judith, *Revelation* (Oxford: Blackwell, 2004); Bray, Gerald (ed.), *Romans: Ancient Christian Commentary on Scripture*, vol. 6 (Downers Grove, IL: IVP, 1998); and Greenman, Jeffrey P., and Larsen, Timothy (eds), *Reading Romans through the Centuries* (Grand Rapids: Brazos, 2005). (Paul Fiddes on Romans has yet to appear.)

[9] Holub, Robert C., *Reception Theory* (London and New York: Methuen, 1984).

any part of the epistle that was positive about the Jews. This seems to be a better indicator of Marcion than attempting to reconstruct a portrait of him solely from those who opposed him. It seems as if he regarded Paul as the very antithesis of Judaism. Like the Gnostics, he drew a contrast between the Old and New Testaments, but he had too distinctive and emphatic a stress on God's grace to be called a Gnostic. He argued, according to his critics, that Christ had abolished the OT and even the God of the OT. Similarly Paul attacks the Jewish law. According to an older but well-known view, Adolf von Harnack quoted Franz Overbeck as suggesting that no one has really understood Paul except Marcion, that even he misunderstood him! Marcion was expelled from his original church of Pontus, and in due course was excommunicated from the church in Rome for his views. His picture of Paul is sometimes known today as that of the Radical Paul.[10] Judith Lieu warns us not to take polemical or rhetorical pictures of Marcion at their face value.[11]

Nevertheless it is very likely that Marcion could never have echoed the approach to Romans championed today, for example, by Dunn and Wright. The latter regards 'God's loyalty to the covenant with Israel' as crucial to Romans, against the background of Abraham and David, and the OT narrative of 'rebellion, decline, and exile of a long period of waiting for restoration; and the eventual new day of liberation that would dawn in God's good time'.[12]

Origen (c.185 – c.254)

The earliest extant commentary on Romans during the patristic period is that of *Origen*, as Cranfield reminds us.[13] The form in which it has come down to us is in the fourth-century Latin translation by Rufinus. Some Greek fragments are also preserved in the *Philocalia*. Origen was immensely learned, but his work on Romans was also prone to digression, and contained long excursi on Paul's use of the OT. Origen argued: 'Those Scriptures alone were inspired by the Holy Spirit, i.e. the Gospels and Epistles, and the law and the prophets, according to the declaration of Christ himself.'[14] Origen had an especially lengthy comment on Romans

---

[10] Meeks, Wayne A., *The Writings of St Paul* (New York: Norton, 1972), pp. 187–98.

[11] Lieu, Judith, *Marcion and the Making of Heretics* (Cambridge: CUP, 2015).

[12] Wright, N. T., 'Romans' in *The New Interpreter's Bible* (*NIB*) (Nashville: Abingdon, 2002), vol. 10, p. 398.

[13] Cranfield, C. E. B., *A Critical and Exegetical Commentary on the Epistle to the Romans*, vol. 1 (Edinburgh: T & T Clark, 1975; ICC), p. 32.

[14] Origen, *De Principiis*, 1.3.2 (Eng., *ANF*, vol. 4, p. 252).

1.1–7, where his interest is both christological and in the timeless nature of gospel truth. Since the gospel of God is what 'he promised beforehand' (Rom. 1.2), the gospel is eternal.[15]

On 'grace and peace' (Rom. 1.7) Origen cited OT parallels, such as the blessing of Noah. On Romans 1.16, 'also to the Greeks', Origen notes various attacks on the gospel made by Greeks, and Paul's need for patience and persistence.[16] On 1.17, he commented, 'None is excluded from salvation', and compared the words of Jesus on this. On 4.8, he called attention to the literal sequence of 'sin forgiven' and 'not imputed'. Forgiveness, he said, comes first, and then good works and maturity. On the law in Romans 7, he explained that the value of the law was to teach us what sin consists in. On 8.11, 'The Spirit of Christ dwells in you', Origen commented on the restoration of the body as the place where Christ dwells.

Ambrosiaster (fourth century)

This writer is anonymous, but of considerable importance. As an exegete he ranks almost alongside Chrysostom for his accuracy, learning and wisdom. We know nothing about Ambrosiaster's identity. Originally he was confused with Ambrose; but his approach to biblical interpretation is different from that of Ambrose. He is easier to characterize than Origen. He had a special interest in Judaism, valuing its privileges, and yet firmly condemning its unbelief in Christ. This dual attitude to our epistle makes Romans especially relevant.[17]

Ambrosiaster clearly understood the grace of God to be utterly independent of human 'works'. Further he compares Paul's missionary zeal in Romans with that of his former zeal as a Pharisee. Jewish Christians, he argues, have a rightful place in the Church, but Jewish rejection of Christ remains without excuse. He regards Rome as the heart of the Gentile world, in the same way as that in which Jews in the OT regarded Babylon and Nineveh as centres of worldly power. He distinguishes between Jewish ceremonial law, the eternal law of God, and 'common law' as reflected in human conscience. He is perhaps at his best on the meaning of the cross. The atonement nullifies sin and alienation. Through faith even Gentiles can become right with God. The wrath of God is a consequence of universal disobedience to the law. Ambrosiaster understands Romans 5—8 as presupposing the sacrifice of Christ, and as fulfilling the OT sacrificial system.

---

[15] Origen, in Migne, PG, vol. 82, col. 48; cf. Bray (ed.), *Romans*, p. 5.

[16] Bray (ed.), *Romans*, p. 29.

[17] Bray, Gerald, 'Ambrosiaster' in Greenman and Larsen (eds), *Reading Romans*, pp. 21–38.

John Chrysostom (c.347–407)

Chrysostom was Bishop of Constantinople, and studied under Diodore of Tarsus. Because of his widely appreciated preaching, he was nicknamed 'Golden-mouth' (Greek *chryso-stoma*). His *Commentaries and Homilies* on Romans are available in English.[18] He usually divides different passages into a first half of careful exegesis, and a second half of applied homilies. He was a passionate admirer of Paul, whom he called a 'spiritual trumpet' who 'roused and warmed me with desire . . . a voice so dear to me'.[19] He read Paul at least twice per week, and often three or four times. He laments, however, 'I grieve and am pained that all people do not know this man, as much as they ought to know him . . . some are ignorant of him'.[20]

Chrysostom expounds very well the need of all humankind for God's grace. When Paul speaks of the grace of apostleship, all humankind stands in need of this grace (Rom. 1.5).[21] He also draws a practical lesson from this. He comments: 'Do not become apathetic, because Paul has called this a gift of grace. He knows how . . . to call even good deeds, "graces"; because even in these, we need much influence from above.'[22] Likewise, Chrysostom helpfully expounds the sovereignty and transcendence of God, especially in his comment on the potter and the clay in Romans 9. On Romans 9.13, he exclaims, 'We must yield to the incomprehensibleness of Providence, for Paul has instructed us all, "never to call God to account for what happens even though what is done may seem to trouble the minds of many".'[23] These are matters too high, he says, for human understanding. To attempt to plumb the depths of God's wisdom and inscrutable providence will only lead to disaster.

At first sight Chrysostom seems to expound justification through faith accurately in contrast to 'works'. But Christopher Hall warns us about what he terms Chrysostom's 'synergism'.[24] On the one hand justification depends on the faithfulness of God and his promise through the law and the prophets. Together with this he has set forth Jesus Christ as the propitiation for our sins (Rom. 3.25).[25] On the other hand Chrysostom makes much of human free choice. This becomes explicit in Romans 1.25,

---

[18] Chrysostom, *Homilies on the Epistle to the Romans*, NPNF, ser. i, vol. 11 (repr. Grand Rapids: Eerdmans, 1975).

[19] Chrysostom, *Homilies on Romans*, p. 335.

[20] Chrysostom, *Homilies on Romans*, p. 335.

[21] Chrysostom, *Homilies on Romans*, Homily 1, pp. 340–1.

[22] Chrysostom, *Homilies on Romans*, Homily 2, p. 345.

[23] Chrysostom, *Homilies on Romans*, Homily 2, pp. 346–7.

[24] Hall, Christopher A., 'John Chrysostom' in Greenman and Larsen (eds), *Reading Romans*, pp. 47–57.

[25] Chrysostom, *Homilies on Romans*, Homily 7, p. 377.

where Chrysostom writes that sin produced its effects 'because the acts of free-will led the way'.[26] On Romans 7.15–16 and 8.7–10, when Chrysostom asks, What does it mean to walk in the Spirit? he answers: '[This comes by] freedom of choice placed in our hands. It rests with you, therefore, to become this or that.'[27] In this context faith becomes a 'contribution' to salvation. Yet on Romans 6, Chrysostom understands baptism as effecting once for all a dying to sin, similar to Christ's death on the cross. It becomes a life free from sin, in which we never again obey it. He writes, 'We may never again remain immovable as a dead man does.'[28] Nevertheless Chrysostom can *never* define human bondage in the way that Paul, Augustine or Luther do. Undoubtedly on the whole Chrysostom is an accurate exegete with abundant homiletical application.

Augustine of Hippo (354–430)

We have already related Augustine's account of his coming to Christian faith in his *Confessions*, partly through Romans 13.13, in our Introduction.[29] He tells us also how, while crying in tears before God, he heard 'the voice of a boy or girl . . . chanting over and over again, pick it up and read it'. He found a Bible, and opened it at Romans 13.13: 'Not in rioting and drunkenness . . . but put on the Lord Jesus Christ, and make no provision for the flesh.' Later he was convinced that this was one of three means of God's grace: Ambrose, Paul in Romans 13.13 and the prayers of his mother Monica. Each had been decisive for him. He was baptized by Ambrose on Easter eve, 387. In 388–9 he returned to North Africa, and was ordained in 391. Whereas Chrysostom had relished Paul and Romans as a regular sweetness in his Christian life, for Augustine they were decisive in bringing him to faith and transforming him.

Three continuous influences on Augustine are of significance. The earliest belongs to his Manichaean period, during which he first encountered Paul's epistles. In his later writings against the Manichees, he quotes the Manichaean Fortunatus as citing part of Romans 7.23–25: 'I see another law in my members, warring against the law of my mind . . . Who shall deliver me from this body of death?' Paul replies, quoting Romans 5.19: 'The grace of God has made me free from the law of sin and death.' Romans 7.23–25 seemed to the Manichaeans to accord with their negative evaluation of the human body. The whole exchange is recounted in English in

---

[26] Chrysostom, *Homilies on Romans*, Homily 4, p. 355.
[27] Chrysostom, *Homilies on Romans*, Homily 13, pp. 428–9, 436.
[28] Chrysostom, *Homilies on Romans*, Homily 8, p. 405.
[29] Augustine, *Confessions*, 8.12.28–29.

Augustine's *Disputation against Fortunatus*.[30] The second major influence was Augustine's encounter with the thought of Tyconius, a leading Donatist intellectual, and author of *The Book of Rules*. Tyconius had asserted: 'No one can ever be justified by works of the law.'[31] Tyconius argues on the basis of several texts in Romans and Galatians, which encouraged Augustine to continue to engage with this issue.

The third issue, which began around 397, was his encounter with Pelagius and the Pelagian controversy. Augustine saw humankind as *either* 'under the law' *or* 'under grace' (Rom. 7.25a, 25b). One of Augustine's major discussions occurs in *On the Spirit and the Letter* (AD 412), which argues that God's help in effecting righteousness consists not in the gift of the law or the 'letter', but in being aided and uplifted by the grace of God and the Holy Spirit. Human incapacity, which is clear from Romans 7, is explained by the doctrine of original sin, drawn mainly from Romans 5.19. Augustine quotes this verse when he comments, 'For as by the disobedience of one man, many were made sinners, so by the obedience of the one, shall many be made righteous.'[32] He repeats this quotation in *On Marriage and Concupiscence*.[33]

Augustine also discusses grace and free will in *On the Spirit and the Letter*, chapter 52 (AD 412). He asks: 'Do we then by grace make void free will? God forbid! . . . Free will is not made void through grace, but is established, since grace cures the will whereby righteousness is freely loved.'[34] Human incapacity is evident from Romans 7.7–25, in which the law cannot overcome sin, or lead to salvation. Further to all this, however, is Augustine's notorious misquotation of Romans 5.12, based on the Old Latin and Vulgate textual reading '*in quo*' (*in whom*), in place of the Greek '*eph' hō*' (usually translated *because*). Augustine followed the Old Latin in reading '*in quo omnes peccaverunt*'. This reading had reached him through Ambrosiaster and Ambrose, as well as Jerome's Vulgate. This misreading was perpetuated in the Catholic and Protestant Churches until it was challenged by Erasmus, who worked directly with the Greek text, in 1516.

Thus the twin themes of the universality of human sin and the supremacy of God's free grace came to dominate Augustine's thinking, not least on the Epistle to the Romans. So voluminous, however, are his writings

---

[30] Augustine, *Disputation against Fortunatus*, NPNF, ser. i, vol. 4, p. 121.

[31] Tyconius, *The Book of Rules*, 3.1.

[32] Augustine, *On Forgiveness of Sins, and Baptism*, 1.19 (15) (Eng., NPNF, ser. i, vol. 5, p. 22).

[33] Augustine, *On Marriage and Concupiscence*, 2.46 (Eng., NPNF, ser. i, vol. 5, p. 302).

[34] Augustine, *On the Spirit and the Letter*, 52 (30) (Eng., NPNF, ser. i, vol. 5, p. 106).

that it would not be wrong to suggest that various other themes in Romans also featured in his work.

The medieval period

Thomas Aquinas (1225–74)

Aquinas was one of the most influential philosophical and theological thinkers of the Middle Ages. Much of his theological material is available in the *Summa Theologiae*, and this can be compared with his commentaries, which included all the Pauline epistles. His work on Romans shows how firmly committed he was to justification by grace through faith (especially in Rom. 5); to the generosity of God's free grace (Rom. 4; 5); to predestination and election (especially Rom. 9—11); to good works (Rom. 12); and to original sin (especially Rom. 1.18–32; 7). His procedure in both commentaries and class instruction was first to divide the text into passages or stages of argument; second, to cite other parallel biblical texts, often in very large quantities. Third, he drew heavily on the Church Fathers, especially but not exclusively on Augustine. He also cited Chrysostom, Jerome and others. Fourth and finally, he drew on, or compared, the thinking of philosophers, especially Aristotle.

Aquinas is always concerned about Scripture, and language and its relation to truth. Sacred doctrine, for Aquinas, is revealed by God, and unfolded by Scripture and human intelligence in contemplation and in love of God. He writes, 'All Scripture inspired of God is profitable to teach, to reprove, to correct, to instruct in righteousness' (2 Tim. 3.16).[35] He continues, 'God destines us for an end beyond the grasp of reason . . . We are in need of being instructed by divine revelation.' Aquinas devotes question 13 of Part I of the *Summa* to theological language, concluding: 'The word "God" . . . is used neither univocally nor equivocally, but analogically.'[36]

Aquinas was especially drawn to Romans 9—11. In contrast to Marcion, he sees the importance of the Jews in salvation history for Paul. This emerges both from his *Summa Theologiae* and his *Commentary on Romans*. He is equally interested in Paul's doctrine of predestination in Romans 9—11. He discusses predestination systematically in *Summa Theologiae* Part I, question 23, in which he discusses passages in Romans. Romans 9.11–12 combines this with Paul's emphasis on pure grace. Paul declares that sheer grace is shown to human beings 'even before they had been

---

[35] Aquinas, Thomas, *Summa Theologiae* (60 vols, Lat. and Eng., Oxford: Blackfriars, 1963), Part I, qu. 1, art. 1 (vol. 1, p. 7).

[36] Aquinas, *Summa*, I, qu. 13, art. 9 (vol. 3, p. 87).

born or had done anything good or bad, so that God's purpose of election might continue, not by works, but by his call'. Aquinas comments on this passage several times, once with reference to Romans 8.30, and once to attack Origen's assumption that grace and predestination depends on foreseen merit.[37]

Aquinas also discusses Romans 9.15, 'I will have mercy upon whom I will have mercy':

> A gloss of Ambrose on Rom. 9:15: 'I will have mercy upon whom I will have mercy', says: 'I will give mercy to him who, I foresee, will turn to Me with his whole heart.' Therefore it seems the foreknowledge of merits is the cause of predestination ... The Apostle, however, rebuts this opinion where he says (Rom. 9:11–12): 'For when they were not yet born, nor had done any good or evil ... not of works, but of Him that calleth, it was said of her: The elder shall serve the younger'.[38]

Aquinas discusses 'hardening' of the heart in Romans 9.17–29. He writes, 'It is written (Isa. 6:10): "Blind the heart of this people, and make their ears heavy," and Rom. 9:18: "He hath mercy on whom He will, and whom He will He hardeneth".'[39] On resistance to the divine will Aquinas quotes Romans 9.19:

> It would seem that the will is moved of necessity by God. For every agent that cannot be resisted moves of necessity. But God cannot be resisted, because His power is infinite; wherefore it is written (Rom. 9:19): 'Who resisteth His will?' Therefore God moves the will of necessity.[40]

Aquinas presses Romans 11.29, 'the gifts and calling of God are without repentance', to serve his reply that no human action can change what God has predestined. He writes:

> Against this is the authority of Scripture. For it is said: 'But the triumpher in Israel will not spare and will not be moved to repentance' (1 Sam. 15:29); and that 'the gifts and the calling of God are without repentance' (Rom. 11:29).[41]

On the doxology of Romans 11.33, Aquinas considers the objection that 'in God there is not knowledge'. He replies, 'On the contrary, the Apostle says, "O the depth of the riches of the wisdom and of the knowledge of

---

[37] Aquinas, *Summa*, I, qu. 23, art. 2; and II-II, qu. 94, art. 1 (also online at <http://www.newadvent.org/summa/>, ed. Kevin Knight, 2006).

[38] Aquinas, *Summa*, I, qu. 23, art. 5, obj. 1.

[39] Aquinas, *Summa*, I-II, qu. 79, art. 3.

[40] Aquinas, *Summa*, I-II, qu. 10, art. 4.

[41] Aquinas, *Summa*, I, qu. 23, art. 8.

God" (Romans 11:33).'[42] He uses the further doxology of Romans 11.36 to answer profound questions about God. He considers the objection: 'Not all beings are from God as from their efficient cause.' He replies, 'On the contrary, It is said (Rom. 11:36): "Of Him, and by Him, and in Him are all things".'[43]

Aquinas' *Commentary on Romans*, together with his *Lectures on Romans*, follows exactly the pattern and themes of the *Summa Theologiae*.[44] In paragraph 764, for example, he cites Romans 9.11–13, commenting that Paul speaks of the children of Isaac and Rebekah 'even before they were born, and concludes, "I have loved Jacob, but I have hated Esau"'. As in the *Summa*, he writes, 'Foreknowledge of merits cannot be the reason for predestination, because the foreknown merits fall under predestination.' Moreover 'Love . . . pertains to God's predestination . . . Nothing in the Divine will is temporal; rather it is eternal . . . It is akin to love or predestination.' In paragraph 773 he is blunt about original sin and damnation:

> Since all men are born subject to damnation on account of the sin of the first parent, those whom God delivers by his grace, He *delivers by His mercy alone*, and so He is merciful to those whom he delivers: just to those whom he does not deliver, but unjust to none.[45]

This is no more 'lenient' or Pelagian than Augustine or Calvin.

We have the assurance of Aquinas specialists that Romans 9—11 was of particular concern to Aquinas for two reasons. First, he links predestination with God's purposes for the world. Second, he has a positive view of 'the Jews and their role in salvation history'.[46] In addition to Boguslawski's work which I have cited in note 46, Coolman, another such specialist, has specifically written on Romans 9—11 and Aquinas on the Jews.[47]

Peter Lombard (c.1100–61) and Nicholas of Lyra (1270–1349)

Peter Lombard worked in Paris from 1136, where he became bishop in 1159, and is best known as a systematic theologian, mainly from his

---

[42] Aquinas, *Summa*, I, qu. 14, art. 1.

[43] Aquinas, *Summa*, I, qu. 44, art. 1.

[44] Aquinas, Thomas, *Super epistolas S. Pauli Lectura* (Turin: Marietti, 1953); Eng., *Aquinas Study Bible: St. Thomas Aquinas on Romans*; online at <http//consolamnipublications/about-cp>; esp. paras 736–952 on Romans 9—11.

[45] Aquinas, *Romans*, para. 773 (my italics).

[46] Boguslawski, Steven, 'Thomas Aquinas' in Greenman and Larsen (eds), *Reading Romans*, pp. 81–2 and 81–99.

[47] Coolman, Holly Taylor, 'Romans 9—11' in Levering, Matthew, and Dauphinais, Michael (eds), *Reading Romans with St. Thomas Aquinas* (Washington, DC: The Catholic University of America, 2012), pp. 101–12.

Sentences. He was influenced by Hugh of St Victor, Haimo of Auxerre and the *Glossa Ordinaria*. Nevertheless, Levy, Krey and Ryan rightly claim, 'He made a major contribution to medieval exegetical tradition', and his *Great Gloss* 'proved to be a mainstay for centuries to come, and was frequently appealed to by the thirteenth- and fourteenth-century exegetes'.[48] He gave probably a more historical and literary interpretation of Paul than any other medieval writer.[49] In his *Preface to the Pauline Epistles* he provided a textual introduction, and declared, 'To understand things more fully, one should first seek their beginnings . . . [and] give an account of their purpose'.[50] Perhaps in contrast to Peter of John Olivi, originality was not his aim, and he often depended on the Latin Fathers. His more intellectual emphasis may owe much to the gradual takeover of the monasteries as centres of biblical interpretation by the universities, of which Paris and Oxford were among the earliest at this very time.

Nicholas of Lyra was administrator in the Franciscan order, and became regent master in the University of Paris in 1309. He is known for his learning and balance in his commentaries. Like Peter Lombard, he paid attention to the literal meaning of the text, and offered verse-by-verse commentaries. He had a rare knowledge of Hebrew, the Church Fathers, Hugh of St Victor and Abelard's writings. But within this context he maintained the tradition of attending to a moral and 'spiritual' meaning also.[51] Indeed Henri de Lubac credits Nicholas with formulating the aphorism: 'The letter teaches events, allegory what you should believe; morality teaches what you should do; anagogy what mark you should be aiming for'.[52] Gillian Evans regards Peter as beginning 'the Road to the Reformation'.[53]

The period of the Reformation

Martin Luther (1483–1546)

Luther was, in effect, the founder of the Reformation. He was born in Eisleben, Saxony. In 1505 he entered the Augustinian monastery at Erfurt, and was ordained priest in 1507. He lived as a devout monk, and professed

---

[48] Levy, I. C., Krey, P. D. W., and Ryan, T., *The Bible in Medieval Tradition: The Letter to the Romans* (Grand Rapids: Eerdmans, 2013), p. 33.

[49] Thiselton, Anthony C., *Hermeneutics* (Grand Rapids: Eerdmans, 2009), p. 119.

[50] Migne, PL, vol. 191, col. 1297.

[51] Thiselton, *Hermeneutics*, pp. 122–3.

[52] Lubac, Henri de, *Medieval Exegesis, vol. 1: The Four Senses of Scripture* (Grand Rapids: Eerdmans, 2000), p. 1.

[53] Evans, Gillian R., *The Language and Logic of the Bible: The Road to the Reformation* (Cambridge: CUP, 1991), p. 95.

vows of poverty, chastity and obedience. In 1508 he was called to the University of Wittenberg. The years 1512–19 were difficult ones, full of heart-searching, doubt and even despair. Monastic 'works' seemed only to deepen his despair. He later recounts, 'I was a monk for twenty years. I tortured myself with prayers, fasting, vigils . . . It caused me pain . . . What else did I seek by doing this but God? . . . I did this all for the sake of God'; but all this gave him no peace or assurance.[54] His lectures on the biblical writings provided one way forward. During 1513–14 he lectured first on the Psalms, and then on Romans. He wrestled with the meaning of Romans 1.17, 'The righteousness of God is revealed through faith for faith, as it is written, "The one who is righteous will live by faith." '

Luther was helped pastorally by John Staupitz, by the biblical work of Peter Lombard and John Chrysostom, and above all by Augustine on grace. Perhaps a year or so later he experienced a more profound engagement with Romans 1.17. We quoted part of Luther's words in Chapter 1 above, but they deserve fuller quotation now. Luther recalled: 'I hated Paul with all my heart', but later,

> by the mercy of God, meditating day and night, I gave heed to the context of the words . . . I began to understand that the righteousness of God is that by which the righteous lives by a gift of God, namely by faith . . . I felt that I was altogether born again and had entered paradise itself through open gates. There a totally other face of the entire Scripture showed itself to me.[55]

This breakthrough was not due to a single intense experience, but to several years of thought, study and prayer. It was the result of a sharp distinction between God's generous grace and human sinfulness and ecclesial 'works'. This became the 'lens' through which Luther now interpreted Romans.

Thus Luther wrote in his famous Preface to Romans,

> This epistle is in truth the most important document in the New Testament, the gospel in its purest expression. Not only is it well worth a Christian's while to know it word for word by heart, but also to meditate on it day by day. It is the soul's daily bread . . . The first thing needed is to master the terminology. We must know what Paul means by the words law, sin, grace,

---

[54] Luther, Martin, *Martin Luthers Werke*, Weimar edition (57 vols, Weimar, 1883–1929 [1527]), vol. 24, pp. 23–4.

[55] Luther, Martin, *Luther's Works* (Eng., 55 vols, St Louis and Phildelphia: Concordia and Fortress, 1955–2015), vol. 34, pp. 336–7.

faith, righteousness, flesh, spirit and the like . . . Faith [for example] is a living, unshakeable confidence in God's grace, so assured and certain that a man would stake his life on it a thousand times.[56]

Luther's *Preface to the Epistle to the Romans* attends to each chapter of the epistle. Chapter 1 asserts the sinfulness of Gentiles. Chapter 2 focuses on Jews, who are likewise 'all sinners'. Like Jesus' teaching on the splinter in a person's eye, and timber in one's own, Paul warns against our judging others.[57] Chapter 3 underlines that no one can be justified before God on the basis of his deeds. In Romans 4 Paul addresses Abraham's faith or trust. Chapter 5 presses the conclusion 'that faith alone justifies us'.[58] Romans 6 reminds us that 'sin . . . means something more than the external works done by our bodily action', and that we are 'struggling against the flesh'. In Romans 7 Paul tells us that 'The first duty of a preacher of the gospel is to declare God's law and describe the nature of sin . . . to show men their own selves and their lamentable state.'[59] Luther insists that to proclaim 'the wrath of God' remains part of the gospel. Chapters 5—8, however, teach us the peace, joy and love towards God that flows from our redemption in Christ. Luther writes, 'In chapter 8, Paul gives comfort to those engaged in this warfare, and says that the flesh shall not condemn them.'[60]

Like Aquinas, Luther regards chapters 9—11 as dealing 'with the eternal providence of God'; 'his providence will not fail'. We must 'concentrate on Christ and His gospel'; nevertheless election and predestination belong to the area of divine providence and governance. In chapter 12 Luther notes, 'All Christians are priests, and . . . the sacrifices they offer are . . . their own selves.'[61] In chapter 13 Paul 'teaches us to respect and obey the secular authorities'. In chapter 14 he teaches us how to deal with any who have an unstable conscience, and to spare them. Chapter 15 cites the example of Christ, and teaches 'that we should bear with others who are weak, even including open sinners'.[62]

The seminal thoughts of the Preface found fuller expression in Luther's *Lectures on the Epistle to the Romans*.[63] Timothy George points out that

---

[56] Luther, Martin, *Preface to the Epistle to the Romans* (Nashville: Discipleship Resources, 1977), pp. 3, 7.

[57] Luther, *Preface*, p. 4.

[58] Luther, *Preface*, p. 5.

[59] Luther, *Preface*, p. 8.

[60] Luther, *Preface*, p. 13.

[61] Luther, *Preface*, p. 14.

[62] Luther, *Preface*, p. 15.

[63] Luther, Martin, *Luther: Lectures on Romans* (Philadelphia: Westminster, 1956; LCC).

Luther's lectures were not read for some 400 years as a result of what James Atkinson has called one of the 'freaks of historical accident'.[64] His lectures show that he depended on a number of medieval commentators, including Alcuin, Anselm of Leon and Nicholas of Lyra; the Church Fathers Ambrose, Augustine, Gregory the Great, Origen and Chrysostom; and finally Erasmus. Yet Luther provides a regular critique of scholastic theology, and of Aristotle. George writes, 'Reformation theology is focused on the promise or the covenant (Latin, *pactum*), through which David heard the word of justification in his day . . . *Fides ex auditu*: faith comes by hearing'.[65] Gerhard Ebeling thus sees Luther as anticipating the New Hermeneutic. He reduced the four senses of Scripture to two.

Luther laid a special emphasis on the nature of sin. Whereas Aquinas had regarded sin simply as the absence of original righteousness, or privation of the good, Luther regarded it as the power of all our faculties of body and soul, in what was later to be called total depravity. Luther's deepened doctrine of the radical nature of sin has been taken up positively by Wolfhart Pannenberg. Pannenberg writes,

> Many modern treatments of sin have been unsuccessful because they have overhastily dismissed Augustine's [and Luther's] teaching . . . Augustine found an autonomy of the will that puts the self in the center, and uses everything else as a means to the self as an end.[66]

According to George, Luther's approach also resonates with Feuerbach and Freud. He comments on Romans 1.20: 'Luther anticipated Feuerbach's critique of religion when he observed that the root of all idolatry is human worship of God, *not* as he is, but as they *imagine* and think him to be'.[67] The Christian alternative, in Watson's words, is to 'let God be God'.

Romans 5 opens with Luther on 'the power of faith, as it proves itself in the justification of believers . . . St Paul speaks in this chapter with great joy and exceeding exultation'.[68] On Romans 8.15, he comments, 'Whoever believes with a firm faith and hope that he is a child of God, *is* a child of God'.[69] On Romans 11.26–27 he writes,

---

[64] Atkinson, James, *Luther and the Birth of Protestantism* (Atlanta: John Knox, 1981), p. 108.

[65] George, Timothy, 'Martin Luther' in Greenman and Larsen (eds), *Reading Romans*, p. 110.

[66] Pannenberg, Wolfhart, *Systematic Theology*, vol. 2 (Grand Rapids: Eerdmans, 1994), pp. 242–3.

[67] George, 'Martin Luther', p. 115.

[68] Luther, Martin, *Commentary on Romans* (Grand Rapids: Kregel, 1954), p. 88.

[69] Luther, *Commentary*, p. 122.

The purpose of the whole passage is to incite the people of God (the Jews) to repentance. To understand the apostle rightly, we recall that his statement extends to the whole lump of the Jewish people. Even if some among them are cast away, nevertheless the lump must be honoured because of the elect.[70]

On Romans 12.1–2, he writes, 'the apostle taught how Priscilla becomes a new man. He has described the new birth which gives us the new being . . . So here follow one upon another: the becoming, being and that working of good deeds.'[71]

John Calvin (1509–64)

Calvin was born at Noyon, Picardy, and studied in the University of Paris in 1523. In 1536, at the age of 26, he had already written the first edition of his *Institutes*. These expounded Protestant Christian doctrine according to the headings of the Apostles' Creed. He completed the first edition of his *Commentary on Romans* in 1539, doubtless based on lectures given in 1536–7. He published a second edition of the *Institutes* in 1539, and the first edition of *Romans* in 1540.[72] He planned a series on the Pauline corpus, beginning (after Romans) with 1 Corinthians. His two aims were to facilitate understanding of the Scriptures, and to expound and defend Reformation doctrine. He kept them apart, as far as possible, although they clearly overlap.

Calvin follows Luther when he comments, 'When anyone gains a knowledge of this epistle, he has an entrance opened to him to all the most hidden treasures of Scripture.'[73] Similarly he writes, 'The subject of these chapters may be stated thus: men's only righteousness is through the mercy of God in Christ, which being offered by the gospel . . . [is] apprehended by faith.'[74] Calvin compares the depths of human sin, from which God rescues us. Anticipating Bultmann's definition of the mind of the flesh, he calls it 'all self-confidence . . . deep self-security', as well as 'ingratitude', failure to give due honour to God, and covering 'inward depravity by the veil of outward holiness'.[75]

Calvin does not begin with the nature of sin because he is obsessed with the subject, but because after a brief comment on grace in 1.17, *Paul* begins

---

[70] Luther, *Commentary*, p. 162.
[71] Luther, *Commentary*, p. 166.
[72] Parker, T. H. L., *Calvin's New Testament Commentaries* (Louisville: Westminster/John Knox, 1993), pp. 15–17; and Demson, David, 'John Calvin' in Greenman and Larsen (eds), *Reading Romans*, p. 138.
[73] Calvin, John, *Calvin's Bible Commentaries: Romans* (London: Forgotten Books, 2007 [1847]), p. 17.
[74] Calvin, *Commentary*, p. 17.
[75] Calvin, *Commentary*, pp. 17–18.

with the universal sin of Gentiles (1.18–32) and Jews (2.1—3.20). Calvin also deals with the other major themes in these chapters, namely the wisdom and knowledge of God. Calvin comments on 1.18–23, 'It behoves us to know of God . . . God accommodates to our small capacities.'[76] To reject knowledge of God is both foolish and immoral. In 2.16 Paul expounds judgement. Calvin comments, 'God will judge the secrets of men . . . those who wilfully hide themselves . . . the most secret thoughts . . . hid in the depths of their hearts, shall be brought forth to light'.[77] On 3.20 he comments, 'Righteousness is not brought to us by the law, because it convinces us of sin and condemns us . . . showing man his sin, it cuts off the hope of salvation'.[78]

Calvin offers entirely positive comments on Romans 5.17. He writes,

> Christ surpasses Adam, the sin of one is overcome by the righteousness of the other; the curse of the one is effaced by the grace of the other . . . By *Adam*'s sin we are not condemned . . . because *we ourselves* are guilty.[79]

On Israel and the Jews (9.13, 15), Calvin comments on God's election that it is all 'through the kindness of God, not through our own merit . . . God is not unjust, because he is merciful to whom he pleases'.[80] Calvin goes further than Paul when he asserts, 'the lot of human beings is assigned to each by the secret will of God'.[81] Yet, George insists, in chapter 11, 'Paul's emphasis is that . . . Jesus Christ is the enactment of God's eternal will to be merciful.'[82]

Calvin begins Romans 12 with the comment, 'First, we are the Lord's, and secondly . . . we ought on this account to be holy.'[83] On Romans 13 he comments, 'Paul was induced to establish, with greater care than usual, the authority of the magistrates.'[84] Chapter 14 is very much 'necessary for the instruction of the Church, that they who have made most progress in Christian doctrine should accommodate themselves to the more ignorant, and employ their strength to sustain their weakness.'[85]

Calvin is broadly an excellent expositor of Pauline thought in Romans, retaining general faithfulness to the text. It is not for nothing that he has

---

[76] Calvin, *Commentary*, p. 47.
[77] Calvin, *Commentary*, p. 70.
[78] Calvin, *Commentary*, p. 96.
[79] Calvin, *Commentary*, p. 155 (my italics).
[80] Calvin, *Commentary*, pp. 260 and 263.
[81] Demson, 'John Calvin', p. 147.
[82] Demson, 'John Calvin', p. 147.
[83] Calvin, *Commentary*, p. 337.
[84] Calvin, *Commentary*, p. 357.
[85] Calvin, *Commentary*, p. 369.

been called the first of the modern commentators. Parker mentions in effect seven methods of interpretation in Calvin, of which I cite six. First, method is only a means to an end; no final and definitive claims should be made for it. Second, Parker argues, 'This method is characterized by two qualities, clarity and brevity. They are juxtaposed in his definitive statement: "The chief virtue of the interpreter lies in clear brevity".'[86] This principle accounts for his rejection of the commentaries by Melanchthon, Bullinger and Bucer as models, even if he praises Melanchthon's learning. Third, Calvin intends that doctrine should not obscure the objectivity of his exegesis. This is why, at the beginning of the second edition of the *Institutes*, he shows that he has so embraced the sum of religion in all its parts that he is able to keep his comments short, direct and to the point.[87] Fourth, he argues that his major duty is to lay open the mind of the writer whom the commentator has undertaken to explain. Fifth, he argues 'skill in interpretation consists . . . in judging whether the passage is to be understood according to its grammatical meaning'.[88] Sixth, likewise the commentator's understanding of the historical element of the Bible is crucial.

The modern period

The contrast between F. C. Baur and Johannes Munck

F. C. Baur (1792–1860) postulated in 1831 a sharp division between the Petrine and Pauline traditions, and in 1836 he applied this contrast to Romans. He regarded the whole epistle as expressing Paul's opposition to Judaism and his defence of the admission of the Gentiles to the Church. He imagined that the church in Rome was predominantly Jewish. He regarded Romans 9—11 as an important part of Paul's argument about the Jews. His view of the contrast between Peter and Paul had first emerged in 1831 in his lectures on 1 Corinthians, when he took literally the so-called party-labels, 'I belong to Paul' and 'I belong to Cephas' (1 Cor. 1.12). In his later work from 1845 Baur began to draw on Hegel's theory of thesis, antithesis and synthesis, to suggest that over against Peter's more 'Judaistic' gospel, Paul opposed this, especially in Galatians and Romans. Finally, a more synthesizing 'catholic' phase emerged in Acts and the later NT writings.

Johannes Munck is well known for his convincing demolition of Baur's theories. He began with Paul's call and commission and his mission

---

[86] Parker, *Calvin's NT Commentaries*, p. 87.

[87] Calvin, John, *Institutes of the Christian Religion*, ed. H. Beveridge (2 vols, London: James Clarke & Co., 1957).

[88] Parker, *Calvin's NT Commentaries*, p. 100.

to the Gentiles. Then he considered Baur and the Tübingen School of the nineteenth century. He commented, 'The bias of his [Baur's] critical theory becomes clear . . . a picture of Paul that is . . . assumed in advance.'[89] He adds, 'From the point of view of source and method, things are thus made to stand on their heads.'[90] The so-called 'parties' in Corinth were not parties at all. They were 'splits' (Greek *schismata*) motivated by power-claims, and not at all by adherence to contrasting doctrines. Corinth is a 'church without factions' in any doctrinal sense.[91] After all, Paul rebukes those who say, 'I am for Paul'. Munck rightly comments, 'Paul is not arguing in chs. 1 – 4 against false doctrine.'[92] In Romans Paul is writing to a *mixed* church. Thus: '[T]he weak and the strong in Rom. 14 – 15.5 [is] a contrast between Jewish and Gentile Christians.'[93] In chapters 12—15, Paul is setting out 'what is God's will for the Gentile's life in Christ'.[94] Munck's approach to Romans is radically different from that of Baur. They express entirely different versions of 'historical-critical' methods.

The approach of Krister Stendahl

Stendahl had studied under Friedrichsen and Riesenfeld in Stockholm, and taught at Uppsala and Harvard. In 1963 he published 'Paul and the Introspective Conscience of the West', which has since been reprinted twice.[95] Like Kümmel, he utterly rejects the notion that Romans 7 can have anything to do with autobiographical reflections. The 'I' of Romans 7.7–25 is not *Paul*. As a Lutheran pastor, Stendahl had witnessed agonies of conscience among some Lutheran students, and was eager to show that such introspection was emphatically not Pauline. Paul, Stendahl argued, did not emphasize personal, individual guilt, but the *corporate sin of humankind*. He admits: 'No one would ever deny that *hamartia*, sin, is a crucial word in Paul's terminology, especially in . . . Romans. Romans 1 – 3 set out to show that *all* – both Jews and Gentiles – have sinned.' But he adds, 'It is much harder to gauge how Paul experienced the power of sin in his life.' Indeed Paul asserts, 'I know nothing against myself'

[89] Munck, Johannes, *Paul and the Salvation of Mankind* (London: SCM, 1959), p. 82.
[90] Munck, *Paul*, p. 83.
[91] Munck, *Paul*, pp. 135–67.
[92] Munck, *Paul*, p. 152.
[93] Munck, *Paul*, p. 196.
[94] Munck, *Paul*, p. 206.
[95] Stendahl, Krister, 'The Apostle Paul and the Introspective Conscience of the West', Paper to the American Psychological Association in September 1961, *HTR* 56 (1963), pp. 199–215; reprinted in Stendahl, *Paul among the Jews and Gentiles* (London: SCM, 1976).

(1 Cor. 4.4), and 'as to righteousness of the law [I am] blameless' (Phil. 3.6). Stendahl concludes that in fact Paul had a 'robust' conscience.

The approach of E. P. Sanders

We noted above that Sanders' work constituted a watershed in Pauline studies for many, but not for all. His insights led to what is generally known as the 'New Perspective on Paul'. He rejected a simplistic understanding of the relationship between Paul and Judaism, which was not simply one of contrast. *Paul remained a Jew*, as well as becoming a Christian. He did not simply 'attack' rabbinic Judaism. Although Sanders often follows Davies, he argued that Davies tended to compare backgrounds, not 'what is essential' in both 'religions'.[96] He aimed at a more 'wholistic' comparison. He criticized especially Weber's notion of an over-clear antithesis between law and grace, and Bultmann's version of this.[97] He especially examined the role of 'obedience' in rabbinic theology.[98] He concluded, 'All Israelites have a share in the world to come unless they renounce it by renouncing God and his covenant.'[99] He adds, 'God has appointed a means of atonement for every transgression, except to reject God and his covenant.'[100] Salvation is received by *remaining within the covenant*. Rabbinic religion was thus corporate and collective as well as personal and individual.[101]

Sanders accepts Schweitzer's proposal that justification by grace through faith is not the sole 'central theme' in Paul.[102] Participation in Christ and cosmic aspects of Christ's Lordship are equally central, as Käsemann maintains. If justification is central, this is not simply the justification of the individual. *Romans 9—11 is no less 'central' than Romans 1—5*. Sanders writes, 'The assumption that the opening argument of Galatians and Romans gives the clue to all of Paul's theology is ultimately misleading.'[103] He prefers to see the starting point for Paul as being (i) 'that Jesus Christ is Lord, that in him God has provided for all who believe', and (ii) 'that he, Paul, was called to be the apostle to the Gentiles'.[104]

A fundamental practical consequence follows. Sanders aimed to *exclude* describing *first, the plight of man* to which, *second*, Paul saw Christ as offering

---

[96] Sanders, E. P., *Paul and Palestinian Judaism* (London: SCM, 1977), pp. 10–11.
[97] Sanders, *Paul*, pp. 42–59.
[98] Sanders, *Paul*, pp. 107–47.
[99] Sanders, *Paul*, p. 147.
[100] Sanders, *Paul*, p. 157.
[101] Sanders, *Paul*, p. 237.
[102] Sanders, *Paul*, p. 434.
[103] Sanders, *Paul*, p. 441.
[104] Sanders, *Paul*, pp. 441–2.

the solution. This is the way chosen by Bultmann, Conzelmann and Born-kamm.[105] On Romans 7 Sanders follows Kümmel, Stendahl and others. The *need* for a Saviour, he urges, 'springs *from* the *prior* conviction that God had provided such a Saviour'.[106] What God is doing is of *cosmic* significance. The gift of the Holy Spirit to Christians is the present guarantee of the future. *Union with Christ* now assumes a fundamental importance. 'In Christ' becomes a central theme, but not in the mystical and personal sense of Deissmann's interpretation. *Participation in Christ*, and in his death and resurrection, is then rightly called by Sanders 'transfer terminology'.[107] The death of Christ 'for us', Sanders concludes, is not only for 'past sins', but also to transfer us into the new creation. The emphasis falls '*not backwards towards the expiation of past transgressions, but towards the assurance of life with Christ*'.[108]

This profoundly influences our interpretation of Romans. To be sure Romans 1—4, and especially Romans 3.25, refers to

> forgiveness of previously committed trespasses . . . the cancellation of former guilt . . . [But] according to Rom. 5:9–10 . . . Paul . . . was thinking more in terms of *a change of lordship* which guarantees future salvation than in terms of the expiation of past transgressions.[109]

This provides a 'new perspective' on the law. The law has 'the function of consigning everyone to sin *so that* everyone could be saved by God's grace in Christ'.[110] The law becomes inoperative with the beginning of the messianic kingdom. If the *law* could save us, *Christ* died in vain (Gal. 2.21). It is *participation in Christ* that assures resurrection with Christ (Rom. 6.5). Paul's view of the ineffectiveness of the law is not the *cause* of salvation in Christ, but, Sanders argues, a *consequence* of the power of the gospel. What is wrong with observance of the law only is that the person or people concerned are not seeking God's way through *Christ* (Rom. 10.2–4; Phil. 3.9).[111]

This affects our understanding of the structure of Romans. Sanders observed, 'The entire theme of 2:12–29 is enunciated in 2:11: "God shows no partiality". Paul must then ask what advantage the Jew has (3.1).'[112]

---

[105] Sanders, *Paul*, p. 442.
[106] Sanders, *Paul*, p. 443 (his italics).
[107] Sanders, *Paul*, pp. 463–72.
[108] Sanders, *Paul*, p. 465 (my italics).
[109] Sanders, *Paul*, p. 466.
[110] Sanders, *Paul*, p. 475.
[111] Sanders, *Paul*, p. 482.
[112] Sanders, *Paul*, p. 489.

Thus, Sanders insists, '*Romans 1 – 4 is against the necessity of keeping of the law.*'[113] Hence the meaning of 'faith' undergoes change. In 3.25 it means *accepting* God's free gift. In Romans 4.16–23 it comes to mean *trust* that God will do what he promises. Sanders added, '*The argument for faith is really an argument against the law.*'[114] In contrast to Schweitzer he argued that no body of Jewish literature expects the abolition of the law with the advent of the Messiah. Hence Paul addresses the question of why God established the law. Good deeds 'do not *earn* salvation', but 'are the *condition of remaining "in"*' the covenant.[115] In Paul this is 'a *transfer term* . . . In Paul's usage "be made righteousness" ("be justified") is a term indicating getting in, not staying in the body of the saved.'[116]

Sanders' work is *defended with modifications* by Dunn, and with yet *further* modifications by Wright. At one time probably the majority of Pauline scholars broadly followed Sanders. However, Seyoon Kim and a significant number express reservations. Kim writes, 'Sanders' definition of Judaism as covenantal nomism is in need of correction, and therefore we cannot simply elevate it to the status of a dogma.'[117] First-century Judaism, he insists, contained an element of works-righteousness within its framework. Some of Sanders' themes remain generally accepted, but certainly not all of them. Cranfield has also expressed strong reservations.

Approaches to a single example passage: Romans 13.1–7

We conclude this account of reception history by reviewing the contrasting ways in which approaches to one instructive sample, Romans 13.1–7, have varied through history. This passage concerns political authority, and retained importance through the centuries. Broadly, the patristic and medieval periods valued Paul's very positive view of what today we should call the state. Origen wrote to Celsus, 'We are not so mad as to stir up the wrath of kings and princes . . . For we read, "Let every soul be subject to the higher powers. There is no power but God . . ."' (Rom. 13.1–2).[118] Chrysostom devotes seven pages (in English) in his *Homily on Romans* to Romans 13.1–7. He pleads that 'all things should not just be carried on in confusion'. For 'Anarchy . . . is an evil'. Will 'authorities punish a person

---

[113] Sanders, *Paul*, p. 490 (his italics).
[114] Sanders, *Paul*, p. 491 (his italics).
[115] Sanders, *Paul*, p. 517 (my italics).
[116] Sanders, *Paul*, p. 544 (his italics).
[117] Kim, Seyoon, *Paul and the New Perspective* (Grand Rapids: Eerdmans, 2002), p. 83.
[118] Origen, *Against Celsus*, 8.14 (Eng., ANF, vol. 4, p. 66).

that is doing well?'[119] The state is on guard, like a soldier. Rulers ensure 'good order and peace'.

Lactantius similarly declared, 'Render to all [authorities] the fear that is due to them, all offerings, all customs, all honour, gifts, and taxes.'[120] Eusebius credits Polycarp with saying, 'We have been taught to render to princes and authorities ordained by God the honour that is due, so long as it does not injure us.'[121] Both Lactantius and Eusebius were in effect imperial court theologians. But the same cannot be said of Athanasius, Basil and Augustine. Athanasius twice wrote, 'Render to all their dues,' on the basis of Romans 13.4.[122] Ambrose declared, 'I will pay the deference due to authority, as it is written, "Honour to whom honour is due, tribute to whom tribute"' (Rom. 13.7).[123] Augustine wrote that the Donatists should not 'resist the ordinance of God'.[124]

During the medieval period the Church and state were often a single authority. Aquinas followed Augustine closely, comparing the state to a household: 'It is ordained for the common good.'[125] He derived his thought from Romans 13.1–7, Augustine and Aristotle, and appealed several times to Romans 13.[126] At the Reformation, Luther's 'Two Kingdoms' theology owed much to Augustine's two Cities. Both have authority within their own sphere. Calvin, however, is emphatically positive about civil authorities on the basis of Romans 13.1–7. He cited Romans 13.4 for the view that laws are just and 'the strongest sinews of government'.[127] He strongly dissented from the Anabaptist tradition.[128]

Yet the Anabaptist tradition held a very different understanding of Romans 13.1–7. Thomas Müntzer understood Romans 13.4 as expelling evildoers from the Church, as 'protection for the pious' and 'to wipe out the godless'.[129] Similarly Obe Phillips declared on the basis of Romans 13.1, 'The higher power has received the sword from God, not that it shall judge therewith in spiritual matters . . . but to protect the pious.'[130] In the twentieth century this view is supported by Yoder, Schlier, Caird (broadly) and Wink.

---

[119] Chrysostom, *Homilies on Romans*, Homily 23, pp. 511–14.
[120] Lactantius, *Constitutions of the Holy Apostles*, 2.13 (Eng., *ANF*, vol. 7, p. 436).
[121] Eusebius, *Ecclesiastical History*, 4.22 (Eng., *NPNF*, ser. ii, vol. 1, p. 190).
[122] Athanasius, *Letter*, 6.5 and 10.1 (Eng., *NPNF*, ser. ii, vol. 4, p. 521).
[123] Ambrose, *Letter*, 40.12 (Eng., *NPNF*, ser. ii, vol. 10, p. 454).
[124] Augustine, *The Letter of Petilian the Donatist*, 2.45 (Eng., *NPNF*, ser. i, vol. 4, p. 540).
[125] Aquinas, *Summa*, I-II. qu. 90, art. 3, reply to obj. 3.
[126] Aquinas, *Summa*, I-II. qu. 96, art. 5.2.2; qu. 88, art. 10, and art. 4, reply to obj. 1.
[127] Calvin, *Institutes*, 4.20.14 and 16.
[128] Calvin, *Institutes*, 4.20.19.
[129] Williams, G. H. (ed.), *Spiritual and Anabaptist Writers* (London: SCM, 1957; LCC 25), pp. 66, 68.
[130] Williams (ed.), *Anabaptist Writers*, p. 253.

The last two have written of the 'principalities and powers' which mark a political authority that has gone beyond God-given limits.[131] The most influential negative approach has been Cullmann, *The State in the New Testament* (1963), which we cite and discuss under Romans 13.1–7.

On the other hand O'Donovan convincingly argues that 'political communities' and their authority are ordained by God, and follows exactly the exegetical logic of Romans 13.1–7.[132] In a later work he writes, 'The authority of government [is] essentially an act of judgment . . . to reward the just and punish the evil.'[133] Judgement is 'an act of moral discrimination.'[134] O'Donovan associates this passage in Romans with 'righteousness', as in the theme of Romans in 1.17 and 1.18—3.20. Under Romans 13.1–7, we also trace this theme in the liberation theologian José P. Miranda. In the mid-twentieth century Emil Brunner insisted that the state is an 'ordinance' of God, of 'preserving grace'.[135] In the same era Reinhold Niebuhr argues for the use of power to oppose abused power.[136] Today, Sarah Coakley insists that the search for justice 'must go on strategically'.[137] Finally, Pannenberg traces the biblical origins of the political order from the Davidic monarchy onwards, and concludes, 'Something in law . . . corresponds to the difference between church and state, for the political order is essentially a legal order.'[138]

The reception of Romans is exemplified strikingly by the polar opposite ways in which Romans 13.1–7 has been interpreted over the centuries. In very broad terms, the patristic and medieval interpreters understood Romans 13.1–7 at face value, and regarded state authorities positively as deserving obedience. Later the Anabaptists and some modern writers, especially Mennonites, viewed it more negatively, stressing the possibility of oppressive totalitarianism. Nevertheless most modern interpreters today regard civil authority as God's ordinance, worthy of obedience, unless or until it lapses into totalitarian forms. This crosses the God-ordained line.

---

[131] Yoder, John, *The Politics of Jesus* (Grand Rapids: Eerdmans, 2nd edn, 1994); Schlier, Heinrich, *Principalities and Powers in the New Testament* (New York: Herder, 1961); Caird, George B., *Principalities and Powers: A Study in Pauline Theology* (Oxford: OUP, 1956); and Wink, Walter, *Naming the Powers, Unmasking the Powers* and *Engaging the Powers* (3 vols, Augsburg: Fortress, 1984, 1986 and 1992).

[132] O'Donovan, Oliver, *The Desire of Nations: Rediscovering the Roots of Political Theology* (Cambridge: CUP, 1996), p. 233 and throughout.

[133] O'Donovan, Oliver, *The Ways of Judgment* (Grand Rapids: Eerdmans, 2005), p. 4.

[134] O'Donovan, *Ways of Judgment*, p. 7.

[135] Brunner, Emil, *Natural Theology* (Eugene, OR: Wipf & Stock, 2002 [1948]).

[136] Niebuhr, Reinhold, *The Nature and Destiny of Man* (2 vols, London: Nisbet, 1941), vol. 1, pp. 221–33.

[137] Coakley, Sarah, *God, Sexuality, and the Self* (Cambridge: CUP, 2013), p. 80.

[138] Pannenberg, Wolfhart, *Systematic Theology*, vol. 3 (Grand Rapids: Eerdmans, 1998) p. 57 and pp. 49–57.

5

The textual criticism and integrity of Romans

If the whole of Romans is relevant to readers, can we be sure that Paul wrote chapters 1—16? In the nineteenth century many writers offered partition theories, but these have been for the most part discredited today. However, problems remain about the place of doxologies within the text and earliest manuscripts in the last three chapters. In order to appreciate these, we must address some basic issues about the Greek manuscripts and textual criticism.

An introduction to basic textual criticism in Romans

Textual criticism often compares early Greek manuscripts which turn out to have only minor significance for the meaning. But in the case of Romans, two issues which do immediately affect meaning are widely known. One concerns Romans 5.1. Where some manuscripts read, '*We have* peace with God' (Greek *echomen*), others read, '*Let us have* peace with God' (Greek *echōmen*). This depends on whether they reflect the Greek present *indicative* or the present *subjunctive* of the verb. The second, as we have mentioned, concerns the placing of the doxologies at the end of chapters 14, 15 and 16, or even in more than one place.

The evidence of variations in the manuscripts derives especially from texts dating from the second century onwards. In the process of copying them, these manuscripts underwent deliberate or accidental variations that necessitate textual criticism. *Accidental* variations might arise when a copyist skipped a word, or mistook one letter for another. *Deliberate* alterations arose from the desire of the copyist either to clarify the passage or to harmonize it with another.

The very earliest manuscripts of the Greek Testament are *the papyri*, mainly discovered in Egypt, which date from the second century. These are earlier than the major uncial codices (i.e. texts written in Greek capitals, discussed below). Two of the oldest manuscripts (MSS) are the papyrus known as P[46]; and, even older, P[52], which is now in the John Rylands Library, Manchester. This provides a fragment of John, which some date as early as around AD 125. The Chester Beatty papyri, which are also very early, include P[45], P[46] and P[47]. These were acquired by Sir Alfred Chester Beatty in 1930–1, and are now housed in Dublin.

The five most important *early uncial codices* are as follows: (i) Codex Sinaiticus (usually identified by the symbol ‭א‬), is a fourth-century manuscript now in the British Museum. It was found in the Monastery of Saint Catherine on Mount Sinai. Konstantin von Tischendorf discovered it in 1844, and it is usually regarded as second in value only to Codex Vaticanus. (ii) Codex Alexandrinus (identified as A) is in the British Museum, and was presented to James I by the then Patriarch of Alexandria. (iii) Codex Vaticanus, called B, dates from the fourth century, and originated in Alexandria. It is the most important and highly valued of the uncial manuscripts, and has been in the Vatican Library since 1481. (iv) Codex Ephraemi Rescriptus (C) dates from the fifth century, and is partly mutilated. It was associated with Ephraem of Syria, and is preserved in Paris. Its full name recalls that it was a palimpsest, i.e. used twice, and overwritten. (v) Codex Bezae (D) also dates from the fifth century, and was presented to Cambridge University by Theodore Beza in 1581.

These are by no means the only important uncial MSS. Another early uncial manuscript (MS) became known as D[2] to distinguish it from D. It dates from the sixth century, but remained one of the leading 'Western' MSS on Paul, together with D, F, G and H, which cover the complete epistles of Paul. Sometimes a MS will be qualified by a second symbol. For example, ‭א‬* signifies the first corrector of ‭א‬. The symbol 33 denotes the earliest and most important 'cursive' Greek MS, i.e. in lower case. Accents emerged in the second century.

By the second and third centuries, (i) *Church Fathers* cited NT passages, and this provided further evidence of early textual readings. The critical apparatus of the Greek Testament included not only papyri, uncials and cursives, but also such pre-Nicene Fathers as Clement, Tertullian, Origen and Cyprian. (ii) Latin, Syriac and Coptic *versions* (VSS) of the Greek text also become significant supplements. Old Syriac dates from the fourth century. The Bohairic version (VS) of the Coptic is the official version of the Coptic Church. The Vulgate is a Latin VS, dating from Jerome, and was traditionally used in the Roman Catholic Church. (iii) The one other major factor concerns *internal reasons* about why the earlier MS may be overridden, but these depend entirely on specific exegesis.

This basic introduction to textual criticism now allows us to consider specific examples in Romans. We need consider most of these only briefly, because we discuss them in our exegesis of the text.

Specific textual issues in Romans

(1)The most famous of all, as we noted, is Romans 5.1, 'We have peace' (Greek *echomen*) or 'Let us have peace' (Greek *echōmen*). As we note in our chapter on Romans 5.1–11, ℵ*, A, B*, C, D, 33, and many other later MSS read the subjunctive *echōmen*, '*let us have* peace with God'. The indicative *echomen*, '*we have* peace with God', is found in ℵ, B², F, Coptic Sahidic VS and other later MSS. Metzger, however, reports that the United Bible Societies (UBS) Committee 'judged that internal evidence should take precedence', especially since Paul is not exhorting here, but 'stating facts'. He adds: 'Only the indicative is consonant with the apostle's argument.'[1] Further, in the age of Hellenistic Greek the difference between the pronunciation of o and ō was almost non-existent. Jewett, Kuss and Porter are in a small minority who adopt the subjunctive.[2] Dunn, Cranfield, Fitzmyer, Wright and most commentators adopt the indicative.[3]

Apart from Romans 5.1 and those verses that relate to the integrity of the epistle, there remain only three or four of comparable significance. (i) The first is also well known. Does Paul say in Romans 8.28, 'All things work together for good for those who love God' (NRSV, Authorized Version/King James Bible (AV/KJB)), or 'God works all things together . . .' (New Jerusalem Bible (NJB), Revised English Bible (REB), New International Version (NIV))? Dodd, Cranfield, Wright and Jewett prefer this. The first reading, which the NRSV supports, is found in ℵ, C, D, G and 33, some Old Syriac VSS and Coptic Bohairic. But 'God' (Greek *ho theos*) is added to the sentence by the earlier P⁴⁶, A, B, Coptic Sahidic VS and Origen. A complication is that P⁴⁶ reads *pan* (singular, *all*). Fitzmyer comments, 'In view of the fluctuation in the text tradition, it is not easy to be certain about which interpretation is better. Any one of them would suit the context.'[4] Dunn also regards both readings as having good support, although 'God' might represent a smoothing out of the text.[5] Dodd commented that 'all things' risks 'a natural tendency towards progress', which is not

---

[1] Metzger, Bruce, *A Textual Commentary on the Greek New Testament* (New York: UBS, 2nd edn, 1994), p. 452.

[2] Jewett, Robert, *Romans: A Commentary* (Minneapolis: Fortress, 2007; Hermeneia), p. 344; Kuss, Otto, *Der Römerbrief übersetzt und eklärt* (3 vols, Regensburg; Pustet, 1957–78), vol. 1, pp. 201–2.

[3] Dunn, James D. G., *Romans 1—8* (Dallas: Word, 1988; WBC 38), p. 245; Cranfield, C. E. B., *A Critical and Exegetical Commentary on the Epistle to the Romans*, vol. 1 (Edinburgh: T & T Clark, 1975; ICC), pp. 257–8; Fitzmyer, Joseph A., *Romans: A New Translation with Introduction and Commentary* (New York: Doubleday, 1992; AB 33), p. 395; Wright, N. T., 'Romans' in the *New Interpreter's Bible* (*NIB*) (Nashville: Abingdon, 2002), vol. 10, p. 515.

[4] Fitzmyer, *Romans*, p. 523.

[5] Dunn, *Romans 1—8*, p. 466.

Paul's view, and Jewett agrees.[6] Yet Nygren, Byrne and Käsemann favour the AV/KJB and NRSV reading ('All things'), against Jewett, Cranfield and Wright, who prefer 'God works', as more consistent with Paul's theology.[7]

(2) Romans 9.5 presents a notorious christological crux. The NRSV has 'the Messiah, who is over all, God blessed for ever'. Its marginal reading, however, suggests: 'the Messiah, who is God over all, blessed for ever'. The stakes may seem high. But the problem is that the different versions depend wholly on differences of punctuation, and, as Metzger comments, 'The earliest manuscripts of the N.T. are without systematic punctuation.'[8] Contrary to the NRSV, a minority of the UBS Committee under Metzger's chairmanship favour 'Christ, who is God over all, blessed for ever'. But the majority of the Committee thought that no consideration was decisive, and that much depended on the theological judgement of whether Paul is likely to have explicitly called Christ 'God' in this context. Most thought that this was unlikely. (See further under 9.5.) It looks as if ℵ, C, D, G and 33 favour the view that Paul does not explicitly call Christ 'God' in this verse.

(3) In 14.19 the NRSV translates: 'Let us then pursue [Greek *diōkōmen*] what makes for peace'. But others read the indicative. Metzger comments that the UBS Committee had great difficulty in reaching a decision about this verse, and grades it 'D', the least certain.[9] The indicative (*diōkomen*) is supported by ℵ, A, B and G. But the Committee believed that the hortatory text was marginally more likely.

All in all, the UBS Committee considered over 60 MS variants, but the vast majority of them are of minimal importance for understanding the meaning of verses in Romans. This brings us to those which raise questions about the integrity of Romans.

The integrity of the epistle

Only a minority of scholars have questioned any division in Romans, except for interruptions and uncertainties about Romans 15 and 16. John O'Neill and Walther Schmithals regularly find interpolations in several letters, and for them Romans is no exception. However, Kümmel reflects the mainstream view when he comments, 'The authenticity and unity of

---

[6] Jewett, *Romans*, p. 526; Dodd, C. H., *The Epistle of Paul to the Romans* (London: Hodder & Stoughton, 1932), p. 138.

[7] Jewett, *Romans*, p. 526; Wright, 'Romans', *NIB*, vol. 10, p. 600; Cranfield, *Romans*, vol. 1, pp. 424–9, expounded in detail.

[8] Metzger, *Textual Commentary*, p. 459.

[9] Metzger, *Textual Commentary*, p. 469.

Rom. 1 – 15 admit of no serious doubt.'[10] He regards the primitive text as running from 1.1 to 16.23, even if Marcion's text ran up only to 14.23, with the minor omission of 'in Rome' in 17 and 1.15.

The doxology in Romans 16.25–27 has been placed in various positions in different MSS. The early papyrus P[61], ℵ, B, C, D and the Old Syriac place it at 16.25–27. But the very early papyrus P[46] places it at the end of chapter 15; and the cursive 33 places it both there and at 16.25–27. G and Marcion omit it altogether. Further, 'the grace' occurs both in 16.20 and also 16.24 in one manuscript, K, while D omits it altogether in 16.20. The early P[46], P[61], ℵ, A and B place it at 16.24. On top of all this, G omits 'in Rome' from Romans 1.7 and 1.15. Among the earlier ante-Nicene Fathers, Tertullian appears to cite 14.10 as being in the concluding section, and never quotes from Romans 15 or 16.

In the light of these textual problems about chapters 15 and 16, some, including Manson, advocate the hypothesis that Paul originally wrote only Romans 1.1—14.23 (probably without the reference to Rome in 1.7 and 1.15). He would have written these chapters as a general epistle to the churches that he had not yet visited. But, so the theory goes, he then added 1.7 and 1.15 and Romans 14.23—16.27, to make it specific to Rome. Cranfield and many others, however, think that this theory is 'most unlikely', especially since Romans 1.8–13 contains more specific references than we might expect to find in a merely 'general' letter.[11]

T. W. Manson has a special theory which may at first seem more plausible. It is well known that Marcion was not well received in Rome. Hence his resentment against the church in Rome, Manson argues, led him to excise the original references to Rome in Romans 1.7 and 1.15. Again, most writers reject this theory as unlikely, but nevertheless certainly possible. Manson argued that Paul wrote Romans 1.1—15.33 for Rome, and then sent a copy to *the church in Ephesus, to which he added chapter 16*. His theory is accepted by Munck, Leenhardt and Bultmann. It rests on the presupposition that the greetings of chapter 16 are more suited to Ephesus, which Paul knew very well, than to Rome, which he had not visited. Romans, he held, is a manifesto of the gospel, which deserves *wide circulation*.

Manson first propounded this theory in 1938, with subsequent reprints and revisions. Donfried has reprinted it in *The Romans Debate*.[12] He argues, 'Romans is a calm and collected summing up of Paul's position as it had

---

[10] Kümmel, Werner G., *Introduction to the New Testament* (London: SCM, 1966), p. 222.

[11] Cranfield, *Romans*, vol. 1, p. 7.

[12] Manson, T. W., 'St. Paul's Letter to the Romans – and Others' in Donfried, Karl P. (ed.), *The Romans Debate* (Grand Rapids: Baker Academic, 2nd edn, 1991), pp. 3–15.

been hammered out in the heat of controversy during the previous months.'[13] The omissions of 'in Rome' are ancient, at least by the mid-second century. But he acknowledges that the text of the very early P[46] presents a problem. He admits that chapter 15 and the commendation of Phoebe seem to be addressed to Rome. Further, the greetings of chapter 16 are supported not only by P[46], but also by ℵ, B, C, Coptic VSS, the Vulgate and the Latin version of Origen. However, he replies, 'The covering note (Ch.16) and the Roman Letter (1–15) were associated from the beginning and presumably formed a single document, which were preserved in the archives of the Ephesian community.'[14] He writes that Paul sent a copy of his letter to his friends in Ephesus, which would be available to the churches of Asia. He then decided to send a copy to Rome, to which he added a statement of his future plans. Manson concludes, 'Looked at in this way, Romans ceases to be just a letter of self-introduction from Paul to the Roman church, and becomes a manifesto of his deepest convictions.'[15]

Many contemporary scholars argue that Romans 15.33 might have once constituted the conclusion of this letter, especially in the light of the discovery of the early P[46]. Metzger considers 'the possibility that Paul may have made two copies of the Epistle, one with and one without chapter 16'.[16] Ephesus arises as a probable or possible destination because Paul had a longer ministry there than anywhere else, and he would have had many friends there. Further, Epaenetus was 'the first convert in Asia' (16.5), and Prisca and Aquila (16.3) would be no less likely to come from Ephesus than from Rome. According to Metzger, the Committee of the United Bible Societies gave serious consideration to both Manson's theory, and the hypothesis of Paul's longer and shorter letters, especially in the light of the varied places of the doxology.[17] In the end, however, like Kümmel and many others, they did not consider it convincing.

Bruce, Cranfield, Wright and Jewett, among many others, argue convincingly for the traditional view that Paul wrote Romans 1—16. The list of names, Cranfield argues, constitutes 'A good way of establishing contact, which is something he is desirous of doing in writing to the Roman church'.[18] It is also more than possible that Paul's friends would have found their way to the imperial capital, and many Jewish Christians would have

---

[13] Manson, 'Romans – and Others', p. 4.
[14] Manson, 'Romans – and Others', pp. 13–14.
[15] Manson, 'Romans – and Others', p. 15.
[16] Metzger, *Textual Commentary*, p. 470.
[17] Metzger, *Textual Commentary*, p. 472.
[18] Cranfield, *Romans*, vol. 1, p. 10.

returned to Rome after the death of Claudius. Jewett also makes a strong and convincing argument about Phoebe and Latin-speaking Spain, which is infinitely more probable than Manson's theory.[19] We consider Jewett's reconstruction elsewhere in this commentary. Bruce comments, 'That a separate letter to the church in Ephesus has somehow been tacked on to a letter addressed to Rome is highly improbable.'[20] Commenting on Paul's thanksgiving for the church, in positive terms, he declares, 'There was a flourishing church in Rome, and many Christians whom Paul had met elsewhere in his travels were now resident in Rome.'[21] *Social mobility in the mid-first-century empire was good.*

---

[19] Jewett, *Romans*, pp. 74–91.

[20] Bruce, F. F., *The Epistle of Paul to the Romans* (London: Tyndale, 1963), p. 266.

[21] Bruce, *Romans*, p. 12.

6

Paul, traveller and citizen of Rome

Paul had grown up in Tarsus, in Cilicia in Asia Minor, which probably boasted a population of 75,000 inhabitants. Greek was its normal language, and the city attracted many foreign traders and tourists. Paul's family was among the more prominent families who had received Roman citizenship. Almost like Corinth, Tarsus was regarded as prosperous and flamboyant. Acts 22.3 tells us that at an early age he was sent to Jerusalem to be trained in the Scriptures and in Judaism, to become a Pharisee. Willem van Unnik argues that this training may have begun as early as in Paul's boyhood.[1] Virtually everyone refers to Paul's triple roots in Judaism, Hellenism (including Diaspora Judaism) and Rome. He would have been accustomed to synagogue worship, in which the Hebrew Bible and the Targums (Aramaic glosses or paraphrases) would have featured.

It is common knowledge that Paul received his call and experienced his conversion on the road to Damascus, after which he visited Arabia for prayer and reflection (Gal. 1.17). Murphy-O'Connor estimates this visit as in AD 33–4, when he stayed with Peter for two weeks.[2] Doubtless, in spite of his disclaimer about learning the gospel from no human source (Gal. 1.11–12), he took the opportunity to hear more from Peter about the life and teaching of Jesus. Dodd dryly observes, 'We may presume that they did not spend all their time talking about the weather.'[3]

The years from AD 36 to 46 are known as 'the hidden years'. The floggings, persecutions and imprisonments listed in 2 Corinthians 11.23–33 may have belonged to this period. The next that we know for certain is that in about AD 46 Barnabas sought out Paul, and found him in Tarsus (Acts 11.25–26), preaching the gospel. Paul then stayed for a year in Antioch, the seat of Roman government of Syria and Cilicia. Antioch was by now the third city of the empire, third only to Rome and Alexandria, perhaps with a population of up to half a million. The church found Antioch to be a 'base' for its early outreach into Asia Minor. Many were

---

[1] Unnik, W. C. van, *Tarsus or Jerusalem* (London: Epworth, 1962).
[2] Murphy-O'Connor, Jerome, *Paul: A Critical Life* (Oxford: OUP, 1997), pp. 7–22.
[3] Dodd, C. H., *The Apostolic Preaching and Its Developments* (London: Hodder & Stoughton, 1936), p. 26.

converted (Acts 11.20). The Church then commissioned Barnabas and Paul to undertake what is widely called 'the first missionary journey', which was based largely in Cyprus. It is crucial to note that Paul was *not a freelance lone individual*. He had been commissioned by the church in Antioch with prayer and the laying on of hands, and then worked collaboratively and collegially with Barnabas and other co-workers (Acts 13.1–2). These may have at first included Barnabas, Mark, Silas and Luke.

Paul would now have drawn on his Greek-speaking background and his use of the Septuagint (LXX). Sergius Paulus, the Roman proconsul of Cyprus, came to Christian faith. With Barnabas, Paul took the gospel to Perga, Pamphilia and Antioch in Pisidia. In his first and second missionary journeys Paul preached 'to the Jews first' (Rom. 1.16); then to the Gentiles (Gal. 1.16). He first began his preaching in Jewish synagogues.

The second noteworthy point is that he was called to be *both a missionary and a pastor*. In spite of hostility, Paul and Barnabas stayed in Iconium 'for a long time' (Acts 14.3). He returned to Lystra and to Antioch and 'strengthened the souls of the disciples, and encouraged them to continue in the faith' (Acts 14.22). They then *appointed elders* in each church (14.23). They returned to Syrian Antioch, and reported to them (14.25–26). After the Council of Jerusalem they revisited believers 'in every city where we proclaimed the word of the Lord' (15.36). Paul spent a further period in Syria and in Cilicia with Silas (1 Thess. 1.1).

Part-way through the second missionary journey Paul received a vision for Greece. At Troas, on the tip of Asia Minor, and facing across the sea to Greece, Paul had a dream in which 'a man of Macedonia' (possibly his companion Luke) pleaded with them, 'saying, "Come over to Macedonia and help us"' (Acts 16.9). Paul was convinced that this constituted the call of God (16.10). Hence they sailed from Troas eventually to Philippi (16.2). This was a leading city of Macedonia, and a Roman colony. They remained in the city for some days (Acts 16.12). There 'the Lord opened the heart' of Lydia (16.14), and they stayed in her home.

When they encountered a fortune-telling slave girl, Paul and Silas were thrown into prison (Acts 16.22–24). This episode culminated in the earthquake which destroyed the prison doors. They now travelled to the second city of Macedonia, namely the seaport of Thessalonica. In many ways it resembled a miniature Corinth, and Paul proclaimed the gospel in the synagogue every Sabbath for three weeks. Some came to Christian faith, 'But the Jews became jealous . . . and set the city in an uproar' (17.4–5). They charged them with 'acting contrary to the decrees of the emperor, saying that there is another king named Jesus' (17.7–8), for the imperial cult loomed large. They took bail for Paul, and after visiting Beroea (17.9–10), he travelled to Athens. Acts 17 recounts Paul's speech to philosophers on Mars Hill, while 1 Thessalonians 1.6 recounts the genuineness of the faith of Paul's Thessalonian converts.

Paul now aimed to visit Corinth, a logical choice, Engels argues, for rapid propagation of the gospel, in view of numerous trade and tourist connections.[4] Corinth also contained a synagogue, as well as many freed persons and householders such as Stephanas. Murphy-O'Connor writes: 'Corinth offered advantages which Athens lacked . . . Athens was no longer productive or creative . . . a mediocre university town', while Corinth was 'a wide-open boom town'.[5] Paul's travel from Athens would amount to some 50 miles, an easy first day on foot to Megara, but then a hazardous second day, amidst dangers from bandits, until he reached the outer territory of Corinth. There in the city he would have encountered jostling crowds, and on the Lechaeum road would pass shops and markets, the Temple of Asklepios, and the Peirene Fountains. It is no wonder that Paul's first preaching was 'in weakness, in much fear, and trembling' (1 Cor. 2.2–3), although Dibelius suggests that at that point Paul was in poor health. Paul renounced the strategy of audience-pleasing rhetoric and 'cleverness', and preached only Christ crucified (1 Cor. 2.1–5).

Paul settled with fellow-Christians Prisca and Aquila, who shared the same trade as Paul. Stephanas, Gaius and Crispus were probably among the first converts (1 Cor. 1.16; 16.15). Paul remained there for some 18 months, between March 50 and September 51. Then he and his co-workers sailed from Cenchreae, one of Corinth's harbours, to Ephesus, back in Asia Minor (Acts 18.11–19).[6] Paul then made Ephesus his pastoral and missionary base during the period 52–3, perhaps up to early 54. Meanwhile Apollos visited Corinth, and brought back disturbing news. During 53–4 Paul received further news from an oral report from Chloe's people (1 Cor. 1.11), and then from a further letter of enquiry from Corinth (1 Cor. 7.1). Thereupon Paul wrote 1 Corinthians. This combines clear-cut pronouncements (1 Cor. 1.10—6.20), which respond to the oral report; and more sensitive, carefully balanced answers to their letter (1 Cor. 7.1—10.33; perhaps also 11.1—15.58). Exactly as in Romans, the epistle is shot

---

[4] Engels, Donald, *Roman Corinth* (Chicago: University of Chicago Press, 1990), p. 20.

[5] Murphy-O'Connor, *Paul*, p. 108.

[6] Thiselton, Anthony C., *The First Epistle to the Corinthians: A Commentary on the Greek Text* (Grand Rapids: Eerdmans, and Carlisle: Paternoster, 2000; NIGTC); Thiselton, Anthony C., *1 Corinthians: A Shorter Exegetical and Pastoral Commentary* (Grand Rapids: Eerdmans, 2006), pp. 23–7; and Thiselton, Anthony C., *The Living Paul: An Introduction* (London: SPCK, 2009), pp. 20–8.

through with recognition of God's undeserved grace and gifts, in the light of which no single group or person can have any ground whatever for claiming superiority over another.

These letters of Paul would have been *read aloud to the assembled church* (or church groups) in question. Paul may have dictated several letters, and the use of secretaries is well established in that era. Some still dispute the date of Galatians, depending largely on whether 'Galatia' signifies the southern area which Paul had visited on his first missionary journey. It is likely that 2 Corinthians (at least 2 Cor. 1—9) was written from Ephesus.

Paul's eyes now turned to Spain (Rom. 15.23–24; 16.28), using Rome as his base. He seeks to prepare the church in Rome for his coming, in his Epistle to the Romans, written probably between November 56 and January 57, from Corinth. He knew, however, that he first had to face a final visit to Jerusalem. This was for the purpose of carrying a gift of money collected from his Gentile converts, to strengthen the bonds and mutual understanding between the church in Jerusalem and Gentile Christians.

Bruce comments,

> In making the choice of a new sphere of activity Paul determined to go on being a pioneer; he would not settle down as an apostle in a new place to which the gospel had already been brought; he would not 'build upon another man's foundation' (Romans 15.20).[7]

That is why Paul's ultimate objective is Spain, not Rome itself, other than as a strong supporting base of operations. However, Jewett adds a most important addition to this comment. Spain was Latin-speaking rather than Greek-speaking, and Paul would heavily rely on the Romans themselves, perhaps overseen by the deacon Phoebe, for the presentation of the gospel in Spain. Paul knew from many contacts with Christians that there was already a flourishing Christian community in Rome.

Paul dictated this epistle to Tertius as secretary. The letter did indeed establish Paul's credentials in Rome. He echoed the teaching of Jesus on the grace and the generosity of God (Rom. 3—5), and applied it pastorally to mutual acceptance and welcome of Jewish Christians by Gentile Christians, and of Gentile Christians by Jewish Christians (Rom. 14—15). He expounded the character of new life in Christ, and how the Holy Spirit inspired and formed the Christ-like life in all Christians (Rom. 6—8). He validated God's faithfulness to his purposes and promises in

---

[7] Bruce, F. F., *The Epistle of Paul to the Romans* (London: Tyndale, 1963), p. 12.

public history to Israel and to the world (Rom. 9—11). He demonstrated the ethical stance that all Christians should adopt (Rom. 12—15). He commended the deacon Phoebe to the church in Rome, and gave warm expression to a network of personal friends, who would doubtless help and support him (Rom. 16).

Paul's plans to visit Rome immediately after he left Jerusalem did not materialize. Agabus prophesied his fate in Jerusalem (Acts 21.10–14). At first the church in Jerusalem had welcomed him warmly. He visited James and the elders of the church, and related God's gracious work among the Gentiles (Acts 21.18–20). But then Jews arrived from Asia Minor, and stirred up the crowd (21.27–30). Paul was rescued from a hostile mob by a Roman tribune, who placed him in protective custody. The next day Paul sought to address the crowd, and Acts 22.1–21 recounts his testimony to his call and conversion.

When Paul reached the point of recounting his call to the Gentiles, riots ensued (Acts 22.22–33), and he was forced to avoid a flogging only by stating that he was a Roman citizen (22.25, 27). In the face of plots to kill him, the tribune escorted Paul to Caesarea with a hundred soldiers, where he could be examined by the Roman governor, Felix (23.23–25). Paul offered his defence to Felix, who kept him under close guard, until he was in due course succeeded by Porcius Festus (24.27). Festus, however, sought to ingratiate himself with the Jews, and, understanding the situation, Paul took the decisive step of appealing to Caesar (25.9–12). God had already assured him: 'You must bear witness also in Rome' (23.11).

The closing chapters of Acts recount Paul's hazardous journey on board ship to Rome, and his eventual arrival, after shipwreck, via Crete and Malta. Acts 18.15–16 tells us that believers from Rome came out to meet Paul and to welcome him on his arrival. At Rome 'Paul was allowed to live by himself, with the soldier who was guarding him' (Acts 28.16). We have no firm evidence of what occurred thereafter. Luke tells us in Acts that Paul continued to preach the gospel, proclaiming, in Luke's words, 'the kingdom of God and teaching about the Lord Jesus Christ' (28.31). Tradition suggests that Paul was martyred in Rome. This is probable, but not historically certain.

7

Paul introduces himself and the
theme of the gospel (1.1–17)

The address and greetings (1.1–7)

Normally, as is well known, the standard form of a letter in the first-century Graeco-Roman world was 'A to B, Greetings', not 'Dear B'. There is nothing sacrosanct about this formula. However, Paul takes the opportunity to insert into this conventional form something about himself, something about the gospel, and something about Christ. The greeting follows in verse 7.

Although the NRSV translates verse 1 as 'Paul, a servant of Jesus Christ . . .' it loses something by failing to translate Greek *doulos* as *slave*. Understandably, it is concerned that modern readers should not misunderstand this term, and according to Danker, *doulos* can mean *servant* as well as *slave*.[1] However, in the ancient Roman world, as Martin convincingly argues, what being a slave amounted to depended entirely on who was the slave's master, and for what purpose he or she was purchased.[2] Thus Jewett points out that many slaves in imperial service 'proudly bore the title "Slave of Caesar"'.[3] Byrne points out that this consciously places Paul in the great tradition of 'God's servants' in the OT such as Moses and David.[4]

Bad masters could indeed regard their slaves as mere 'things', with little freedom and dignity. Wright stresses that Paul gladly opted for a title that readily implied 'social degradation'. He adds, 'Slaves had no rights, no property, and no prospects.'[5] But many slaves were literate and educated, and could become trusted managers of households or estates. Some of these could have 'prospects'. Best of all, a slave could enjoy the *security of 'belonging'* to a good master. His master could provide for his family if he was ill. The name of his master could protect him from robbers, and

---

[1] Danker, Frederick, *A Greek-English Lexicon of the New Testament and Other Early Christian Literature* (BDAG) (Chicago and London: University of Chicago Press, 3rd edn, 2000), p. 260.
[2] Martin, Dale B., *Slavery as Salvation* (New Haven: Yale University Press, 1990), pp. 15–22, 50–85, 122–4, 145–9, and throughout.
[3] Jewett, Robert, *Romans: A Commentary* (Minneapolis: Fortress, 2007; Hermeneia), p. 100.
[4] Byrne, Brendan, *Romans* (Collegeville: Liturgical Press, 1996 and 2007; Sacra Pagina 6), p. 38.
[5] Wright, N. T., 'Romans' in the *New Interpreter's Bible* (*NIB*), (Nashville: Abingdon, 2002), vol. 10, p. 415.

provide security, to an extent far better than if he were a free man, or she, a free woman. Hence, some deliberately bought themselves into slavery. For Paul, therefore, to call himself 'a slave/servant of Jesus Christ' meant that he *belonged* to Jesus; Jesus *had the care of him*; he would be secure as Christ's slave. Weiss comments, 'What appears in the Greek as ignoble or servile appears in the Semitic as a proud title . . . The believer can rely on him [Jesus] in every situation.'[6] The earlier sociological researches in slavery by Deissmann have been proved to be unreliable; Combes and others corroborate Martin.[7]

At the same time Paul defines himself as 'a called apostle, set apart for the gospel of God' (v. 1). The Greek *klētos apostolos* means 'a called apostle', rather than called *to be* an apostle. *Call* draws attention to the sovereignty of God, as in 2 Corinthians 4.6: 'It is the God who said, "Let light shine out of darkness", who has shone in our hearts to give the light of the know-ledge of the glory of God in the face of Jesus Christ.' God's call is creative.

Apostle denotes one who was sent as an envoy on behalf of another, here on behalf of God. It is Paul's regular greeting (1 Cor. 1.1; 2 Cor. 1.1; Gal. 1.1; Eph. 1.1; Col. 1.1) and is alluded to in Romans 11.13 and 1 Corinthians 9.1–2. In Luke–Acts and the Synoptic Gospels the term is often used of the Twelve. Other theories suggested that it primarily drew attention to apostolic authority. But more recently J. A. Crafton and others have compared apostles to 'windows' who transparently convey to others the image of Christ.[8] Paul insists that apostles are witnesses to Christ, especially to his resurrection (1 Cor. 9.1; 15.5–6).

Rengstorf appealed to the rabbinic background of 'sent' (Semitic *shaliach*) in the saying, 'A man's *shaliach* is like himself' (*Berakoth* 3.5). But Rengstorf's view has been criticized by Käsemann, Barrett and others. Holmberg urges that Paul's concept is *collaborative*.[9] Best stresses both the significance of apostles as founders of the community, and also, like Crafton, as *a term of humility*.[10] Pannenberg concludes, 'In the first beginnings of the Church, the authority of the apostles kept the churches in their faith in the crucified and risen Lord.'[11]

Finally in verse 1, Paul says that he has been 'set apart for the gospel of God' (Greek *aphōrismenos eis euaggelion theou*). Munck and Jeremias regard

---

[6] Weiss, Johannes, *Earliest Christianity* (2 vols, New York: Harper, 1959 [1937]), vol. 2, pp. 458–61.

[7] Combes, I. A. H., *The Metaphor of Slavery in the Writings of the Early Church* (Sheffield: Sheffield Academic Press, 1998; JSNTSS 156), pp. 72–93.

[8] Crafton, J. A., *The Agency of the Apostle* (Sheffield: Sheffield University Press, 1991), pp. 53–103.

[9] Holmberg, Bengt, *Paul and Power* (Lund: Gleerup, 1978).

[10] Best, Ernest, 'Paul's Apostolic Authority', *JSNT* 27 (1986), pp. 3–25.

[11] Pannenberg, Wolfhart, *Systematic Theology*, vol. 3 (Grand Rapids: Eerdmans, 1998), p. 377.

this as a conscious allusion to the call of Jeremiah (Jer. 1.5). It may imply God's eternal decree before all time. In Paul's case, this was the call to be apostle to the nations. At the very least this refers to 'the promises of God beforehand through his prophets in the holy scriptures' (v. 2). Paul emphasizes the continuity of the Old and New Testaments.

Paul now expounds the Christ-centred nature of the gospel. Paul anchors the gospel in public history, namely Christ's Davidic descent. Jesus was descended from David (Greek *kata sarka*). The NRSV translates this literally as 'according to the flesh'; the NJB has 'in terms of human nature'. It means 'as far as physical descent is concerned'. Dunn comments, this is a common theme in the NT (Matt. 1.1–16, 20; Luke 1.27, 32, 69; 2.3; 3.23–31).[12] Wright urges that this phrase does not simply indicate the humanity of Christ, to complement his divinity in verse 3, but his messianic role for Israel.[13]

More problematic is verse 4: 'and was declared to be Son of God with power according to the spirit of holiness by resurrection from the dead.' 'Declared to be' might be acceptable as long as we recognize that it is *God* who declares this. The Greek uses *horisthentos*, which may also denote *appoint, constitute* or *define*. Danker proposes *define* as his first meaning, and *determine* or *appoint* as his second. But he concludes that *declared* is right for Romans 1.4.[14]

Cranfield argues that the remainder of this verse bristles with problems. If it meant the human spirit of holiness, this could denote a psychological attitude. But this would be out of place in this context. He and Wright argue that this is a Semitism which denotes 'the Holy Spirit'.[15] Elsewhere in Paul the Holy Spirit is the normal meaning of *spirit*. 'Power' has special significance in the light of awareness of imperial power.

Barrett and Leenhardt are right in seeing the verse as precluding adoptionism. Bruce, Leenhardt and Best see the phraseology as looking back to a common *pre-Pauline* formulation. The dead (Greek *nekrōn*) is a generalizing *plural* as Bruce points out, which also shows the *inclusiveness* of the term. Nygren comments, 'For Paul the resurrection of Christ is the beginning of the resurrection of the dead. Through Christ the resurrection Age has burst upon us.'[16]

---

[12] Dunn, James D. G., *Romans 1—8* (Dallas: Word, 1988; WBC 38), p. 12; Fitzmyer, Joseph A., *Romans: A New Translation with Introduction and Commentary* (New York: Doubleday, 1992; AB 33), p. 234.

[13] Wright, 'Romans', *NIB*, vol. 10, pp. 416–18.

[14] Danker, BDAG, p. 723.

[15] Wright, 'Romans', *NIB*, vol. 10, p. 419.

[16] Nygren, Anders, *Commentary on Romans* (London: SCM, 1952), p. 50.

The opening christological clause brings together the *prophetic* promises of an *anointed Davidic king,* which Wright stresses, and the *apocalyptic expectations of God's intervention* to bring in the new creation, which Käsemann stresses.

In verses 5–6 Paul considers the *effects* of Christ's work and the gospel. This includes the wonder of God's generous, free grace in Christ and his apostleship. For all Christians this consists not only in God's grace, but also in the obedience which involves faith. Paul never ceases to wonder at the generosity of God's grace to him, for God called and commissioned one who, in his words, 'persecuted the church of God. But by the grace of God I am what I am' (1 Cor. 15.9, 10; cf. 1 Cor. 3.10). His ministry was to bring about 'the obedience of faith' (Greek *eis hupakoēn pisteōs*). The meaning of *eis* (*with a view to,* or *to bring about*) is clear. Cranfield lists seven ways of understanding *obedience of faith*.[17] Fitzmyer opts for 'faith that manifests itself as obedience', which is similar to Cranfield's 'obedience which consists in faith'. Both see *faith* as 'obedience that springs from faith'.[18] Wright comments that this 'obedience' is 'not a list of moral good works', but 'obedience to Christ's Lordship'.[19] In Dunn's words, 'To clarify what faith is . . . is one of Paul's chief objectives in this letter.'[20]

Garlington declares, 'The pivotal point of the introduction [to Romans] is v. 5 – the obedience of faith.'[21] He writes: 'Rom. 1:5 can be looked upon as a programmatic statement of the main purpose of Romans,' also citing Wright.[22] He also approves the conclusion of Paul Minear that 'the obedience of faith' derives from the transfer of new life under Christ's Lordship.[23] The acknowledgement of Jesus as Lord (1 Cor. 12.3) lies at the heart of obedience that springs from faith. Garlington concludes, ' "*The obedience of faith" in Romans is perseverance in Christ . . . a perseverance requisite to eschatological salvation.*'[24]

To view faith in the NT as primarily *one thing* has confused many writers. In justification by grace through faith, it is reception and appropriation

---

[17] Cranfield, C. E. B., *A Critical and Exegetical Commentary on the Epistle to the Romans,* vol. 1 (Edinburgh: T & T Clark, 1975; ICC), p. 66.

[18] Fitzmyer, *Romans,* p. 237.

[19] Wright, 'Romans', *NIB,* vol. 10, p. 420.

[20] Dunn, *Romans 1—8,* p. 17.

[21] Garlington, Don, *Faith, Obedience, and Perseverance: Aspects of Paul's Letter to the Romans* (Eugene, OR: Wipf & Stock, 2009; reprinted from Mohr: Tübingen, 1994; WUNT 79), p. 1.

[22] Garlington, *Faith, Obedience, and Perseverance,* p. 10.

[23] Minear, Paul, *The Obedience of Faith: The Purposes of Paul in the Epistle to the Romans* (London: SCM, 1971; SBT), p. 65.

[24] Garlington, *Faith, Obedience, and Perseverance,* p. 3 (his italics).

of God's gift. Often, as Luther urged, it entails bold action. In some contexts faith constitutes a special 'gift of the Spirit' which is given only
to some, not to all (1 Cor. 12.9). What faith *is* in given situations *varies
from context to context.* But it is never mere 'intellectual assent' as it often
is in James.

In verse 5 Paul also refers to *the Gentiles.* He regularly addresses Jewish
Christians and Gentile Christians in co-equal terms. Here he alludes to
his special commission as an apostle to carry the gospel to the Gentiles,
including to the far west. Paul's motivation is 'for the sake of his [Christ's]
name'. In verse 6 Paul classes the Christians of Rome among the Gentiles
(Greek *ethnē*).

The important word here is *called*: 'who are called to belong to Jesus
Christ'. The NRSV is probably correct to treat this as a genitive of possession. God has taken the initiative in calling them to belong to Christ.
Nygren notes that the modern world stresses 'coming to Christ' as a *human*
activity; while Paul stresses *God's calling.*[25]

The UBS Committee under Metzger regards verse 7, 'To all God's
beloved in Rome', as a 'certain' MS grading. In Marcion this address is
lacking, as in some minor MSS and in Origen. This could be either
accidental, or in Marcion's case deliberate and replicated by an anti-Rome
copyist. It is included by the very early P^{10}, $\aleph$, B and C.[26] We discussed
the destination of the epistle under its integrity (see Chapter 5), where
Manson holds a special theory. 'Beloved' may replicate Christ's title as
the Beloved Son in Mark 1.11. On 'called to be saints', Fitzmyer comments,
'[Saints] Gk. *hagios* has to be understood in its O T sense, "dedicated,
consecrated", i.e. separated from the profane aspects of life for an encounter
with the awesome presence of God.'[27]

Grace and peace (v. 7) is the normal Pauline substitute for the secular
greeting *chairein*, literally 'May you have joy'. *Grace and peace* occur in
1 Thessalonians 1.1; Galatians 1.3; 1 Corinthians 1.3; 2 Corinthians 1.2;
and Philippians 1.2. *Peace* (Greek *eirēnē*) here does *not* mean inner tranquillity of mind, but describes the *objective relationship of reconciliation
with God.* It represents the Hebrew notion of *shālōm*, while *grace* conveys
the theme of God's generous favour. Grace and peace come both from
God and Jesus Christ.

---

[25] Nygren, *Romans*, p. 56.

[26] Metzger, Bruce, *A Textual Commentary on the Greek New Testament* (New York: UBS, 2nd edn,
1994), p. 446.

[27] Fitzmyer, *Romans*, p. 239.

Thanksgiving for the Christians in Rome, and missionary plans (1.8–15)

Paul is always ready to give thanks to God (v. 8). The Greek word-group *eucharistō* occurs 46 times in the Pauline corpus (e.g. 1 Cor. 1.4; 1 Thess. 1.2; Phil. 1.3; Col. 1.3). Many regard the 'thanksgiving' as a conventional form in ancient Greek letters, but Paul specifically gives thanks to God for the well-known faith of the Roman Christians. Wright comments, 'Hyperbole it may be, but it is still no mean thing to say that the faith of the Roman church was proclaimed "in all the world".'[28] Schubert undertook extensive research into thanksgiving forms in Greek papyri in 1939. He argued that these forms were 'typical of normal social life' in this era.[29] But in 1977 Peter O'Brien argued that while purely formal similarities exist with the Graeco-Roman letter-form, the content was usually distinctive to Paul, and often reflected a Jewish background.[30]

Paul's ground of thanksgiving is 'because your faith is proclaimed throughout the world'. Since Rome was the capital and focal point of the empire, it is easy to imagine that Christians would readily pass on good news about the Christian community in Rome. 'All of you' anticipates one of the themes of Romans: Jewish and Gentile Christians stand together as co-equal recipients of God's free grace. Here, but not in every passage, 'your faith' means simply, as Sanday and Headlam argue, 'your Christianity'. Thanksgiving is especially heartfelt in view of the imperial demands and pressures of Rome.

Paul reiterates in verse 9 his *constancy in prayer* for the church. He prays for them 'without ceasing'. Why does Paul invoke God as a witness to this? In 2 Corinthians 1.23 he appeals to God as his witness concerning his motives and reasons for his travel, and in 2 Corinthians 11.31 God witnesses to his boasting 'of the things that show my weakness'. In Galatians 1.20, again, 'before God, I do not lie' concerns his independent revelation and call. This also concerned his stay with Peter, in which he heard the corporate testimony of the Church, and of the historical Jesus. God can genuinely witness to this. Cranfield understands this as equivalent to 'Paul's oaths', although God's witness to the hidden processes of the heart and Paul's prayer constitute the main point.[31]

---

[28] Wright, 'Romans', *NIB*, vol. 10, p. 422.
[29] Schubert, Paul, *Form and Function of the Pauline Thanksgivings* (Berlin: Töpelmann, 1939), esp. pp. 39–94 and 156–73.
[30] O'Brien, Peter T., *Introductory Thanksgiving to the Letters of Paul* (Leiden: Brill, 1977; NovTSup 49), esp. pp. 107–40.
[31] Cranfield, *Romans*, vol. 1, p. 75.

'God, whom I serve with my spirit' also raises difficulties. This is because, although he sometime alludes to 'spirit' as a human capacity, Paul more characteristically uses the term to denote the Holy Spirit. If it is used in the former sense, its relevance may lie in Paul's comment about his inner, secret, life. Elsewhere Paul says that he serves God in costly action in the public world; here he states that his prayer life and inner reflection equally serve God.

In verses 10–13 Paul expresses his deep longing to succeed in visiting the Christians in Rome, implying that he would have done this sooner if he had been free to do so. This desire forms part of his prayers. The English VSS, including the NRSV and Danker, suggest 'succeed in coming to you' for the future of the Greek verb.[32] The verb can mean *to have things turn out well*. But why does Paul not now mention his intention to use Rome as a supportive 'base' for his mission to Spain? Leenhardt observes,

> He does not wish it to be thought that Rome will be merely a halt, soon forgotten, in his march towards the west. He counts rather on making Rome a base where he may strike roots. He hopes to create . . . deep spiritual bonds which will bear fruit.[33]

Rome, Paul hopes, will be the crucible in which his missionary projects will come to birth.

Jewett, we have noted, sheds much light on this. To say that he wants to use Rome as a 'base' for missionary outreach would be to understate Paul's hopes. Paul is aware, through his contacts, of 'the cultural situation in Spain'.[34] Latin was the main language generally spoken, in contrast to Greek in the eastern Mediterranean. Communication would be difficult for anyone who did not readily speak Latin. Paul's hope is to introduce Phoebe as someone who could mastermind and partly finance the mission to Spain (16.1–2). Thus he hopes that the Roman church will itself undertake this mission, as those well equipped to speak the main language, and to liaise with Roman administrators in Spain.[35] Here he would have in mind especially the more gifted Christians in Rome. Jewett writes, 'The word *prostatis* describing Phoebe's role in 16:2 is a technical term for *an upper-class benefactor*.'[36]

Hence in verse 11 Paul longs *to share* 'some spiritual gift to strengthen you'. 'Spiritual gift' (NRSV) literally translates *charisma . . . pneumatikon*,

---

[32] Danker, BDAG, p. 410.
[33] Leenhardt, Franz J., *The Epistle to the Romans* (London: Lutterworth, 1961), p. 43.
[34] Jewett, *Romans*, p. 80.
[35] Jewett, *Romans*, pp. 74–91.
[36] Jewett, *Romans*, p. 89.

which is reminiscent of 'the gifts of the Holy Spirit' in 1 Corinthians 12.6–10. Paul qualifies verse 11 by verse 12: 'Or rather so that we may be *mutually* encouraged by *each other's* faith'. Paul uses the powerful infinitive *symparaklēthēnai* which is a double compound verb, meaning 'to receive encouragement or comfort *together*'. Paul is concerned to underline the two-sided bond which he seeks with the Christians in Rome, and to equip some to undertake the evangelization of Spain.

In verse 13 Paul spells out more explicitly how his hands were tied in his desire to come to Rome sooner. The NRSV 'I want you to know' conceals a double negative: 'I do not want you to be unaware', a construction which Paul usually reserves for emphasis (1 Thess. 4.13; 1 Cor. 10.1; 12.1). Wright comments that this is because he hopes that no one will accuse him of 'building on another's foundation'. 'Brothers' (NRSV 'brothers and sisters') occurs at Romans 7.1; 8.12; 10.1; and so on. It is used by Christians to denote their close relationship with one another (Rom. 8.29; 1 Cor. 5.11; Eph. 6.23; etc.). Hitherto Paul has been prevented from coming because of missionary duties, as 15.22–24 will explain. His visit to Jerusalem will take many months or years. Although there are Jewish Christians in Rome, Paul tends to think of Rome as part of his special ministry to the Gentiles. Hence he speaks of 'you . . . [and] the rest of the Gentiles'.

Verse 14 explicates Paul's allusion to the Gentiles. He states, 'I am a debtor both to Greeks and to barbarians'. *Barbarian* is onomatopoeia for those whose language was unintelligible to Greeks or Romans (sounding only like *bar-bar-bar*; 1 Cor. 14.11). 'Greeks' may either mean simply 'Greeks' or 'cultured Romans with interests in things Greek'.[37] The two terms, Fitzmyer suggests, denote Paul's 'debt to the non-Jewish world'.[38] Cranfield regards the two pairs as solemnly denoting 'the whole of Gentile humanity'.[39] To them all, Paul knows that he has a debt, an obligation that God has laid upon him as 'apostle to the Gentiles'. Paul preaches to 'all sorts and conditions' of people.

An English-speaking reader might not suspect that the NRSV has smoothed out awkward Greek syntax in verse 15. Sanday and Headlam propose 'as far as it rests with me . . . I am ready to preach'. Probably it simply means 'I am eager to proclaim the gospel to you also who are in Rome'. Fitzmyer proposes 'hence my eagerness to preach the gospel to you'.

---

[37] Danker, BDAG, p. 318.
[38] Fitzmyer, *Romans*, p. 250.
[39] Cranfield, *Romans*, vol. 1, p. 83.

The theme of the epistle: God's gracious act in Christ (1.16, 17)

Luther believed that the Prologue to Romans ended at verse 15, and verse 16 showed that the gospel 'is through God and from God'.[40] Nygren devotes nearly 30 pages to these two verses.[41] 'I am not ashamed' reminds us of how different the first-century society was, before 'Christendom' became established in the empire in *c.*313. In Origen's lifetime Celsus was still pouring scorn on the notion of a crucified God. Rome, as we have noted, was the centre of the imperial cult.

The word *gospel* (Greek *euaggelion*) had already occurred in Romans 1.1. In 1 Corinthians 1.18 Paul had already acknowledged that 'the message about the cross is foolishness to those who are perishing, but to us who are being saved it is the power of God'. Romans repeats this theme. The *power* of God through the gospel will stand in marked contrast to the weakness or *ineffectiveness* of the law. Power in Paul often means 'what is *effective*'. 'Power . . . for salvation' is 'God's effective power'.[42] Wright and Jewett see this as standing in contrast to the secular force of imperial Rome.[43] Käsemann comments: 'It creates salvation in a manner which determines the whole person in time and eternity.'[44] In Romans 11.23 it means ability to do something, and in 1 Corinthians 1.18 'the power of God' stands in contrast to the ineffectiveness of human wisdom or human capacities. God *effectively* creates salvation, whereas the law and human aspiration fail to do so. In Romans 8.3, Paul declares, '*God* has done what the law . . . could not do by sending his Son' (italics mine). If this is *God's method*, Paul can only *glory in it*.

'To the Jew first and also to the Greek' (v. 16) partly reflects verse 14, but goes further. It reflects Paul's experience in Corinth when he declared in the face of Jewish hostility, 'From now on I will go to the Gentiles' (Acts 18.6). But it had always been normal practice to proclaim the gospel in the Jewish synagogues, and he does not intend to abandon them. Dodd interprets verse 16 as a simple reference to historical fact: the gospel was first preached to the Jews.[45] Munck argues that both Jesus and Paul regarded the gospel as in due time embracing the whole of humankind, both Jews and Gentiles. Munck is opposing the nineteenth-century theory of F. C. Baur about a radical division within the wider Church. He writes,

---

[40] Luther, Martin, *Commentary on Romans* (Grand Rapids: Kregel, 1954; repr. 1976), p. 39.
[41] Nygren, *Romans*, pp. 65–92, esp. 66–73.
[42] Cranfield, *Romans*, vol. 1, p. 89.
[43] Jewett, *Romans*, p. 139.
[44] Käsemann, Ernst, *Commentary on Romans* (London: SCM, 1980), p. 22.
[45] Dodd, C. H., *The Epistle of Paul to the Romans* (London: Hodder & Stoughton, 1932), p. 9.

These observations seem to show that Romans is essentially a summing-up of the point of view that Paul had reached during the long struggle that begins in 1 Corinthians ... [Romans] becomes a manifesto presenting his deepest convictions on vital points.[46]

The majority of Christians in Rome, Munck argues, were Gentiles, and had become 'God's true Israel', or the remnant within Israel. Barrett asserts, 'The extension of the Gospel to the Gentiles was the result not of easy-going charity, but of theological conviction.'[47]

The word *salvation* occurs especially in relation to how we relate with *God*. By contrast *deliverance* is used more widely. Like the word 'redemption', it readily suggests being saved *from* some oppression or misery, *to* some state of safety and security, *by* some costly saving act or event. The book of Judges clearly explained the term: 'saviours' were raised up by God to be his agents to deliver Israel from oppression by the Philistines, and provide them with security. Othniel (Judg. 2.16; 3.9), Ehud (3.15), Deborah (4.4) and Gideon (6.11—8.32) are such examples. In the NT God anoints Jesus Christ to deliver Christians *from* alienation from God and consequent sin and death, *by* or *through* his life, death and resurrection, *to* a new life of salvation. In this section of Romans, 'It is salvation from the final eschatological manifestation of the wrath of God ... It is the restoration of the *doxa* (glory) which sinful men lack.'[48]

'To everyone who has faith' (v. 16) occurs in Greek as the participle of the verb: 'to all who believe'. Both *faith* and *belief* reflect the same Greek stem. Virtually all commentators insist that faith does not constitute a 'prior qualification'. In this context *faith* is a *response* to God's initiative of pure grace. Dunn notes that the Greek for 'has faith' uses a *present* participle, not a past one.[49] The main thrust is on 'everyone'. Paul stresses once more that Jews and Gentiles are equal in the light of the gospel.

In verse 17 Paul begins to explain that in the gospel *the righteousness of God is revealed*. Paul has inherited the term from the OT, where the Hebrew *ts-d-q* is used over 500 times. The term denotes *being in accordance with a norm; fundamentally, with the character of God*. Secondarily it may refer to *ethical conduct*. God reveals himself as the One who is 'absolute in righteousness and truth' (Ps. 7.8–11).[50] The ethical use became prominent

---

[46] Munck, *Paul and the Salvation of Mankind* (London: SCM, 1959), p. 199.
[47] Barrett, C. K., *The Epistle to the Romans* (London: Black, 1957), p. 29.
[48] Cranfield, *Romans*, vol. 1, p. 89.
[49] Dunn, *Romans 1—8*, p. 40.
[50] Vriezen, T. C., *Outline of Old Testament Theology* (Oxford: Blackwell, 1962), p. 162; cf. Rad, Gerhard von, *Old Testament Theology*, vol. 1 (Edinburgh: Oliver & Boyd, 1962), pp. 370–6.

in the eighth-century prophets, where Amos condemns exploitation of the poor. Ziesler claims that in Paul the abstract noun *righteousness* (Greek *dikaiosunē*) and adjective *righteous* (Greek *dikaios*) tend to refer to ethical righteousness, while the verb (*dikaioō*) tends to refer to 'putting things right'.[51] But most scholars regard this as an overstatement. The range of meanings is complex, and Danker illustrates *nine* meanings from NT passages. In Romans 1.17 (with 3.21–26; 1 Cor. 1.20; 2 Cor. 3.9; 5.21) there has long been debate about whether 'of God' is *objective genitive*, meaning 'righteousness that *God bestows*'; or subjective genitive, meaning 'righteousness *belonging to God*'. So great has been the controversy that Cranfield lists an additional seven pages of bibliography on this issue.

We have already noted Luther's initial loathing of the word *righteousness* as expressing demands which he could not meet. His earlier understanding was thus primarily ethical. But his entire world changed when he saw *righteousness* as something *that God gave*. At this point, we recall, he felt that he had entered paradise. But then he studied and reflected, 'I began to understand that the righteousness of God is that by which the righteous live by a gift of God . . . I felt that I was altogether born again.'[52] This understanding is liberating, but strictly requires 'the righteousness *of God*' to be *objective* genitive, righteousness 'which God bestows'.

Dunn explains why Luther's interpretation does not totally exclude the subjective genitive. He rightly argues that 'righteousness' is a covenant term, and comments, 'God is "righteous" when he fulfils the obligations he took upon himself to be Israel's God, that is, to rescue Israel . . . (Exod. 9:27; 1 Sam. 12:7; Dan. 9:16; Mic. 6:5) – "righteousness" as "covenant faithfulness" (3:3–5, 25; 10:3).'[53] He adds that righteousness thus explicates 'the power of God for salvation' (v. 16). He concludes that this in effect removes the traditional debate about subjective or objective genitive; it 'is not a strict either – or, but both – and'.[54] The distinction features in Ridderbos and Cranfield, but recently Holland and Wright have urged the importance of a covenantal understanding of righteousness, as inherited from Isaiah and other parts of the OT.[55]

---

[51] Ziesler, John, *The Meaning of Righteousness in Paul* (Cambridge: CUP, 1972).

[52] Luther, Martin, *Luther's Works* (Eng., 55 vols, St Louis and Philadelphia: Concordia and Fortress, 1955–2015), vol. 34, pp. 336–7.

[53] Dunn, *Romans 1—8*, p. 41.

[54] Dunn, *Romans 1—8*, p. 41.

[55] Holland, Tom, *Romans: The Divine Marriage* (Eugene, OR: Pickwick, 2011), pp. 22 and 43–4; Wright, N. T., *Paul and the Faithfulness of God* (London: SPCK, 2013), pp. 795–804; cf. also his earlier work, *The Climax of the Covenant: Christ and the Law in Pauline Theology* (Edinburgh: T & T Clark, 1991), and 'Romans', *NIB*, vol. 10, pp. 425–6.

Most scholars now view the earlier debate about whether justification primarily means *to count righteous* or *to make righteous* as having lost some of its sharpness and an alleged Protestant–Catholic polarity. *Righteousness* is to be seen as a term of *relationship* in this *covenant context*. The term, however, remains *verdictive*, in J. L. Austin's words; i.e. it relates to the giving of the *verdict*, such as 'put in a right relationship with God'. Because this is essentially an eschatological verdict, it means 'right with God' within the framework of eschatology. Being 'counted righteous' anticipates God's verdict at the Last Judgement.[56] But because Christians still sin and still inherit the results of past history, within the framework of history they are still sinners. Hence Luther's dictum 'both righteous and sinners' (Latin *simul iustus et peccator*) is *neither a logical contradiction nor a paradox*, but a simultaneous divine judgement, each aspect of which functions within a different frame of reference. This helps to explain why in Romans 1.16, 17 and 1.18–32, Paul uses 'righteousness' in *both* senses: as a gift and as behaviour: the eschatological and the ethical.

In Romans 5—8 Paul insists that God's eschatological act of conferring righteousness as a gift carries with it the obligation to seek ethical righteousness through the gift of the Holy Spirit. Hence, as the old slogan goes, Christians are 'to be what they are to become'. Traditionally these two modes of response to God have been called *justification* and *sanctification*. The life of faith, as Luther himself declared, is not to be divorced from deeds. This is why verse 17 includes 'through faith for faith' (NRSV; Greek *ek pisteōs eis pistin*). The NRSV misses the force of the word *eis* as denoting direction or goal. Cranfield admits that this phrase has 'been understood in many different ways', and he provides more than seven examples.[57] He rightly regards it as connected with the quotation from Habakkuk, which follows in the same verse. Fitzmyer identifies the phrase as coming from Psalm 84.8, where the prepositions 'express passage from one degree to another, a meaning that Paul uses elsewhere (2 Cor. 2:16; 3:18)'.[58] He rightly emphasizes a more perfect faith as the Christian grows. The initial gift of faith, through which God *bestows* righteousness, nurtures a faith which *begins to live out* righteousness. Wright argues, 'In the light of 3.21–22 . . . its most natural meaning is "from God's faithfulness to human faithfulness".'[59]

---

[56] Thiselton, Anthony C., *The Two Horizons* (Exeter: Paternoster, and Grand Rapids: Eerdmans, 1980), pp. 415–22.

[57] Cranfield, *Romans*, vol. 1, p. 99.

[58] Fitzmyer, *Romans*, p. 263.

[59] Wright, 'Romans', *NIB*, vol. 10, p. 425.

This does much to help us to understand what could otherwise constitute a puzzle in Paul's handling of Habakkuk 2.4. Paul introduces the quotation from Habakkuk with the regular phrase 'As it is written'. Since the perfect tense denotes a past event with effects remaining in the present, Luther rendered it 'it stands written' (cf. 2.24; 3.4; 4.17; etc.). The NT arguably offers three versions of Romans 1.17: (i) *ho de dikaios ek pisteōs zēsetai* can be understood as 'The righteous person on the basis of faith [possibly faithfulness] shall live'; (ii) the Masoretic or Hebrew text of Habakkuk 2.4 reads *wᵉtsadîq bᵉ 'mûnātō yich ᵉyeh*, 'the righteous person by *his* faithfulness [or faith] shall live'; (iii) the LXX has *ho de dikaios ek pisteōs mou zēsetai*, 'The righteous person on the basis of *my* faithfulness [or faith] shall live.' (i) has 'faith'; (ii) has 'his' faith; (iii) has 'my' (God's) faith or faithfulness.

Why is there such controversy about the variant versions of this verse? Stanley is a specialist on Paul's use of the language of Scripture. He argues that Paul uses OT passages in a variety of ways. Sometimes he recalls a genuine quotation; *but he also uses paraphrase, allusion and reminiscence.*[60] He adds that the reason and purpose for which Paul uses these texts vary. This should save us from jumping to conclusions about 'loose' quotations. Occasionally variations may be due to different versions of the LXX text in the first century. But Paul varies quotations for his own purposes. Paul was educated amid uses of the Aramaic Targums in the Jewish synagogue, which were often paraphrases. Any mere generalizing solution for all texts, Stanley insists, cannot stand up. Paul very often does use the LXX, not the Hebrew text, with an eye on the understanding of his audience, as if an exposition today might quote the NRSV or NIV for more ready communication than the AV/KJB or the original language. It is not adequate simply to say that Paul 'sits loose' to the wording of the OT.[61] He highly prizes the authority of Scripture, but he does not *always* use it to establish a *doctrine*.

Specifically on Romans 1.17 Stanley points out that the LXX of Habakkuk 2.4 provides three different readings, as we have seen. Paul's omission of *my* need not surprise us, although Koch insists that 'my' after *faith* is original.[62] Stanley concludes that Paul adapts the text broadly to match the thrust of his current discussion. The word *my* might have distracted readers from seeing Paul's main point.[63]

---

[60] Stanley, Christopher D., *Paul and the Language of Scripture: Citation Technique in the Pauline Epistles and Contemporary Literature* (Cambridge: CUP, 1992; SNTSMS 74), p. 5.

[61] Stanley, *Paul and the Language of Scripture*, pp. 338, 340, 342, 346, 348.

[62] Stanley, *Paul and the Language of Scripture*, p. 83.

[63] Stanley, *Paul and the Language of Scripture*, p. 260.

Fitzmyer broadly agrees with Stanley's argument. First, he traces the role of Habakkuk 2.4 in first-century Jewish thought; especially in the quotation in the Dead Sea Scrolls (1QpHab 7.5—8.3), in which the emphasis is firmly on *fidelity*, which would accord with Wright's faithfulness.[64] Second, Paul's words correspond neither with the Masoretic (Hebrew) text nor with the LXX; he 'understands *pistis* in the sense of "faith", and "life", as a share in the risen life of Christ'.[65]

Does *through* or *by* faith qualify *righteous one*, or *shall live*? At least six writers, Barrett, Barth, Black, Cranfield, Kuss and Nygren, follow the latter, *shall live*. At least four, Godet, Leenhardt, Michel and Murray, follow the former, *righteous one*. The matter can be argued either way. Dunn rightly argues that Paul would not wish 'to exclude' the different meanings.[66] He offers the judicious comment:

> When *pistis* (faith) is understood as '*trust*', better sense can be made of *both* the chief alternative forms of the text: that is to say, for Paul the counterpart of God's faithfulness is not man's *faithfulness* ... but *faith*, his trust in, and total reliance upon, God.[67]

This sets the scene for Paul's main argument in Romans. Faithfulness or faith is no longer observance of the law. It is *trust in God's provision* of righteousness and life through sharing in the crucified and risen life of Jesus Christ. This is the effective power of God which results in salvation for both Jewish and Gentile believers in Christ. Nygren declares, 'One's faith is evidence that the gospel *has* exercised its power on him [the Christian] ... It is the power of the gospel that makes it possible for one to believe.'[68] Romans 1.16–17 precisely anticipates what Paul later asserts in Philippians 3.9: 'Not having a righteousness of my own that comes from the law, but one that comes through faith in Christ, the righteousness from God based on faith'.[69]

---

[64] Fitzmyer, *Romans*, p. 264.
[65] Fitzmyer, *Romans*, p. 265.
[66] Dunn, *Romans 1—8*, p. 45.
[67] Dunn, *Romans 1—8*, p. 46 (his italics).
[68] Nygren, *Romans*, p. 71.
[69] 'Based on' is the NRSV translation of the verse. But is this quite right? The Greek is *epi tē pistei*. *Epi* with the dative may have a wider meaning. Danker suggests 'is', 'on', 'in consideration of' or other 'markers' of relation (Danker, BDAG, pp. 363–7).

8

The Gentile world judged and alienated from God (1.18–32)

The wrath of God: Gentiles are without excuse (1.18–23)

Paul speaks of the wrath and judgement of God, but also makes use of common material from a standard Jewish synagogue sermon on the iniquities of the Gentile world. This use of Jewish homily material extends through the chapter to verse 32. Examples of this material occur in Jewish literature, for example in Wisdom of Solomon 13.1–10; 14.9–31; and 15.18–19. Wright sees this as a courtroom scene: 'It opens with a sentence being passed; it moves back to explain the grounds for this verdict . . . Romans 1:18 – 3:20 . . . is all about God's righteousness . . . God is the Judge.'[1] It is, he says, not only about the plight of *humanity*, but about *God's problem and plan*.

Paul introduces the revelation of *the wrath of God* in verse 18. Stählin comments that in the NT, as in the OT, all motives for divine wrath can be traced back to one fundamental notion, namely human contempt for God. It is also related to a rejection of the love of God. He provides a full and detailed examination of its nature, causes and effects in *TDNT*.[2] He concludes:

> That which is a *cause* of wrath becomes its *effect*. In this respect Romans 1 goes far beyond the O T statements . . . A threefold *paredōken* (he gave them up) corresponds to the threefold *ēllaxan* (they exchanged, vv. 23, 25, 26). Here cause and effect are one and the same.[3]

Jewett writes, 'The "revelation of wrath" relentlessly exposes the awful truth that the human race constantly attempts to suppress . . . the true nature of its relationships.'[4]

---

[1] Wright, N. T., 'Romans' in the *New Interpreter's Bible* (*NIB*) (Nashville: Abingdon, 2002), vol. 10, p. 428.

[2] Stählin, G., ' *orgē, opgizomaï*, in Kittel, G., and Friedrich, G. (eds), *Theological Dictionary of the New Testament* (*TDNT*) (10 vols, Grand Rapids: Eerdmans, 1964–76), vol. 5, pp. 382–447 (with O. Grether and others).

[3] Stählin, G., '*orgē*', *TDNT*, vol. 5, p. 444 (my italics).

[4] Jewett, Robert, *Romans: A Commentary* (Minneapolis: Fortress, 2007; Hermeneia), p. 151.

In other words the very godlessness and moral chaos that provokes the wrath of God becomes the fruit of this wrath. It is expressed later in Romans 5.10: 'While we were enemies . . .', and Romans 8.7: 'The mind that is set on the flesh is hostile to God'.

It is a mistake to understand *wrath* as the opposite of *love*. *The opposite of love is not wrath, but indifference.* The attitude of parents and grandparents readily illustrates this. If their child or grandchild is bent on what leads to self-destruction, through foolishness, laziness, or entering into bondage under drugs or excessive drink, parents may feel anger, because they hope for good for their child. Indeed only an indifferent or indulgent parent would remain calm and unaffected by such conduct. By analogy, God shows wrath only because *he loves* what he has created, and *longs for the best for it*.

We cannot complete our examination of 'the wrath of God' without noting the notorious comments on these verses by Dodd. Dodd insists that Paul never says that God is 'angry', yet does use the phrases 'vessels of wrath' (Rom. 9.22), 'day of wrath' (Rom. 2.5), 'the wrath to come' (1 Thess. 1.10); and 'the Law works wrath' (Rom. 4.15).[5] He also examines 'wrath' in the OT. He concludes that Paul 'retains it [the term], not to describe the attitude of God to man, but to describe an *inevitable process of cause and effect in a moral universe*'.[6]

Most scholars since 1932 have reacted in two ways to Dodd's comments. First, Dodd is entirely correct to suggest that often the consequences of human actions can be 'internal', i.e. bring their penalty with them. If someone refuses to learn at school, a time will come when needed qualifications for a job will be lacking. Numerous philosophers, biblical exegetes and theologians endorse this principle.

Second, most writers nowadays recognize that Dodd has undervalued the *personal* dimension of wrath. We have observed that self-destruction can provoke wrath as a sign that God really *cares* for the person who is destroying his or her life. Wrath can constitute a manifestation of *love*. Wright points out that the older liberal approach understandably wanted to avoid any suggestion that God is a malevolent despot, but, he says, 'the tide has turned now', partly because of 'the great wickedness of the twentieth century'.[7]

Paul states that God's wrath 'is revealed . . . against all ungodliness and wickedness' among those who 'suppress the truth' (v. 18). Schlatter

---

[5] Dodd, C. H., *The Epistle of Paul to the Romans* (London: Hodder & Stoughton, 1932), p. 21.

[6] Dodd, *Romans*, p. 23 (my italics).

[7] Wright, 'Romans', *NIB*, vol. 10, p. 431.

related 'ungodliness and wickedness' to the two tables of the law, sin against God, and sin against fellow humans. Like the Gospel of John, Paul sees this as wilful suppression of the truth (Greek *katechontōn* means *to hold imprisoned*). Although Paul draws directly on synagogue sermon material, W. L. Knox comments: 'Paul gives us an excellent sample . . . of the conventional philosophy borrowed by the Jews from the Greeks.'[8] Knox continues, 'This form is a deliberate parody of the portentous grandiloquence with which the synagogue preacher encouraged his hearers "to thank God that they were not as other men were", and to encourage Gentiles to become proselytes.'[9]

It is true that Paul uses the word *humankind* (Greek *anthrōpōn*), which in verse 18 is simply rendered as 'those' in the NRSV. In verses 18–32, Fitzmyer notes, Paul looks at 'the totality of the cosmos'. God's wrath concerns humankind without the gospel. Yet Paul is not being ironic when he declares, as Judaism does, that 'ungodliness' leads to idolatry and moral corruption.

In verse 19 Paul initiates the theme of 'no excuse'. 'What can be known' is unusual in Paul, but regularly occurs in the LXX. Wisdom 12—15 implies that God can be known to some degree. The verse reflects the speech in Acts 17.23–28, even if some follow Schweitzer in regarding these verses as un-Pauline. Plato and Aristotle acknowledge that some knowledge of God can be inferred from creation.[10] Similar themes are found in Philo, Josephus and Cicero.[11]

What is 'plain to them' signifies this. Leenhardt comments, 'Paul is serious in affirming that natural man has a knowledge of God', although this knowledge is 'certainly also ignorance'.[12] Human beings vaguely know God, but not clearly so; they do *not* recognize God '*as God*' (v. 21). The second clause, 'God has shown it to them', implies that they have sufficient knowledge to remain 'without excuse' for their godlessness.

Paul explains in verse 20 that God is both '*invisible*', and yet can be 'seen through the things he has made.' The physical invisibility of God is affirmed in John 1.18; Colossians 1.15; and Hebrews 11.27. 'From the creation of the world' has a temporal sense. 'Eternal' (Greek *aïdios*) occurs also in Wisdom 7.26 and Jude 6. The word *invisible* (Greek *aorata*) is matched in

---

[8] Knox, W. L., *Some Hellenistic Elements in Primitive Christianity* (London: OUP and British Academy, 1944), p. 31.

[9] Knox, *Some Hellenistic Elements*, p. 32.

[10] Plato, *Timaeus*, 28A–30C, 32A–35A; Aristotle, *De Mundo*, 6.387B–398B.

[11] Philo, *De Somn.* 1.11; Josephus, *Jewish War*, 7.8.7; and Cicero, *Tusculan Disputations*, 1.29.70.

[12] Leenhardt, Franz J., *The Epistle to the Romans* (London: Lutterworth, 1961), p. 62.

a deliberate word-play with *kathoratai* (*are perceived*; NRSV 'understood').
It is almost a hypothetical endorsement of the cosmological argument for
the existence of God. The world is not self-sufficient; it does not contain
a ground for its own cause. Barrett comments, 'Observation of created life
is sufficient to show that creation does not provide the key to its own
existence . . . [Gentiles] did not (for the most part) deny the existence of
deity; but they did fail (v. 21) to give God due honour and praise.'[13] 'So'
expresses purpose: 'So they are without excuse'.

Gentile – or world – responsibility is that people 'did not honour him'
or 'give thanks to him'. Greek *doxazō* means both *honour* and *glorify*. It
is a firm conviction both in Judaism and in Paul that humankind is
obligated to give God glory, and to thank him for his benefits (as in Calvin).
Paul may be quoting explicitly from Jewish sources. Because there is a
mismatch between the actions of human beings and what deep down they
know, 'they became futile in their thinking, and their senseless minds were
darkened.' Paul recognized the valuable place of *reasoning among Christians*,
as Bornkamm, Stowers and Pannenberg emphasize. But in the unbelieving world reason is corrupted and darkened. The word for argumentative
reason (Greek *dialogismoi*) is qualified by *emataiōthēsan*, made *futile*, or
worthless, which is cognate with the adjective *mataios*, meaning *empty*,
fruitless.[14]

Heart (v. 21), as Dunn affirms, is broader and deeper than in modern
parlance. The New English Bible (NEB) translates 'their misguided minds',
but the word denotes more than intellectual capacity. Jewett examines
Paul's uses of the term exhaustively, and includes *mind, attitude, thoughts*
and *desires*, not least in Romans 1.21.[15] Fitzmyer alludes to Ephesians
4.17–18: 'The Gentiles live in the futility of their minds. They are darkened
in their understanding, alienated from the life of God.'[16] Only the gospel
can penetrate this darkness.

In verse 22 there are parallels to 'Claiming to be wise, they became fools'.
In Jeremiah 10.14 'all human beings have become fools'. More specifically,
'The message about the cross is foolishness' (1 Cor. 1.18); 'I will destroy
the wisdom of the wise' (1 Cor. 1.19); 'Where is the one who is wise? . . . Has
not God made foolish the wisdom of the world?' (1 Cor. 1.20); 'God chose

---

[13] Barrett, C. K., *The Epistle to the Romans* (London: Black, 1957), pp. 35, 36.
[14] Danker, Frederick, *A Greek-English Lexicon of the New Testament and Other Early Christian Literature* (BDAG) (Chicago and London: University of Chicago Press, 3rd edn, 2000), p. 621.
[15] Jewett, Robert, *Paul's Anthropological Terms* (Leiden: Brill, 1971), p. 448.
[16] Fitzmyer, Joseph A., *Romans: A New Translation with Introduction and Commentary* (New York: Doubleday, 1992; AB 33), p. 282.

what is "foolish" in the world to shame the "wise"' (1 Cor. 1.27). Welborn examines this theme in Corinthians.[17]

This part of Paul's argument reaches a climax in verse 23, 'They exchanged the glory of the immortal God for images resembling a mortal human being or birds or four-footed animals or reptiles.' This verse shows the depths of the folly of the Gentile world. It also reflects the language of the OT (Ps. 105.20 LXX; 106.20 Hebrew text), where it refers to Israel's making of the golden calf (Exod. 32). It also reflects Jeremiah 2.11 and Deuteronomy 4.16–18, as well as themes in Isaiah. Deuteronomy 4.16–18 contains the same Greek words for 'images resembling'.

Pagan temples often contained images which represented the deities they worshipped. Oriental and Egyptian images included animals and reptiles. God had given Israel the vocation of representing *God* as *his people*. The prohibition of images was not only to inhibit pagan idolatry; it was also because Israel and God's people, in contrast to a block of wood or stone, were *intended to be his image*.[18]

Pagan images not only degraded the conception of God, but violated God's declaration, 'My glory I give to no other' (Isa. 42.8). The *glory* of the immortal God is, in Fitzmyer's words, 'the radiant external manifestation of his presence', initially in the OT in the tabernacle or Temple.[19] The Hebrew word for glory (*kābôdh*) denotes literally *weight*, but then *what makes a person impressive, weighty* or *having gravitas*. It includes 'honour, splendour, and glory'.[20] Danker gives as his third NT meaning *fame, honour, prestige*, as extensions of the original meaning, *shining*. Finally it denotes 'a transcendent being deserving honour'.[21] One example concerns Stephen, who 'gazed into heaven and saw the glory of God' (Acts 7.55). In Hebrews, Christ is 'the reflection of God's glory' (1.3).

In classical Greek the word *doxa* often denoted *reputation*. This understanding does not disappear in the NT. God's glory manifests his reputation or name on the basis of his character and past acts. In Romans 1.23 Paul argues that the Gentile world without Christ has parted with all that, exchanging it for petty images which compare the deity with reptiles or quadrupeds!

---

[17] Welborn, L. L., *Paul, the Fool of Christ: A Study of 1 Corinthians 1—4 in the Comic Philosophical Tradition* (London and New York: T & T Clark International/Continuum, 2005), pp. 1–24, 49–253.

[18] Moltmann, Jürgen, *God in Creation* (London: SCM, 1985), pp. 215–43; and Clines, D. J. A., 'The Image of God in Man', *Tyndale Bulletin* 19 (1968), pp. 53–103; Lossky, V., *The Image and Likeness of God* (London: Mowbray, 1974).

[19] Fitzmyer, *Romans*, p. 283.

[20] Brown, F., Driver, S. R., and Briggs, C. A., *Hebrew and English Lexicon of the Old Testament* (BDB) (Lafayette, IN: Associated Publishers, 1980), pp. 458–9.

[21] Danker, BDAG, pp. 256–8.

Further consequences of the alienation of the Gentile world: 'God gave them up' (1.24–32)

'God gave them up' (v. 24) means, according to Ernest Best, that sin not only brings its own punishment, but God takes steps to implement his judgement. Bruce cites C. S. Lewis as expressing 'an impressive modern statement of this principle' in Lewis' words that the lost 'enjoy forever the horrible freedom they have demanded, and are therefore self-enslaved'.[22] Nygren makes a similar comment: Paul 'does not say that God withdraws His blessing'. Further: 'When they turn to sin, they follow their own choice.'[23] They have not thereby escaped God.

Fitzmyer comments: 'The rhetorical triple use of *paredoken* ('gave them up', vv. 26, 28) . . . shifts the discussion from the question of guilt to that of punishment . . . Impiety brings its own retribution.'[24] Käsemann argues, 'This passage is indispensable to an understanding of the righteousness of God . . . [and] the faithfulness of the Creator to his creation.'[25] He adds on the same page: 'Paul paradoxically reverses the cause and the consequence: moral perversion is the result of God's wrath, not the cause of it', as we saw in Stählin.[26]

'Degrading of their bodies' (v. 24) touches a sensitive nerve in Paul's theology. *Body* is an important term for Paul. Käsemann expounds this brilliantly. He regards the body (Greek *sōma*) as 'the earliest gift of our Creator to us', which allows us to be a *visible* part of the world, involving *'ability to communicate'*. It is not merely 'physical' or 'outward', but our *'public face'*. Hence:

> In the bodily obedience of the Christian . . . in the world of everyday, the lordship of Christ *finds visible expression*, and only when this *visible* expression takes personal shape in us does the whole thing become *credible* as Gospel message.[27]

Thus Christians must 'glorify God in your body' (1 Cor. 6.20), and 'present your bodies as a living sacrifice' (Rom. 12.1). But in Romans 1.24, the Gentiles *degrade* their bodies.

---

[22] Bruce, F. F., *The Epistle of Paul to the Romans* (London: Tyndale, 1963), p. 85; cf. Lewis, C. S., *The Problem of Pain* (London: Bles, 1940), pp. 115–16.

[23] Nygren, Anders, *Commentary on Romans* (London: SCM, 1952), p. 110.

[24] Fitzmyer, *Romans*, p. 284.

[25] Käsemann, Ernst, *Commentary on Romans* (London: SCM, 1980), p. 47.

[26] Stählin, 'orgē', *TDNT*, vol. 5, p. 444.

[27] Käsemann, Ernst, 'Primitive Christian Apocalyptic' in *New Testament Questions of Today* (London: SCM, 1969), p. 135 (my italics).

In the Gentile world people enter bondage to the 'lusts of their hearts' (v. 24); they become in bondage to their own desires. The whole cycle of cause and effect has the consequence of their *dishonouring* themselves. Paul, as in Judaism, insists on the causal link between practical atheism and immorality, even if this is unpopular today.

It also results in their exchanging 'the truth about God for a lie' (v. 25), thereby serving the creature in place of the Creator. Again there are echoes of Wisdom 14.22–31 and Paul's earlier verses. Paul also reflects Isaiah 44.19–20: '"Shall I fall down before a block of wood?" . . . a deluded mind has led him astray, and he cannot . . . say, "Is not this thing in my right hand a fraud?"' Augustine cites the folly of giving worship to a creature rather than to God who created it. All first-century Jews would instantly concur with the utter folly of worshipping the creation of their own hands, or any *created* being.

'God . . . who is blessed for ever! Amen' (v. 25) is, in Dunn's words, 'A thoroughly and typical Jewish benediction (Gen. 9.26; 14.20; 1 Sam. 25.32; 2 Sam. 18.28; 1 Kings 1.48'.[28] Paul would declare God's blessedness in his daily prayers, just as the Jews recited the Eighteen Benedictions (2 Cor. 1.3; Eph. 1.3). 'Amen' expresses the speaker's or writer's *commitment* to the truth expressed. Hence it falls under the heading of a speech-act, in which J. L. Austin includes 'commissives'.[29]

In verse 26 Paul considers sexual perversion in the Gentile world. Paul calls them 'degrading passions'. He considers 'unnatural' intercourse between women; in verse 27, unnatural intercourse between men, which constitutes 'shameless acts'. Many modern readers may ask whether this is 'homosexuality', or specifically acts with call-boys or temple prostitutes. Cranfield acknowledges that the Greek *chrēsis* is a recognized periphrasis for sexual intercourse.[30] Leenhardt comments that Paul is concerned that deviation from God leads to deviation from the right and proper use of nature.[31] A huge array of scholarly literature has addressed this issue, including works by Bailey, Furnish, D. F. Wright, Hays, Scroggs, Boswell and Joseph Ratzinger (Pope Benedict XVI). We have denominational statements from Anglicans, Lutherans, Presbyterians, the United Methodist Church and the Southern Baptist

---

[28] Dunn, James D. G., *Romans 1—8* (Dallas: Word, 1988; WBC 38), p. 63.

[29] Austin, J. L., *How to Do Things with Words* (Oxford: Clarendon, 1962), pp. 88–107 and throughout.

[30] Cranfield, C. E. B., *A Critical and Exegetical Commentary on the Epistle to the Romans*, vol. 1 (Edinburgh: T & T Clark, 1975; ICC), p. 125.

[31] Leenhardt, *Romans*, p. 69.

Convention.[32] Bailey's work is useful in distinguishing between 'possible references' and 'definite references' in biblical passages. He concludes that there are six 'definite' allusions, including Leviticus 18.22; 20.13; Romans 1.26–27; 1 Corinthians 6.9, 10; and 1 Timothy 1.9–10.

A careful report, *Some Issues in Human Sexuality*, was published in 2003 under the authority of the House of Bishops of the Church of England.[33] The chairperson was the eminent ethicist Richard Harries, then Bishop of Oxford. Among other evidence, the group scrutinized Romans 1.28–32, considering the major commentaries. After examining issues of context and Paul's aim, the bishops concluded:

> Rom. 1:26–27 . . . have traditionally been seen to teach clearly that both male and female forms of same-sexual activity are shameful and contrary to the natural order established by God. The consensus among the commentators is still that this is a correct reading of the text.[34]

They quote Fitzmyer as writing, 'Homosexual behaviour is the sin of rebellion against God, an outward manifestation of inward and spiritual rebellion. It illustrates human degradation.' Dunn comments, 'Paul's attitude to homosexual practice is unambiguous', and Wright declares: 'Paul notes homosexual practice, both female and male . . . Out of the many things Paul could have highlighted in the pagan world, he has chosen same-sex erotic practices.'[35]

The main exponent of a 'Minority Report' on the opposite side of the debate had been Boswell, a historian rather than a NT specialist, supported by Scroggs. They propose three arguments. (i) Boswell argued that homosexual relationships were tolerated in some periods of church history.[36] But most historians reject this argument; at best it is highly controversial. (ii) Boswell and Scroggs argue that what Paul really condemned was 'pederasty', or intercourse between a man and boy, probably a call-boy.

[32] Bradshaw, Timothy (ed.), *The Way Forward?* (London: Hodder & Stoughton, 1997) with essays from Oliver O'Donovan and others; Bailey, D. S., *Homosexuality and the Western Tradition* (New York: Longmans Green, 1955); Wright, David F., 'Homosexuality', *EQ* 61 (1989), pp. 291–300; Scroggs, Robin, *The New Testament and Homosexuality* (Philadelphia: Fortress, 1983); Boswell, J., *Christianity, Social Tolerance and Homosexuality* (Chicago: University of Chicago Press, 1980) and Siker, Jeffrey S., *Homosexuality in the Church: Both Sides of the Debate* (Louisville: John Knox, 1994); Gagnon, R., *The Bible and Homosexual Practice* (Nashville: Abingdon, 2001).

[33] Church Report, *Some Issues in Human Sexuality: A Guide to the Debate* (London: Church House Publishing, 2003).

[34] Church Report, *Some Issues*, p. 133.

[35] Wright, 'Romans', *NIB*, vol. 10, p. 433.

[36] Boswell, J., *Christianity, Social Tolerance and Homosexuality*, and *Same-Sex Unions in Pre-Modern Europe* (New York: Villard Books, 1994).

Scroggs claims, 'Biblical judgments against homosexuality are not relevant to today's debate.'[37] (iii) They argue that Paul inherited his strong disapproval from the united witness of Judaism, whereas these relationships were widely accepted in the Hellenistic world. On the other hand the bishops' report and others insist that Paul is speaking with his *Christian voice*. They refer to my argument on 1 Corinthians 6.9–10 that Paul reflects a Christian catechetical tradition, and is neither idiosyncratic nor reflecting simply Jewish cultural prejudices.[38] These are dehumanizing practices, which do not reflect God's 'order' for nature. Questions about intermediate environmental or genetic causes do not detract from this.

Some Issues in Human Sexuality is an exceedingly thorough study, which includes a large bibliography and a multitude of footnotes. It is clear and readable, written by four scholarly and well-informed bishops, alert to biblical scholarship.

In verses 28–29 Paul proceeds to anti-social sins among the Gentiles. He repeats that 'God gave them up to a debased mind and to things that should not be done'. They further 'did not see fit to acknowledge God'. There is clearly a word-play in the Greek between *adokimon* (*worthless*) and *edokimasein* (*to see fit*) which the English misses. The word *adikomos* means *not standing the test*, but then comes to mean *worthless*.[39] The verb *dokimazō* means *to make a critical examination of something* or *to approve*, or in Romans 1.28 *to see fit* (*to have a true knowledge*).[40] The purpose of the word-play is to stress the correspondence between the sin and the penalty. The Gentile world without Christ did not consider it fit or proper to keep God in mind, by praising him and serving him. Wright comments that idolatry is as relevant today as ever it was. He writes:

> Our generation has seen the resurgence, in the Western world, of various forms of paganism. The worship of blood and soil . . . The worship of Mammon . . . the god of sexual love, claims millions of devotees.[41]

Schlatter and Jewett conclude that *mind* (*nous*) is 'the constellation of thought and assumptions which makes up the consciousness of the person and acts as the agent of rational discernment and communication'.[42] As a tool for Christian reflection, as Bornkamm, Jewett and Pannenberg

---

[37] Scroggs, *New Testament and Homosexuality*, pp. 126–7.
[38] Thiselton, Anthony C., *The First Epistle to the Corinthians: A Commentary on the Greek Text* (Grand Rapids: Eerdmans, and Carlisle: Paternoster, 2000; NIGTC), pp. 599–611.
[39] Danker, BDAG, p. 21.
[40] Danker, BDAG, p. 255.
[41] Wright, 'Romans', *NIB*, vol. 10, p. 435.
[42] Jewett, *Paul's Anthropological Terms*, p. 450.

insist, Paul has the highest evaluation of this Spirit-directed capacity. This makes his statement about the *debased mind*, apart from Christ, all the more forceful.

In verses 29–31 Paul piles *anti-social vices* one on top of the other. These include *wickedness, evil, covetousness, malice, envy, murder, strife, craftiness* and so on. Catalogues of vice are well known in the ancient world.[43] They are reflected in Stoic writings and in such Hellenistic-Jewish literature as Wisdom 14.22–26. Philo lists no fewer than 140 such vices.[44] Paul lists 21 such vices in 1 Corinthians 5.9–11. Easton then argues that these catalogues were primarily derived from the Stoics. Vögtle took this further in 1936.[45] Wibbing developed this yet further in 1959, except that he stressed the background in Greek-speaking Judaism.[46] On this basis Conzelmann argued that these lists are not specifically Pauline.

Dodd argued in 1951, however, that the basis of Paul's ethics must be 'sharply distinguished from that of contemporary Greek moralists'.[47] Carrington and Selwyn agree that much is owed to common Christian catechism, which became a *Sitz im Leben* for such references as Romans 1.28–29.[48] In Germany Kamlah developed the approach of Dodd, Carrington and Selwyn.[49] Parallels to Paul do readily exist in Hellenistic and Hellenistic-Jewish sources. But, as Sandmel has argued, parallels do not guarantee *borrowings*. Romans 1.28–29 are Paul's own.

Dunn comments on verse 29: 'The positioning of "unrighteousness" at the head of the list is no doubt deliberate'.[50] *Greed (pleonexia)* denotes *always wanting more*, as do *envy* and *covetousness*. In verse 30, 'slanderers' denotes *speaking ill*, whereas 'gossips' (v. 29 NRSV) denotes *secret slander*, or, as Danker renders it, *rumourmonger*, or *tale-bearer*.[51] 'God-haters' (v. 30) was translated as 'hateful to God' in the Revised Version (RV), but as 'haters of God' in the Revised Standard Version (RSV). Danker endorses the NRSV.[52] 'Boastful' (v. 30; Greek *alazonas*) really means a *braggart*, or

---

[43] Dunn, *Romans 1—8*, p. 67.

[44] Philo, *Sac.*, 32.

[45] Vögtle, A., *Die Tugend- und Lasterkataloge im der Neuen Testament* (Münster: Aschendorff, 1936).

[46] Wibbing, S., *Die Tugend- und Lasterkataloge im der Neuen Testament und ihre Traditionsgeschichte* (Berlin: Töpelmann, 1959; BZNW 25).

[47] Dodd, C. H., *Gospel and Law* (Cambridge: CUP, 1951), p. 10; cf. pp. 10–21.

[48] Carrington, Philip, *The Primitive Christian Catechism* (Cambridge: CUP, 1940); Selwyn, E. G., *The First Epistle of St Peter* (London: Macmillan, 1947), pp. 365–466.

[49] Kamlah, R., *Die Form der katalogischen Paränese im Neuen Testament* (Tübingen: Mohr, 1964; WUNT 7), esp. pp. 11–14 and 27–31.

[50] Dunn, *Romans 1—8*, pp. 67–8.

[51] Danker, BDAG, p. 1098; cf. p. 519.

[52] Danker, BDAG, p. 453.

one who swaggers. This denotes those who disrupt social relations. 'Foolish' looks back to verse 21, where the word really means *uncomprehending,* and is linked with Greek *asunthetous,* which really means *those who deal treacherously.* This is stronger than NRSV's 'faithless'.[53] NRSV's 'heartless' (v. 31) is the opposite of a person who *shows family affection,* and therefore it means *without natural affection.*

The climax of verses 18–31 finds expression in verse 32: the Gentiles indirectly 'know God's decree', but practise those evils which his decree excludes. Paul even adds, 'They . . . applaud others' who do them, but 'those who practise such things deserve to die'. Some commentators find this verse difficult. Cranfield, however, insists, 'The man who applauds and encourages others in doing what is wicked is . . . not only as guilty as those who do commit it, but very often more guilty than they.'[54] *Death* is introduced for the first time, although it will feature especially in chapters 6—8.[55] The whole argument of 1.18–32 depends on separation and alienation from God, who is the *source of all life.* Hence *death* is literally the *embodiment of godlessness,* or of *being without God.*

---

[53] Cranfield, *Romans,* vol. 1, pp. 118 and 133.
[54] Cranfield, *Romans,* vol. 1, p. 135.
[55] Dunn, *Romans 1—8,* p. 69.

9

The Jewish world as moral critic (2.1—3.8)

God is impartial: the moral critic also stands under judgement (2.1–11)

The stance of the Jews as moral critics of the Gentiles is fully understandable. For one thing, Gentile polytheism and often flagrant immorality did seem in many cases to set Jew and Gentile apart. 'Good-living' Gentiles like Cicero and Seneca constituted the exception rather than the rule. Jewish inter-Testamental sacred writings encouraged this judgmental attitude. Wisdom 12.2–5 declares: 'You correct . . . those who trespass, and you remind and warn them of the things through which they sin . . . their works of sorcery and unholy rites, their merciless slaughter of children' (i.e. infanticide).

Many of the sins listed in Wisdom 12.6, 10, 23–26; 13.10, 13–18; 14.8–14, 22–31; and 15.10–19 reflect Paul's own 'catalogue of vices' in Romans 1.18–32. Hence in 1.18–32 Paul's denunciation of the Gentile world would strike a chord with most Jewish readers. It is reminiscent of Amos' strategy in denouncing 'the transgressions of Damascus . . . Gaza . . . Tyre . . . Edom . . .' (Amos 1.3—2.3), and then suddenly changing to 'transgressions of Judah' (Amos 2.4). Nodding approval would suddenly be stung into shock: 'Us, too?' Commentators from Dodd to Cranfield, Dunn, Fitzmyer and Jewett underline this approach.[1] Wright observes that God's judgement is 'addressed to anyone who . . . tries to adopt a superior posture'.[2]

Dunn and Jewett rightly refer to Paul's 'vigorous diatribe style'.[3] Whereas some find difficulty in interpreting 'therefore' (2.1; Greek *dio*), Dunn and Jewett explain that recognition of the diatribe style shows how this section constitutes 'a challenge to anyone who thought himself exempt from the

---

[1] Cranfield, C. E. B., *A Critical and Exegetical Commentary on the Epistle to the Romans*, vol. 1 (Edinburgh: T & T Clark, 1975; ICC), pp. 137–40; Dunn, J. D. G., *Romans 1—8* (Dallas: Word, 1988; WBC 38), pp. 79–80; Fitzmyer, Joseph A., *Romans: A New Translation with Introduction and Commentary* (New York: Doubleday, 1992; AB 33), pp. 296–9; Jewett, Robert, *Romans: A Commentary* (Minneapolis: Fortress, 2007; Hermeneia), pp. 197–8.

[2] Wright, N. T., 'Romans', in the *New Interpreter's Bible* (*NIB*) (Nashville: Abingdon, 2002), vol. 10, p. 437.

[3] Dunn, *Romans 1—8*, p. 78; Jewett, *Romans*, pp. 196–7.

preceding indictment'.[4] Paul repeats 'without excuse' (Greek *anapologētos*) from 1.20. 'Whoever you are' (NRSV) renders Greek *ei, ō anthrōpe* (vocative). Paul deliberately uses the haranguing style of popular preachers. Stowers emphasizes this, and cites parallels with Epictetus.[5] Paul writes as if he were accosting 'an imaginary interlocutor, who applauds what he has been saying about the pagan in 1:18–32'.[6] The challenge comes in the phrase 'in passing judgement on another you condemn yourself' (v. 1). It is reminiscent of the Jesus tradition about removing the speck or splinter from another's eye, while there is a log or plank in one's own eye (Matt. 7.3–5; Luke 6.41–42).

In verse 2 the interlocutor speaks explicitly, and Paul quotes what could be selected from an abundance of Jewish literature and synagogue sermons. In passing such judgements, he confirms that he knows the law of God, and is therefore doubly 'without excuse'. Moreover, in judging the Gentiles, the Jewish critic tries to place himself in the position of *God, the Judge of all*. It is a human trait to use blaming others as a cloak for our own failures.

In verses 2–5 Paul states four reactions and counter-reactions. The first exchange takes the form: (i) 'Yes, I agree; the Gentiles are sinners; and they will pay for it.' Counter-reply (v. 3): 'Do you imagine that, if you do these things yourself, *you* will escape the judgement of God?' (ii) Within the 'reply' in verse 3, it is implied that 'to know' God or the law of God is to be 'acquainted with complete righteousness'. Wisdom 15.3 states, 'To know you is complete righteousness'. The counter-reply would be: 'You see yourself on God's side, assenting to his judgement. You gladly say with Psalm 79.6: "Pour out your anger on the nations . . . that do not call on your name." But will *you* escape God's judgement?'

(iii) The third exchange comes in verse 4. Paul imagines the Jewish reply: 'God has "given up" the Gentile world, but there is no evidence that he has given *me* up!' Paul suggests the counter-reply: 'God's kindness, forbearance and patience is meant to *lead you to repentance*' (v. 4). The fact that God has *postponed* the hour of judgement does *not* show that God will judge us favourably.

(iv) The fourth exchange centres on 'storing up', whether merit or wrath. In Judaism there was a common belief that merit could be stored up to result in a *reward*. God judges the *heathen* (Wis. 11.9–10). The final counter-reply comes in verse 5: 'By your hard and impenitent heart

---

[4] Dunn, *Romans 1—8*, p. 79; Jewett, *Romans*, pp. 196–8.

[5] Stowers, Stanley K., *The Diatribe and Paul's Letter to the Romans* (Chico: Scholars Press, 1981; SBLDS 57), pp. 85–93, 103–14, 213; see Epictetus, *Discourses*, 2.21.11–12, 3.2.14–16.

[6] Fitzmyer, *Romans*, p. 299.

you are "storing up" *wrath* for yourself on the day of wrath, when God's righteous judgement will be revealed.'

Some particular words require comment. 'Do you *despise* [Greek *kataphroneis*] the riches of his kindness . . . ?' means, 'Do you *look down upon*', as if the moral critic is still scrutinizing everything![7] The Greek piles up *riches, kindness, forbearance* and *patience* in a long single clause, before the verb comes as a sharp rebuke: in verse 5 'hard and impenitent heart' translates *sklērotēta sou kai ametanoēton kardian.* The stem *sklēro-* denotes *dry* or *rough*, and the NEB translates 'rigid obstinacy'.[8] The adjective *ametanoēton* denotes *being incapable of turning round.*

'He will repay according to each one's deeds' (v. 6) echoes the language of Psalm 62.12 (61.13 LXX), and Proverbs 24.12. Wright suggests that the psalm 'sees God's just judgment . . . as an expression of God's power and mercy'.[9] Cranfield argues that this principle is repeated frequently in the NT no less than the OT (Matt. 7.21; 16.27; 25.31–46; John 5.28, 29; 2 Cor. 5.10; 11.15; Gal. 6.7–9).[10] Verse 7 looks at the other side of the coin. Those who set their sights on *God* and values beyond the self will receive *eternal life.* Goodness is *not a single act, but a steady persistent habit*, as Aquinas argues. The Greek of verse 8 is more complex than the NRSV translation. It comes to mean 'those who are self-seeking'; but Barrett renders the more complex Greek: 'those who are out for a quick and selfish profit on their own account'. The Greek *eritheia* is a condemnation of selfish ambition. In the last clause of verse 8 the syntax changes abruptly. 'Wrath and fury' appear in the nominative, suggesting NRSV's 'there will be'.

The NRSV translation 'for everyone' (v. 9) is correct. The Greek is *epi pasan psuchēn anthrōpon*, but any older attempt to interpret *psuchēn* as '*soul* of man' is wrong. As Fitzmyer observes, this is too Hellenistic an interpretation.[11] Like the Hebrew *nephesh* (*life*, or *soul*; Lev. 24.17; Num. 19.20), it is much more likely to refer to the *life* of a person. 'Anguish and distress' (v. 9) convey similar ideas. Greek *thlipsis* (*anguish*) comes from the verb *to squeeze*, and *stenochōria* denotes painful pressure from narrowing confines. '[To] the Jew first and also the Greek' indicates that Jews and Gentiles are in the same boat. The clause balances that of verse

---

[7] Danker, Frederick, *Greek-English Lexicon of the New Testament and Other Early Christian Literature* (BDAG) (Chicago and London: University of Chicago Press, 3rd edn, 2000), p. 529, has *look down upon, despise, scorn, treat with contempt.*

[8] Danker, BDAG, p. 930, has *an unyielding frame of mind, hardness of heart, obstinacy, stubbornness,* as the meaning.

[9] Wright, 'Romans', *NIB*, vol. 10, p. 439.

[10] Cranfield, *Romans*, vol. 1, p. 146.

[11] Fitzmyer, *Romans*, p. 302.

10, where they can also enjoy 'glory and honour and peace' co-equally in a new situation in Christ. Verse 11 expresses the theme of this section: 'God shows no partiality.' This reflects verses 6–10. Some have argued that this might imply justification by works, but Romans 3.20 emphatically declares, 'No human being will be justified . . . by deeds . . .'. The Greek *prosōpolēmpsia* (*partiality*), is of special interest. Moulton and Milligan find it in the papyri, but not in the LXX. They comment, 'It may be reckoned amongst the earliest definitely Christian words.'[12]

The same divine judgement befalls both Jews and Gentiles (2.12–16)

Wright comments that Paul in verses 12–16 'explains further what is involved in vv. 7–11'.[13] With respect to the Gentiles, to sin 'apart from the law' implies to 'perish apart from the law' (v. 12a). Co-equally, to sin 'under the law' implies that Jews 'will be judged by the law' (v. 12b). Paul has now introduced the word *nomos* (*law*). But this word can mean *several different things*.

(i) Sometimes 'the law' is equivalent to the Hebrew *Torah*, or the *Law given through Moses*. As in Judaism, it may denote the Pentateuch in contrast to the Prophets and the Writings. (ii) Sometimes this word can mean *Jewish interpretation* of the Law, as in the *Mishnah* or rabbinic writings. (iii) It may also denote *the whole OT*, as in 'What is written in the Law?' (iv) It may also denote *the will of God*, as in 'O how I love thy law' (Ps. 119.97 AV). (v) Sometimes the word may denote a *principle* of any kind, as in 'The law of the Spirit of life in Christ Jesus has set you free from the law of sin and of death' (Rom. 8.2), although some contest this meaning. (vi) The law may denote the *means* through which God does *not provide justification* and righteousness (Gal. 3.10).[14] Wright declares, in summary: 'The law is meant to be *obeyed*, not merely listened to,' while for many Jews 'It had become . . . (merely) a badge of privilege, a talisman, a sign that Israel was inalienably God's people.'[15]

---

[12] Moulton, James H., and Milligan, George, *The Vocabulary of the Greek Testament* (London: Hodder & Stoughton, 1952 [1930]), p. 553.

[13] Wright, 'Romans', *NIB*, vol. 10, p. 440.

[14] Whiteley, D. E. H., *The Theology of St. Paul* (Oxford: Blackwell, 1970), pp. 76–86; Dunn, James D. G., *The Theology of Paul the Apostle* (Edinburgh: T & T Clark, 1998), pp. 128–61; Wright, N. T., *Paul and the Faithfulness of God* (London: SPCK, 2013), pp. 90–5, 485–95, 505–16, 892–902, 1032–8; and Danker, BDAG, pp. 677–8.

[15] Wright, 'Romans', *NIB*, vol. 10, p. 440.

Paul introduces explicitly in verse 13 the contrast between a theoretical familiarity of the law ('hearing it'), and acting upon the law ('doing it'). The next verse (v. 14) recognizes that the Gentiles do not 'possess' the law, but may 'do instinctively what the law requires'. *Instinctively* is not in the Greek, but Greek *phusei* (*by nature*), can amount to *instinctively*, if Paul uses it in the Stoic sense of 'living in harmony with the natural order'. Leenhardt, Dunn, Fitzmyer and the NRSV construe 'by nature' as qualifying what follows it, i.e. 'do by nature the [things] of the law'.[16] Cranfield recognizes that we cannot be certain, but opts for the phrase that precedes it: 'not possess the law by nature'. *The practical point is that the 'decent' Gentile feels a twinge of unease when he (or she) does certain things that he knows in his heart are wrong.* The 'twinge' is because this is how God has made him. Paul does not subscribe to the notion of 'natural law' in Stoic philosophy.

Paul introduces *conscience* (Greek *suneidēsis*) for the first time in Romans. He has already used it extensively in 1 Corinthians (1 Cor. 8.7, 10, 12; 10.25, 27–29; cf. 2 Cor. 1.12; 4.2; 5.11), and will use it in Romans 9.1 and 13.5. The term is also used in Acts 23.1 and 24.16, Hebrews and 1 Peter. It comes from the popular language of the time, usually with the sense of *remorse* or *freedom from remorse*. Only from the third century onwards does it come to mean an arbitrating capacity, largely for good conduct. In the OT, Hebrew uses the term *heart* (Hebrew *lēbh*) some 600 times.[17] Holtzmann (1911) argued that Paul borrowed the term from Hellenism. Bultmann and Dupont (both 1948), and recently Wright (2002), note affinities, but not necessarily borrowings, from Stoic thought.

A new stage of research, however, began with C. A. Pierce in 1955.[18] He argued that any dependence on Stoicism rests on 'insufficient evidence'. Conscience has nothing to do with a supposed 'divine voice'. In Paul it denotes 'the pain consequent upon the inception of an act believed to be wrong'.[19] It is mainly *retrospective*, concerning only *past* acts. A second step came with Thrall's modification to Pierce. She argued that sometimes the word could be more positive, and could concern *future* action.[20] A third advance came with the research of Horsley (1978), Eckstein (1983), Gooch

---

[16] Fitzmyer, *Romans*, pp. 309–10; Dunn, *Romans 1—8*, pp. 98–9, as against Cranfield, *Romans*, vol. 1, pp. 136–7.

[17] Brown, F., Driver, S. R., and Briggs, C. A., *Hebrew and English Lexicon of the Old Testament* (BDB) (Lafayette, IN: Associated Publishers, 1980), p. 525; Wolff, Hans W. *Anthropology of the Old Testament* (London: SCM, 1974), p. 40.

[18] Pierce, C. A., *Conscience in the New Testament* (London: SCM, 1955), esp. pp. 13–20 and 111–30.

[19] Pierce, *Conscience*, p. 22.

[20] Thrall, Margaret, 'The Pauline Use of *Suneidēsis*', *NTS* 14 (1967), pp. 118–25.

(1987) and Gardner (1994). They argued that *self-awareness* often provided a more accurate translation, especially in 1 Corinthians 8—10.[21]

This sub-section ends in verse 16 with a reminder of the Jewish teaching that 'God . . . will judge the secret thoughts of all.' Paul adds 'through Christ' and 'according to my gospel'. The first addition shows Paul's already *cosmic* Christology: Christ, together with God, will be Judge of all. The second shows that teaching on the Last Judgement constitutes a fundamental doctrine of his gospel. There is no contradiction between the judgement of *all* and justification by free grace, as many have shown.[22] Justification is often thought of as the anticipation of the verdict of the Last Judgement, appropriated in advance through faith. Theissen has also provided an illuminating discussion about the relation between the *heart*, or 'the *secret thoughts* of all' (v. 16) and modern post-Freudian notions of the subconscious or unconscious.[23]

Reliance on the law and circumcision gives no security, but everything depends on God (2.17—3.8)

In verse 17 Paul explicitly addresses his dialogue-partner as a Jew (Greek *Ioudaios*). This is the normal term for Jews. The verb 'rely on' (Greek *epanapauē*) is used only here in the NT, but is crucial. It means 'to rest one's hopes on', as a double compound. Roberts suggests 'the picture of a blind, mechanical, reliance on the Mosaic law'. The MSS א, B and D* omit the definite article. 'You boast of your relation to God' reflects literally 'You glory in God', almost as if it were a national asset for the Jews.

Verses 17–20 and beyond not only constitute an ironic paraphrase of many Diaspora synagogue sermons, but also anticipate what Paul will say about his attitude as a Pharisee in Philippians 3.4–6: 'Circumcised on the eighth day, a member of the people of Israel . . . a Hebrew born of Hebrews, as to the law, a Pharisee . . . as to righteousness under the law, blameless.' In Philippians 3.7–8, however, he adds: 'Yet whatever gains I had, these I have come to regard as loss . . . I regard them as rubbish'. On verse 18 Fitzmyer comments, 'To know God's will concerning his people was a matter of great pride in Jewish piety.'[24]

---

[21] Horsley, R. A., 'Consciousness and Freedom among the Corinthians: 1 Corinthians 8—10', *CBQ* 40 (1978), pp. 574–89; Eckstein, H.-J., *Der Begriff Syneidesis bei Paulus* (Tübingen: Mohr, 1983); Gooch, P. D., '"Conscience" in 1 Corinthians 8 and 10', *NTS* 33 (1987), pp. 244–54; and Gardner, Paul D., *The Gifts of God and the Authentication of a Christian* (Lanham, MD; University Press of America, 1994).

[22] Yinger, Kent L., *Paul, Judaism, and Judgment According to Deeds* (Cambridge: CUP, 1999; SNTSMS 105), esp. pp. 134–260.

[23] Theissen, Gerd, *Psychological Aspects of Pauline Theology* (Edinburgh: T & T Clark, 1987), esp. pp. 177–266.

[24] Fitzmyer, *Romans*, p. 316,

The next four or five phrases reflect typical Jewish attitudes: 'A guide to the blind, a light to those who are in darkness, a correction of the foolish' etc. (vv. 19–20), which abound in Jewish literature and in rabbinic homilies as a distinctive ministry to the Gentile world (Sir. 17.11; 45.5; Baruch 3.36; 4.1). 'A teacher of children' (v. 20) is literally 'a teacher of babes', which may refer to the instruction of proselytes to Judaism.

In grammatical terms Paul is so carried away by passion in verse 21 that he breaks off, leaving the syntactical protasis in the air. Technically this is called *anacoluthon*. Here Paul expresses the nub of his point: 'You, then, that teach others, will you not teach yourself?' If you preach against stealing, do you steal? Cranfield comments, '21 and 22 consist of four sentences which can be read either as statements, or – more naturally – as accusatory rhetorical questions.'[25] Rabbinic writings, he adds, often cite individual teachers whose teaching is contradicted by their actions.[26] Fitzmyer understands Paul's reference to idolatry in verse 22 figuratively, as if to say: 'Do you succumb to the idolatry of elevating the Mosaic law to a position of unwarranted devotion?'[27] Cranfield, by contrast, understands this as 'the use by Jews of articles stolen . . . from idol-shrines'.[28] Dunn similarly understands Greek *hierosulein* to mean *to rob a temple*, although he recognizes that it may also mean *to commit sacrilege*.[29]

Romans 2.24 presents a problem in that Paul seems to be quoting Isaiah 52.5 from the LXX, where the Hebrew has neither 'because of you' nor 'among the Gentiles'. Lightfoot, however, argues that the additions 'give the correct sense'. Does 'because of you' mean (as in Isaiah) because God has given them up to exile, or (as in Paul) because of what the Jews fail to do? Stanley discusses this.[30] Cranfield similarly notes that the LXX's variations from the Hebrew make Paul's *application* easier.[31]

Paul turns to the subject of circumcision in 2.25–29. It is as if his dialogue-partner were saying: 'Well, granted that what you say about the law is correct, what about circumcision? *That* can't be undone by disobedience to the law!' Paul takes up his opponent's point by replying that even in the case of circumcision, its value as a sign of belonging to God can still

---

[25] Cranfield, *Romans*, vol. 1, p. 168.
[26] Strack, Hermann L., and Billerbeck, Paul, *Kommentar zum Neuen Testament aus Talmud und Midrasch* (München: Beck, 1969), vol. 3, pp. 106–7.
[27] Fitzmyer, *Romans*, p. 318.
[28] Cranfield, *Romans*, vol. 1, p. 169.
[29] Dunn, *Romans 1—8*, p. 114.
[30] Stanley, Christopher D., *Paul and the Language of Scripture: Citation Technique in the Pauline Epistles and Contemporary Literature* (Cambridge: CUP, 1992; SNTSMS 74), pp. 84–6, 254–6.
[31] Cranfield, *Romans*, vol. 1, p. 171.

be contradicted by one's *inner attitude*: 'Real circumcision is a matter of the heart – it is spiritual and not literal' (v. 29); it is not 'something external and physical' (v. 28). Barrett comments, 'Paul challenges the Jew's complacent reliance upon circumcision as a certain passport to salvation.'[32] Verse 25 states the principle: 'Circumcision . . . is of value *if* you obey the law; but *if* you break the law, your circumcision has become uncircumcision.' Even the OT spoke of 'Circumcising your hearts' (Deut. 10.16), as Holland points out.[33]

In verses 27–28 the contrast between 'inner' and 'external' is not characteristic of Paul, because we have seen with reference to Käsemann that the *body* is where Christians manifest the Lordship of Christ credibly and publicly. Here, however, the contrast, as Cranfield indicates, is 'between the person who is to all outward appearance a Jew and the person who is inwardly a Jew'.[34] Paul argues that the latter, not the former, is a *genuine Jew*. In addition to Deuteronomy 10.16, we may also cite Leviticus 26.41; Deuteronomy 30.6; Jeremiah 4.4 and 9.26 for the same idea. Paul's allusion to the Gentiles in verse 27 is a rhetorical inversion of the Jews' 'judging' Gentiles: in this respect the Gentiles may 'judge' Jews! Nygren expounds this point: 'Thus the positions are reversed'; it is as if Paul recalled the tradition, 'The people of Nineveh will rise up at the judgement with this generation and condemn it' (Matt. 12.41).[35]

The contrast between Spirit and letter (or the literal, v. 29) recalls 2 Corinthians 3.6–11. The NEB renders verse 29, 'not by written precepts but by the Spirit'. In verse 29b Leenhardt sees a possible play on words between 'praise' and 'Judah', since *Judah* means *praise* (Gen. 29.35; 49.8).[36]

Romans 3.1–8 constitutes the third stage of Paul's argument from 2.17 to 3.8. It concerns the advantages of the Jews (3.1–2) and the faithfulness and justice of God (3.8). God's *covenant faithfulness becomes a major theme in Romans 9—11.*[37] Paul argues, first, that to reduce the Jews to the level of the Gentile world would nullify all that the revelation of the Old Testament stands for. 'What advantage has the Jew?' (v. 1) could be understood in either of two ways. Either Paul asks: 'What is the personal advantage of being a Jew?' Or Paul asks: 'What is the advantage (profitable function) of Israel in God's purposes?' Käsemann, Barrett and most writers choose

---

[32] Barrett, C. K., *The Epistle to the Romans* (London: Black, 1957), p. 58.

[33] Holland, Tom, *Romans: The Divine Marriage* (Eugene, OR: Pickwick, 2011), p. 69.

[34] Cranfield, *Romans*, vol. 1, p. 175.

[35] Nygren, Anders, *Commentary on Romans* (London: SCM, 1952), p. 133.

[36] Leenhardt, Franz J., *The Epistle to the Romans* (London: Lutterworth, 1961), p. 89.

[37] Wright, 'Romans', *NIB*, vol. 10, p. 452.

the second. Käsemann paraphrases: Paul 'asks whether the precedence of the Jews in salvation history has been completely cancelled according to 2.12–29'.[38] Fitzmyer observes that 3.1–8 represent a 'dialogue element', like a teacher 'using diatribe'.[39] 'The oracles' of God (v. 2) means primarily here Scripture.

Fitzmyer asserts that verse 3 poses the leading question and dominates the whole discussion. Surprisingly Dodd suggests that it merely adds obscurity. But 'the faithfulness of God' constitutes a major theme in Paul's argument, as Wright stresses. Moreover this is closely relevant to a hypothetical reply: 'You are suggesting that the Scripture cannot be applied.' Paul anticipates the conclusion of Romans 9—11. Nygren comments, 'It is *by* man's falseness, not in spite of it, that the truthfulness of God is glorified.'[40] The Greek *apistia* probably means *unbelief* here, but it may also mean *lack of trust*. Cranfield suggests a word-play in English between 'they were entrusted', 'they refused to trust', and God's 'trustworthiness'.[41] It is unthinkable that God's faithfulness to his covenant should be rendered ineffective.

In verse 4 'Everyone is a liar' reflects the psalmist's dismay in Psalm 116.11 (115.2 LXX). Against God's truthfulness, all humanity seems to be lying. The phrase 'As it is written' refers to what follows from Psalm 51.4 (50.6 LXX). The psalmist confesses his sin against God, and God's righteousness and truth stand over against the sinfulness of humankind. The LXX of Psalm 51.4 uses the middle voice (Greek *krinesthai*) in an active sense, *contend*; the AV/KJB is mistaken in translating it as passive, 'Thou art judged'. NRSV 'prevail' (Greek *nikēseis*) means here *to win a lawsuit*.

The following verse (v. 5) continues the diatribe style by anticipating the objection: 'You seem to be making unrighteousness a good thing, as a foil for God's righteousness.' Hence, the objector continues, 'God would not be fair to punish me!' But, Paul replies, this is a false inference. Admittedly it is human unbelief that shows up God's righteousness and faithfulness. But God, to be true to himself and his nature, *cannot* (logical *cannot*) be unjust, to inflict wrath on humankind. Because of the complexity of his rejoinder, Paul adds: 'I speak in a human way', i.e. this is the best that human language can do. Dunn comments, 'Paul thus uses covenant language to reaffirm the basic covenant concepts of the Jewish Scriptures.'[42]

---

[38] Käsemann, Ernst, *Commentary on Romans* (London: SCM, 1980), p. 78.

[39] Fitzmyer, *Romans*, p. 325.

[40] Nygren, *Romans*, p. 138.

[41] Cranfield, *Romans*, vol. 1, p. 180.

[42] Dunn, *Romans 1—8*, p. 134.

Paul's speaking 'in a human way' also relates to the blasphemous thought that God could ever be unjust.

Hence verse 6 begins with a passionate negative. The NRSV 'By no means!' hardly captures it fully. The Greek *mē genoito*, literally 'May it never come to pass' (optative mood), is used for emphatic negation: 'Perish the thought!' Cranfield comments,

> Paul rejects the notion that God is guilty of injustice on the ground that to ascribe injustice to God is essentially absurd, since it is tantamount to a denial of what must be held to be axiomatic, namely that God is the eschatological [final] Judge of the world.[43]

If we really imagine that we can be the arbiter of God's acts, how could it then make sense to speak of God as a definitive Judge? Verses 7–8 in effect repeat this argument, except that in verse 8 Paul refers to his misreported teaching: 'Let us do evil so that good may come.' The syntax is a little awkward. Perhaps, as Dunn suggests, Paul was running out of patience.[44] The point is that such a sensitive doctrine can too easily be turned upside down, to imply that Paul taught what he could *never have said*!

---

[43] Cranfield, *Romans*, vol. 1, pp. 184–5.
[44] Dunn, *Romans 1—8*, p. 143.

10

Judgement and grace on all:
redemption and atonement (3.9–31)

The universal sin of humankind (3.9–20)

The rhetorical question, 'What then?' prepares for an inference to be drawn from Romans 2.1—3.8. We might suggest: 'Well, now . . . Are we any better off?' Danker observes that the Greek middle voice has the same meaning as the active.[1] The word appears only here in the NT, and occurs in ℵ, B and 33, so is fairly secure. The NRSV 'not at all' is a more accurate translation of Greek *ou pantōs*, than 'not altogether'. Romans 1.18–31 and 2.1—3.9 respectively have proved that both Jews and Gentiles are under the power of sin.

Paul follows this general statement with a string of ten quotations from the OT (vv. 10–18). Verses 10–12 concern the relation between humankind and God; verses 13–14 concern the human heart and human speech; and verses 15–17 concern human sin against fellow-humans. Paul probably uses a topical, *shared collection* of Scripture passages, along the lines proposed by Harris.[2] Fitzmyer declares, 'Paul makes use of a Palestinian Jewish literary form at this point, adopting the sub-form called *testimonia*.[3] This form was well known among the Church Fathers, and is evidenced in the Dead Sea Scrolls (4Q *Testimonia*). The whole block of ten quotations witnesses to the sinfulness of humankind. Paul's dialogue-partner might protest that only *Gentiles* fall under such condemnation, but in verse 19 Paul replies, 'It speaks to those *who are under the law*, so that every mouth may be silenced.'

On the details of the quotations, verse 10 constitutes a free quotation of Ecclesiastes 7.20 and Psalm 14.1 (LXX) or 13.2–3 (Hebrew text); then he quotes from Psalm 14.53, and moves on to Psalm 5.10. He also uses

---

[1] Danker, Frederick, *A Greek-English Lexicon of the New Testament and Other Early Christian Literature* (BDAG) (Chicago and London: University of Chicago Press, 3rd edn, 2000), p. 869.

[2] Harris, J. R., *Testimonies* (2 vols, Cambridge: CUP, 1916–20), and Harris, 'St. Paul's Use of Testimonies in the Epistle to the Romans', *Expositor* 8.17 (1919), pp. 401–14.

[3] Fitzmyer, Joseph A., *Romans: A New Translation with Introduction and Commentary* (New York: Doubleday, 1992; AB 33), p. 333.

snatches of Psalm 139.4; verse 14 of Psalm 9.15–17, 28; and some of Isaiah 59.7–8. The LXX is followed in every case. Dunn sets out the Greek of the LXX and of Paul in parallel columns for easy comparison of the wording.[4] On Isaiah 59, Wright comments, 'Of all the chapters in the Hebrew Scriptures, this is the one that most strikingly depicts YHWH discovering that there is no righteousness to be had in the world', and so only to put on the clothes of righteousness will rescue God's people.[5] Several phrases call for comment. Psalm 13 (14) judges 'Fools' who say '"There is no God"', and is cited in Anselm's 'Ontological Argument'. In Romans 3.12 the NRSV translation 'become worthless' (Greek *ēchreōthēsan*) reflects a Hebrew word which means *to go sour* like bad milk. In 3.13 'Their throats are opened graves' suggests the stench of a newly opened grave, while 'to deceive' is in the imperfect to suggest regular habit. Verse 16 speaks of 'ruin and misery', where *ruin* (Greek *suntrimma*) suggests a rubbing together until an object is crushed to destruction.

Again, verse 19 confirms that God's condemnation extends to Jews as well as Gentiles, hence the Scriptures speak 'to those who are under the law'. In verse 20 'No human being will be justified in his sight' comes from Psalm 143.2. This psalm is a call to God to have mercy 'in his righteousness'. Paul adds 'by deeds prescribed by the law' to the quotation, to clarify the psalmist's statement. This also shows that, as Cranfield comments, justification itself is not rendered impossible, but justification 'on the basis of [his] deserts'.[6] Paul's statement, 'Through the law comes the knowledge of sin', anticipates what he will argue about the law in Romans 7.

God's righteousness manifested through Jesus Christ (3.21–26)

Paul's theme that under judgement we are 'without distinction' continues as 'without distinction' *under grace* through Jesus Christ. The coming of Christ inaugurates a new age in the history of humankind. This new event will make possible a *right relation between God and humankind*. Here this right relation is *justification by grace through faith*. Elsewhere Paul speaks of salvation and reconciliation. Wright comments, 'Justification, in this passage, is clearly a law-court term.'[7] He also calls it, 'This world-righting

---

[4] Dunn, James D. G., *Romans 1—8* (Dallas: Word, 1988; WBC 38), p. 349.

[5] Wright, N. T., 'Romans' in the *New Interpreter's Bible* (*NIB*) (Nashville: Abingdon, 2002), vol. 10, p. 458.

[6] Cranfield, C. E. B., *A Critical and Exegetical Commentary on the Epistle to the Romans*, vol. 1 (Edinburgh: T & T Clark, 1975; ICC), p. 197.

[7] Wright, 'Romans', *NIB*, vol. 10, p. 459.

covenant faithfulness'.[8] Where God is present, there is 'life', as Romans 5—8 makes clear. Schweitzer argued, 'Christ's resurrection inaugurates the End-events of history.' 'Now' (v. 21) is temporal, and marks this new stage of history.[9]

The statement 'the righteousness of God has been disclosed' (v. 21) is the converse of 'the wrath of God is revealed' in Romans 1.18. As against the later claims of Marcion, Paul insists that this stands not in discontinuity with the OT, but 'is attested by the law and the prophets'. Even so, 'a person is justified . . . apart from works prescribed by the law' (3.28). The verb 'disclosed' conveys the sense of *being known*. The passive voice can mean *to become visible*, which occurs literally in Jesus Christ.[10] Jüngel makes this point dramatically: in Christ God becomes 'conceivable' and 'speakable'.[11]

In verse 22 Paul repeats the phrase 'the righteousness of God' to show that all that follows comes from *God*. Leenhardt explains, 'The righteousness of God is disclosed outside the sphere of what man himself can contribute . . . Every man can . . . *receive*.'[12] 'Faith in Jesus Christ' translates a simple genitive 'of Jesus Christ' in the Greek, which Wright and others interpret as a subjective genitive, i.e. the faith that Christ has, or, in Wright, the fidelity of Christ. Wright comments, 'Jesus has offered to God, at last, the faithfulness Israel had denied.'[13] He thinks that 'all who believe' would otherwise become redundant. But most insist, with Fitzmyer, that this 'runs counter to the main thrust of Pauline theology'.[14] *Faith* (Greek *pistis*) denotes in this passage the way that believers respond to and appropriate the gospel. But it would be a mistake to imagine that *faith* always means the same thing in Paul's writings. For example, Bultmann declares, 'Paul understands faith primarily as obedience.'[15] Sometimes faith stands in contrast to sight, as in 'we walk by faith, not by sight' (2 Cor. 5.7). Sometimes it is a special gift for chosen individuals, as in, 'To another [is given] faith by the same Spirit' (1 Cor. 12.9). Luther declares that faith includes stance and action. He writes,

---

[8] Wright, 'Romans', *NIB*, vol. 10, p. 470.

[9] Leenhardt, Franz J., *The Epistle to the Romans* (London: Lutterworth, 1961), p. 98.

[10] Danker, BDAG, p. 1047.

[11] Jüngel, Eberhard, *God as the Mystery of the World* (Edinburgh: T & T Clark, 1983), pp. 111, 220–1 and 229.

[12] Leenhardt, *Romans*, p. 99 (my italics).

[13] Wright, 'Romans', *NIB*, vol. 10, p. 470.

[14] Fitzmyer, *Romans*, p. 345.

[15] Bultmann, Rudolf, *Theology of the New Testament*, vol. 1 (London: SCM, 1952), p. 314.

Faith is a living and unshakeable confidence, a belief in the grace of God, so assured that a man would die a thousand deaths for its sake . . . [It] makes us joyful . . . Hence the man of faith . . . willingly and gladly seeks to do good to everyone, serve everyone.[16]

What faith *is* depends on to whom it is directed, and the purpose for which God gives it. Nevertheless Wright's interpretation, 'the faithfulness of Christ', should be carefully weighed.

Paul deliberately adds 'for *all* who believe. For there is no distinction'. Just as he has deliberately emphasized that *all* stand under judgement, and that there is no distinction between Jew and Gentile, so now he urges that *all* may stand under grace, receiving God's righteousness 'without distinction', on the same basis for all.

'All' is repeated in 3.23, 'Since *all* have sinned'. *Glory* (Greek *doxa*, Hebrew *kābôdh*), like *faith*, has many nuances of meaning. In terms of word history the Hebrew meant *heavy* or *weighty*, *being impressive* or *having gravitas* or *majesty*. But by NT times it usually denoted a *visible manifestation* of this impressiveness or majesty. Hence Leenhardt is correct in understanding the *lack* (Greek *husteroō*) of this as signifying the incapacity of fallen humankind to appreciate what could be visible of God's majesty as Creator.[17] Earlier modern commentators, including Hunter, Knox, Vaughan and Liddon, discuss the notion of 'original righteousness'; but this belongs more to speculative aspects of systematic theology than to Paul.

Paul declares a complementary truth of the gospel in verse 24: 'They are now justified by his grace as a gift.' The two operative words are *grace* (Greek *charis*) and *free gift* (Greek *dōrean*, *gratis*). Bultmann rightly regards *grace* here not as 'timeless kindness,' but as a decisive *event*. Here, he says, ' "grace" means the territory of the divine deed's sway'.[18] Volf expounds the free, sovereign grace of God at a pastoral level under the title *Free of Charge*, which also paints the picture of Romans 1—3.[19] God is not merely indulgent, but has a way whereby humans may receive free grace, even if in another sense it is not without cost.

This is the first time that *grace* (*charis*) has appeared in Romans, except for the greeting-form in Romans 1.7, where Paul also refers to the grace of apostleship in 1.5. Hence a note on *charis* is in order. *Charis* occurs 20 times in Romans 3.24—16.24. It has occurred 18 times in 1 and 2

---

[16] Luther, Martin, *Preface to the Epistle to the Romans* (Nashville: Discipleship Resources, 1977), p. 7.

[17] Leenhardt, *Romans*, p. 100.

[18] Bultmann, *Theology of the NT*, vol. 1, p. 290; cf. pp. 289–92.

[19] Volf, Miroslav, *Free of Charge* (Grand Rapids: Zondervan, 2005).

Corinthians and seven times in Galatians. The OT uses the Hebrew *chēn* (*grace* or *favour*) and *chānan* (*to show favour*); and the term *chesed* (*grace*, or *loving kindness*). *Chesed* often occurs in contexts of covenant love. God is 'merciful and gracious, slow to anger, and abounding in steadfast love' (Exod. 34.6). God declares, 'I will be gracious to whom I will be gracious' (Exod. 33.19). In Isaiah God is uniquely gracious, because he will abundantly pardon: 'For my thoughts are not your thoughts, nor are your ways my ways, says the Lord' (Isa. 55.8). God's grace is uniquely above all possible comparisons with human forgiveness.

The idea is not unique to Paul in the NT. The parables of the Labourers in the Vineyard (Matt. 20.1–16), of the Pharisee and the Tax-collector, and of the Prodigal Son (Luke 15.11–32) anticipate the idea that the generosity of grace eclipses 'deserts' or 'works'. In 1 Corinthians 15.8–10 Paul declares, 'By the grace of God I am what I am.' Since God called him when he was like 'a prematurely born dead foetus' (Munck), God's grace gives life to the dead (Gal. 1.13, 15). The word is given its most distinctive meaning in 1 Corinthians 4.7: 'What do you have that you did not receive? And if you *received* it, why do you boast *as if it were not a gift?*' In 2 Corinthians 8.1–9 Paul spells out further the generosity of grace as sheer gift. It can inspire the churches to be generous, in turn. When he experiences weakness, or has reached the end of his resources, God tells Paul, 'My grace is sufficient for you' (2 Cor. 12.9). Hence Conzelmann comments on Romans, 'Grace is not just the *basis* of justification (Rom. 3:24–25; 5:20–21); it is also *manifested* therein.'[20]

Cranfield interprets 'this grace in which we stand' as 'this state of being the objects of [God's] favour' (Rom. 5.2).[21] In 5.17 Paul speaks of receiving 'the abundance of grace'. In 8.2 he explains that God's grace has made us 'free from the law of sin and of death'; while in 8.38–39 *grace has the last word*: we *cannot be separated from God's love* in Christ. In 9.28–33 sovereign grace makes possible the salvation of a remnant of Israel. We find a definitive statement in Ephesians 2.8–9: 'By grace you have been saved through faith, and this is not of your own doing; it is the gift of God – not the result of works.' Whether grace is 'prevenient' is the stuff of later post-Pauline debate from Augustine and Pelagius onwards.

The same verse (v. 24) uses *justified* (Greek *dikaioumenoi*), although *dikaioō* was already introduced in Romans 2.13; 3.4; and 3.20 (with *righteousness*

---

[20] Conzelmann, Hans, '*charis*' in Kittel, G., and Friedrich, G. (eds), *Theological Dictionary of the New Testament* (*TDNT*) (10 vols, Grand Rapids: Eerdmans, 1964–76), vol. 9, p. 395; cf. pp. 372–402.

[21] Cranfield, *Romans*, vol. 1, p. 259.

in Rom. 1.17; 3.5, 21, 22). We therefore produced an extended note on justification in 1.17, which we need not repeat. Paul now introduces a *third* theological term, *redemption* (Greek *apolutrōsis*), which appears for the first time in Romans in 3.24. It will appear again in Romans 8.23, and was used in 1 Corinthians 1.30. Wright rightly observes, '"Redemption" . . . is not simply one term among others, a metaphor chosen at random . . . It stands at the head of the dense statement that follows.'[22]

Redemption and *redeem* have a strong background in the OT (Hebrew verbs *gā'al* and *pādah*; LXX usually *agorazō, to redeem,* or *to purchase*). The Hebrew and Greek almost always have three distinct aspects: to redeem *from* bondage, oppression or jeopardy; to redeem *by* a costly event or act of redemption; and to redeem *to* a new state of freedom, security or new ownership.[23] The classic paradigm of redemption is the exodus event. Israel was redeemed *from* bondage, *by* a saving act, *to* safety in the promised land. A number of liberation theologians have reflected and written on this, especially Severino Croatto. The OT term *go'el* is associated with the special task of the near-relative, the *go'el-haddam* (*redeemer of blood*). Such a person could 'redeem' his kinsman from accidental sin against a fellow-Israelite (Lev. 25.25–28; 27.20; Ruth 4.4, 6). Redemptive acts of God are celebrated in Exodus 6.6; Isaiah 43.1; 44.22, 23; and Hosea 13.14.

In the NT *agorazō* is the normal word for making purchases in the market. In theological terms, Christ redeemed believers from the curse of the law (Gal. 3.13; 4.5). They are 'bought with a price' (1 Cor. 6.20). An outdated view was promoted by Deissmann, citing analogies from pagan deities' 'redeeming' slaves, according to inscriptions at Delphi. This has been overtaken by Martin's emphasis on redemption to a new 'Lord', Jesus Christ. The redeemed *belong to* Christ *as their Lord*, who takes *responsibility* for them and has the *care* of them. Paul's terminology also reflects the traditions of the Synoptic Gospels. In Mark 10.45, Jesus gives his life as a ransom (Greek *lutron*) for many. It is taken up in 1 Peter 1.18–19. Clement of Rome, Irenaeus, Gregory of Nyssa and others use the term. Gregory, however, misunderstood the metaphor by asking *to whom* the ransom price should be paid, even answering 'to the devil'. Most theologians reject this understanding as too anthropomorphic. The question would not have occurred to Paul.

---

[22] Wright, 'Romans', *NIB*, vol. 10, p. 471.

[23] Brown, F., Driver, S. R., and Briggs, C. A., *Hebrew and English Lexicon of the Old Testament* (BDB) (Lafayette, IN: Associated Publishers, 1980), pp. 145, 804; Danker, BDAG, p. 117; Dunn, James D. G., *The Theology of Paul the Apostle* (Edinburgh: T & T Clark, 1998), pp. 227–8; Wright, N. T., *Paul and the Faithfulness of God* (London: SPCK, 2013), pp. 1070–3.

In verses 24–25 Paul makes it clear that the major emphasis falls on Christ Jesus. In verse 25 Paul introduces yet a further major theological term, which the NRSV translates 'a sacrifice of atonement by his blood' (Greek *hilastērion . . . en autou haimati*). The vast quantity of modern writing on the word may seem disproportionate, since within the NT the noun *hilastērion* occurs only once (here) in Paul and in Hebrews 9.5 (even if *hilasmos* occurs twice in 1 John 2.2; 4.10, and the verb *hilaskomai* in Luke 18.13 and Heb. 2.17). Even the NRSV margin gives a note which suggests 'place of atonement' instead of 'sacrifice of atonement'. This is close to Nygren's proposal that *hilastērion* alludes to *the mercy seat* as 'the place where God manifested his presence to Israel. In Exod. 25:22 God said to Moses, "There will I meet with thee".'[24] This suggestion is followed by Wright, on the basis of Leviticus 16.2.[25] On the other hand most argue that *hilastērion* denoted either a *propitiatory sacrifice* or an *expiatory sacrifice*. The major debate is whether the term means primarily *expiation* or *propitiation*. The proposal *place of meeting*, if it is adequate, would take the sting out of this sometimes acrimonious debate. Yet Pannenberg observes that we cannot abandon the genuinely biblical meaning of a term simply because it requires an understanding of the biblical background and history.

Expiation, or expiatory sacrifice, derives from that class of sacrifice which *covered sin*, without further specific reference. Dodd defined it as 'an act (such as the payment of a fine or the offering of a sacrifice) by which . . . guilt is annulled . . . Such acts were felt to have the value, so to speak, of a disinfectant.'[26] Dodd's analogy lets the cat out of the bag. Although there are admittedly problems about *propitiation*, the problem about *expiation* is that it *depersonalizes* the process, making it almost a mechanical process of cause and effect. Dodd's major criticism of *propitiation* is that in secular Greek it may denote 'placating' a person or a deity, and this cannot be said of the God who is the Father of Jesus Christ.

A number of writers, however, reject Dodd's view as too simplistic. Denney, Hill, Klausner and Morris led the way in arguing this. As Hill asserts, '*Propitiation* is primarily and directly orientated towards the deity or the offended person.'[27]*Expiation* 'is directed towards that which has caused the breakdown in relationships; it deals with sin'. Dodd, Hill argues, has deprived himself of important contexts. *Propitiation* therefore, he declares, 'emphasize[s]

---

[24] Nygren, Anders, *Commentary on Romans* (London: SCM, 1952), p. 157.

[25] Wright, 'Romans', *NIB*, vol. 10, p. 474.

[26] Dodd, C. H., *The Epistle of Paul to the Romans* (London: Hodder & Stoughton, 1932), p. 54.

[27] Hill, David, *Greek Words and Hebrew Meanings* (Cambridge: CUP, 1967; SNTSMS 5), p. 23; cf. pp. 23–48.

the *personal* nature of the breach with God'.[28] He rejects the claim that the term always means *expiation* in the LXX. Since the context of Romans 3.25 is 'so dominated by the themes of judgment and wrath, it seems plausible to find a trace of the idea of propitiation in the meaning of the term'.[29] It may indeed also translate the Hebrew *kapporeth* (*mercy seat*), as Manson, Nygren and Wright have argued, although Morris finds this unconvincing. Hill also alludes to 4 Maccabees 17.22, where it clearly means a *propitiatory* death, although this cannot be dated with certainty. Hill concludes, 'This investigation has revealed throughout the importance of the study of context.'[30]

In 1955 Morris devoted 60 pages to a discussion of this term.[31] He, like Hill, declares, 'More than expiation is required, for to speak of expiation is to deal in *sub-personal* categories.'[32] He combs through Jewish inter-Testamental writings, and in modern thought Forsyth, Baillie and Denney. He quotes Denney's comment, 'If the propitiatory death of Jesus is eliminated from the love of God . . . it is robbed of apostolic meaning.'[33] In practice both terms may *complement* each other. *Expiation* ensures that there is *no idea of merely appeasing an angry God, unless at the initiative of his love; propitiation ensures that we are addressing a deeply personal relation between God and humankind.*

In the most recent literature Vidu defends the idea of propitiation with reference to Augustine. He writes,

> Atonement is conceived as being primarily Godward . . . Augustine recognizes that the cause of the problem is the relationship between humankind and God. This is a clear penal substitutionary element . . . Christ's death . . . represents a fitting sacrifice, which propitiates God.[34]

He adds, 'Although Augustine talks about propitiation, he is careful to avoid the notion of a Father who, on account of the sacrifice of his Son, turns from wrath to love.'[35] Augustine, Vidu points out, uses these valid models of the atonement as complementary, not as exclusive alternatives.

Cranfield argues for *propitiation*, after four pages of detailed argument.[36] He convincingly criticizes Dodd and defends Morris. However, Dunn refers

---

[28] Hill, *Greek Words*, p. 37 (my italics).
[29] Hill, *Greek Words*, p. 39.
[30] Hill, *Greek Words*, p. 47.
[31] Morris, Leon, *The Apostolic Preaching of the Cross* (London: Tyndale, 1955), pp. 125–85.
[32] Morris, *Apostolic Preaching*, p. 169 (my italics).
[33] Morris, *Apostolic Preaching*, p. 182; Denney, James, *The Death of Christ* (London: Hodder & Stoughton, 1950), p. 152.
[34] Vidu, Adonis, *Atonement, Law and Justice* (Grand Rapids: Baker Academic, 2014), p. 33.
[35] Vidu, *Atonement*, p. 35.
[36] Cranfield, *Romans*, vol. 1, pp. 214–18.

to the whole debate as 'the older dispute', which suffered from 'an unnecessary polarizing of alternatives'.[37] He appeals here to Young and Hofius.[38]
Our conclusions above have also proposed that these are not alternatives;
rather, that *propitiation* must be retained, even if in conjunction with
expiation. Barrett favours *expiate* here, even though, he says, the normal
meaning is *propitiate*; but, again, God *initiates* the atonement.[39] Leenhardt
simply translates 'bloody sacrifice'.[40] The commentators speak with a
divided voice. Here exegesis and linguistics run out, and the final decision
is probably partly a theological one.

As Fitzmyer has indicated, the term 'put forward' (NRSV) translates
Greek *proetheto*, which may mean 'designed [Christ] to be', or (with the
stress on the prefix *pro*) would mean 'set [Christ] forth'. Holland translates
this as 'publicly displayed', alluding to the Passover victim.[41] Cranfield
points out that this verb occurs only three times in the NT (Rom. 1.13;
3.26; Eph. 1.9). He argues for 'God's gracious purpose of election', following Origen, Ambrosiaster and Chrysostom.[42]

In verse 25 the NRSV translates, 'He [God] did this to show his righteousness'. Verse 26 amplifies this: 'It was to prove at the present time that
he himself is righteous, and that he justifies the one who has faith in Jesus'.
Wright regularly renders 'righteousness' (partly for the English reader's
benefit) as 'God's faithfulness to the covenant', and 'faith' as 'the faithfulness of Jesus'. This may move the text away from modern theological
controversies, and place the emphasis on God and his covenant redemption. On the other hand, it reflects a careful understanding of Paul as
conveyed to the modern reader, rather than strictly conveying the text
word by word.[43] Denney has memorably paraphrased this in the following
words: '*Something is done which enables God to justify the ungodly who believe
in Jesus, and at the same time to appear signally and conspicuously a righteous
God.*'[44] The NRSV 'to prove that' is a technically accurate translation of
the Greek *eis endeixin*, but the word also regularly means *to show forth*.

---

[37] Dunn, *Romans 1—8*, p. 171.

[38] Young, N. H., '"*hilaskesthai*" and Related Words in the New Testament', *EQ* 55 (1983), pp. 169–76;
and Hofius, O., 'Sühne und Versöhnung: Zum paulinischen Verständnis des Kreuzestodes Jesu' in
Maas, E. (ed.), *Versuche, das Leiden und Sterben Jesu zu verstehen* (Munich: Schnell & Steiner, 1983),
pp. 25–46.

[39] Barrett, C. K., *The Epistle to the Romans* (London: Black, 1957), p. 77.

[40] Leenhardt, *Romans*, pp. 105–6.

[41] Holland, Tom, *Contours of Pauline Theology* (Fearn: Mentor, 2004), p. 170.

[42] Cranfield, *Romans*, vol. 1, p. 209.

[43] Wright, 'Romans', *NIB*, vol. 10, pp. 472–4.

[44] Denney, *Death of Christ*, p. 167 (my italics).

Cranfield rejects this, arguing that it means 'showing, not in the sense of proving, but in the sense of offering, making available'.[45]

The last clause of verse 26, 'the one who has faith in Jesus' (NRSV), is also crucial to Paul's argument. Fitzmyer comments: 'Even though the most important aspect of salvation is what Jesus did in dying and rising, the benefits are shared only "through faith", i.e. through a proper response to the gospel.'[46] On this phrase the Greek MSS are divided. Greek *dia pisteōs* is found in P[40], ℵ, C*, D* and F; *dia tēs pisteōs* (through *the* faith) is found in B, C[3] and D[2]. Metzger reports that the UBS Committee had difficulty in deciding the issue.[47] Paul's addition of 'the present time' indicates, again, the *event* of grace in the inauguration of the new age of the gospel.

The exclusion of human 'boasting' among both Jews and Gentiles (3.27–31)

It is almost a relief to turn from some weighty theological terms to Paul's clear, practical conclusion. In verse 27 he declares, 'Boasting ... is excluded.' The aorist passive with an intensive compound, *exekeisthē*, according to Robertson means 'completely shut out'. Jewett relates 'boasting' to the cultural setting of honour and shame, and imperial glory.[48] This section (vv. 27–31), according to Cranfield, 'affirms that all glorying that is ... to establish a claim on God on the ground of one's works, has been ruled out'.[49] Here again are allusions to what Paul has written in 1 Corinthians: 'So let no one boast about human leaders' (1 Cor. 3.21); 'Who sees anything different in you? ... Why do you boast as if it were not a gift?' (1 Cor. 4.7). Both Romans and 1 Corinthians use the Greek *kauchaomai*, which re-emerges in chapter 10.

Verse 28 sums up Paul's argument: 'A person is justified by faith apart from works prescribed by the law.' But Paul then applies this in verse 29 to the relation between Jews and Gentiles: 'Is he not the God of Gentiles also?' 'Yes', Paul replies, for both are *equally* justified 'through that same faith' (v. 30). Sanders and Dunn are right to perceive this as *corporate* boasting or *corporate* pride. It is as if the *Jews* said, 'Hands off! He is *our* God!' This recapitulates Paul's pastoral argument about the equality of

[45] Cranfield, *Romans*, vol. 1, p. 211.
[46] Fitzmyer, *Romans*, p. 350.
[47] Metzger, Bruce, *A Textual Commentary on the Greek New Testament* (New York: UBS, 2nd edn, 1994), p. 449.
[48] Jewett, *Romans*, pp. 295–6.
[49] Cranfield, *Romans*, vol. 1, p. 218.

Christian Jews and Christian Gentiles. The purpose of the law is to silence boasting (3.19). But the same goes for faith, which shifts the ground of confidence from the self to God in Christ.

Romans 3.27–31 continues the diatribe style. The debate continues: 'Is God the God of Jews only?' The reply is: he is 'the God of Gentiles also'. Even circumcision is of no special avail: salvation is '*on the ground of faith*' (Greek *ek pisteōs*, v. 30) and '*through* faith' (Greek *dia tēs pisteōs*, v. 30). But faith is no substitute for grace. Such a person relies on grace, but appropriates grace as source through faith as means. Barrett adds: 'The Cross anticipates the results of the Last Judgment: the Judge of all the earth is seen to do right, and . . . he is able righteously to justify those who believe.'[50] We have already noted that *law* (*nomos*) denotes at least three things: *principle* or religious system; *Scripture* or the Pentateuch; and the *Jewish* law. Wright seeks to steer a middle course between the 'New Perspective' and the Lutheran view of justification by faith. Here he writes, 'It is important to say that the battles of Augustine and Luther were not entirely mistaken. Paul's whole thought is characterized by the free grace of God.'[51]

Paul's opponent in the rhetorical dialogue quite rightly raises the question in verse 31: 'Do we then overthrow the law by this faith?' Paul replies: 'By no means! On the contrary, we uphold the law.' Many commentators regard verse 31 as a transitional verse, which looks forward to chapter 4. Fitzmyer interprets *the law* in verse 31 as 'the Mosaic legal corpus', including 'deeds prescribed by the Pentateuch'.[52] As we noted on 3.4, 'By no means' (Greek *mē genoito*) is the most emphatic negative. The Mosaic revelation is workable *only through Christ*. According to Dunn, 'Paul has the law as such, the whole law, in view.'[53] In verse 31, NRSV 'we uphold the law' is better translated by Dunn and others as 'we establish the law', i.e. 'We are placing the law on its true footing'.[54] Dunn, Fitzmyer, Cranfield and many others (especially, in their age, the Puritans) insist that this verse constitutes a rejection of the simplistic popular antinomian picture that Paul 'abandoned' the law altogether.

---

[50] Barrett, *Romans*, p. 80.
[51] Wright, 'Romans', *NIB*, vol. 10, p. 479.
[52] Fitzmyer, *Romans*, p. 366.
[53] Dunn, *Romans 1—8*, p. 186.
[54] Dunn, *Romans 1—8*, p. 190.

11

The promise of the covenant God; trust, the test case of Abraham (4.1–25)

Wright declares, 'The chapter is ... [an] exposition of the covenant [that] God made with Abraham in Genesis 15, showing at every point how God always intended and promised that the covenant ... would include Gentiles as well as Jews.'[1] Paul continues his diatribe style, as indicated by, 'What then are we to say ...?' (vv. 1, 3, 9, 10). This diatribe style is interwoven with a *midrash* or Pauline commentary on Genesis 15.6, and probably secondary texts from Psalm 31 (LXX) in Romans 4.7–8. The word 'ancestor' (NRSV) or 'forefather' (KJB/AV) occurs in א*², A, B and C*, but some change this to the more familiar *father* (א¹, C³). The contrast in this chapter will be between *work* (Greek *ergon/ergazesthai*), *circumcision* and *faith*. 'Ancestor according to the flesh' (v. 1) denotes purely physical descent.

The prostasis, 'If Abraham was justified by works', constitutes a false hypothesis. It is false, because it is denied in 3.20.[2] *Works* stands for 'works of the law'. Paul explicitly rules out the traditional rabbinic doctrine of the merits of Abraham, to which John the Baptist alludes in Luke 3.8 ('We have Abraham as our ancestor'). The rabbinic claim is explicitly embodied in 1 Maccabees 2.52: 'Abraham was found faithful ... and it was reckoned to him as righteousness', as Jewett points out.[3] Hence Paul sees the battleground as an issue of 'boasting'. Cranfield and Fitzmyer see *boasting* as the antithesis of faith: 'Glorying has been excluded.'[4] Fitzmyer observes that contemporary Judaism embellishes the story of Abraham, 'making him an observer of the Mosaic law even before it was promulgated, and ascribing his uprightness, not to his faith, but to his loyalty when tested' (Gen. 22.9–10, the 'sacrifice' of Isaac; *Jubilees* 6.19; 23.10; Wis. 10.5; 1 Macc. 2.52; *2 Bar.* 57.2).[5]

---

[1] Wright, N. T., 'Romans' in the *New Interpreter's Bible* (*NIB*) (Nashville: Abingdon, 2002), vol. 10, p. 487.
[2] Dunn, James D. G., *Romans 1—8* (Dallas: Word, 1988; WBC 38), p. 200.
[3] Jewett, Robert, *Romans: A Commentary* (Minneapolis: Fortress, 2007; Hermeneia), p. 309.
[4] Cranfield, C. E. B., *A Critical and Exegetical Commentary on the Epistle to the Romans*, vol. 1 (Edinburgh: T & T Clark, 1975; ICC), pp. 224 and 224–32; Fitzmyer, Joseph A., *Romans: A New Translation with Introduction and Commentary* (New York: Doubleday, 1992; AB 33), pp. 369–72.
[5] Fitzmyer, *Romans*, p. 372.

In his book *From First Adam to Last* Barrett writes, 'Though all the patriarchs had by their virtue and obedience to God laid up a store of merit on which Israel as a whole was able to draw, this was pre-eminently true of Abraham ... "our father".'[6] He alludes to the collection of material in Strack-Billerbeck.[7] According to rabbinic sources: 'With ten temptations was Abraham our father tempted, and he stood steadfast in them all', especially in his readiness to sacrifice Isaac, his only son (Gen. 22). Schoeps confirms the importance of this event. In Hellenistic Judaism Philo also regards Abraham as full of virtues. This overflowing merit was available only for Jews.

Yet Paul's exegesis of the Abraham passages draws the opposite conclusion. The point made by 'scripture' (Rom. 4.3) is that 'Abraham *believed* God and it was reckoned to him *as righteousness.*' Abraham is not a labourer receiving 'wages' (v. 4; Greek *misthos, reward*), for God is not indebted to him, but it comes 'as a *gift*' (Greek *kata charin*). Thus 'to one who, without works, *trusts* [Greek *pisteuonti*] him who justifies the ungodly, such faith is reckoned *as righteousness.*' Denney regards this single sentence as a summary of the whole gospel. This is specifically *trust in God's promise*, later exemplified in the promise of resurrection. As with Habakkuk 2.4, Paul gives a different interpretation to the verse than that of contemporary Judaism. The verses show the contrast between 'pay' (*misthos*) and 'reckoning' (*logizesthai*), and between what is due (*opheilēma*) and grace (*charis*). Jewett cites Gerhard von Rad as viewing 'reckoned' as 'a declaration of acceptance'.[8] The antithesis between gift and obligation, he suggests, was widely assumed in the ancient environment.[9] In verse 5 the term 'ungodly' further sharpens the contrast, since Paul has used this word in 1.18.

Verses 6–8 probably allude to Psalm 32.1, 2 (31.1, 2 LXX), in which 'David' pronounces a blessing on those whose 'transgression is forgiven, whose sin is covered. Happy are those to whom the LORD imputes no iniquity.' Greek *makarizō* means *to pronounce blessed*, and is used in Luke 1.48. As in Rabbi Hillel's seven rules of interpretation, Paul explicates Genesis 15.6 in the light of Psalm 32 (31 LXX).

In verses 9–12 Paul makes a double argument. First, he points out that in the Abraham narrative, *faith precedes circumcision.* Second, circumcision is a *sign* of this faith and justification, *not an instrument which brings*

---

[6] Barrett, C. K., *From First Adam to Last: A Study in Pauline Theology* (London: Black, 1962), p. 31.
[7] Strack, Hermann L., and Billerbeck, Paul, *Kommentar zum Neuen Testament aus Talmud und Midrasch* (Munich: Beck, 1969), vol. 1, pp. 117–21; Barrett, *From First Adam*, pp. 22–45.
[8] Jewett, *Romans*, p. 311.
[9] Jewett, *Romans*, p. 313.

faith and justification. The first half of verse 9 takes up the point that the blessing pronounced by the author of Psalm 32 (31 LXX) extends to both Jews *and Gentiles*. The second part of the verse highlights the fact that in Abraham's case it is faith or trust that was 'reckoned as' *righteousness*. As in 4.3, the verb means 'was credited', as 'a book-keeping term figuratively applied'.[10] The argument about the priority of faith over circumcision arises from comparing Genesis 15.6 with Genesis 17. Dunn compares Paul's thought in Galatians 3.15–18.[11] In verse 11 'sign' (Greek *sēmeion*) also means 'distinguishing mark, by which something is known'.[12] Paul does not deny that circumcision *may* constitute a 'work', but it is the fruit of a *prior* call and a *prior* faith.

Circumcision is also a *seal* (Greek *sphragis*). Lampe explores the development of the term. It originally denoted the stone of a signet ring; then the design which it bears; and finally the stamp made by the seal on wax. It is thus an outward confirmation or authentication.[13] Danker suggests similar headings.[14] The *Psalms of Solomon* depict it as the eschatological stamping for recognition during the ambiguities of the world. In Jewett's words, it 'confirms validity of a reality already present that is righteousness through faith'.[15] Paul provides an insightful paraphrase of Genesis 17.11 and of that chapter. In Genesis 17.1 Abraham is said to be 99 years old when God promised him covenantal blessings, but according to Jewish chronology Abraham's circumcision was 29 years *after* the promise of Genesis 15.6.[16] Barrett sums this up: 'Abraham was a Gentile when God counted him righteous.'[17]

NRSV is probably correct in interpreting verse 12 to mean that Abraham is ancestor of both Jews and Gentiles, namely all who 'also follow the example of faith that our ancestor Abraham had'. Leenhardt, however, comments, 'The construction of v. 12 is uncertain. Is Paul speaking to two classes of people?' Or are 'Jews referred to in *both* parts of the clause'?[18] Jewett, Cranfield and Fitzmyer interpret the syntax as making

---

[10] Fitzmyer, *Romans*, p. 373.

[11] Dunn, *Romans 1—8*, p. 208.

[12] Dunn, *Romans 1—8*, p. 209.

[13] Lampe, G. W. H., *The Seal of the Spirit* (New York and London: Longmans Green, 1951), pp. 8–9; more broadly pp. 15–18.

[14] Danker, Frederick, *A Greek-English Lexicon of the New Testament and Other Early Christian Literature* (BDAG) (Chicago and London: University of Chicago Press, 3rd edn, 2000), pp. 980–1.

[15] Jewett, *Romans*, p. 319.

[16] Cranfield, *Romans*, vol. 1, p. 235; and *Seder Olam*, R. 1.

[17] Barrett, *From First Adam*, p. 34.

[18] Leenhardt, Franz J., *The Epistle to the Romans* (London: Lutterworth, 1961), p. 119.

Abraham the father of 'all humanity'.[19] The *example* of Abraham suggests *footmarks, steps*, in Greek.

Paul now introduces a third line of argument in verses 13–22. The theme becomes *the promises of God*. The very concept of a 'promised inheritance' excludes any notion of legal payment. The key words become *promise* (Greek *epaggelia*) and *inheritance* (*klēronomon*). Paul's rhetoric replies to the *unspoken* response: 'Very well; *faith* may have been prior to circumcision, but the *promise* came *after* it!' Hester has shown how well the word *inheritance* coheres with Paul's argument from Genesis. (i) It denotes something which is conveyed normally by legal testament. (ii) It comes to mean inalienable property, which is secure to the beneficiary. (iii) It comes to mean a common family possession. (iv) It can be conveyed through adoption to people outside the family, like the Gentiles inheriting by adoption that which the Jews regarded as 'their' inheritance.[20] Hester relates it especially to Genesis chapters 12, 15 and 17, and eventually to a 'spiritual' reality and possession.[21]

In verse 13 Cranfield understands Greek *dia* to be instrumental in the phrase *dia*, '*by means of the law*': 'It was not through the instrumentality of the law but through the righteousness of faith that the promise was to be appropriated.'[22] This stands in striking contrast to the rabbis. *Seed* may refer to Christ, he continues, as the true seed of Abraham, as in Galatians 3.16. God's promises to Abraham occur in Genesis 12.7; 13.15–16; 22.17–18. In particular God promises Abraham that he will be given a numberless progeny, and all the nations shall be blessed in him or his seed. Ecclesiasticus 44.21 takes up this promise: 'He assured him by an oath ... that he would ... exalt his seed as the stars, and cause them to inherit from sea to sea.'[23]

The OT passage from which this is derived is Genesis 22.17, 18:

> I will indeed bless you, and I will make your offspring as numerous as the stars of heaven and as the sand that is on the seashore. And your offspring shall possess the gate of their enemies, and by your offspring shall all the nations of the earth gain blessing for themselves, because you have obeyed my voice.
>
> (NRSV)

---

[19] Fitzmyer, *Romans*, pp. 381–2; Dunn, *Romans 1—8*, p. 211; Jewett, *Romans*, p. 320; Cranfield, *Romans*, vol. 1, pp. 237–8.

[20] Hester, J. D., *Paul's Concept of Inheritance: A Contribution to the Understanding of Heilsgeschichte* (Edinburgh: Oliver & Boyd, 1968; *SJT* Occasional Paper 14), p. vii.

[21] Hester, *Inheritance*, pp. 22, 33.

[22] Cranfield, *Romans*, vol. 1, p. 239.

[23] Cranfield, *Romans*, vol. 1, p. 239.

Sanday and Headlam comment, 'St. Paul brings up the key-words of his own system: Faith, Promise, Grace', which he marshals against the leading points of Jewish thought: 'Law, Works . . . Merit'.[24]

In our introduction to historical-critical studies of Paul we claimed that the research of Sanders and the 'New Perspective' constituted a landmark in the history of Pauline studies. Does the comment from Sanday and Headlam, at the end of the nineteenth century, now require revision? Sanders' study post-dates Cranfield's magisterial commentary. But Cranfield made no secret of his strong reservations about the 'New Perspective'. Fitzmyer and Jewett make relatively little reference to Sanders. On the other hand Dunn includes a section of some ten pages on the New Perspective, and on Paul on the law, and refers to Sanders also in his exegesis.[25] But Dunn is not uncritical of Sanders. He shares his view of Paul's pastoral concern about the relation between Gentile Christians and Jewish Christians, and agrees that too often a Lutheran grid of hermeneutics has been imposed on Pauline exegesis. Paul's polemic, he says, against assumptions about 'works' in Judaism has been too readily assimilated into Luther's polemic against medieval indulgences. On the other hand he regards Sanders as too sweeping in his claims, especially when he argues that Paul's view of works and the law is incoherent. Wright is sympathetic with much of the New Perspective, but remains uncompromising on 4.13. He writes,

> The point of v. 13, then, that this inheritance promised repeatedly to the Gentiles was not to be made over to Abraham's . . . descendents (*sic*) . . . [is] accurate enough . . . The Torah, coming later than the promise, cannot be allowed to annul it.[26]

Jewett's comment is helpful. He writes, 'Representatives of the "New Perspective" deny that Paul is "opposing a view of a legalistic Abraham", whose virtues legitimate boasting.'[27] He continues,

> Yet the antithesis between Paul's view of Abraham and that of Jewish religion-
> ists in his period . . . is sharply delineated by the wording of 4:2, and fails
> to do justice to the explicit references to boasting and justification by works
> by substituting a politically correct emphasis on God's mercy.[28]

---

[24] Sanday, William, and Headlam, Arthur C., *Critical and Exegetical Commentary on the Epistle to the Romans* (Edinburgh: T & T Clark, 1902; ICC), p. 110.

[25] Dunn, *Romans 1—8*, pp. lxiii–lxxii, 187–8, 191, 195, 214 and elsewhere.

[26] Wright, 'Romans', *NIB*, vol. 10, p. 496.

[27] Jewett, *Romans*, pp. 309–10; Sanders, E. P., *Paul, the Law, and the Jewish People* (Philadelphia: Fortress, 1983), p. 33; Räisänen, Heikki, *Paul and the Law* (Tübingen: Mohr, 1983; WUNT 29).

[28] Jewett, *Romans*, p. 310.

If Abraham had been put right on the basis of works, he adds, he would have had grounds for 'boasting', but Paul's preceding argument from Romans 1.18 onwards showed that *all* people fall short of a glory required for boasting. With Jewett, we conclude that Romans 4 maintains the antithesis that Paul suggests.

Paul argues in Romans 4.14 that if Abraham was justified, or put right, by law, the promise is nullified. Attention shifts from Abraham himself to the promise to his descendants. Paul hammers home the point in verse 15: the regime of the law brings wrath, not least because it would engender a false pride or boasting. Paul asserts that far from regarding the law as a possible ground for being set right, it turns sin, as Cranfield observes, 'into conscious transgression, and so rendering it more exceeding sinful'.[29] The last phrase of verse 15, 'Where there is no law, neither is there violation', clarifies this point. Law makes us *aware* of sin as sin.

Paul further underlines the closeness of promise and grace in verse 16, and shows how this affects *all of us* as spiritual descendants of Abraham. Paul writes: 'that the promise may rest on grace and be guaranteed to all his [Abraham's] descendants'. He argues that the promise is sure of fulfilment. If the promise had depended on the keeping of the law, it would have then been empty.

The word *promise* (*epaggelia*) occurs more than 50 times in the NT, and is especially prominent in Romans 4.13–21; Galatians 3.14–29; and Romans 9.4–9. In the OT *dābār* often has the meaning of *promise*, as well as *say*, especially in Deuteronomy and 1 Kings. Characteristically it occurs in the context of the covenant. In Genesis 22.16 and Exodus 13.5, 11; 32.15; 33.1, God confirms his promise with an oath. This troubled Philo. How can God pronounce an oath when his word is already certain? In these passages and in Hebrews 7.20–21 the promise-by-oath *makes more explicit the pledge*, or in Austin's language, the commissive speech-act.[30] If God promises to take a specific action, he 'cannot' (in the logical sense) simultaneously perform an act which contradicts this. In this sense God 'cannot' tell a lie. In the history of theology, promise has occupied a prominent place in Luther, Tyndale, Barth, Rahner, Moltmann and Pannenberg. Pannenberg observes 'The concept of promise links our present to God's future'.[31] Promise always involves a *personal commitment*. God's promise to Abraham, to Israel or to the Church excludes any action which might detract from it or contradict it. For human recipients of the promise, it

---

[29] Cranfield, *Romans*, vol. 1, p. 241.
[30] Austin, J. L., *How to Do Things with Words* (Oxford: Clarendon, 1962), pp. 63 and 69.
[31] Pannenberg, Wolfhart, *Systematic Theology*, vol. 3 (Grand Rapids: Eerdmans, 1998), p. 545.

may be a life-changing utterance; a transformative speech-act, which bestows assurance, a new status and a new task. Holland shows how closely this is bound up with God's *covenant*, especially in Genesis 15.6.[32]

Wright argues, 'Romans 4 is not [simply] a "proof from scripture" of "justification by faith" . . . it is an exposition of the covenant God and the way in which the covenant promises to Abraham were fulfilled.'[33] Paul's use of the term 'the father of all of us' shows that God's promise is without discrimination between Jews and Gentiles. But, as Jewett and others rightly argue, here 'faith is not a virtue . . . [or] a theological accomplishment. It is defined by grace . . . Faith is nothing more than the acceptance of this unearned honour.'[34] Paul's 'not only . . . but also' shows that this faith embraces both Jewish Christians and Gentile Christians within the promise to Abraham. It reinforces Paul's use of 'all', and prepares for later discussion in Romans 9—11.

Genesis 17.5, quoted in verse 17, follows the LXX: 'I have made you the ancestor of a multitude of nations'. The Hebrew *gôyim* and Greek *ethnōn* mean either 'nations' or 'Gentiles'. Jewett suggests: 'a plurality of nations, including Israel'.[35] Dunn explains the purpose of the perfect tense, 'I have made you' (*tetheika*) as having 'full force'.[36]

The connecting thread with the next clause is that *Abraham took God at his word*, believing 'the (humanly) impossible'. But even more spectacular and capable of demonstration is that God through his sovereign power '*gives life to the dead* and *calls into existence* things that do not exist.' This reflects Paul's personal experience in 2 Corinthians 1.9, in which God, to whom Abraham and Paul direct their faith, acts with creative power, to bring into existence that which could not contribute to its own life. Like Ezekiel's valley of dry bones (Ezek. 37), God created anew what was dried up and non-existent. Similarly, God brought life out of Abraham's and Sarah's withered bodies, and in Genesis 1 he created the world from nothing. Dunn comments, 'Paul . . . has more immediately in view the deadness of Abraham's body and of Sarah's womb . . . The broader usage of *zōopoiein* [*gives life to*] . . . can denote God's creative, sustaining . . . or renewing power.'[37]

In verse 18, as Chrysostom suggests, Paul explained that what normally surpasses human hope becomes possible in hope from God. The Greek

---

[32] Holland, Tom, *Romans: The Divine Marriage* (Eugene, OR: Pickwick, 2011), pp. 127–49.

[33] Wright, 'Romans', *NIB*, vol. 10, p. 497.

[34] Jewett, *Romans*, p. 329.

[35] Jewett, *Romans*, p. 333.

[36] Dunn, *Romans 1—8*, p. 217.

[37] Dunn, *Romans 1—8*, p. 217.

phrase *par' elpida* can mean 'either "beyond hope" . . . or "against hope"'.[38] Abraham believed God, when it was hardly a human possibility to hope. This is precisely how Paul expounds the resurrection in 1 Corinthians 15. The whole phenomenon depends for its credibility on whether we have 'knowledge of God', of his infinite power and resourcefulness. If God has created the world in its infinite variations, how can anyone doubt that God can bring into existence varied life in the wondrous world of the resurrection? In 2 Corinthians 1.9 Phillips paraphrased Paul's hope in God as taking place 'when he came to the end of his tether'. God had compared the numbers of Abraham's descendants to the stars of the sky and to infinite grains of sand on the shore. The later MSS F and G add those phrases.[39]

Fitzmyer comments on verse 19 that one might expect faith to *weaken* when it was confronted with mounting problems and difficulties. Abraham's age of about 100 meant that from the point of view of childbearing he and Sarah were 'already as good as dead'. The MS reading B omits *ēdē* (*already*), while A, C, D and 33 retain it. More significantly, ℵ, A, B and C read the positive 'he considered', whereas D, G and 33 read the negative 'he did not consider'. Cranfield, Fitzmyer and Metzger commend the positive reading, although they agree that both readings come to the same thing. Metzger explains: the positive means 'His faith did not weaken when he considered'; the negative means, 'He was so strong in faith that he did not consider'. But the negative is 'less appropriate in the context'.[40] This verse and the following three characterize Abraham's faith as having *lack of doubt*. Dunn and Nygren well sum up Paul's point: 'Faith is strong precisely because it looks solely to God, and does not depend on human possibilities.'[41]

Paul repeats this theme (v. 20). 'No distrust made him waver concerning the promise of God'. Part of the meaning of faith in this context is that it is faith-in-God's-promise. Often today people speak of 'my faith' as if it were a synonym for religion or for 'being a Christian'; but Paul generally does not use 'faith' in the abstract, apart from its being *faith-in-God and in his promises. It is not a human construct or aspiration in Paul.* Hence, because faith-in-God was possible for him, Abraham 'gave glory to God' by the very fact that he showed faith. 'Faith' depends for its exact

---

[38] Cranfield, *Romans*, vol. 1, p. 245.

[39] Fitzmyer, *Romans*, p. 387.

[40] Metzger, Bruce, *A Textual Commentary on the Greek New Testament* (New York: UBS, 2nd edn, 1994), p. 451.

[41] Dunn, *Romans 1—8*, p. 220; Nygren, Anders, *Commentary on Romans* (London: SCM, 1952), p. 181.

meaning upon its precise context. I have argued this elsewhere.[42] In the same vein, Wright comments, 'Abraham's faith was not just a general religious belief . . . It was trust in specific promises that the true God had made.'[43] The Greek for 'did not waver' (*ou diekrithē*) could also mean 'did not dispute with himself', depending on whether the verb is passive or middle voice. In the active the word means *to distinguish between* or *to separate*, and hence can mean *to be divided in one's mind* (middle) or *to waver*. Jewett and Fitzmyer favour *waver*; Cranfield calls both meanings 'the active rejection of faith'.[44]

Paul stresses that Abraham's faith was directed to the God *who* had promised, not simply to *what* he had promised (v. 21). His faith recognized that God's almightiness, love and faithfulness was enough to guarantee the fulfilment of what he had promised. The phrase 'fully convinced' indicates that Abraham had no reservations about this. Verse 22 draws out the full meaning of Genesis 15.6 (LXX). The word 'therefore' suggests that because Abraham *trusted* (in) God, this trust 'was reckoned to him' as righteousness. B, D*, F and G omit *and* before the verb.

In verses 23–24 Paul stresses that Genesis does not merely recount an ancient narrative about Abraham, but that it was written 'not for his sake alone, but [v. 24] for ours also.' Aageson uses Paul's phrase as the title of a book on biblical interpretation, citing Romans 4.23–24 and Galatians 4.29.[45] Paul uses the first-person plural 'ours', thereby identifying himself with Jewish and Gentile Christians in Rome. All share Abraham's trust in God. The context of this trust or faith is God, 'who raised Jesus our Lord from the dead', in parallel with Abraham's faith that he would beget descendants in his old age. Jewish and Gentile Christians alike may regard Abraham's story and faith as 'our' story and faith.

Paul explicitly refers to *God's raising Christ* in Romans 8.11 and 10.9, as well as 1 Corinthians 6.14 and 15.15. The idea occurs also in Acts 3.15 and 1 Peter 1.21. Käsemann underlines that 'not for his sake alone' constitutes 'an appeal to the reader'.[46] He adds that verse 24b 'mentions the correspondence on which the typology rests'.[47] The NRSV translation 'It will be reckoned to us' assumes that Greek *hois mellei logizesthai* must be

---

[42] Thiselton, Anthony C., *The Two Horizons* (Exeter: Paternoster, and Grand Rapids: Eerdmans, 1980), pp. 407–9.

[43] Wright, 'Romans', *NIB*, vol. 10, p. 499.

[44] Cranfield, *Romans*, vol. 1, p. 248.

[45] Aageson, James W., *Written Also for Our Sake: Paul and the Art of Biblical Interpretation* (Louisville: Westminster/John Knox, 1993).

[46] Käsemann, Ernst, *Commentary on Romans* (London: SCM, 1980), p. 125.

[47] Käsemann, *Romans*, p. 128.

understood as future. Some, however, understand *mellei* as present in the sense of 'must certainly be reckoned'. Jewett opts for the future meaning.[48]

Most commentators follow Dunn when he describes verse 25 as 'a well-established formulation in earliest Christianity'.[49] We may compare Romans 8.32; Galatians 2.20; and Ephesians 5.2, 25. He rightly regards it as a meeting point between the two strands of Christian tradition, namely the Passion narratives and reflection on the Suffering Servant of Isaiah 53. Many writers, including notably Vanstone, have repeatedly called attention to the double meaning of *paredothē*, which means both 'handed over' and 'betrayed'. Dunn cites at least seven biblical passages which reflect this ambiguity, including Mark 9.3 (primarily 'betrayed') and Acts 3.13 (primarily 'handed over'). Vanstone expounds *'was handed over'* as Jesus' releasing control of his life.[50] The two aorist passives 'was handed over' and 'was raised' are notable. Wright also favours *'handed over'* in this context.[51] Dahl stresses that in the resurrection *God* is virtually always *the active and creative cause*. Christ and the dead in Christ remain *passive recipients* of this gift of new life.[52]

Cranfield, following Neufeld and others, also regards Romans 4.25 as 'a quotation of a traditional formula . . . formulated under the influence of Isa. 52:13—53:12'.[53] The first clause comes directly from Isaiah 53.12. Commentators are virtually unanimous in regarding this as a pre-Pauline formulation or common apostolic creed, and in insisting, with Bultmann and Käsemann, that 'handed over to death for our trespasses' and 'was raised for our justification' constitutes 'a single event'; they are *not* two sequential events.[54] As a pre-Pauline formula, Romans 4.25 is often placed by NT scholars alongside Romans 1.3–4; 10.8–9; and 1 Corinthians 13.13. Many distinguish it from the formal *paradosis* in 1 Corinthians 15.3–6 and 11.23–25. In accordance with his emphasis on shame and honour, Jewett regards the two clauses as closely related to each other: 'transgressions' (NRSV 'trespasses') look back to shame; 'justification' looks forward to honour.

---

[48] Jewett, *Romans*, p. 341.

[49] Dunn, *Romans 1—8*, p. 224.

[50] Vanstone, W. H., *The Stature of Waiting* (New York: Morehouse, 1982 and 2006; and London: DLT, 2004), ch. 3.

[51] Wright, 'Romans', *NIB*, vol. 10, p. 503.

[52] Dahl, M. E., *The Resurrection of the Body* (London: SCM, 1962), pp. 96–100.

[53] Cranfield, *Romans*, vol. 1, p. 251; Neufeld, V. H., *The Earliest Christian Confessions* (Leiden: Brill, and Grand Rapids: Eerdmans, 1963), pp. 48–9.

[54] Bultmann, Rudolf, *Theology of the New Testament*, vol. 1 (London: SCM, 1952), p. 82; Käsemann, *Romans*, p. 129.

12

Peace with God (5.1–11)

Many regard this chapter as opening the second major section of Romans, namely from chapter 5 to chapter 8. They argue that Romans 1.18—4.25 largely concerns those who are righteous by faith, while chapters 5—8 focus on the theme of 'shall live'. This, at least, is the view of Cranfield, Fitzmyer and Jewett. Some regard 5.1–11 as belonging to the thrust of chapters 1—4. Wright points to differences between Romans 5—8 and 1—4; and calls 5—8 'a majestic statement of some of Paul's greatest themes'.[1] Yet much of the *vocabulary* of chapter 5 is common to 1—4, especially 'righteous' (*dikaios*), 'righteousness' (*dikaiosunē*) and 'put right', or 'to justify' (*dikaioō*). By contrast, others regard the *content* as more clearly matching that of 5—8. Cranfield observes:

> In each of the four chapters [5—8] the first sub-section is a basic statement concerning the life promised for a man who is righteous by faith . . . being reconciled to God, being sanctified, being free from the law's condemnation, and being indwelt by God's Spirit.[2]

While Nygren, Käsemann, Cranfield, Wright and Fitzmyer champion the view which we adopt, namely placing chapter 5 with 6—8, Bruce and Dunn, for almost equally good reasons, take the opposite view, associating chapter 5 with 1—4. Black and Jewett understandably call it 'both an introduction to the themes of Romans 5—8 and a development of the preceding argument'.[3] Much can be said on behalf of both sides, which are complementary rather than contradictory. Wright describes 5—8 as inaugurated eschatology, in which 'the three tenses of salvation are . . . unveiled'.[4]

Romans 5.1 presents one of the best-known textual debates in this epistle. The manuscripts ℵ*, A, B*, C, D, 33 and many later MSS read the subjunctive *echōmen* ('*let us have* peace with God'). The indicative *echomen* ('*we have* peace with God') is found in ℵ[1], B[2], F and other MSS. Although

---

[1] Wright, N. T., 'Romans' in the *New Interpreter's Bible* (*NIB*) (Nashville: Abingdon, 2002), vol. 10, p. 508.

[2] Cranfield, C. E. B., *A Critical and Exegetical Commentary on the Epistle to the Romans*, vol. 1 (Edinburgh: T & T Clark, 1975; ICC), p. 254.

[3] Jewett, Robert, *Romans: A Commentary* (Minneapolis: Fortress, 2007; Hermeneia), p. 346.

[4] Wright, 'Romans', *NIB*, vol. 10, p. 514.

the reading of the subjunctive receives better support, Metzger reports that the UBS Committee 'judged that internal evidence should take precedence', since Paul is not exhorting here, but 'stating facts'. He adds: 'Only the indicative is consonant with the apostle's argument.'[5] Further, in the age of Hellenistic Greek the difference between the pronunciation of *o* and *ō* was 'almost non-existent'. Dunn, Cranfield, Fitzmyer, Byrne, Wright and most commentators adopt the indicative, while Kuss, Jewett and Porter insist on the subjunctive.[6]

Peace denotes not an inner feeling of tranquillity or calm, but the *objective state* of being at peace with God, rather than being alienated from him. It denotes the reversal of the effects of sin and alienation set out from Romans 1.8 to 3.20. God's justification brings reconciliation.

On the word *reconciliation* (Greek *katallagē*), apart from two references in the LXX, this term shows Paul's distinctive ingenuity in coining a word to preach the gospel intelligibly to the Gentiles. *Everyone* knows what *reconciliation* means, in the ancient world in wars and political programmes, and in the modern world, in family relationships, industrial and business relationships, wars and so on. The gospel (in Paul) is 'the word of reconciliation' (Rom. 11.15; 2 Cor. 5.19), and Christians are those who 'receive reconciliation' (Rom. 5.11). The verb (Greek *katallassō, to reconcile*) occurs in 2 Corinthians 5.18, 20, as well as in Romans 5.10. It occurs in Philo and Josephus, and in classical Greek in Heroditus, Aristotle and Plato. Clearly in Romans 5.10 it stands in contrast to being *enemies* (Greek *echroi*) of God. For the Christian, hostility against God has been 'overcome through the death of his Son'. The Greek stem *allos* means *other*, and hence reconciliation denotes a changed relationship of personal harmony, welcome and intimacy with one who was once 'other'.

The broad equivalent in Hebrews is the liturgical one of opening *a way of approach*. Today reconciliation is one of the most easily understandable terms for the effect of the gospel, especially in view of South Africa, Northern Ireland, Israel and Palestine, and industrial relations. Barth wrote the whole of *Church Dogmatics* volume IV (four volumes in English) under this heading, citing 'God with us' as 'at the heart of the Christian message'.[7]

---

[5] Metzger, Bruce, *A Textual Commentary on the Greek New Testament* (New York: UBS, 2nd edn, 1994), p. 452.

[6] Dunn, James D. G., *Romans 1—8* (Dallas: Word, 1988; WBC 38), p. 245; Cranfield, *Romans*, vol. 1, pp. 257–8; Fitzmyer, Joseph A., *Romans: A New Translation with Introduction and Commentary* (New York: Doubleday, 1992; AB 33), p. 395; Wright, 'Romans', *NIB*, vol. 10, p. 515; Kuss, Otto, *Der Römerbrief übersetzt und eklärt* (3 vols, Regensburg: Pustet, 1957–78), vol. 1, pp. 201–2.

[7] Barth, Karl, *Church Dogmatics* IV.1; Eng., vol. 9, *The Doctrine of Reconciliation* (Edinburgh: T & T Clark, 1957), sect. 57, pts 1 and 2, pp. 3–67.

He wrote: reconciliation is 'the resumption of a fellowship which once existed but was then threatened with dissolution'.[8]

Reconciliation is a result of justification, not least because justification denotes being in a right relationship with God. The Greek for 'with God' is *pros theon*, which Jewett translates as 'with' or 'toward' God. He urges that justification and reconciliation are given entirely as gifts; they also suggest the possibility of a status of honour.[9] The phrase 'through Jesus Christ our Lord' is repeated again and again in chapters 5—8, as Barth also stresses (Rom. 5.10, 11, 21; 6.23; 7.25; 8.39).

In 5.2 Paul further explicates peace with God in terms of 'access', as in Ephesians 2.18. But *grace* is no less a key word. This denotes here 'this state of being objects of God's favour'.[10] Robertson construes 'let us rejoice' (Greek *kauchōmetha*) as present middle subjunctive, meaning 'we keep on enjoying peace with God and keep on exulting in the hope of the glory of God'.[11] Michel endorses this.[12] Some MSS add 'in faith' after 'access'. But the phrase does not occur in B, D, F or G, although it is supported by ℵ[2] and 33. 'Our hope of . . . the glory' may refer back to Romans 3.23, where alienation from God means that we fall short of this glory.

The glory of God denotes primarily *the manifestation of God's presence*. Thus it entirely coheres with reconciliation and 'God with us'. Jesus Christ in Hebrews is the reflection of God's glory (Heb. 1.3), just as Paul declares that God's shining in our hearts gives 'the light of the knowledge of the glory of God in the face of Jesus Christ' (2 Cor. 4.6). Originally the Hebrew for *glory* (*kābôdh*) meant *weighty* in the sense of having *gravitas*, and in Greek came to mean what makes someone *impressive*. This is not simply God's *majesty*, but also *God's love in the cross* of Christ. Thus Luther sees this not merely as triumphal glory, but as the glory of the cross: the Christlikeness of God in his humility and hiddenness. Moltmann understands 'to glorify God' as 'to enjoy God as he is in himself'.[13]

In 5.3 Paul provides a new way of regarding sufferings. We can even 'boast' in them, because 'suffering produces endurance', when we are also heartened and strengthened by the vision of the previous verses. We certainly know

---

[8] Barth, *Church Dogmatics*, vol. 9, sect. 57, p. 22.

[9] Jewett, *Romans*, p. 349.

[10] Cranfield, *Romans*, vol. 1, p. 259.

[11] Robertson, A. T., *Word Pictures in the New Testament, vol. 4: Romans* (New York: R. Smith, 1931), p. 356.

[12] Michel, O., *Der Brief an die Römer* (Göttingen: Vandenhoeck & Ruprecht, 4th edn, 1966), p. 130.

[13] Moltmann, Jürgen, *The Coming of God* (London: SCM, 1996), p. 323, and more broadly pp. 323–30; and Hurst, L. D., and Wright, N. T. (eds), *The Glory of Christ in the New Testament* (Oxford: OUP, 1987).

that suffering in no way signals alienation from God. Suffering (Greek *thlipsis, tribulation, affliction*) promotes perseverance and endurance. Paul may be reflecting on his own experiences (2 Cor. 11.23–29; 2 Cor. 1.4–11; 1 Cor. 4.11–13). These in no way led Paul to doubt God's love. God can readily use these experiences to make us grow. NRSV 'we also boast' may be translated *let us boast.*

'Character' (*dokimē*) in verse 4 is an exclusively Pauline word in biblical Greek, used in the sense of 'being approved', or of tested character. Pannenberg comments that qualities such as *faithfulness* can be evidenced *only over time.* The end product of this ascending chain is hope. This looks beyond the present age to the world to come.

In verse 5 Paul elaborates this point: 'Hope does not disappoint us' (Greek *kataischunei*). Dunn observes that this verb can mean either 'to be achieved' or 'to put to shame'.[14] Far from shame, hope suggests vindication. Hope is shown not to be illusory. The second half of verse 5 is one of the most widely known in Paul, and is sometimes called 'the Pauline Pentecost'. God's love is 'poured' (Greek *ekkechutai*), and is rendered 'floods' by Moffatt. Life-giving water can be poured out (Isa. 44.3). These metaphors of pouring or filling do not 'de-personalize' the Holy Spirit, but qualify personhood for him who, as God, is 'suprapersonal'.

The *heart* is the seat of human emotion, intellect and will. It is important, however, as Thornton has painstakingly argued, that we do not give this verse a merely psychological, emotional and subjective interpretation, as his exact exposition of Paul's use of tenses here clarifies.[15] Admittedly the heart (Hebrew *lēbh*; Greek *kardia*) may denote depth of feeling, including exultation (1 Sam. 2.1; Ps. 4.7; and sensitivity, Ezek. 36.26); but may also denote obstinacy of will (Deut. 2.30; 15.7; Ps. 75.8). More explicitly, it can denote *the core of one's being* (Deut. 6.5; 1 Sam. 16.7; Matt. 11.29; Luke 12.34; Acts 8.21). However, Calvin, Bultmann and Theissen have shown that it often denotes the *hidden depths* of one's being. Calvin rightly declared, 'The human heart has so many crannies where vanity hides, so many holes where falsehood lurks . . . that it often deceives itself.'[16] For this reason it is precisely the area in which the Holy Spirit and love of God is most needed.

In our post-Freudian era, Bultmann and Theissen rightly compare its use in Paul with the *unconscious* or *subconscious.* Bultmann declares that

---

[14] Dunn, *Romans 1—8*, p. 252.

[15] Thornton, Lionel S., *The Common Life in the Body of Christ* (London: Dacre, 3rd edn, 1950), pp. 81–91.

[16] Calvin, John, *Institutes of the Christian Religion*, ed. H. Beveridge (2 vols, London: James Clarke & Co., 1957), 3.2.10.

the heart in Pauline usage 'need not penetrate into the field of consciousness at all, but may designate the hidden tendency of the self'.[17] Theissen insists, 'Paul is familiar with the idea of unconscious influences within human beings.'[18] He appeals to such passages as 1 Corinthians 4.1–5; 14.20–29; and Romans 2.16. In 1 Corinthians 14.20–25 the key phrase is 'the secrets of the heart'. In Romans 2.12–16 the secrets of the heart are known to God. Hence, again, the Holy Spirit does his transformative work here, sent by the love of God.

Thornton dismissed a purely 'subjective' understanding of Romans 5.5, and insisted that a string of commentators and English versions of the Bible had misrepresented Paul's careful use of tenses. He calls Sanday and Headlam's paraphrase of 5.5b,

> deplorable ... [it] suggests floods of emotion ... Worse still, where the apostle writes about the love of God, his interpreters substitute our 'consciousness of the love of God'. What a difference! ... [Paul's] picture emphasizes the 'givenness' of God's love as it ... enters our hearts.[19]

The Greek *ekkechutai* (*poured out*) reflects, Thornton argues, the story of Cornelius in Acts 10.44–45, in which the Holy Spirit was 'poured out' on the Gentiles, reflecting in turn the outpouring of the Spirit at Pentecost in Acts 2, and Joel 2.17, 18 and 28–32.[20] Many commentators, he adds, miss the aorist tense of *given to us*, where 'the gift of the Spirit is assigned to a definite moment in the past', as well as the perfect tense of 'has been poured out' as past with effects remaining in the present.[21] Chrysostom, Bengel, Cranfield and Byrne make similar comments.[22]

In Romans 5.1–5 Paul has stated the facts of his case. He now explains the nature of the love to which verse 5 referred (vv. 6–8). 'At the right time', Wright stresses, matches Galatians 4.4, 'When the time had fully come'. The main thrust is the fulfilment of God's plan, even if the *pax Romana* and the universality of the Greek language were additional factors.[23] The main thrust of these three verses is that the love of God is unmotivated and undeserved. This is a central theme of Nygren's famous *Agapē and Eros*. In his *Commentary on Romans* he writes, 'In Christ, God's love ... has

---

[17] Bultmann, Rudolf, *Theology of the New Testament*, vol. 1 (London: SCM, 1952), p. 223.

[18] Theissen, Gerd, *Psychological Aspects of Pauline Theology* (Eng., Edinburgh: T & T Clark, 1987), p. 57.

[19] Thornton, *Common Life*, p. 83.

[20] Thornton, *Common Life*, p. 85.

[21] Thornton, *Common Life*, p. 88.

[22] Cranfield, *Romans*, vol. 1, p. 263; Byrne, Brendan, *Romans* (Collegeville: Liturgical Press, 1996 and 2007; Sacra Pagina 6), p. 167.

[23] Wright, 'Romans', *NIB*, vol. 10, p. 518.

poured forth from the heart of God and sought its way to our hearts, true to the very nature of love.'[24] Here, he says, we see 'the deepest meaning of God's love'.[25] He adds, 'It is proper to call it "unmotivated" because there is in the object to which it is directed nothing at all to which appeal can be made to explain this love.'[26] We are 'weak' (v. 6), neither righteous nor good (v. 7), and 'sinners' (v. 8), when God 'proves his love for us' through the death of Christ (v. 8).

In *Agapē and Eros* Nygren writes, '*Agapē* is spontaneous and unmotivated.'[27] He calls it 'the most striking feature of God's love as Jesus represents it', as well as Paul. We look in vain for *an explanation* of God's love; God's love is 'groundless', as in Deuteronomy 7.7: God loved you . . . 'because he loved you'. *Agapē* is also 'indifferent to value' and 'creative', or a 'value-creating principle'.[28] It is showered upon the weak, unrighteous and sinners, and creates beloved children of God. Admittedly Nygren places too much weight on the distinctiveness of the Greek *word* for the love of God, namely *agapē*. But he is generally right about how Paul *uses* this word. The LXX *agapaō* and *agapē* translate the Hebrew words '*ahēbh* and '*aheʰbhāh*. In Deuteronomy 7.7–11 and Hosea 3.1 love is shown to the unlovely. Stauffer correctly calls it in the NT, 'a matter of will and action', not mere emotion, for emotion *cannot be commanded*.[29] Of human love, Jesus commanded, 'Love your enemies' (Matt. 5.44). Paul's great argument from Romans 5—8 concludes that nothing 'will be able to separate us from the love of God in Christ Jesus our Lord' (Rom. 8.39). Spicq also expounds the numerous effects of love.[30]

Verses 7–8 contain two further points. One concerns Paul's comparisons of the good and righteous person; the other concerns the love of *God* through Christ, in distinction from Christ's own love. In Judaism dying for the righteous has a tradition in the context of martyrdom (Hab. 2.4; Wis. 10.20). The good person (Greek *agathos*) traditionally denoted a person of more warmth and compassion than the righteous one; but this difference has been challenged recently. Jewett suggests that this term may denote a *benefactor*, who brings well-being to others.[31] The second point is that

---

[24] Nygren, Anders, *Commentary on Romans* (London: SCM, 1952), p. 199.

[25] Nygren, *Romans*, p. 200.

[26] Nygren, *Romans*, p. 201.

[27] Nygren, Anders, *Agapē and Eros* (London: SPCK, 1957 [1932]), p. 75.

[28] Nygren, *Agapē and Eros*, pp. 77, 78.

[29] Stauffer, E., '*agape*' in Kittel, G., and Friedrich, G. (eds), *Theological Dictionary of the New Testament* (*TDNT*) (10 vols, Grand Rapids: Eerdmans, 1964–76), vol. 1, pp. 94–5.

[30] Spicq, C., *Agapē in the New Testament* (3 vols, London: Herder, 1963), vol. 2, pp. 139–81.

[31] Jewett, *Romans*, p. 360.

God shows *his* love in *the death of Christ*. This coheres with the insistence of Baillie, Jüngel and Moltmann (as well as others) that *God himself* is deeply involved in Christ's atonement, as the expression of his initiative and love. The title of Baillie's book, *God Was in Christ*, says it all. Baillie writes: 'While God is in Himself incomprehensible, unknowable, yet it is His very nature to reveal Himself . . . even to the point of incarnation . . . It was *God* who became man in Jesus Christ.'[32]

More recently Jüngel has declared that the 'speakability' of God became possible only in the cross. He writes, 'We can also say that the word of the cross is the self-definition of God in human language.'[33] Moltmann declares, 'The history of Jesus the Son cannot be grasped except as part of the history of the Father and the Spirit.'[34] Because it was God who, in one sense, 'died' at Calvary, this makes God's love unique. Moltmann writes, 'A God who cannot suffer cannot love either. A God who cannot love is a dead God.'[35] Finally, Morris points out that *God himself* is especially prominent in Romans. He writes, 'No other book in the NT has this same concentration on the God-theme.'[36] God's name appears 153 times in Romans, which Morris claims is more than in any other book. He adds: 'There is not the same emphasis in Romans on Christ as on God.'[37] In practice God's love is closely co-ordinated with Christ's. Christ's action is God's action. Paul piles up the terms: *helpless* and *ungodly* (v. 6), *sinners* (v. 8) and *enemies of God* (v. 10). This heightens the striking contrast between divine and human. In human love there is usually some hint of reciprocation or return; the love of God is pure, undeserved, grace.

Paul then sets out the conclusion of his argument in verses 9–11. Having been put right with God by Christ's blood, 'much more surely' we will be saved (future) through Christ from God's wrath (v. 9). Present justification guarantees future salvation. (We discussed 'wrath' above under 1.18.) In this sense hope cannot disappoint, but is gloriously fulfilled in our final or completed salvation. 'Blood' in verse 9 is parallel with 'death' in verse 10.

In verse 10 Paul calls alienated humankind 'enemies' of God. This makes explicit human hostility towards God and alienation from him, caused by sin and guilt. These lead us to shrink away from God and to hide, as Adam

---

[32] Baillie, Donald M., *God Was in Christ* (London: Faber & Faber, 1948), p. 124.

[33] Jüngel, Eberhard, *God as the Mystery of the World* (Edinburgh: T & T Clark, 1983), p. 229.

[34] Moltmann, Jürgen, *The Trinity and the Kingdom of God* (London: SCM, 1981), p. 16.

[35] Moltmann, *The Trinity*, p. 38.

[36] Morris, Leon, 'The Theme of Romans' in Gasque, W. Ward, and Martin, Ralph P. (eds), *Apostolic History and the Gospel: Presented to F. F. Bruce* (Exeter: Paternoster, 1970), pp. 249–63.

[37] Morris, 'Theme of Romans', p. 252.

did in the Garden of Eden. Hence the key need is for *reconciliation*, which the rest of verse 10 unfolds. 'We were reconciled . . . through the death of his [God's] Son', is followed by: since we *have been* reconciled, we will be 'saved by his life.' Knox, Cranfield, Dunn and Fitzmyer understand reconciliation to be mutual or two-sided.[38] Jewett is more cautious about whether even raising this issue goes beyond the text, and focuses on 'human hostility against God'.[39] He also points out that it is God, the offended party, who takes the *initiative* in seeking reconciliation. (We discussed *reconciliation* above under 5.1.) Martin has shown that Paul uses *reconciliation* as a comprehensive term for the basis and larger context of salvation.[40]

'Much more surely . . . saved by his life' is highly debated. The traditional understanding is that Christ's resurrection life makes his death doubly effective. The Greek *en tē zōē* is instrumental. Nygren relates it to living in oneness with the living, raised Christ.[41] Dunn, Cranfield and Fitzmyer insist that we should view Christ's death-and-life as one event, and that the 'much more' flows on from the previous verse.[42] Jewett relates it to the paradoxes of life and death in 2 Corinthians 4.10, including new life in Christ (Rom. 5.15–21; 6.2–10), as do Tannehill and Hanson.[43]

'We even boast' (v. 11) reflects later MSS. Earlier MSS read the participle 'boasting' (*kauchōmenoi*, ℵ, B, C, D), making it continue the previous clause. *God* is the one in whom we boast (as 1 Cor. 1.31), not least because salvation is guaranteed. The verse gathers up the whole of the previous paragraph in a grand climax. Paul then concludes that it is all 'through our Lord Jesus Christ' that we have now received reconciliation. He stresses Christ's role as Mediator.

---

[38] Cranfield, *Romans*, vol. 1, p. 267; Dunn, *Romans 1—8*, p. 258; and Fitzmyer, *Romans*, p. 401.

[39] Jewett, *Romans*, p. 364.

[40] Martin, Ralph P., *Reconciliation: A Study of Paul's Theology* (London: Marshall, and Atlanta: John Knox, 1981).

[41] Nygren, *Romans*, p. 205.

[42] Dunn, *Romans 1—8*, p. 260.

[43] Jewett, *Romans*, p. 366; Hanson, A. T., *The Paradox of the Cross in the Thought of St. Paul* (Sheffield: Sheffield Academic Press, 1987); and Tannehill, R. C., *Dying and Rising with Christ: A Study in Pauline Theology* (Eugene, OR: Wipf & Stock, 2006).

13

Christ and Adam: humanity and the new humanity (5.12–21)

The exegesis and syntax of verses 12 and 14 are complex and much debated. Hence they require more detailed comment than usual. Paul is now concerned to urge the universal significance and effects of Christ's work in history. He begins to draw a parallel between the effects of the *Adam event* for *humanity* and the effects of *Christ's work* for the *new* humanity. His introductory *therefore* (Greek *dia touto*) may refer backwards to 5.1–11 or alternatively to the whole argument from 1.17 to 5.11. Wright indicates this complexity when he comments, 'The next paragraph is as terse and cryptic as the previous one was flowing and lucid . . . Paul paints with a few, large, sweeping strokes on a giant canvas.'[1] On verse 12, he comments, 'Straightforward in some ways it may be. But it has created huge problems of interpretation for subsequent readers.'[2] Hence our comments refer to more scholarly opinions than usual.

Paul's theme is 'the many in the one', which corresponds to the respective roles of Adam and of Christ. In verse 12 'through one man' (Greek *di' henos anthrōpou*) clearly alludes to Adam and to Christ, but stands in the clearest contrast to the twice-repeated 'all' (Greek *eis pantas anthropous . . . eph' hō pantes hēmarton*). In this verse 'sin came into the world through *one* man' (Adam), but 'death spread to all'. Paul will expound this in verses 13–14. Although the first-person plural was used in 5.1–11, here Paul returns to the third person.

Nygren shows special enthusiasm for this passage. He writes,

> This passage is actually the high point of the epistle, in the light of which the whole is best understood . . . It is complained that Paul does not at all demonstrate the parallelism between Christ and Adam, to which he appeals. But . . . Paul is expounding something which he considers decisive and axiomatic. It is too basic to be capable of formal demonstration. One does not prove an axiom.[3]

---

[1] Wright, N. T., 'Romans' in the *New Interpreter's Bible* (*NIB*) (Nashville: Abingdon, 2002), vol. 10, p. 523.
[2] Wright, 'Romans', *NIB*, vol. 10, p. 525.
[3] Nygren, Anders, *Commentary on Romans* (London: SCM, 1952), p. 20.

For Nygren, this is primarily because Paul thinks in terms of aeons or realms. Two realms stand over against each other: the age of Adam, and the age of Christ and the dominion of Christ. He adds, 'When Adam departed from God, it was not something which concerned him only as an individual; but in his act sin and death were made regnant in the cosmos.'[4]

However, is Paul thinking of Adam as a named individual in Genesis, or as humanity-as-a-whole, or even its first instantiation in Adam? Barrett comments,

> Paul learnt to think in Hebrew, and knew that the name Adam (*'ādām*) means *man*. The result of this is not only an inevitable (even when subconscious) tendency to interpret the story of Adam anthropologically, but also that wherever in Paul we meet the word *man* . . . we may suspect that Adam is somewhere in the background.[5]

Wright comments,

> Paul clearly believed that there had been a single first pair, whose male, Adam, had been given a commandment, and had broken it . . . We have consigned Adam and Eve entirely to the world of mythology, but we are still looking for their replacements.[6]

Brown, Driver and Briggs (BDB) list the main meanings of the Hebrew *'ādām* as *man, mankind* (very occasionally as a name); *the first man*; and even *ground* or *territory*.[7] Their numerous biblical references include Genesis 1.26; 2.5, 7, 8, 15–19, 22; 3.17, 19–21; 4.25; 5.1–4; and many more. A considerable surprise awaits us when we consult the Hatch-Redpath *Concordance to the Septuagint.*[8] We find that the word *Adam* does *not appear in the LXX even by transliteration*, but that the Hebrew *'ādām* is regularly translated as *anthrōpos, man*. Even the passage from which Paul quotes in Genesis 2.7: 'Man became a living being' (NRSV), or 'Adam became a living being' (1 Cor. 15.45 NRSV), is rendered by the Greek Septuagint of Genesis 2 by *man* (Greek *anthrōpos eis psuchēn zōsan*). This makes the Hebrew word *'ādām* very complex to translate in the OT, as well as for determining the meaning of the Greek word for Paul.

---

[4] Nygren, *Romans*, p. 21.

[5] Barrett, C. K., *From First Adam to Last: A Study in Pauline Theology* (London: Black, 1962), p. 6.

[6] Wright, 'Romans', *NIB*, vol. 10, p. 526.

[7] Brown, F., Driver, S. R., and Briggs, C. A., *Hebrew and English Lexicon* (BDB) (Lafayette, IN: Associated Publishers, 1980), pp. 9–10.

[8] Hatch, Edwin, and Redpath, Henry A., *A Concordance to the Septuagint* (2 vols, Athens: Beneficial Book Publishers, 1977; abbreviated as Hatch-Redpath).

There are a few counter-examples. In Genesis 4.25 we read, 'Adam knew his wife again', after which Seth was born. It is unclear whether this is the named Adam, or merely the first man. Genesis 5.1 even less clearly gives a list of his descendants. On the other hand, Genesis 5.3, 4, 5 give estimates of a life span in terms of a measure of years. The personal name is used by the NEB in Genesis 3.2; and by the Jerusalem Bible (JB), REB and NRSV in 4.25. In their commentaries on Genesis, Wenham believes that 4.1, 25 is probably a personal name, because *'ādām* lacks the definite article, while Speiser interprets 4.23 and 5.2 as a personal name.[9] Admittedly Philo and rabbinic sources use 'Adam' to denote a personal individual at times, so this use is not unknown to Paul. Philo refers to him as 'the true, beautiful, and good'.[10] Adam was 'most beautiful to behold'. But this is partly to show God's skill as Creator, partly to see Adam as a copy of archetypal man, and may refer to primal humankind. Philo comments, 'The Creator excelled'. The rabbis more often referred to the fall of Adam, citing idolatry and sexual perversion as a consequence of this, accompanied by a distinct loss of knowledge of God, as Paul does in Romans 1.18–32.[11]

Moberly stresses that there is a *firm tradition*, especially in Origen, for understanding the early chapters of Genesis 'not "literally" (Gk. *sōmatikōs*)'.[12] He comments, that is, not in terms of 'the familiar categories of space and time', because Origen 'is indeed attentive to the letter of the text'.[13]

Second, Moberly insists that we must take account of the *literary conventions of the day*. For example, the discredited theory that people spoke Hebrew before Babel was due to the problems of 'the assumption that Genesis's portrayal of speech in Hebrew must be historicized . . . When Shakespeare depicts all characters in *Julius Caesar* or *Coriolanus* as speaking Tudor English in the context of ancient Rome, one would be unwise to assume that Shakespeare was making a historical claim about the language of ancient Rome.'[14]

Third, Moberly considers that our modern obsession with cosmogony and teleology, while not wrong, has put us off track in our interpretation

[9] Wenham, Gordon J., *Genesis 1—15* (Waco: Nelson/Word, 1987), p. 32; and Speiser, E. A., *Genesis* (New York: Doubleday, 1964), p. 40.

[10] Philo, *De Opificio Mundi*, 136 and 138; Gk and Eng. in Colson, F. H., and Whitaker, G. H. (eds), *Works*, vol. 1 (Cambridge, MA: Harvard University Press, 1929), pp. 106–11.

[11] Levison, J. R., *Portraits of Adam in Early Judaism: From Sirach to 2 Baruch* (Sheffield: JSOT Press, 1998), esp. pp. 47–8, 61–2; 96–7, 113–27; and Scroggs, R., *The Last Adam* (Oxford: Blackwell, 1966), pp. 22–9.

[12] Moberly, R. W. L., *The Theology of the Book of Genesis* (Cambridge: CUP, 2009), pp. 1–120, esp. pp. 21–41.

[13] Origen, *De Principiis*, 4.16 (Eng., ANF, vol. 4, pp. 239–584); and Moberly, *Genesis*, p. 23 n. 3.

[14] Moberly, *Genesis*, p. 35.

of Genesis 1—3. Everything depends on 'how one pictures the world'.[15] He warms to the interpretation of Levenson. Levenson observes, '*The point of creation is not the production of matter out of nothing, but rather the emergence of a stable community in a benevolent and life-sustaining order.*'[16] Moberly regards Levenson's approach as significantly responding to the claims of Richard Dawkins and others about the supposed dethronement of the teleological argument for the existence of God, not least in the light of certain evolutionary theories. Moberly argues that '*God*' *is not an* '*explanation*' of the world, which would by implication fuel the 'god of the gaps' approach.[17] He concludes that the Israelite creeds concerning the God of creation *do not depend on teleology*, but on divine *sovereignty to order the world*, and thus to make possible the *covenant, covenant faithfulness and love.*

Finally, Moberly, incidentally, shows how closely the Genesis narrative relates to Paul. He complements Levenson's interpretation by regarding '*trust in God*' *as the key to the narrative.* God warned the 'Adam' figure that the consequences of disobedience would be death. The 'serpent' denied the word of God. Sin entered the world when the human response to God's word turned on lack of trust, rather than some particular action.[18] Moberly understands Genesis 1 and the Adam narrative as cohering with Paul's argument in Romans 4, and as helping to explain the word 'therefore' in 5.1.

Paul's parallel between Christ and Adam in verse 12 implies that Christ does not only 'determine the existence of believers: it is also the innermost secret of the life of every man'.[19] The third person (in contrast to the first person in verses 1–11) implies that more than Christians are involved. Jewett alludes to the apocalyptic background, which shows the cosmic and universal scope of Paul's concern.[20] He comments, 'Paul depicts Adam's act as decisively determining the behaviour of his descendants.'[21]

The preposition *eph' hō*, which the NRSV translates as '*because*' ('because all have sinned'), has been strongly contested. It is well known that Augustine translated the word *hō* as masculine, to translate, '*in whom* all sinned', following the Vulgate. Most modern commentators, however, render the

---

[15] Moberly, *Genesis*, p. 42.

[16] Levenson, Jon Douglas, *Creation and the Persistence of Evil* (Princeton: Princeton University Press, 1994), p. 12 (my italics).

[17] Moberly, *Genesis*, p. 62.

[18] Moberly, *Genesis*, pp. 75–86.

[19] Cranfield, C. E. B., *A Critical and Exegetical Commentary on the Epistle to the Romans*, vol. 1 (Edinburgh: T & T Clark, 1975; ICC), p. 269.

[20] Jewett, Robert, *Romans: A Commentary* (Minneapolis: Fortress, 2007; Hermeneia), pp. 374–5.

[21] Jewett, *Romans*, p. 375.

word as neuter, to mean *because*. Augustine renders the verse: 'So death passed upon all men, for in him [one man, Adam] all have sinned.' His phrasing is complex, but we quote his words. He regards his rendering as the

> very clear and manifest words of the apostle ... Adam was the first to sin ... afterwards [people] found an example for sinning in him ... He [Paul] used the phrase 'by one man', from whom the generation of men, of course, had its beginning, in order to show us that original sin had passed upon all men by generation.[22]

Augustine is even more explicit elsewhere. He writes that this means

> Either in that 'one man' all have sinned ... because when he sinned *all were in him*; or that ... 'all have sinned' because *that was the doing of all in general* ... All die in ... sin ... Sin is the sting of death.[23]

This approach is usually known as the *seminal headship* of Adam, and Augustine is said to have invented the term *original sin* to explain it. This view can also readily be traced to Origen. He examines the Adam narrative carefully, although many claim that his view of Adam is 'purely allegorical'. On the other hand, as we have seen, Moberly challenges this.[24] Moxon comments, 'Origen also, like Irenaeus, held the doctrine of the solidarity of mankind, and was the first to account for this by the conception of the seminal presence in Adam of all his posterity.'[25] He quotes Origen's Latin: '*Si Levi ... in lumbis Abrahae fuisse perhibetur, multo magis omnes ... in lumbis erant Adae, cum adhuc esset in paradiso*', i.e. 'How much more were all in the loins of Adam'. In contrast to most modern commentators, Fitzmyer maintains that *because* (neuter) was not supported as a translation of *eph' hō* prior to the sixth century. The translation *in whom* is based on the Vulgate 'commonly used in the Western Church since Ambrosiaster'.[26]

Fitzmyer gives no fewer than 11 possible ways in which *eph' hō* has been interpreted.[27] But on examination, it appears that only two or three of these are significantly distinctive: (i) '*in whom*' (*in quo*, Vulgate and Augustine); (ii) '*because of whom*' (Chrysostom and others); and (iii) '*to the extent that*' (Cyril of Alexandria), or more explicitly '*with the result*

---

[22] Augustine, *On Marriage and Concupiscence*, 2.45 (Eng., *NPNF*, ser. i, vol. 5, p. 301).

[23] Augustine, *Against Two Letters of the Pelagians*, 4.7 (Eng., *NPNF*, ser. i, vol. 5, p. 419) (my italics).

[24] Moxon, R. A., *The Doctrine of Sin* (London: Allen & Unwin, 1922), p. 27, uses the words 'purely allegorical'.

[25] Moxon, *Doctrine of Sin*, p. 29.

[26] Fitzmyer, Joseph A., *Romans: A New Translation with Introduction and Commentary* (New York: Doubleday, 1992; AB 33), pp. 413–14.

[27] Fitzmyer, *Romans*, pp. 413–17.

that. All underline the phrase 'through one man', which Paul repeats 12 times. Davies argues,

> Paul accepted the traditional rabbinic doctrine of the unity of mankind in Adam. That doctrine implied that the very constitution of the physical body of Adam ... was symbolic of the real oneness of mankind ... The 'body' of Adam includes all mankind.[28]

But Fitzmyer shows that Davies based his evidence on selected texts, many of which post-date Paul.[29] On the other hand Paul does allude to contemporary Jewish belief about Adam's influence (Wis. 2.24; *2 Apoc. Bar.* 17.3; 23.4; 48.42; 54.15; *4 Ezra* 3.7, 21; 7.118).

The two most often quoted passages express two sides of a major problem with which the rabbis and Paul would wrestle, and which resonates today. The writer of *4 Ezra* 7.118 exclaimed, '*O Adam, what have you done? Although it was you who sinned, the fall was not yours alone; but ours too*, who are your descendants.' But *2 Apocalypse of Baruch* 54.19 expressed the other side of the well-known dilemma: 'Thus Adam was *not the cause, except for himself only*; each one of us is his own Adam.'[30]

Paul asserts the truth of *both* sides. Some imagine a hypothetical dialogue-partner in the diatribe responding in Romans 5.12: 'But that's not fair. Why should all humanity suffer because Adam sinned?' Paul would then reply: 'Well, we have all *endorsed* Adam's sin. Sin *entered* the world with the *first* man, but *we all sin* in the same way as the Adam figure.' This dilemma is thus theoretical. The comparison or analogy between Christ and Adam serves to show primarily the *differences* between the two respective corporate solidarities. Cranfield rightly observes on this comparison:

> He [Paul] desires, while drawing the analogy, at the same time to deny emphatically that there is even the remotest semblance of equilibrium between them, for as Chrysostom observes, 'Sin and grace are not equivalents, nor yet death and life ... the difference between them is infinite'.[31]

The point of the analogy is to bring out clearly the universal significance of Christ's work. Jewett endorses Cranfield's argument that Paul clearly asserts 'both Adamic causation and individual responsibility for sin'.[32]

Cranfield also notes that in verse 12,

[28] Davies, W. D., *Paul and Rabbinic Judaism* (London: SPCK, 1948, 2nd edn, 1955), pp. 53–7.
[29] Fitzmyer, *Romans*, p. 412.
[30] The modern translation comes from Fitzmyer, *Romans*, p. 413 (my italics).
[31] Cranfield, *Romans*, vol. 1, p. 273.
[32] Jewett, *Romans*, p. 376.

Human death is the consequence of human sin . . . That is difficult for those who are in the habit of thinking of death as natural . . . It is not *only in modern times* that the difficulty of this doctrine has been felt.[33]

At the end of his second volume Cranfield further addresses this problem about *death and the natural world*. He suggests that it is 'not necessarily obscurantist' to believe that the first man could have gained extended life or even immortality, had he been obedient and trustful, and retained his intimacy with God. But as it was, he chose a different path, which placed him alongside all the rest of natural creation, which faced death in due course. Cranfield speaks of the first man's missing

a God-given summons to a human life such as did not need to be ter-minated by the death which we know, that is, a death which is for all men objectively . . . death-as-the-wages-of-sin, whether or not they subjectively know it as such.[34]

He adds that it is only in the death of Jesus Christ that we see the reality and seriousness of human death, and that only Jesus Christ did not merit death.

This approach to the problem is different from that of Bultmann. Bultmann declares, 'Death grows out of the fleshly life like a fruit – organic-ally, as it were . . . (Rom. 7:5). Death is the "end" of the "fruit" of sinful life.'[35] He argues that the 'justice conception of death as the punishment for sin and the conception of death as a fruit organically growing out of sin are not harmonized with each other'.[36] In his essays on myth Bultmann explicitly discusses Romans 5.12, in which 'this world' is 'the world of corruption and death', since 'Death is the wages of sin (Rom. 6:23).' Paul, he argues, ascribes these to the fall of Adam 'as the ancestor of the human race'. He then argues that 'For that all sinned (Rom. 5:12) . . . stands in contradiction to the Adam theory.'[37] But 'contradiction', for Bultmann, is a sign and symptom of myth. The 'scientific' approach regards death as a natural phenomenon; the 'mythological' approach regards it as an 'objective' event of God's judgement.[38] In 1980, I argued that Bultmann's notion of myth is itself self-contradictory and untenable, although we cannot rehearse

---

[33] Cranfield, *Romans*, vol. 1, p. 291.

[34] Cranfield, C. E. B., *A Critical and Exegetical Commentary on the Epistle to the Romans*, vol. 2 (Edinburgh: T & T Clark, 1979; ICC), p. 845.

[35] Bultmann, Rudolf, *Theology of the New Testament*, vol. 1 (London: SCM, 1952), p. 247.

[36] Bultmann, *Theology of the NT*, vol. 1, p. 249.

[37] Bultmann, Rudolf, 'New Testament and Mythology' in Bartsch, Hans-Werner (ed.), *Kerygma and Myth* (Eng., London: SPCK, 1953), p. 17.

[38] Bultmann, 'New Testament and Mythology', p. 18.

these lengthy arguments here.[39] He readily confuses myth, symbol and analogy, too often reduces de-objectification to an evaporation of ontology. He mistakes what Ramsey calls 'models and qualifiers' for 'contradiction'. We cannot unpack this compressed criticism, except to say that Cranfield's approach makes it *unnecessary to pit a 'scientific' view against biblical language* in this verse.

Dunn also rejects the notion that Paul alludes to one *mythical* man. He points out that '"sin" and "death", appearing here for the first time as interdependent categories, will dominate the discussion for the next three chapters ("sin" 42 times between 5:12 and 8:10; "death" 19 times between 5:12 and 8:6)'.[40] He agrees with Cranfield that the allusions to Adam do not diminish human responsibility. Similarly Jewett comments, 'That humans are responsible for the spread of sin throughout the world is clearly implied by the expression *pantes hēmarton* ("all have sinned")'.[41]

Romans 5.13 provides an *explanation of verse 12*. Sin appeared in the world long before the laws of Moses. But in 13b Paul declares that this sin was not 'reckoned'. The Greek is the present passive of a unusual verb, *ellogaō*, which means *to put down in the ledger to one's account*. There are examples in inscriptions and papyri.[42] Robertson implies that 'infants and idiots' do not therefore have responsibility, but this claim seems speculative.[43] Cranfield explains that without the law, 'Sin is not the clearly defined thing . . . that it becomes when the law is present.'[44]

In verse 14 Paul clarifies the point that the reality of sin between Adam and Moses means that 'death exercised dominion'. There is much debate over 'those whose sins were not like the transgression [Greek *tēs parabaseōs*] of Adam' (v. 14). So, once again, we have to cite a number of scholars. In what sense is it 'not like'? Sanday and Headlam and Cranfield suggest that Adam's sin was disobedience to a 'clear and definite' command. Leenhardt and Whiteley distinguish between 'solidarity in guilt' and 'solidarity in the

---

[39] Thiselton, Anthony C., *The Two Horizons* (Exeter: Paternoster, and Grand Rapids: Eerdmans, 1980), pp. 252–92; see Hepburn, R. W., 'Demythologizing and the Problem of Validity' in Flew, A., and MacIntyre, A. (eds), *New Essays in Philosophical Theology* (London: SCM. 1955), pp. 227–42; and Macquarrie, John, *The Scope of Demythologizing: Bultmann and His Critics* (London: SCM, 1960), throughout.

[40] Dunn, James D. G., *Romans 1—8* (Dallas: Word, 1988; WBC 38), p. 273.

[41] Jewett, *Romans*, p. 376.

[42] Moulton, J. H., and Milligan, G. exemplify this in *The Vocabulary of the Greek Testament* (London: Hodder & Stoughton, 1952 [1930]), p. 204, e.g. Pap. Ryl. II. 243.11; and Danker, Frederick, *A Greek-English Lexicon of the New Testament and Other Early Christian Literature* (BDAG) (Chicago and London: University of Chicago Press, 3rd edn, 2000), p. 319 (*ellogéo*, Philem. 8).

[43] Robertson, A. T., *Word Pictures in the New Testament, vol. 4: Romans* (New York: R. Smith, 1931).

[44] Cranfield, *Romans*, vol. 1, p. 282.

consequences of the original transgression'.[45] Jewett rejects any distinction between 'sin' and 'transgression'; since *paraptōma* is used of Adam as much as *parabasis*, 'the distinctions remain murky'.[46] Probably Paul is simply warning us not to over-press the comparison between Adam and Christ.

Paul elaborates that Adam is 'a type [Greek *tupos*] of the one who was to come.' 'Type' in the third century clearly denotes a correspondence between *persons* or *events*, whereas, according to Hanson, allegory denotes only a correspondence between *ideas*.[47] But does this distinction apply as early as in Paul? He also uses the word *tupikōs* of Israel's drinking from the cleft rock in the wilderness in 1 Corinthians 10.6, 11, and in the LXX and Philo the term is used with the meaning *pattern* or *model*.[48] The word also occurs in Hebrews 7.1–3 for the parallel between Christ and Melchizedek, and in the later *Epistle of Barnabas* and the *Didache*.[49] The term fluctuates between historical correspondence and analogy, and thus denotes both similarity and difference, which are expounded in verse 15.

The phrase 'one who was to come' is messianic. Since death is the 'last enemy' to be destroyed (1 Cor. 15.26), it is appropriate that Christ will put an end to 'the reign of death' (v. 14), which Nygren calls 'not only an event' but 'a power, a ruler'.[50] Death will have humanity in its grip until the victory of Christ is fully realized at the Last Day. In Nygren's words, it is personified as a power alongside wrath, law and sin.

Paul begins to expound *grace* further in verse 15: 'The free gift is not like the trespass.' The similarity is that in both cases what began with '*one* man' spread to '*the many*'; and that the free gift of grace 'abounded' (Greek *eperisseusen*). Grace was also 'even more so' (Greek *mallon*) in the sense of 'much more surely', as the NRSV expresses it. Not for the first time Paul uses an *a fortiori* argument. Lightfoot explains that God delights *so much more* to show grace and mercy than to punish sinners. Grace surpasses both sin and its effects. Dunn comments that Paul 'intends to hold together the grace of the Christ-event and the grace actually received by those who believe in Christ'.[51]

Often verse 15 is understood as a statement, but Jewett understands it as a rhetorical question.[52] He also quotes Moo's comment: 'The act of each

[45] Leenhardt, Franz J., *The Epistle to the Romans* (London: Lutterworth, 1961), p. 145.

[46] Jewett, *Romans*, p. 378.

[47] Hanson, R. P. C., *Allegory and Event* (London: SCM, 1959), pp. 6–8.

[48] Danker, BDAG, pp. 1019–20; and Goppelt, L., *Typos* (Grand Rapids: Eerdmans, 1982).

[49] *Epistle to Barnabas*, 99; *Didache* 9.2.

[50] Nygren, *Romans*, p. 216.

[51] Dunn, *Romans 1—8*, p. 280.

[52] Jewett, *Romans*, p. 379.

is considered to have determinative significance for those who "belong" to each.'[53] This does not exhaust the dissimilarities between the two. Barrett reminds us that the one act is a purely human act, while the other is God's intervention of grace.[54] Best stresses the difference between the cause–effect chain of sin and death, and grace, which operates on an entirely different basis. Adam begins from a 'neutral' situation in the sense of having no predecessor, whereas Christ reverses the pre-existing chain of sin and death, cancelling cumulative sin, to initiate the new creation. Hence, in Barrett's words, grace abounds because grace *more than undoes* the effects of sin. The Greek phrase *hē dōrea en chariti* denotes 'the gift prompted by grace'.

Romans 5.16 lacks verbs, which indicates Paul's compressed style. We may supply *esti* (*is*) in the first part of the verse and *egeneto* (*brought into being*), for the second part (as NRSV). The participial construction *di' henos hamartēsantos* denotes 'the having sinned one [person]', the first man. The word *dikaiōma* usually means *righteous act*, but often in Romans also denotes a verdict. Here it means a verdict of *acquittal*, and stands in parallel with *condemnation*, which occurs nine words later. Moffatt renders the Greek: 'Nor did the gift correspond in any way with the effects of one man's sin.' Cranfield writes, 'His [God's] grace is infinitely more effective than man's sin.'[55] In Greek there is conscious word-play between *krima* (*judicial verdict*) and *katakrima* (*condemnation* or *penalty*).[56]

In verse 17 Paul gives support to verse 16a, emphasizing especially the initiative of divine grace. The structure of the protasis and apodosis is inverted. Cranfield explains,

> The effectiveness and unspeakable generosity of the divine grace are such that it will not merely bring about the *replacement* of the reign of death by the reign of life, but will make those who receive its riches to *become kings*.[57]

Barth is at his best here. He calls 5.12–21 'The New World', comparing the contrast between humankind and the new humanity in Christ. The latter, he suggests, is like 'streams at the watershed of the Alps', which can flow in *two directions*. In the *old world* humans lie

> under the mechanical necessity of destiny ... confined in a circle of meaningless growth, and decay, of false security, and bitter disappointment ... of abortive optimism and abortive pessimism ... Death ... is suspended over our heads like a sword of Damocles ...

---

[53] Moo, Douglas J., *The Epistle to the Romans* (Grand Rapids: Eerdmans, 1996; NICNT), p. 334.

[54] Barrett, C. K., *The Epistle to the Romans* (London: Black, 1957), p. 114.

[55] Cranfield, *Romans*, vol. 1, p. 285.

[56] Danker, BDAG, pp. 518 and 567.

[57] Cranfield, *Romans*, vol. 1, p. 288.

In the *New World* they

> reign in life . . . are made new; . . . it is rehabilitation . . . and complete free-
> dom . . . They discover the free purpose of life . . . His [the new humanity's]
> nobility is immeasurable, and to his worth there is no limit.[58]

Paul states the conclusion of the argument (vv. 18–19). He recapitulates
the parallels and contrasts between Christ and Adam. In this context,
'one man' must refer to Adam, or the first man. 'All' corresponds with 'the
many' in verse 15. Barrett observes, '"Condemnation" and "justification" are
in their ordinary use ultimate and mutually exclusive terms. At the last
judgement a man [a person] is either condemned or justified [acquitted].'[59]
On '*justified*', we might explain: 'put in a right relation with God'. The double
use of 'all' is not a contradiction, for Paul presupposes the meaning 'all
in [or with] Adam' and 'all in Christ'. Nevertheless Fitzmyer regards *henos*
(*one*) as neuter, which would mean 'one offence'.[60] This verse would then
match 'through the justifying act' (Greek *dikaiōma*). Dunn argues that
both remain possible on exegetical and grammatical grounds.[61]

The climax of the comparison is reached in verse 19, which echoes
5.12. The formal effects of Adam's disobedience make 'all' sinners. Paul
uses here a third term for the sin of Adam, namely Greek *parakoē*
(*disobedience*), in contrast to Christ's *hupakoē* (*obedience*).[62] In 5.12–13
Paul uses *hamartia*, the regular word for *sin*. In 5.15, he uses *paraptōma*
(*offence* or *wrongdoing*).[63] But, as we noted, Jewett regards the distinctions
between these three terms as at best 'murky'. Greek is utterly unlike Hebrew,
where the three main words for sin are the verbs *chātā'* and *chattā'th*
(*to miss the mark/to transgress*); *pasha'* (*to rebel against God*); and *āwōn*
(*iniquity, depravity*, or *distortion*). Each Hebrew word has a different force.

Paul's other statement declares, 'Many will be constituted righteous
[Greek *dikaioi katastathēsontai*] through Christ's obedience.' The old
Greek verb *kathistēmi* means *to render* or *to constitute*, which Paul uses
here in the future passive. Fitzmyer comments: 'This is the climax . . . The
influence of Christ is overwhelming and knows no bounds.'[64] Cranfield
declares, 'Since God has in Christ identified himself with sinners and taken
upon himself the burden of their sin, they will receive as a free benefit

[58] Barth, Karl, *The Epistle to the Romans* (Eng., Oxford: OUP, 1933), pp. 180–1.
[59] Barrett, *Romans*, p. 116.
[60] Fitzmyer, *Romans*, p. 420.
[61] Dunn, *Romans 1—8*, p. 283.
[62] Danker, BDAG, pp. 766–7.
[63] Danker, BDAG, p. 770.
[64] Fitzmyer, *Romans*, p. 421.

from him that status of righteousness, which Christ's perfect obedience alone has deserved.'[65] The term *obedience* covers Christ's whole life, and not just his death.

Paul provides a qualifying postscript to the main argument (vv. 20–21). The law does not imply that all that has gone before in 5.12–18 is undermined or invalidated. The law 'came in' (NRSV; Greek *pareisēlthen*). The verb is a double compound, indicating the intervention of an interloper. Danker proposes *to slip in, to come in as a side issue*.[66] Sanday and Headlam translate this as 'came in as a sort of "afterthought", a secondary and subordinate stage in the divine plan'.[67] Its effect was that 'the trespass multiplied'. The last clause of verse 20 hammers home the main lesson of Romans 5.12–17: 'Where sin increased, grace abounded all the more'. Paul will explain and expand this further in chapter 7. The result is confirmed in verse 21: sin exercised dominion in death, but grace exercises dominion through justification. The risen Lord gives his people a share in eternal life. Sin is the usurper, but grace is triumphant, overflowing, and reigns for ever.[68]

---

[65] Cranfield, *Romans*, vol. 1, p. 291.

[66] Danker, BDAG, p. 774.

[67] Sanday, William, and Headlam, Arthur C., *Critical and Exegetical Commentary on the Epistle to the Romans* (Edinburgh: T & T Clark, 1902; ICC), p. 139.

[68] Jewett, *Romans*, p. 389, concludes in the same vein.

14

Dead to sin; alive to God (6.1–23)

Union with Christ (6.1–11)

The heading 'Dead to sin' constitutes a reply to the hypothetical question 'Does grace encourage sin?' Hence Paul continues his diatribe style with the hypothetical rhetorical question: 'What then are we to say? Should we continue in sin in order that grace may abound? By no means!' Paul's fundamental reason for this is: 'How can we who died to sin go on living in it?' (Rom. 6.1–2). 'Are we to continue' is a deliberative subjunctive. There is support for the subjunctive reading in A, B, C, D, F and 33, but the indicative, 'shall we remain', is supported by ℵ. Most support the deliberative subjunctive. Wright comments on this passage, 'Granted justification by grace through faith, what is the place of ethics, and of moral effort, in the Christian life?'[1] The passage has some broad parallel with 1 Corinthians 6.12–20.

The phrase 'died to sin' (6.2) has been amplified in 5.21 as 'the dominion of sin'. Paul does not say that Christians cannot *in fact* sin, but that sin cannot (logical *cannot*) *be a ruling principle* for Christians. Only a perverse person could understand Paul as implying that then 'grace may abound' (6.1). In 5.20 he said that grace could abound 'all the more', so the question must be raised. 'By no means' (Greek *mē genoito*) is emphatic: the equivalent might be 'Perish the thought!' In Luther's day the 'left-wing' or 'radical' pietist reformers seemed to defend what Paul utterly rejects. But Paul will later support his conclusion that we cannot (logical *cannot*) sin because we belong to Christ.

'Belonging to Christ' explains why Paul now makes so much of Christian baptism (6.3–11). Bultmann rightly observes, '"Sinlessness" is not a magical guarantee against the *possibility of sin* . . . but release *from the compulsion of sin*.'[2] He declares,

> The believer . . . no longer 'belongs to himself' (1 Cor. 6:19). He no longer bears the care for himself . . . but lets this care go, yielding himself entirely to the grace of God; he recognizes himself to be the property of God.

---

[1] Wright, N. T., 'Romans' in the *New Interpreter's Bible* (*NIB*) (Nashville: Abingdon, 2002), vol. 10, p. 533.
[2] Bultmann, Rudolf, *Theology of the New Testament*, vol. 1 (London: SCM, 1952), p. 332 (his italics first, then mine).

Bultmann then cites Romans 14.2–8, 'None of us lives to himself . . . If we live we live to the Lord . . .'[3] To remain in sin would be self-contradictory.

Wright observes that 'Do you not know?' (v. 3) shows that Paul does not use 'a rhetorical trick'.[4] Paul makes it clear that 'all of us' who have been baptized 'have been baptized into Christ Jesus . . . were baptized into his death.' Baptism was involved with coming to faith from the earliest NT times. Jewett comments, 'Baptism would be regarded as establishing Christ's proprietary rights over the baptized person.'[5] That is true, but Dunn elsewhere adds a caution. He writes: 'It is important to grasp that the subject of Rom. 6 is not baptism, but death to sin and the life which follows from it.'[6] This is why he calls baptism a 'conversion-initiation event'.[7] *Water-baptism may not always coincide with the event of conversion* chronologically; the two are not to be identified.

It is important not to overrate parallels between Romans 6.3–4 and baptismal initiation into the Isis cult. Wagner has criticized making too much of this parallel on several grounds.[8] One concerns the respective dating of Paul and many cults, including the Isis cult; another concerns how close alleged parallels genuinely are. Dunn continues, 'The critique of Wagner in particular has been influential in providing a corrective to the overstatements of earlier history-of-religion hypotheses.'[9] On the other hand he recognizes some counter-criticisms of Wagner. He adds, 'It is unfortunate that the discussion has to depend so heavily on . . . one text', namely on Apuleius' description of the Isis cult in *Metamorphoses* 11.[10] Lucius Apuleius Madaurensis (*c*.125–80) travelled in Italy, Asia Minor and Egypt, and wrote an irreverent, bawdy novel, *Metamorphoses*, otherwise known as *The Golden Ass*. Alleged parallels merely establish that related concepts would have been familiar to Paul's readers; not that Paul *borrowed* from such notions, especially given the clearly pagan nature of the cult.[11]

The heart of the alleged parallel is that ritual initiates are said to be 'born again' after a voluntary death.[12] But in Paul, unlike John, death-and-

---

[3] Bultmann, *Theology of the NT*, vol. 1, p. 331.

[4] Wright, 'Romans', *NIB*, vol. 10, p. 534.

[5] Jewett, Robert, *Romans: A Commentary* (Minneapolis: Fortress, 2007; Hermeneia), p. 433.

[6] Dunn, James D. G., *Baptism in the Holy Spirit* (London: SCM, 1970), p. 139.

[7] Dunn, *Baptism*, pp. 104–5 and 116–31, esp. 120–3.

[8] Wagner, Günther, *Pauline Baptism and the Pagan Mysteries: The Problem of the Pauline Doctrine of Baptism in Romans VI.1–11 in the Light of Its Religio-Historical 'Parallels'* (Edinburgh: Oliver & Boyd, 1967).

[9] Dunn, James D. G., *Romans 1—8* (Dallas: Word, 1988; WBC 38), p. 308.

[10] Dunn, *Romans 1—8*, p. 309.

[11] Wagner, *Pauline Baptism*, pp. 100–3.

[12] Apuleius, *Metamorphoses*, 11.16, 21, 23.

resurrection with Christ and new creation remain key concepts and terms, *rather than rebirth*. If Paul shows any consciousness of the mystery cults, he regularly *avoids* the term 'rebirth', in favour of 'new creation'. Cranfield adds a further comment:

> While the mysteries were concerned with the union of the participant with a nature-deity, baptism had to do with the relationship of the believer to the historical event of God's saving deed in Christ; while the dying and rising of a nature-deity were conceived as something recurring again and again, the historical event to which baptism pointed was *a once for all, unique, event*.[13]

Many comments on verse 3 apply to Paul's argument about baptism in verses 3–11. Our next comment, however, concerns the NRSV translation of verse 3, 'baptized into Christ'. This faithfully reproduces the Greek *eis Christon*. But Robertson insists, '*Eis* [into] is at bottom the same word as *en* [in] . . . Here *into his death* means in relation to his death.'[14] Danker has ten categories of use, each of which is subdivided into up to seven sub-sections.[15] The classic study of baptism in Pauline thought is still that by Schnackenburg. He asserts that whether *eis* denotes movement or motion remains disputed. If it means *into*, he says, it denotes 'into the body of Christ'; but if it denotes *in*, he says, it signifies allegiance to Christ.[16] He also insists that *baptizein eis* is often in parallel with *pisteuein eis* (*believe in*), which indicates 'the *direction of faith*'.[17]

Schnackenburg calls Romans 6.3–11 'the *locus classicus*' of Paul's teaching on baptism as 'salvation-event'.[18] He first points out that 'Do you not know that?' (v. 3), and 'we believe' (v. 8), demonstrate the familiarity of readers with Paul's appeal to the meaning of baptism.[19] To be baptized into (or in) Christ's death (v. 3) immediately leads to 'buried with . . . raised . . .' in verse 4 (Greek *synetaphēmen*). He comments, '"Buried with" expresses more clearly the complete succumbing to death.'[20] Hence the Christian is 'dead' to the reign of sin. In turn, 'planted with' (v. 5, Greek *sumphutoi*,

[13] Cranfield, C. E. B., *A Critical and Exegetical Commentary on the Epistle to the Romans*, vol. 1 (Edinburgh: T & T Clark, 1975; ICC), p. 302 (my italics).

[14] Robertson, A. T., *Word Pictures in the New Testament, vol. 4: Romans* (New York: R. Smith, 1931), p. 361.

[15] Danker, Frederick, *A Greek-English Lexicon of the New Testament and Other Early Christian Literature* (BDAG) (Chicago and London: University of Chicago Press, 3rd edn, 2000), p. 288.

[16] Schnackenburg, Rudolf, *Baptism in the Thought of St. Paul* (Oxford: Blackwell, 1964), pp. 21–6.

[17] Schnackenburg, *Baptism*, p. 23.

[18] Schnackenburg, *Baptism*, pp. 30–61.

[19] Schnackenburg, *Baptism*, p. 33.

[20] Schnackenburg, *Baptism*, p. 34.

NRSV 'united with') leads on to 'a resurrection like his', and also how our old self was crucified with him (v. 6, Greek *synestaurōthē*) so that 'the body of sin might be destroyed' (v. 6); that 'we' might no longer be enslaved. Schnackenburg observes, 'The *sun*-sayings emerge here in immediate connection with baptism "to Christ" and "to his death" . . . Baptism brings us into closest relation to Christ and his dying.'[21] Hence Christian believers then share his life and resurrection. The old world in which sin 'reigns' is left behind in the Christ-centred new life.

Elsewhere in his book Schnackenburg discusses these leading themes that have come to be associated with baptism in the NT. Perhaps surprisingly for many, the theme of baptism as *cleansing* plays a minimal role for Paul.[22] Both the second and third themes are prominent: baptism as incorporation into the body of Christ, and baptism as sharing with Christ in a 'salvation event', as in death and resurrection.[23] Romans 6 mainly concerns the third of these, although it also overlaps with the second. Wright calls baptism 'being "co-buried" with Christ'.[24]

To walk 'in newness of life' confirms Paul's answer to his question, 'Are we to remain in sin?' Cranfield points out that the term 'walk' is the OT and Jewish term for the *moral life* (Hebrew *hālakh*, verb, and *hālakhāh*, noun).[25] The ingressive aorist *peripatēsōmen* indicates beginning the new life. The Greek *kainos* (*new*) is often associated with eschatological newness.[26] Paul's metaphor 'planted with' (v. 5) leads on to that of 'grafting' in Romans 11.17. Thornton argues that the two entities are a single organism, but they grow together more and more inextricably and are intimately bound together as one organism, as time goes by.[27]

The eschatological character of *newness* is confirmed by the eschatological significance of *baptism*. We appeal especially to Richardson and to Moule. Moule writes, 'If Baptism is a voluntary death, it is also a *pleading guilty*, and acceptance of the sentence' (of the Last Judgement).[28] Similarly Richardson declares, 'To be baptized is to accept God's verdict of "guilty",

---

[21] Schnackenburg, *Baptism*, p. 35.

[22] Schnackenburg, *Baptism*, p. 35.

[23] Schnackenburg, *Baptism*, pp. 18–29 and 30–61 respectively.

[24] Wright, 'Romans', *NIB*, vol. 10, p. 538.

[25] Cranfield, *Romans*, vol. 1, p. 305.

[26] Harrisville, R. A., 'The Concept of Newness in the New Testament', *JBL* 74 (1955), pp. 69–79; and *The Concept of Newness in the New Testament* (Minneapolis: Augsburg, 1960).

[27] Thornton, Lionel S., *The Common Life in the Body of Christ* (London: Dacre, 3rd edn, 1950), pp. 62–5 and 144–8.

[28] Moule, C. F. D., 'The Judgment Theme in the Sacraments' in Davies, W. D., and Daube, E. (eds), *The Background to the New Testament and Its Eschatology: In Honour of C. H. Dodd* (Cambridge: CUP, 1956), pp. 465 and 464–81.

and so to be brought past the great assize and final "judgment".[29] The aspect of solidarity with Christ is underlined by Holland and Zwiep in their insistence that baptism is a *corporate concept*, not an individualistic one, especially in the light of Romans 6.3–11 and 1 Corinthians 12.13. Holland comments: baptism is 'modelled on the baptism of Israel into Moses when Israel came into a covenant relationship with Yahweh. In Romans 6 . . . Paul is demonstrating how the old order has been brought to an end.'[30] Zwiep underlines the *corporate* nature of both water-baptism and Spirit-baptism.[31] Marcel and Cullmann stress that baptism constitutes an *effective sign* of the covenant relationship.[32] The Christian believer is 'in' Christ, not like a pebble in a box, but in living, organic union with Christ. Expressed negatively, this transference effects a rupture in the malevolent solidarity which made humankind enslaved to sin, and being grafted into the new.

From verse 5b to verse 8 Paul expounds the future implications of union with Christ. This Christ-union carries with it being 'certainly . . . united with him [Christ] in a resurrection like his'. 'In the likeness' is not in the Greek (*tēs anastaseōs esometha*), but is understood. Barrett and Fitzmyer call this a *logical future* in the sense of the conditional sentence: 'If *x* happens, *y* will follow.'[33] Cranfield assumes that *likeness* in verse 5 means 'assimilated to the form of'.[34] Robinson suggests 'fused into the mould of'.[35]

In verse 6 'We know that' may refer to the practical experience of committed Christians, namely that our fallen human nature has been 'crucified with Christ'. Paul appeals to a shared understanding with most readers. Rather than using 'our old self' (NRSV), Jewett suggests 'obsolete self'.[36] The theme is drawn from the Adam–Christ contrast in 5.12–21. 'Body of sin' is taken by Jewett to refer to the human body in a general sense. Bruce, Robinson and Tannehill expound this as the corporeity of the old Adam.[37]

---

[29] Richardson, Alan, *Introduction to the Theology of the New Testament* (London: SCM, 1958), p. 341.

[30] Holland, Tom, *Contours of Pauline Theology* (Fearn: Mentor, 2004), p. 152.

[31] Zwiep, Arie W., *Christ, the Spirit, and the Community of God* (Tübingen: Mohr, 2010; WUNT II.293), pp. 100–19.

[32] Marcel, Pierre C., *The Biblical Doctrine of Infant Baptism* (London: James Clarke & Co., 1953), esp. pp. 63–138; Cullmann, Oscar, *Baptism in the New Testament* (London: SCM, 1950), pp. 44–6.

[33] Barrett, C. K., *The Epistle to the Romans* (London: Black, 1957), p. 124; Fitzmyer, Joseph A., *Romans: A New Translation with Introduction and Commentary* (New York: Doubleday, 1992; AB 33), p. 435.

[34] Cranfield, *Romans*, vol. 1, p. 308.

[35] Robinson, J. A. T., *Wrestling with Romans* (London: SCM, 1979), p. 70.

[36] Jewett, *Romans*, pp. 402–3.

[37] Tannehill, Robert C., *Dying and Rising with Christ: A Study in Pauline Theology* (Berlin: Töpelmann, 1967; BZNW 32), p. 24; Robinson, J. A. T., *The Body: A Study in Pauline Theology* (London: SCM, 1952; SBT 5), p. 29; Bruce, F. F., *The Epistle of Paul to the Romans* (London: Tyndale, 1963), p. 139.

Paul's argument repeats here his thought about being 'crucified with Christ' in Galatians 2.19–20. The purpose of this union with Christ is that 'we might no longer be enslaved to sin.'

In verse 7 'justified' is a perfect passive verb, and hence we could well translate it as 'stands justified', to convey effects remaining in the present. The NEB renders verse 7, 'A dead man is no longer answerable for his sin.' Jewett and Cranfield argue that this summary saying may well reflect a rabbinic legal principle, namely that death pays all debts.[38] Paul repeats this principle in verse 8. Again he uses the preposition *sun* (*with*). If (the logical *if*) we died with Christ, Paul states, 'we believe that we will also live with him.' This leads to eschatological glory.

Paul stresses that Christ's resurrection is not merely 'being raised' to an extension of the same life (v. 9), as was the case with Lazarus in John 11. He urges, as the writer to Hebrews does, that Christ's death and resurrection is *once-for-all* (Greek *ephapax*). Older theologians often called this 'the finished work of Christ'. It is symbolized in Hebrews by Christ's taking his seat. In this sense 'Christ dies no more' or (NRSV) 'Christ . . . will never die again'. It is also noteworthy that 'being raised' (Greek *egertheis*) is always in the passive voice in Paul, because it is God who raises Christ, and this logic applies to believers being raised with Christ. Dahl, among others, makes this point with care and force.[39] Death has no more dominion over Christ, for Christ is Lord, and has been raised 'out of' the old humanity.

In verses 10–11 Paul presses home the point. He explicitly uses the term 'once-for-all' (Greek *ephapax*), as it is also in Hebrews 9.26–27. He declares, 'The death he died, he died *to sin*', not just to the *penalty* for sin. Death has no more hold on Christ; he eternally lives to God. The theme is parallel with that in Romans 4.25; 5.6–8; and 8.3. In Romans 8.3 God 'condemned sin in the flesh'. Two kinds of existence are diametrically opposed. Jewett calls these verses two *enthymemes*, part of logical syllogisms. Verse 11 completes the argument: 'So you also must consider yourselves dead to sin and alive to God in Christ Jesus', as our heading indicates. Paul introduces verse 11 by 'so also are you'. 'Consider' (NRSV) translates *logizesthe*, meaning *to reckon*, but also 'to determine by a mathematical process . . . to take into account, evaluate, estimate, look upon as', by 'a deliberate . . . judgment'.[40]

---

[38] Cranfield, *Romans*, vol. 1, pp. 310–11.

[39] Dahl, M. E., *The Resurrection of the Body* (London: SCM, 1962), pp. 96–7.

[40] Danker, BDAG, pp. 597–8; and Cranfield, *Romans*, vol. 1, p. 315, respectively.

Freedom for a new commitment (6.12–23)

The opening imperative in verse 12 is in fact a third-person present imperative in Greek, 'Let not sin continue to reign', as it did once (5.12). In Nygren's view, it gives the ground on which the Christian has to be *active*. He rightly comments, 'The indicative and the imperative do not clash ... The imperative is spoken because the indicative is true.'[41] Again, Paul does not imply freedom from every actual sin (or that we should not need to confess sins), but freedom from the *power* of sin. Cullmann draws a parallel with deliverance from the *power of death*, not actual dying, as the word 'mortal' implies. Bultmann argues that the imperative not only 'does not contradict the indicative of justification ... but results from it'.[42] Whiteley illustrates freedom from the decisive reign of sin alongside 'lapses into sin' with reference to coming out of the cold into a warm room. The heat in the room is decisive for the person in question; but there may still remain pockets of cold, which take time for the decisive heat to penetrate.[43]

Hence Paul adds, 'No longer present your members to sin as instruments of wickedness' (v. 13). In positive terms, 'Present your members to God as instruments of righteousness.' *Instruments* (Greek *hopla*) strictly means *weapons*. This is the first in a series of antitheses:

> wickedness ... righteousness (v. 13); under the law ... under grace (vv. 14–15); sin leading to death ... obedience leading to righteousness (v. 16); freed from sin ... slaves of righteousness (v. 18); slaves to impurity ... slaves to righteousness (v. 19) ... the end is death ... the end is eternal life (vv. 21–22); the wages of sin is death ... the free gift of God is eternal life (v. 23).[44]

Alongside these contrasting characteristics of the old and new order are the exhortations or imperatives (vv. 12, 13a, 16, 19, 21) which are based on the indicatives (vv. 13b, 14, 17–18).

Human capabilities (v. 13) can be used as weapons for good or ill, for obedience or disobedience. NRSV 'instruments' loses Paul's military metaphor, as when many traditional baptism liturgies speak of 'manfully fighting under his banner', which some today criticize. Similarly the power of sin is personified, as in 6.23. But under grace sin 'will have no dominion over you' (v. 14), or will not reign as a decisive force. 'Present your members to God' in this context means 'Give God control of yourselves'. The aorist

---

[41] Nygren, Anders, *Commentary on Romans* (London: SCM, 1952), p. 241.
[42] Bultmann, *Theology of the NT*, vol. 1, p. 332.
[43] Whiteley, D. E. H., *The Theology of St Paul* (Oxford: Blackwell, 1970), pp. 126–7.
[44] Dunn, *Romans 1—8*, p. 335 (Dunn has the Greek phrases).

(Greek *parastēsate*) signifies 'Present completely'. Barrett compares the 'upward striving' of human religion with the reception of God's grace.[45]

Paul's theme in verses 15–23 concerns the moral consequences of the Christ-union expounded above. Wright observes, 'This time the emphasis is far more on actual behaviour and far less on status.'[46] In Leenhardt's words, 'The believer is not free to surrender himself to the authority of a master, because he is dead as far as the old authority is concerned.'[47] Since Paul now uses the metaphor of being 'obedient slaves' of Christ, it is worth noting again the important research on slavery in Martin.[48] In legal terms a slave was merely a 'thing' (Latin *res*), not fully a 'person'. Slavery could involve oppressive misery. Torture and corporal punishment could occur. On the other hand, as we noted in 'Strategies of interpretation' under the socio-scientific approach, many voluntarily sold themselves into slavery, because literate slaves were often appointed as secretaries or managers of estates, with the security of 'belonging' to their master.

Everything depended on what kind of lord or master the slave belonged to. Wiedemann and others demonstrate this. This makes Paul's language about being 'slaves of the one whom you obey, either of sin ... or ... of righteousness' (vv. 16–18) especially poignant. To *belong* to the Lord Jesus Christ is a totally different matter from being a slave to sin, whose 'wages' are death (v. 23).

In verse 19 Paul makes it clear that the analogy, while valid and very useful, has limitations, and is not to be unduly pressed. Hence, he says, 'I am speaking in human terms because of your natural limitations.' Origen and Calvin called this 'accommodation' to human capacities. In verses 19–23 Paul presses home the difference between the two 'slaveries' in terms of their consequences. Paul has dismissed the sometimes illusory concept of 'freedom' which many hold. 'Having been set free' from sin (v. 18), one does not simply please oneself in neutral autonomy; one is 'enslaved' (*edoulōthēte*), this time, to righteousness.

The analogy is valid, but this is also why Paul underlines its limitations in verse 19. Nevertheless, Dunn and Bartchy remind us, 'The slave was not (legally) a "person", and so had no choice as to whether he was freed or refused freedom.'[49] Thus the former slavery meant handing over your

---

[45] Barrett, *Romans*, p. 129.

[46] Wright, 'Romans', *NIB*, vol. 10, p. 544.

[47] Leenhardt, Franz J., *The Epistle to the Romans* (London: Lutterworth, 1961), p. 170.

[48] Martin, Dale B., *Slavery as Salvation* (New Haven: Yale University Press, 1990), pp. 15–22, 50–85, 122–4 and 145–9; and Wiedemann, T. E. J., *Greek and Roman Slavery* (London: Groom Helm, 1981) and *Slavery: Greece and Rome* (Oxford: OUP, 1997), pp. 1–46.

[49] Dunn, *Romans 1—8*, p. 345; and Bartchy, S. S., *Mallon Chrēsai: First-Century Slavery* (Missoula: Scholars Press, 1973), pp. 98 and 106–10.

bodily capacities (Greek *melē*, *members* or *limbs*) as slaves to uncleanness and to lawlessness. Paul may have in mind literally giving bodily parts, including eyes, limbs and sexual organs, to immoral acts (v. 19b). But the new 'slavery', or being under the new Lord as owner, meant 'presenting them for righteousness and sanctification'. So far Paul has expounded righteousness. Now he introduces *sanctification*. The preposition *eis* indicates the goal or purpose of the transference. The term primarily means *belonging to God*, but has moral implications. The term *sanctification* first occurred in 1 Thessalonians 4.3, 4, 7 and 1 Corinthians 1.30, and then in Romans 6.19 and 22. On the other hand the adjective *hagios*, usually in the sense of *saints*, appears a dozen times in 1 Corinthians, and occurs in Romans 1.2, 7; 5.5; 7.12; 8.27; 9.1; as well as in other epistles. In Romans 5.5 it was used of the Holy Spirit. Robertson observes concerning sanctification: 'It is a life-process of consecration, not an instantaneous act.'[50]

Robertson's argument is much debated, especially among Pentecostals. I have given much space to discussing it in my book *The Holy Spirit*. I note, for example, that Zinzendorf accused John Wesley of confusing two senses of sanctification. One sense of the word (as here in Paul) comes with being-in-Christ; the other (as also in Paul) depends on a long process of the Holy Spirit's work.[51] The Hebrew for holiness (*q-d-sh*) stands in contrast to *common* or *profane* (*chōl*), just as Greek *hagios* stands in contrast to *koinos*. Clearly all Christians are holy or sanctified in this primary sense. All Christians belong to the Lord. Nevertheless *to become holy*, *to grow in holiness*, is also the object of God's command. Luther lamented that the 'radical reformers' did not understand it as a progressive struggle to 'become like Christ'. O. R. Jones defined growth in holiness as 'a disposition to behave in a certain way with respect to certain situations', which requires 'undaunted perseverance and unflinching decision'.[52]

Paul concludes by reinforcing the consequences of each kind of 'slavery'. Fitzmyer comments, 'One can be deluded by what one thinks is freedom', which is the point of verse 20.[53] To be slaves of sin and free of righteousness leads to moral anarchy, as described in Romans 1.18–32. In verse 21 Paul invites self-reflection: what advantage resulted from the old slavery?

---

[50] Robertson, *Word Pictures*, vol. 4, p. 365.

[51] Thiselton, Anthony C., *The Holy Spirit: In Biblical Teaching, through the Centuries, and Today* (Grand Rapids: Eerdmans, and London: SPCK, 2013), p. 405.

[52] Jones, O. R., *The Concept of Holiness* (London: Allen & Unwin, and New York: Macmillan, 1961), pp. 44 and 69; and Webster, John, *Holiness* (London: SCM, and Grand Rapids: Eerdmans, 2003), throughout.

[53] Fitzmyer, *Romans*, p. 451.

Strictly he uses the continuous imperfect: *tina oun karpon eichete tote*; 'What fruit then *used you to have* at that time? The memory of this brings shame, and their value seems like emptiness and ashes!'

A textual variant occurs in the placing of the question mark. The UBS, following Theodore of Mopsuestia, places it after 'then', understanding verse 21b as Paul's answer. The Vulgate understands the first two parts of verse 21 as a question, restricting Paul's answer to verse 21c. NRSV appears to favour the latter, with P[94], $\aleph^2$, B, D* and F; while $\aleph$*, A, C, D[2] and 33 place the question mark after 'them'. Godet and Jewett regard the first alternative as weakening the force of the diatribe, and disguising 'the neat contrast between the fruit of freedom from righteousness in v. 21a and the fruit of freedom from sin in v. 22'.[54] Cranfield also has 'not much doubt' about the reading adopted by Theodore.[55] Calvin comments:

> The light of the Lord alone can open our eyes to behold the filthiness which lies hid in our flesh. He only, then, is imbued with the principles of Christian philosophy, who has well learnt to be really displeased with himself, and to be confounded with shame for his own wretchedness.[56]

In verse 22 sanctification is again prominent. It replaces 'lawlessness', and culminates in eternal life. Käsemann stresses both 'the break between past and present' and 'the ethical development of character', the twin aspects of holiness.[57]

Paul reaches the climax in verse 23: 'The wages [Greek *to opsōnia*] of sin is death, but the free gift [*to charisma*] of God is eternal life'. Sin is personified as the employer paying wages, like 'a general who pays wages to his soldiers'.[58] God, however, does not pay wages, but *gives a free gift*, which is eternal life. Tertullian contrasted 'wages' for the soldiers with the emperor's or general's largesse (Latin *donativum*).[59] The contrasts of verses 16–23 reach their climax in the double contrast between *unmotivated fresh grace*, and reaping the 'wages' of *past acts and attitudes*.

---

[54] Jewett, *Romans*, p. 422.
[55] Cranfield, *Romans*, vol. 1, p. 328.
[56] Calvin, John, *Calvin's Bible Commentaries: Romans* (London: Forgotten Books, 2007 [1847]), p. 177.
[57] Käsemann, Ernst, *Commentary on Romans* (London: SCM, 1980), p. 185.
[58] Cranfield, *Romans*, vol. 1, p. 329.
[59] Tertullian, *The Resurrection of the Flesh*, 47 (Eng., ANF, vol. 3, p. 580).

15

Free from the condemnation of the law (7.1–25)

Paul's argument about the law runs throughout Romans 7. It can be divided into three stages. First, he cites the analogy of the effect of death on legal liability (7.1–3), and applies it to the Christian transference to the new order in Christ (7.4–6). Second, Paul insists that the *law as such* does not *cause* sin, but nevertheless has *provocative effects* (7.7–13). Third, he expounds the impotence of the law to call forth the good, and its tendency to leave humankind in a 'wretched' state (v. 24). This carries us to the end of the chapter (7.14–25). Romans 7 belongs integrally to the argument of the epistle.

The meaning of the term 'the law' is complex, as we have already noted. A superficial reading of Paul may lead us to think that he is being inconsistent, but this is largely due to his using the term *the law* with different meanings. For example, he calls it one of Israel's privileges in Romans 9.4; and (in Gal. 3.24) a 'tutor' (Greek *paidagōgus*) to bring us to Christ. On the other hand it multiplies law-breaking in Romans 5.20; while in Galatians 3.1, reliance on the law is a curse.

Whiteley made some simple working distinctions some years ago, although since that time Sanders, Dunn and others have made more nuanced distinctions. Whiteley suggested that a *first* meaning of the law (Greek *nomos*) is *Holy Scripture* (1 Cor. 14.21). It may in this sense denote God's supreme revelation. It is God's gift, and can be a source of thanksgiving. Thus Paul calls it 'holy and just and good' (7.12).[1] Particular meanings emerge within this first category. For instance, 'the law' may denote *the Law of Moses*, or the Pentateuch, or a source of ethical guidance and knowledge of God. Wright stresses that Paul provides a 'vindication of the Torah'.[2] As Whiteley expresses it, it can in a *second* sense be '*a moral indicator*', as when Paul asserts in Romans 3.20: 'No human being can be justified in the sight of God for having kept the law: law brings only consciousness of sin' (Rom. 7.7 and 5.13).[3] Whiteley adds, 'Wrongdoing . . . must be crystallized into

[1] Whiteley, D. E. H., *The Theology of St. Paul* (Oxford: Blackwell, 1970), p. 79.
[2] Wright, N. T., 'Romans' in the *New Interpreter's Bible* (*NIB*) (Nashville: Abingdon, 2002), vol. 10, p. 551.
[3] Whiteley, *Theology of St. Paul*, p. 80.

conscious sin.' On top of these fundamental two differences of meanings, *third*, the law is not the *exclusive* possession of Israel, but can, in another sense, be extended to Gentiles. *Fourth*, in Christ the '*curse of the law*' (Gal. 3.13) is abrogated in the new creation, as a means of justification before God.

Leenhardt suggests all these features characterize the law in Romans 7. First, he says, 'The law itself does not claim more than a temporary function'; second, it 'does not pretend to do more than provide knowledge of what sin is'; and third, 'Experience confirms the powerlessness of the law to commit man decisively to the way of holiness and obedience.'[4]

These are only introductory comments. Sanders, Dunn and Wright have written at great length on the subject, as well as a host of others, including Hübner, Räisänen and many more. From within Judaism, Schoeps has made a notable contribution, and within 'Messianic Jewish' (Christian Jewish) theology, Harvey offers a careful survey of views.[5]

The analogy of death as freedom from legal liability (7.1–6)

In verses 1–3 Paul sets out the analogy of a married woman's being free from the law when her husband dies. In verses 4–6 he explains the theological applications. It is easily forgotten how often Paul appeals to analogies for clarification or easier communication. His style is unfavourably compared with the use of parables by Jesus. But in his book on the subject, Gale sets out 34 uses of analogy in the generally undisputed letters of Paul.[6] He cites six in Romans, ten in 1 Corinthians, nine in 2 Corinthians and four in Galatians. He uses *analogy* 'to refer to any picture of a phenomenon or life-situation that is presented to the reader ... to suggest ... something that corresponds to what is being said.'[7] In Romans he considers

---

[4] Leenhardt, Franz J., *The Epistle to the Romans* (London: Lutterworth, 1961), p. 177.

[5] Sanders, E. P., *Paul, the Law, and the Jewish People* (Philadelphia: Fortress, 1983); Sanders, *Jesus and Judaism* (London: SCM, 1985), pp. 245–69; Sanders, *Paul and Palestinian Judaism* (London: SCM, 1977), pp. 475–97; Dunn, J. D. G., *Paul and the Mosaic Law* (Tübingen: Mohr, 1998; WUNT 89); Dunn, James D. G., *The Theology of Paul the Apostle* (Edinburgh: T & T Clark, 1998), pp. 128–61; Wright, N. T., *Paul and the Faithfulness of God* (London: SPCK, 2013), Part III, pp. 851–79; 892–914; 1002–18; 1033–4; and 1436–7; Hübner, H., *Law in Paul's Thought* (Edinburgh: T & T Clark, 1984); Räisänen, Heikki, *Paul and the Law* (Tübingen: Mohr, 1983; WUNT 29); Räisänen, *Jesus, Paul, and the Torah* (Sheffield: Sheffield Academic Press, 1992); Thielman, F., *Paul and the Law: A Contextual Approach* (Downers Grove, IL: IVP, 1994); Schoeps, H. J., *Paul: A Theology of the Apostle in the Light of Jewish History* (London: Lutterworth, 1961), pp. 168–218; and Harvey, Richard, *Mapping Messianic Jewish Theology* (Milton Keynes and Colorado Springs: Paternoster, 2009), pp. 140–222.

[6] Gale, Herbert M., *The Use of Analogy in the Letters of Paul* (Philadelphia: Westminster, 1964); see also Straub, Werner, *Die Bildersprache des Apostels Paulus* (Tübingen: Mohr, 1937).

[7] Gale, *Use of Analogy*, p. 18.

the figure of Abraham (4.4); attitudes towards self-sacrifice (5.7); several images for not continuing in sin so that grace may abound (6.1–14); analogies from slavery (6.15–23); the analogy of marriage and death (7.1–6); the potter and the clay (9.20–24); and the first fruits and the branches (11.16–24).[8]

On 7.1–6, Gale declares, 'Paul now introduces the picture of marriage to show that the Christian lives no longer in that condition where law – and human sin – prevails.'[9] Law and sin are inextricably bound together. The law is 'binding' (Greek *kurieuei, has dominion*) only while the person in question is alive. If a wife lives with another man while her husband is alive, she will be called 'an adulteress' (v. 3). But if the husband has died, she may 'belong to another' (v. 4). Nevertheless, Gale concludes, the analogies cannot be pressed in every detail, but 'in a very general way only'.[10]

In 7.1 'the law is binding', as we noted, translates *kurieuei (reigns over)*. Some take 'those who know the law' to include Gentile readers.[11] Most contemporary commentators, however, insist that Paul is appealing to the Jewish Torah.[12] Paul assumes a reasonable knowledge of the Torah among Gentile Christians, because the OT is the Christian 'Bible'. Some treat this analogy as an allegory, with identifications of the wife (v. 2) as the true self, the husband as fallen humanity, and so on. In Jewish law the wife would not be free to remarry immediately on the death of her husband; she would have to wait for a year to elapse. The important principle is that 'she is discharged from the law concerning the husband' (v. 2). 'The law concerning the husband' (v. 2 NRSV) is simply a genitive in Greek (*tou nomou tou andros*). The NRSV makes the most obvious interpretation. Barrett interprets the two terms as in apposition, as if the husband represents the law, but Cranfield rejects this as 'unlikely'.[13]

In verse 3 the Greek may seem complex. But a straightforward genitive absolute renders 'while her husband is alive'. Paul used this analogy in 1 Corinthians 7.39–40. In verse 4 Paul applies what was formulated as a

[8] Gale, *Use of Analogy*, pp. 173–215.

[9] Gale, *Use of Analogy*, p. 190.

[10] Gale, *Use of Analogy*, p. 192.

[11] Käsemann, Ernst, *Commentary on Romans* (London: SCM, 1980), p. 187; Sanday, William, and Headlam, Arthur C., *Critical and Exegetical Commentary on the Epistle to the Romans* (Edinburgh: T & T Clark, 1902; ICC), p. 172.

[12] Dunn, James D. G., *Romans 1—8* (Dallas: Word, 1988; WBC 38), p. 359; Jewett, Robert, *Romans: A Commentary* (Minneapolis: Fortress, 2007; Hermeneia), p. 430; Fitzmyer, Joseph A., *Romans: A New Translation with Introduction and Commentary* (New York: Doubleday, 1992; AB 33), p. 455.

[13] Barrett, C. K., *The Epistle to the Romans* (London: Black, 1957), p. 136; Cranfield, C. E. B., *A Critical and Exegetical Commentary on the Epistle to the Romans*, vol. 1 (Edinburgh: T & T Clark, 1975; ICC), p. 333.

principle in verses 2–3 to the Christian life. 'You have died to the law' picks up the theme of Romans 6.2, in which believers have died to sin. This event leaves open the way to Christ-union. The phrase 'to another, to him who has been raised from the dead' (v. 4) denotes union with the glorified Christ, whom God raised from the dead. In union with the raised Christ we might therefore 'bear fruit for God.' This may further press the analogy with marriage, which leads to 'bearing fruit', or producing children, from this union.

In verses 5–6 Paul recapitulates his argument. In verse 5 he reminds his readers that under their now obsolete regime, 'while we were living in the flesh', the law simply aroused their sinful passions. In verse 6 Paul assures his readers that they are now 'dead' to their former slavery. NRSV 'which held us captive' marks Paul's use of the imperfect *kateichometha*, and could therefore more accurately be translated 'which *used to* hold us captive'. Paul's uses of the term *flesh* are many-sided. We distinguish between (i) *physical flesh* as a mode of existence; (ii) the *weakness* of the flesh; and (iii) *flesh* in the full *theological sense*. Bultmann rightly defines this third sense as 'trust in oneself as being able to procure life by the use of the earthly and through one's own strength' (Rom. 8.7), and 'the self-reliant attitude of the man who puts his trust in his own strength'.[14] Jewett argues that in 7.5 the full theological sense is most likely, to convey an attitude of sin (Rom. 7.14).[15]

In verse 6, by contrast, Paul uses the eschatological '*now*' which will be resumed in 8.1. NRSV 'We are discharged from the law' represents Greek *katērgēthēmen*, for which Barrett suggests 'We are done with the law'. Where NRSV has '*dead* to that which held us captive', ℵ, A, B and C (the best MSS) read *dying* (*apothanontes*); while D, G and Old Latin read *of death* (*tou thanatou*). Paul introduces 'the new life of the Spirit', which will be expounded in Romans 8. As in 2 Corinthians 3.6–8, Spirit and 'letter' are parallel here with 'new' and 'old'. Cranfield observes that Paul does not oppose the law as such (7.14), but 'the *misuse* of the law'.[16]

The provocative effects of the law (7.7–13)

Paul clarifies in detail his main theses about the law. The rhetorical 'What then should we say?' continues the diatribe style, by addressing

---

[14] Bultmann, Rudolf, *Theology of the New Testament*, vol. 1 (London: SCM, 1952), pp. 239 and 240; cf. pp. 232–46; Jewett, Robert, *Paul's Anthropological Terms* (Leiden: Brill, 1971), pp. 49–166 and 154–6.
[15] Jewett, *Romans*, p. 436; Fitzmyer, *Romans*, p. 459.
[16] Cranfield, *Romans*, vol. 1, pp. 339–40; Dunn, *Romans 1—8*, p. 373.

objections from hypothetical opponents. The crux of these objections would be that 'the law is sin'. But yet again Paul responds with his frequent phrase in Greek, *mē genoito*, 'Perish the thought!' The crucial distinction is between *causing* sin, and *making us aware* of what sin is. Hence if there were no law, 'I would not have known sin' (v. 7). For example, 'I would not have known what it is to covet' (v. 7). In this sense, 'Apart from the law sin lies dead' (v. 8).

Paul's use of 'I' in this chapter has raised extensive debate about whom Paul identifies. Wright is illuminating on this issue. He comments,

> The 'I' of 7.7–25, which on any showing is a remarkable rhetorical feature, may then be approached within Paul's two main *controlling narratives*: (a) the story of Adam and the Messiah, and (b) the new exodus. Torah intrudes within the first [i.e. Adam and Christ] (5:20); Sinai is a key moment in the second. Within these, Paul appears to be speaking of *Israel*: of Israel under the Torah.[17]

He later observes,

> The point of the 'I' as a rhetorical device then becomes clear . . . Such language could be used for purposes *other than* literal descriptions of *one's own actual experience* . . . It is a way of not saying 'they', of not distancing himself from the problem, from the plight of Israel.[18]

Wright also draws attention to the change between the past tense in verses 7–12 and the present tense in verses 14–25.

Many of the Greek Fathers, however, understood 'I' to represent Paul's *autobiographical* experiences before his conversion, or pre-Christian experience in general; while many modern scholars, especially since Dodd, Bultmann and Kümmel, take it to refer to the pre-Christian life in general, in a *corporate, not autobiographical* sense. In the course of devoting six pages to the issue, Leenhardt concludes, 'In speaking of himself [Paul] spoke of man in general; when he said "I", he implied "we" . . . the heirs of Adam . . . in their collective condition.'[19] Barrett and Black agree: 'I' could represent 'any one in general'.[20]

The 'autobiographical' or 'psychological' understanding of 'I' is discredited by modern commentators. Fitzmyer regards it as a 'debatable' proposal; Cranfield says that it 'should surely be rejected'; and Käsemann

---

[17] Wright, 'Romans', *NIB*, vol. 10, p. 552 (my italics).
[18] Wright, 'Romans', *NIB*, vol. 10, p. 533 (my italics).
[19] Leenhardt, *Romans*, p. 184.
[20] Barrett, *Romans*, p. 152; Black, Matthew, *Romans* (London: Oliphants, 1973; NCB), p. 101.

insists, 'We do not have an autobiographical reminiscence.'[21] The nearest to the autobiographical approach today is probably Theissen, who argues that the 'I' in Romans 7 'combined personal and typical traits'.[22] Jewett makes the important point that even where he refers to a pre-Christian experience, Paul does so *only* in the light of *post*-Christian insights.[23] He also allows that 'Paul points explicitly to his own personal experience.'[24] The most probable solution is that this is not 'pure' autobiography, but that the 'rhetorical "I"' reflects the experience of both Paul and others. He also has to play more than one role.

Wright is quite specific about verse 11: 'Sin . . . deceived me'. He convincingly understands this as referring to the fall of Genesis 3, especially Genesis 3.13, in conjunction with Paul's citation of Adam in Romans 5.12–21. This also suggests that his reference to 'covet' in verse 7 refers not to the tenth commandment of Exodus 20.17 and Deuteronomy 5.21, but to the wider, primal sin of 'desire' or 'grasping what is not mine'. Thus sin seized 'an opportunity in the commandment'. Adam or humankind found God's law provocative, and yielded to deception and death.

Paul has been so eager to distinguish the law from sin that he states categorically in verse 12, 'The law is holy, and the commandment is holy and just and good.' In verse 11 (as in v. 8) Greek *aphormē* denotes a *starting point* or *handle* which sin can use. As such, the law is not to blame for humanity's predicament. This verse fits well with Sanders' argument about the law in Judaism and the 'New Perspective', and predictably Dunn confirms this. He comments, 'In describing the law as *hagios* [holy], Paul could hardly use a stronger word to affirm the law as God's law . . . Paul's critique of the law [is] understood within the Judaism of his own day.'[25] The commandment is 'just and good' because it defines the covenant relation with God. Watson believes that these adjectives are 'damning the law with faint praise'.[26] In the Puritan tradition Kevan spoke rightly of *The Grace of Law*, and attacks the infiltration of antinomianism into Puritan theology.[27]

This middle section of the chapter concludes with the lengthy verse 13. Could these arguments, Paul begins, imply that what is good can 'bring

---

[21] Fitzmyer, *Romans*, p. 463; Cranfield, *Romans*, vol. 1, p. 342; Käsemann, *Romans*, p. 192.

[22] Theissen, Gerd, *Psychological Aspects of Pauline Theology* (Eng., Edinburgh: T & T Clark, 1987), p. 201.

[23] Jewett, *Romans*, p. 443.

[24] Jewett, *Romans*, p. 450.

[25] Dunn, *Romans 1—8*, p. 385.

[26] Watson, Francis, *Paul, Judaism, and the Gentiles* (Cambridge: CUP, 1986; SNTSMS 56), p. 156.

[27] Kevan, Ernest F., *The Grace of Law: A Study in Puritan Theology* (Grand Rapids: Baker, 2003 [1965]).

death to me?' Again he replies, 'Perish the thought!' (v. 13a). Again he distinguishes the law as such from sin: 'It was sin, working death in me' (v. 13b). The law served to 'show' *sin to be sin* (v. 13c). This led to sin 'beyond measure' (v. 13d, Greek *kath' huperbolēn*). Again, the verse may look back to 5.20–21. Sin 'abounds', but to attribute this to God's gift of the law is superficial. Paul may be indicating that Gentile Christians should not belittle Jewish Christians' pride in the law as God's gift. Wright compares this with Romans 8.3: the law can deal with sin 'fully and finally', so that Christians may escape the chain of cause and effect in the effects of the law.[28] Paul does not imply what Marcion taught in the second century, namely that law and gospel are simply contrary to each other. The law, Paul asserts, *serves God's deepest purposes.*

The importance of the law to call forth good (7.14–25)

Fitzmyer, Nygren and a multiplicity of others call attention to the contrast between the past tense in 7.7–13 and the present tense in 7.14–25.[29] Nygren vehemently insists that chapter 7.14–25 does 'not refer to the pre-Christian life . . . Paul is here describing a divided and discordant state of the soul which characterizes the Christian life.'[30] Only the Christian in Paul's judgement 'delight[s] in the law of God in [his or her] inmost self' (7.22); nevertheless, together with all creation believers still 'groan inwardly while we wait for adoption, the redemption of our bodies' (8.23).

Because the law is from God, it is 'spiritual' (7.14), while 'I' am 'of the flesh' (Greek *sarkinos*), 'sold . . . under sin' (v. 14). Käsemann regards *the flesh* as part of 'the cosmic fallenness of the world'.[31] It may mean 'behaving like ordinary human people', as in 1 Corinthians 3.1.[32] Nygren points out that the Christian is '*not* isolated from the influence of the Spirit', but nevertheless 'belongs at the same time to both the new and the old aeons'.[33] However, could 'sold into slavery under sin' ever describe the Christian's present existence?

---

[28] Wright, 'Romans' in *NIB*, vol. 10, p. 566.

[29] Fitzmyer, *Romans*, p. 473; Knox, John, 'Romans', *Interpreter's Bible* (*IB*) (Nashville: Abingdon, 1954), vol. 9, p. 499; Nygren, Anders, *Commentary on Romans* (London: SCM, 1952), pp. 292–3.

[30] Nygren, *Romans*, p. 292.

[31] Käsemann, *Romans*, p. 199.

[32] Thiselton, Anthony C., *The First Epistle to the Corinthians: A Commentary on the Greek Text* (Grand Rapids: Eerdmans, and Carlisle: Paternoster, 2000; NIGTC), pp. 287–93; Danker, Frederick, *A Greek-English Lexicon of the New Testament and Other Early Christian Literature* (BDAG) (Chicago and London: University of Chicago Press, 3rd edn, 2000), p. 914.

[33] Nygren, *Romans*, pp. 295 and 296 (his italics).

Spiritual in Paul almost always denotes 'of the Holy Spirit', as in 1 Corinthians 2.12–16 and 15.44. Dunn understands the phrase to refer to 'everyman in the present' as embodied in the flesh.[34] He adds, 'The split Paul is about to expound is one between the epochs of Adam and Christ'.[35] Cranfield insists that to treat this present passage and Romans 8 as concurrent, not sequential, does justice 'to the facts of Christian living . . . only if we resolutely hold chapters 7 and 8 together . . . as . . . two contemporaneous realities'.[36] He concludes, 'The more seriously a Christian strives to live from grace . . . *the more sensitive he becomes to the fact of his continuing sinfulness*'.[37] This entirely accords with Luther's comments. He writes, 'The spiritual and wise man . . . knows that he is carnal, and he is displeased with himself; indeed he hates himself and praises the Law of God, which he recognizes because he is spiritual'.[38] Similarly Calvin declares, 'He [Paul] sets before us an example in a regenerate man, in whom the remnants of the flesh are wholly contrary to the law of the Lord, while the spirit would gladly obey it'.[39]

Paul further explains this principle in verse 15: 'I do not do what I want, but I do the very thing I hate.' Cranfield comments, 'Verses 15–23 as a whole . . . explain what it means to be "sold under sin".'[40] The Greek is 'I do not know' (v. 15, *ou ginōskō*), but can mean, 'I do not understand' (NRSV). Robertson observes, 'The dual life pictured here by Paul finds an echo in us all'.[41] Wright regards this as Paul's 'explanation' of previous verses, pointing out that the NRSV and NIV mistakenly omit the word 'for' (*gar*) at the beginning of verse 15.[42] The 'I', he observes, is intellectually puzzled by its behaviour. But Wright has more doubts than Cranfield in seeing verses 15–16 as referring to *conflict* within the Christian. He reserves Paul's focus on the 'I' to 7.13–20.[43] It does not seem to me that these views are mutually exclusive, rather than complementary, given the range of Paul's concerns.

Verses 16–17 recount Paul's aversion to his sinful acts. In view of the prominence of *confession* at virtually every church service, this should not

---

[34] Dunn, *Romans 1—8*, p. 387.

[35] Dunn, *Romans 1—8*, p. 388.

[36] Cranfield, *Romans*, vol. 1, p. 356.

[37] Cranfield, *Romans*, vol. 1, p. 358 (my italics).

[38] Luther, Martin, *Commentary on Romans* (Grand Rapids: Kregel, 1954; repr. 1976), p. 112.

[39] Calvin, John, *Calvin's Bible Commentaries: Romans* (London: Forgotten Books, 2007 [1847]), p. 191.

[40] Cranfield, *Romans*, vol. 1, p. 358.

[41] Robertson, A. T., *Word Pictures in the New Testament, vol. 4: Romans* (New York: R. Smith, 1931), p. 369.

[42] Wright, 'Romans', *NIB*, vol. 10, p. 566.

[43] Wright, 'Romans', *NIB*, vol. 10, p. 567.

surprise us. But the force which pulls at the Christian is 'external', even though the believer remains responsible for his or her actions. 'Within' the Christian, he or she finds acknowledgement of the rightness of God's commandments, through the work of the Holy Spirit. It is no longer the 'I' who 'brings about' the sinful action; but indwelling sin.[44] Paul's verses demonstrate that sin involves a deep *attitude of mind*, not simply an act. 'I' remains responsible for it. Dunn comments: 'The ambivalence of the imagery reflects the ambivalence of the experience of sin – always as a power exercising great compulsion on the individual.'[45] It is *less two 'selves'* in conflict, than *will and action in conflict*. Nygren comments, 'The will to do right is always present in him, but he steadily falls short in performance.'[46]

In verse 18 Paul may well speak of 'me', as this is viewed apart from God. The major Reformers called this 'total depravity', *not* meaning 'wholly sinful', but sinful *in every aspect*. This verse repeats the same contrast between will and deed, and verses 19–20 repeat it again. Paul is preparing for the need for the Holy Spirit to be active in our hearts, which Paul expounds in chapter 8.

In verse 21 the most controversial issue is the meaning of *law*. Probably the majority, including Fitzmyer, Danker, Denney, Käsemann, Murray, Black and others, regard it as meaning *principle* (as NEB and JB).[47] Dunn, however, considers that Paul 'returns to his main apologetic concern with the law' as the Jewish law; as does Wright.[48] Jewett goes further, speaking of 'nomistic zealotism'.[49] Barrett and Moffatt are inclined to this view. Each side presses its case with vigour. Is the practical difference as crucial as the passion of the debate seems to suggest?

'I delight' (v. 22 NRSV) translates Greek *sunēdomai*.[50] It technically means 'rejoicing with' (*sun-*), so Jewett regards this as rejoicing 'with fellow Pharisees in the performance of the law'.[51] If he is right, this underlines Paul's concern to unite Jewish and Gentile Christians. Psalm 19.8 declares,

---

[44] Danker, BDAG, p. 531.

[45] Dunn, *Romans 1—8*, p. 390.

[46] Nygren, *Romans*, p. 293.

[47] Whiteley, *Theology of St. Paul*, p. 79; Fitzmyer, *Romans*, p. 475; Danker, BDAG, p. 542; Godet, F. L., *Commentary on St. Paul's Epistle to the Romans* (New York: Funk & Wagnalls, 1883), pp. 286–7; Sanday and Headlam, *Romans*, p. 182; Käsemann, *Romans*, p. 205; Murray, John, *The Epistle to the Romans* (Grand Rapids: Eerdmans, 1997), p. 205; Black, *Romans*, p. 107.

[48] Dunn, *Romans 1—8*, p. 392; Wright, 'Romans', *NIB*, vol. 10, p. 570.

[49] Jewett, *Romans*, p. 469.

[50] Danker, BDAG, p. 971.

[51] Jewett, *Romans*, p. 469.

'Blessed is the person . . . who delights in his commandments.' 'My inmost self' (NRSV) has long been the subject of research. Paul does *not share a dualistic or partitive view of human nature with most Greek philosophers.* But he does use this phrase, 'inmost self', even if rarely (2 Cor. 4.16–18). In the nineteenth century Baur identified the other self with the body, and the inmost self with the mind, and Lüdemann developed this. But in the twentieth century Bultmann and Stacey rejected this approach as too Platonic and dualistic for Paul. Jewett, however, initially insisted that Paul took over these terms from 'Corinthian Gnostics'.[52] But in his more recent commentary some 36 years later, he seems to have abandoned this view.[53] Wright insists that Paul is being 'deliberately paradoxical'.[54]

In verse 23 'another law' raises once more the debate about the meaning of *law*. Whiteley and Fitzmyer again translate it as 'principle', but this time Fitzmyer calls it 'none other than indwelling sin'.[55] On the other hand 'the law of my mind' recognizes the good as God's will. The oldest MSS (ℵ, B, D, G, 33) read *en tō nomō*, but A and C omit the preposition. 'Captive' recalls 'sold under sin' (7.14).

The last verses of the chapter (vv. 24–25) constitute a bridge to the joyous contrast of chapter 8. The captivity to sin makes a person *wretched* (Greek *talaipōros*) or miserable.[56] The best exposition of this word, and its use in Romans 7.24, comes from Pannenberg. He wrote,

> The root of this misery lies in death's opposition to our human destiny of fellowship with *God* . . . Misery, then, is the lot of those who are deprived of the fellowship with God that is the destiny of human life . . . To speak of human misery is better than using the classical doctrine of sin to describe our situation of lostness when we are far from God. The term 'misery' sums up our detachment from God.[57]

Nygren and Barrett argue that people are 'wretched' because they are subject to two sets of forces.[58] But, Nygren adds, this is not a cry of despair because of what follows it. Yet Jewett flatly rejects Nygren's 'conflict' interpretation. He writes,

---

[52] Jewett, *Paul's Anthropological Terms*, pp. 396–401 and 460.

[53] Jewett, *Romans*, p. 470.

[54] Wright, 'Romans', *NIB*, vol. 10, p. 571.

[55] Fitzmyer, *Romans*, p. 476.

[56] Danker, BDAG, p. 988.

[57] Pannenberg, Wolfhart, *Systematic Theology* (3 vols, Edinburgh: T & T Clark, and Grand Rapids: Eerdmans, 1991–8), vol. 2, pp. 178–9.

[58] Nygren, *Romans*, p. 301; Barrett, *Romans*, p. 151.

Paul's exclamation cannot refer to the tension between the two aeons . . . The sentiment of hopeless misery resonates with Paul's admission in 1 Cor. 15:9, 'For I am . . . unfit to be called an apostle, because I persecuted the church of Christ.'[59]

'Body of death' (v. 24) is also a source of debate. Barrett understands it as 'the body of human nature'.[60] Robinson insists that it must denote the corporate 'body' of 'the whole mass of fallen human nature in which we share as men [human beings]'.[61] Further, Dodd and Jewett clash head-on about the implied answer to the rhetorical question. Jewett claims, 'The rhetorical question about who can deliver such a miserable person is posed in such a way as to require the answer, "Nobody can!" '[62] Dodd asserts, 'It would stultify his [Paul's] whole argument if he now confessed that at the moment of writing he was a miserable wretch . . . When Paul could do nothing, God did everything for him.'[63]

Dodd's case is strengthened by his firm insistence that verse 25a, 'Thanks be to God through Jesus Christ our Lord', was originally in Paul's 'rapid dictation' intended to come as the grand climax after verse 24, while verse 25b, 'with my mind I am a slave to the law of God, but with my flesh I am a slave to the law of sin', came before the triumphant thanksgiving. He admits *that no textual MS supports this.* But he follows Moffatt's translation which reflects the supposedly 'logical position'.[64] He argues that a copyist mistook a marginal note which incorporated verse 25b, and copied it into the text *after* the thanksgiving. Fitzmyer agrees, 'It is certainly a more logical place for it'; the text as it stands is 'scarcely conceivable'.[65] Dunn, however, thinks that Paul ends by stressing 'the eschatological tension' of the situation, and Wright agrees that verse 25b 'is not an anti-climax, nor . . . a dislocated verse'.[66] Cranfield wisely concludes that Dodd's suggestion 'cannot be ruled out', but remains 'exceedingly hazardous'.[67] For the Christian has *not yet already been entirely delivered* from sinful seductions. Nevertheless *the glorious themes of Romans 8 follow immediately.* He concludes, 'God will surely accomplish . . . *deliverance in His good time,* as reflected in v.25a.'[68]

---

[59] Jewett, *Romans*, p. 471.
[60] Barrett, *Romans*, p. 151.
[61] Robinson, J. A. T., *The Body: A Study in Pauline Theology* (London: SCM, 1952; SBT 5), p. 30.
[62] Jewett, *Romans*, pp. 471–2.
[63] Dodd, C. H., *The Epistle of Paul to the Romans* (London: Hodder & Stoughton, 1932), pp. 108 and 116.
[64] Dodd, *Romans*, p. 114.
[65] Fitzmyer, *Romans*, p. 477.
[66] Dunn, *Romans 1—8*, p. 411; Wright, 'Romans', *NIB*, vol. 10, p. 572.
[67] Cranfield, *Romans*, vol. 1, p. 368.
[68] Cranfield, *Romans*, vol. 1, p. 369 (my italics).

16

Life characterized by the Holy Spirit's indwelling (8.1–17)

The 'flesh' and the Spirit (8.1–8)

The theme which Paul announced in 5.1–11 was first developed negatively from 5.12 to 7.24, and then becomes expounded positively in chapter 8. The Christian is freed from the death of sin (5.12–21), from death in relation to sin (ch. 6) and from the condemnation of the law (ch. 7). Now Paul begins, 'There is therefore now [Greek *ara nun*) no condemnation for those who are in Christ Jesus.' Chapter 8 is *thoroughly Trinitarian* because God has purposed this destiny, while it is 'in Christ and is effected by the Holy Spirit.' In 8.26 Christians address prayers *to God by* the agency of the Spirit *through* Christ. The word 'Spirit' occurs 21 times in chapter 8, in contrast to only five times in chapters 1—7, and eight times in chapters 9—16. The believer is characterized by the indwelling of God's Spirit. For all 21 uses of *pneuma*, Cranfield rightly judges the word to refer to the Holy Spirit.[1]

As in the closing verses of chapter 7, some have proposed that 8.1 should be located after 8.2, which might seem to link more clearly with 7.1–25. But Wilckens has replied that 8.2 is tightly connected with 8.3 also.[2] MS readings support the traditional sequence, and 8.1 does run on from 7.25a. Certainly 8.1 makes excellent sense where it stands. 'Now' means since Christ has died and been raised once-for-all.

'The law of the Spirit of life' (v. 2) returns us to the debate about the different meanings of *law*. The majority of scholars understand it here as *principle* (see above under 7.21). Murray, Nygren, Leenhardt, Käsemann and Fitzmyer could not make sense of the verse if *law* refers to the Mosaic law.[3] Cranfield, Dunn, Wright, Hübner and Jewett, however, find no problem

---

[1] Cranfield, C. E. B., *A Critical and Exegetical Commentary on the Epistle to the Romans*, vol. 1 (Edinburgh: T & T Clark, 1975; ICC), p. 371.

[2] Wilckens, Ulrich, *Der Brief an die Römer* (3 vols, Zurich: Benzinger, 1978–82; EKKNT), vol. 2, p. 119.

[3] Leenhardt, Franz J., *The Epistle to the Romans* (London: Lutterworth, 1961), pp. 201–2; Nygren, Anders, *Commentary on Romans* (London: SCM, 1952), p. 312; Käsemann, Ernst, *Commentary on Romans* (London: SCM, 1980), p. 216; Fitzmyer, Joseph A., *Romans: A New Translation with Introduction and Commentary* (New York: Doubleday, 1992; AB 33), pp. 482–3.

in seeing why, as interpreted and applied by the Holy Spirit, the God-given law revealed in Scripture should not lead to life.[4] The syntax may seem awkward but one does not have to subscribe to the 'New Perspective' to believe that the Holy Spirit uses the biblical law for our sanctification and to please God. It was only because the whole of humankind was 'under sin' that the law became distorted.

Paul 'links the Torah and the Spirit in a positive way', not least because of 'the eschatological thrust of the context'.[5] This eschatological context helps us to interpret 'in Christ Jesus' in verse 1. Deissmann had interpreted the phrase mainly as one of religious *experience* or *mysticism*, but Wikenhauser has demonstrated that it is primarily *eschatological: we are transferred* 'in Christ' to the solidarity of the new creation.[6] The meaning of this phrase can vary in accordance with its context, and Weiss has identified up to five such contexts.

In verse 3 Paul summarizes the point of his previous arguments: 'For God has done what the law, weakened by the flesh, could not do'. This came about 'by sending his own Son in the likeness of sinful flesh, and to deal with sin'. There are three long-standing problems.

(1) The Greek syntax of 'what the law could not do' (*to adunaton tou nomou*) is awkward. It means strictly 'the impossibility of the law' which is probably 'nominative absolute' or 'accusative of general reference'. Robertson explains, '[It is] as if it had no syntactical connexion with the rest of the sentence.'[7] As an accusative of respect it could mean, 'As to the incapacity of the law, God brought about . . .' Whatever the syntax, the sense of the verse is clear.

(2) The most problematic phrase of verse 3 is 'in the likeness [*en homoiō-mati*] of sinful flesh'. Weiss claims that this 'grazes the later heresy of Docetism'.[8] But *likeness* qualifies *sin, not flesh*. In 2 Corinthians 5.21 Paul has asserted 'He [Christ] knew no sin'. As in Philippians 2.7 Paul is at pains to assert *Christ's full humanity in every respect, except that of sin*. The question: 'Was *Christ* really human?' misses the point. Since he is the model of sinless humanity, Christ poses to us the question: 'Are *we* really human?' Barrett states, 'Christ took precisely the same fallen nature that we ourselves

[4] Dunn, James D. G., *Romans 1—8* (Dallas: Word, 1988; WBC 38), pp. 416 and 417.

[5] Dunn, *Romans 1—8*, pp. 416 and 417.

[6] Deissmann, Adolf, *St Paul: A Study of Religious and Social History* (Ger., 1911: Eng., London: Hodder & Stoughton, 1926), p. 161; Wikenhauser, Alfred, *Pauline Mysticism* (New York: Herder, 1961), pp. 93 and 49–108.

[7] Robertson, A. T., *Word Pictures in the New Testament, vol. 4: Romans* (New York: R. Smith, 1931), p. 372.

[8] Weiss, Johannes, *Earliest Christianity* (New York: Harper, 1937), vol. 2, p. 490.

have, [but] he remained sinless because he constantly overcame a pro-
clivity to sin.'[9] Robinson underlines this point.[10] Paul's emphasis on
God's 'sending' and on Christ's full humanity and divine origin verges
on anticipating John.

(3) The phrase 'to deal with sin' (v. 3 NRSV) is probably a good translation, but the Greek is simply *peri hamartias*, followed by 'condemned
sin in the flesh' (*katekrinen tēn hamartian en tē sarki*). The first Greek
phrase is best understood as a compressed way of expressing 'God sent
his Son to deal with sin'; alternatively we can understand *sin* (*hamartia*)
as 'sin offering' (NIV), which it regularly denotes in the LXX. Cranfield
cites Leviticus 14.31 (LXX); Psalm 40.6 (39.7 LXX); and Isaiah 53.10 (LXX),
which respectively translate *chattā'th*, *chᵃthā'āh* and *'āshām*. NJB and
NEB translate 'as a sacrifice for sin'. Denney, Käsemann, Dunn and
Wright all support this understanding.[11] Although he does not adopt
this translation, Jewett urges that each way of understanding the word
comes to the same thing.[12] Thornton and Whiteley oppose the meaning
sin offering, and Cranfield doubts it.[13] But it does have precedent in
the LXX and perhaps 2 Corinthians 5.21. Whichever view we take, Paul
declares that God has broken the domain of sin through Jesus Christ
and his work.

If 8.3 has been *kerygma*, or gospel preaching, Fitzmyer views verses 4–7
as *catechesis*, or a pre-Pauline tradition of common accepted moral teaching.[14]
'Just requirement' (NRSV) is an accurate translation of Greek *dikaiōma*,
and these verses spell out how Christians are required to live (Hebrew
'walk'): 'not according to the flesh but according to the Spirit . . . [with]
minds on the things of the Spirit' (vv. 4–5). 'The law' clearly denotes the
will of God here. This common tradition for Christian instruction goes
back to Galatians 5.16–18, where the wording is almost identical: 'Live by
the Spirit . . . and do not gratify the desires of the flesh. For what the flesh
desires is opposed to the Spirit', as Paul continues in Romans 8.6–7. Francis
and Sampley similarly cite parallels in 1 Corinthians 3.1–4; 2 Corinthians
3.7–11; and Colossians 3.1–4.[15]

---

[9] Barrett, C. K., *The Epistle to the Romans* (London: Black, 1957), p. 156.

[10] Robinson, J. A. T., *The Human Face of God* (London: SCM, 1973), pp. 3–91, and throughout.

[11] Denney, James, 'Romans' in *Expositor's Greek Testament* (*ExGrT*) (5 vols, Grand Rapids: Eerdmans, [1910]), vol. 2, pp. 645–6; Wright, N. T., 'Romans' in the *New Interpreter's Bible* (*NIB*) (Nashville: Abingdon, 2002), vol. 10, pp. 578–9; Dunn, *Romans 1–8*, p. 422; Käsemann, *Romans*, p. 216.

[12] Jewett, Robert, *Romans: A Commentary* (Minneapolis: Fortress, 2007; Hermeneia), p. 486.

[13] Cranfield, *Romans*, vol. 1, p. 382.

[14] Fitzmyer, *Romans*, p. 487.

[15] Francis, F. O., and Sampley, J. P., *Pauline Parallels* (Minneapolis: Fortress, 2nd edn, 1984), p. 29.

Bultmann declares, '"Fixing the mind on the things of the flesh" is to be at war against God (Rom, 8:7) . . . "Flesh" is the self-reliant attitude of the man who puts his trust in his own strength and in that which is controllable by him.'[16] We refer the reader to the range of meanings of *flesh* under 7.5–6. Robinson calls *flesh* 'life in pursuit of its ends', 'trusting in ourselves' and 'human self-sufficiency'.[17] Jewett endorses this in his earlier work, and states that in Galatians it means '*self-reliance*' in the context of the law and (equally) *self-indulgence* in relation to antinomianism.[18] In several *other* contexts, but not here, 'the flesh' can be used to denote humankind, especially in its weakness and mortality.

In verse 6 'the mind [*to phronēma*] of the flesh' and 'the mind of the Spirit' denote the outlook, assumptions, values and purposes of the flesh and of the Holy Spirit respectively. Verse 7 then explains that the 'mind' of the flesh is at war with God, and desperately in need of reconciliation with him. Of 'those who walk according to the Spirit', Wright comments, 'Through the action of the Spirit in the present, those who are in Christ are walking on the road that will lead to the resurrection of the body.'[19] Walking according to the Spirit leads to life and peace (v. 6). The mind of the flesh is against the law and against God (vv. 7–8). Danker translates *phronēma* (NRSV 'mind') as 'the faculty of fixing one's mind on something, way of thinking, mind set'.[20]

Every Christian receives the Holy Spirit in union with Christ (8.9–11)

'You are in the Spirit' (v. 9): Paul makes it clear that this is the Spirit of God, the Holy Spirit. Fee argues painstakingly that in Paul the Holy Spirit denotes *not only* the Holy Spirit as such, *but also* God's own presence and power.[21] The term certainly does *not* denote some vague pantheistic 'force' or mystical 'spiritual' presence. Paul does not use the term in this way, nor is it generally a biblical concept. The second part of verse 9 specifically identifies the Holy Spirit as 'the Spirit of Christ', indwelling the believer. Here is another affinity with John. The Christ-like Holy Spirit of God

---

[16] Bultmann, Rudolf, *Theology of the New Testament*, vol. 1 (London: SCM, 1952), pp. 239 and 240.

[17] Robinson, J. A. T., *The Body: A Study in Pauline Theology* (London: SCM, 1952; SBT 5), pp. 25–6.

[18] Jewett, Robert, *Paul's Anthropological Terms* (Leiden: Brill, 1971), pp. 5–116.

[19] Wright, 'Romans', *NIB*, vol. 10, p. 581.

[20] Danker, Frederick, *A Greek-English Lexicon of the New Testament and Other Early Christian Literature* (BDAG) (Chicago and London: University of Chicago Press, 3rd edn, 2000), p. 1066.

[21] Fee, Gordon, *God's Empowering Presence: The Holy Spirit in the Letters of Paul* (Peabody: Hendrickson, 1994, and Milton Keynes: Paternoster, 1995), throughout.

brings about a change in orientation. 'In the flesh' cannot be purely loca-
tive, for Christians still live in the physical world, any more than 'in the
Spirit' indicates (here) 'an inspired state'.[22]

In his earlier book *Baptism in the Holy Spirit*, Dunn comments clearly
and bluntly on Romans 8.9: 'Anyone who does not have the Spirit of Christ
does not belong to him.' Dunn declares that this verse rules out the possibility *both* of a non-Christian's possessing the Spirit *and* of a Christian's
not possessing the Spirit.[23] The logic is parallel with that of Galatians 4.6,
'Because you are children, God has sent the Spirit of his Son into our
hearts, crying, "Abba! Father!"' Similarly Whiteley calls the Holy Spirit 'the
hallmark of the Christian'.[24] He and others admit that often in the OT the
Spirit is an 'occasional' gift, given to perform special tasks, as seen in the
judges (e.g. Othniel, Judg. 3.10; Gideon, Judg. 6.12–16; Jephthah, Judg.
11–29). Filson points out that the OT and Pauline schemes *overlap* and
are valid in the NT. He declares, 'It is likewise true that chosen individuals are given the Spirit for special tasks, but this does not mean that some
are left without the Spirit.'[25]

Paul's logic is that *if a person is 'in Christ', he or she must have received
the Holy Spirit*, not least because 'No one can say "Jesus is Lord" except by
the Holy Spirit' (1 Cor. 12.3). From the converse point of view, it is because
we are 'in Christ' that we can derive Christ's Sonship from him, whereby
the Holy Spirit enables the Christian to say 'Abba! Father!' (Rom. 8.15–16,
26). If we are 'in Christ', *God will raise us by his Spirit together with Christ*, in
the general resurrection (Rom. 8.11). Thornton magnificently writes, '*When
the Messiah was in the tomb, Israel was in the tomb . . . When Christ rose, the
Church rose from the dead*.'[26]

Nygren underlines differences between Paul and Greek thought here.
He comments, 'Tension will cease *not* [because] the spirit is to be freed
from the body – as many under the influence of the Greek way of think-
ing have held – but rather that the Spirit will give life to the body.'[27] The
Spirit is alive and gives life 'because of righteousness' (v. 10). Hence the
Holy Spirit becomes the *pledge or guarantee of the resurrection of believers*

[22] Dunn, *Romans 1—8*, p. 428.
[23] Dunn, James D. G., *Baptism in the Holy Spirit* (London: SCM, 1970), p. 95; and Thiselton, Anthony C., *The Holy Spirit: In Biblical Teaching, through the Centuries, and Today* (Grand Rapids: Eerdmans, and London: SPCK, 2013), p. 71.
[24] Whiteley, D. E. H., *The Theology of St. Paul* (Oxford: Blackwell, 1970), p. 124.
[25] Filson, Floyd V., *The New Testament against Its Environment* (London: SCM, 1950), p. 78.
[26] Thornton, Lionel S., *The Common Life in the Body of Christ* (London: Dacre, 3rd edn, 1950), p. 282 (my italics); the theme occurs on pp. 34–65, 66–95, 127–87, and throughout.
[27] Nygren, *Romans*, p. 323.

(v. 11). This verse refers to the *co-working of all persons of the Holy Trinity*. God the Father 'raised Jesus from the dead' through the agency of God the Holy Spirit. The Father and the Spirit co-act on Christ to raise him, and on believers who have union with Christ, the Son. Once God's purposes of grace have begun, *nothing can stop them*; hence the gift of the Holy Spirit is a *pledge* or *guarantee* of resurrection-with-Christ to all Christian believers.

The Holy Spirit 'dwells in you' (Greek *oikei en humin*) and thereby achieves our liberation. Dunn comments, 'The *oikeō* is probably chosen to denote a settled relation, rather than the more transitory state of possession.'[28] In verse 10 Paul also asserts 'Christ is in you'. Both are true. Hence 'the body' is dead, not in the sense of individual physical bodies, but as what characterizes fallen humanity. Giving life to 'your mortal bodies' confirms that 'The Spirit's life is not confined to the spiritual realm divorced from the material and social.'[29]

Union with Christ involves sharing Christ's Sonship through the Spirit (8.12–17)

Some commentators regard verses 12–13 as beginning a new sub-section (Cranfield, Murray, Dunn, Käsemann and Wright). On the other hand Fitzmyer, Byrne and Jewett view them as continuing the argument. At first sight verse 12 seems only to repeat previous verses. But 'So then, brothers and sisters, we are debtors, not to the flesh' draws out *the consequences* of living not in the flesh, but in the Spirit. Not only has this transference from the realm of the flesh to the realm of the Spirit brought justification, but also it has brought ethical obligations and consequences. Christians must now 'live according to' the influence which now controls them. Wright comments on verses 12–30, 'This passage is the completion of the basic statement about God's righteousness ... [and] covenant faithfulness.'[30] The Greek *ara oun* (*so then*) is emphatic. NEB translates, 'It follows that ...' Fitzmyer warns us, 'It is still possible for even justified Christians to conduct themselves as self-oriented ... individuals.'[31] But this would be the way that leads to death. The syntax of verse 12 is not complete, but is left hanging. Perhaps this is because Paul recoils from the notion that justified Christians could go on following the way of death. In verse 13 Robertson

---

[28] Dunn, *Romans 1—8*, p. 429.
[29] Dunn, *Romans 1—8*, p. 429.
[30] Wright, 'Romans', *NIB*, vol. 10, p. 590.
[31] Fitzmyer, *Romans*, p. 492.

translates Greek *mellete apothnēskein* as 'you are on the point of dying'.[32] The NRSV rendering 'by the Spirit' correctly understands *en pneumati* as a dative of instrument. The Holy Spirit achieved this destruction of the 'flesh', because this is the will of God.

Paul's thought in verse 14 is not discontinuous with previous verses. Byrne calls verses 14–17 'a kind of bridge to the new stage of the argument', namely life and sonship.[33] Union with Christ, who is the Son of God, entails the sharing of Christ's Sonship. In the sense in which God remains Father of all that he creates, we may speak of the universal Fatherhood of God (Deut. 32.6; Ps. 103.13; Jer. 3.19–20; Hos. 11.3; Mal. 2.10). Here, by contrast, God is *not* referring to any 'natural' sonship, but to a distinctively *derived and shared sonship* which is given not by nature, but by *union with Christ*, who is pre-eminently the *Son*. This unique sonship belongs by grace to 'all who are led by the Spirit' (v. 14). Again, Thornton helpfully devotes a chapter to 'Partakers of Christ's Sonship', in which he discusses 'fellowship' or 'sharing' (Greek *koinōnia*), the witness of the Spirit, access to the Father, and verses 11–30.[34] On the indwelling of the Holy Spirit, he comments, 'The same power is at work in us as in Jesus Christ . . . The Holy Spirit of the anointed Messiah will produce in the messianic community effects which were produced in the Messiah.'[35]

In verse 15 Paul spells out the degree of intimacy shared between God the Father and Christ, which can now also become *ours*. 'Abba' is uniquely the Aramaic word for 'Father' used by Jesus (Mark 14.36; Gal. 4.6). In 1955 Jeremias argued:

> *Abba* is not used in Jewish prayers as an address to God; to a Jewish mind it would have been irreverent . . . It was something new, unique and unheard of, that Jesus dared to take this step, and speak with God as a child speaks with his father, simply, intimately, securely.[36]

He added: 'Abba as an address to God is . . . an authentic and original utterance of Jesus.'[37] Today, Dunn and many others recognize that Jeremias may have pressed his case too far, but remains fundamentally correct with this minor qualification.

---

[32] Robertson, *Word Pictures*, p. 374.

[33] Byrne, Brendan, *Romans* (Collegeville: Liturgical Press, 1996 and 2007; Sacra Pagina 6), p. 248.

[34] Thornton, *Common Life*, pp. 156–87.

[35] Thornton, *Common Life*, pp. 183 and 184.

[36] Jeremias, Joachim, 'Abba' in *The Central Message of the New Testament* (Eng., London: SCM, 1965), p. 21 and pp. 9–30.

[37] Jeremias, 'Abba', p. 30.

Jewett insists that 'Abba' was the regular Aramaic word for *father*, and that in this context it may well be ecstatic. 'Cry' (Greek *krazō*), he says, has 'a noisy and ecstatic' quality.[38] Dunn agrees that it may be 'ejaculatory', but argues that it is 'not necessarily ecstatic'.[39] But Cranfield, probably rightly, points out that while *krazō* is used in the LXX for urgent prayer, it is *not* indicative of ecstatic utterance.[40]

Adoption (Greek *huiothesia*) is also of major importance in verse 15. Although the term stands in contrast to 'spirit of slavery', Cranfield is right to interpret Greek *pneuma* here as the Holy Spirit. The Holy Spirit is not the Spirit of slavery, but the Spirit of (who brings) adoption.[41] The aorist signifies the particular moment when readers became Christians. The moment when they became united with Christ by the Holy Spirit, they shared Christ's special Sonship. In the very moment when the Holy Spirit became the controlling principle of their lives, they should not 'fear', or imagine that they face a restricting 'slavery', but rejoice in receiving the Spirit, who made them especially precious to God as his children in Christ. Both Jewish and Gentile Christians receive the special sonship of loving care, which is regarded as a Jewish privilege in Romans 9.4.[42]

In verse 16 the NRSV skilfully uses 'that very Spirit' where the AV/KJB wrongly translates Greek *auto to pneuma* as the woodenly lateral 'the spirit *itself*', as if the Holy Spirit were an impersonal 'thing'. Spirit as *paraklētos* in John 16.13, 26 is masculine; the Hebrew *ruach* (*spirit*) is feminine; *pneuma* happens to be *neuter by another accident of grammar*. But the Holy Spirit in the NT is clearly a Person, representing God himself. It verges on the blasphemous to think of the Holy Spirit merely as a 'force' or a 'thing', as if he were part of the created order. He is above and beyond gender, like God himself, and certainly a 'person', even if a 'person' above and beyond human persons. Elsewhere I have used the term 'suprapersonal'; he is certainly and emphatically not 'sub-personal'.[43] Bultmann is one of those who have misunderstood biblical uses of 'filled' or 'poured out' as if this indicated supposedly sub-personal categories. As Ian Ramsey rightly insists, 'person' is the primary *'model'* but *'qualifiers'* (such as 'filled' or 'poured out') are used to show how his personhood *transcends merely*

---

[38] Jewett, *Romans*, p. 499.
[39] Dunn, *Romans 1—8*, p. 453.
[40] Cranfield, *Romans*, vol. 1, p. 399.
[41] Cranfield, *Romans*, vol. 1, p. 396.
[42] Byrne, *Romans*, p. 250.
[43] Thiselton, *The Holy Spirit*, pp. 120–2, 407–8 and 469.

human categories. In Romans 8.15, the NJB and NIV helpfully translate 'the Spirit himself'; the NEB has 'the Spirit of God'.[44]

'Bearing witness with our spirit' (v. 16a, Greek *summarturei tōi pneumati hēmōn*) explains Paul's introducing 'adoption'. The Holy Spirit *assures us that we are God's children.* The witness of the Holy Spirit, Cranfield comments, 'is something which we cannot impart to ourselves: it has to be given to us *from outside and beyond ourselves*'.[45] It anticipates the maxim: 'The Holy Spirit is the Beyond who is within.' Dunn comments on adoption, 'The metaphor of adoption occurs only in the Pauline literature (8:15, 23; 9:4; Gal. 4:5; Eph. 1:5), and is drawn from his experience of Greco-Roman law and custom, since it was not a Jewish practice.'[46] *Adoption* underlines the gulf between *son* and *slave*, since many Roman citizens gave special status and privilege to those whom they had adopted as sons.

This is expounded in verse 17: 'If children, then heirs, heirs of God and joint heirs with Christ'. Christians are fellow-heirs with the Messiah. They not only share in Christ's prayer, love and Lordship, but also share in Christ's commission to bring redemption to the world.[47] Two particular contributions on inheritance in Paul are especially notable: the work of Hester and Wright on this concept.[48] Both trace the continuity of the inheritance through the OT; Hester, on the kingdom of God; and Wright, on God's promise to Abraham, the theme of exodus, and the promise and possession of the land. Hence Christians do not return to 'slavery' (as in Egypt), but Jewish and Gentile Christians inherit the promises to Abraham.

In verse 17 Paul uses three compound verbs (Greek prefix, *sun-*) to denote 'joint heirs . . . suffer-with . . . glorified-with . . .' These emphasize, first, intimate union with Christ, past, present and future; and second, that sharing in Christ's resurrection is accompanied by also sharing his suffering. Cranfield reminds us that this is 'not . . . understood as a condition, but rather as stating a fact'.[49]

---

[44] Ramsey, Ian T., *Religious Language: An Empirical Placing of Theological Phrases* (London: SCM, 1957), pp. 49–89; and Ramsey, *Models for Divine Activity* (London: SCM, 1973); Barr, James, *The Semantics of Biblical Language* (Oxford: OUP, 1961), pp. 39–40; as against Bultmann, *Theology of the NT*, vol. 1, pp. 155 and 156.

[45] Cranfield, *Romans*, vol. 1, p. 402 (my italics).

[46] Dunn, *Romans 1—8*, p. 452; and Cranfield, *Romans*, vol. 1, pp. 397–8; Fitzmyer, *Romans*, p. 500.

[47] Wright, 'Romans', *NIB*, vol. 10, p. 594.

[48] Hester, James D., *Paul's Concept of Inheritance: A Contribution to the Understanding of Heilsgeschichte* (Edinburgh: Oliver & Boyd, 1968; *SJT* Occasional Paper 14); and Wright, N. T., 'The New Inheritance According to Paul', *The Bible Review* 14.3 (1998).

[49] Cranfield, *Romans*, vol. 1, p. 407.

17

The renewal of all things: suffering and future glory (8.18–39)

The chapter title 'The renewal of all things' is borrowed from Wright. This is not to underrate the importance of suffering, but to bring into prominence Paul's vision throughout the second part of chapter 8.

The groaning of creation, expectation of glory, and the Spirit as first fruits (8.18–25)

For the Christian for whom God has prepared such a magnificent, unsurpassable destiny, suffering in the present can be viewed in a new light. It cannot compare in intensity with what lies ahead, and testifies in cosmic terms to the incompleteness of this present age. Paul's introductory word 'I consider' (Greek *logizomai*) is understood by Leenhardt and Dunn to denote a deliberate solemn calculation, not a passing opinion.[1] Leenhardt and Fitzmyer also stress that 'Suffering is, as it were, a sign and a proof of the authenticity of our Christian condition'.[2] In his development of creation's bondage and groaning, Paul alludes to Genesis 3.17–19 and 5.29, where the earth has been cursed because of Adam's transgression. Corruption came through sin and death (5.12–14) and bondage to decay (8.19–23). We have already commented on *glory* above.

Nevertheless through Christ creation (Greek *ktisis*) may recover its intended orientation (v. 19). It 'waits with eager longing' (Greek *apokaradokia*) for the revealing of the children of God. Fison paraphrases the word as 'stands on tip-toe'. Danker observes that the word is unique to Christian writers, deriving from *kara* (*head*) and *dokeō* (*imagine*); possibly, it denotes *stretching forward* or *craning the neck to see in anticipation*. The notion of straining forward reflects eschatological tension. *Creation* includes angels as well as inanimate objects and animals. It is all that God has created.

---

[1] Leenhardt, Franz J., *The Epistle to the Romans* (London: Lutterworth, 1961), p. 218; Dunn, James D. G., *Romans 1—8* (Dallas: Word, 1988; WBC 38), pp. 467–8.

[2] Leenhardt, *Romans*, p. 218; Fitzmyer, Joseph A., *Romans: A New Translation with Introduction and Commentary* (New York: Doubleday, 1992; AB 33), p. 505.

It is remarkable that creation should 'crane its neck' to see the revealing of the sons of God. This implies that such will be the future glory and status of Christian believers that all creation will long to see this transformation. Since humankind is part of creation, 'creation' may hope to have a share in this spectacular transformation. A number of theologians who specialize in animal theology speculate in this direction, especially in the light of some OT prophecies and apocalyptic.[3] McLaughlin cites, for example, Isaiah 11.6–9: 'The wolf shall live with the lamb, the leopard shall lie down with the kid, the calf and the lion and the fatling together'.[4]

Pannenberg observes, 'Creaturely reality is a plurality of creatures, making up the world . . . [God creates] a productive principle of diversity.'[5] He continues,

> The goal of God's purpose is that all might be reconciled in him (Col. 1:20; Eph. 1:10) . . . The destiny of all creation is at stake (Rom. 8:19–23) . . . The relation of non-human creatures to their Creator thereby also comes to fulfilment.[6]

God will, as it were, reveal our true nature by stripping away our untransformed disguise. Once again, humankind is restored to its intended destiny, as described in the image of God (Gen. 1.26–27; Ps. 8.5–8).

In verses 20–21 Paul describes the cosmic bondage to which creation was subjected when sin entered the world. This is its 'bondage to decay' (v. 21), and its being 'subjected to futility' (v. 20, Greek *tē metaiotēti hē ktisis hupetagē*). *Futility, emptiness*, or *fruitlessness*, is emphatic at the beginning of the sentence, and Paul draws it from Ecclesiastes 1.2; and from his use of the word in Romans 1.21, 'to describe the frustration and destructiveness of persons or groups who suppress the truth and refuse to recognize God'.[7] As in Genesis 3.17–19, in which God 'cursed' the ground in relation to Adam, God changed humanity's relation to the natural world. Jewett, Wright, Cranfield and Dunn all ascribe the agency of this subjection to God.[8] The

---

[3] Thiselton, Anthony C., *Systematic Theology*, ch. 5, sect. 3, 'The Creation and Status of Animals' (Grand Rapids: Eerdmans, and London: SPCK, 2015).

[4] McLaughlin, Ryan Patrick, *Christian Theology and the Status of Animals* (New York: Macmillan/ Palgrave, 2014), pp. 128–31; Wennberg, Robert N., *God, Humans, and Animals* (Grand Rapids: Eerdmans, 2003); and Clough, David L., *On Animals* (London and New York: Bloomsbury, 2012).

[5] Pannenberg, Wolfhart, *Systematic Theology* (3 vols, Edinburgh: T & T Clark, and Grand Rapids: Eerdmans, 1991–8), vol. 2, pp. 61 and 62.

[6] Pannenberg, *Systematic Theology*, vol. 2, pp. 72–3.

[7] Jewett, Robert, *Romans: A Commentary* (Minneapolis: Fortress, 2007; Hermeneia), p. 51.

[8] Dunn, *Romans 1—8*, pp. 470–1; Jewett, *Romans*, pp. 513–14; Cranfield, C. E. B., *A Critical and Exegetical Commentary on the Epistle to the Romans*, vol. 1 (Edinburgh: T & T Clark, 1975; ICC), p. 414; Wright, N. T., 'Romans' in the *New Interpreter's Bible* (*NIB*) (Nashville: Abingdon, 2002), vol. 10, p. 596.

phrase 'not of its own will' excludes any Gnostic view of the world and matter as evil or against God, and can mean 'not involuntarily'.

By contrast with Gnosticism, Cranfield interprets Paul as viewing creation as 'the whole magnificent theatre of the universe together with all its splendid properties and all the chorus of sub-human life, created to glorify God, but unable to do so fully'.[9] 'Unable' arose because in order to fulfil its destiny it needed humanity to reflect the restored image of God, and to order creation as God willed. The most pressing question for many people today is: did Paul envisage a 'cosmic fall'? One of the most thoughtful and subtle treatments of this problem which I have encountered is Bimson, 'Reconsidering a "Cosmic Fall"', published in 2006.[10] Bimson acknowledges that through the centuries many have ascribed the less appealing aspects of nature to human sin. Calvin, for example, declares, 'Frost, thunders, unseasonable rains, drought, hail and whatever is disorderly in the world, are fruits of sin.'[11] Calvin also places such phenomena 'within the purposes of a loving God'. In the sixteenth and seventeenth centuries Milton's notion of a 'cosmic fall' in *Paradise Lost* became influential.[12] Bimson rejects two themes in some Christian thought which are intended to 'solve' the problem of a so-called cosmic fall. There is no actual biblical evidence, he argues, of a fall of rebellious angels long 'before' the creation of humankind, and he also rejects the 'Creation Science' approach as involving 'poor hermeneutics and bad science'.[13]

We cannot simply brush aside notions of a cosmic fall. Bruce is a powerful advocate of this idea in Romans 8.[14] This is the traditional way of understanding the 'cursing of the ground' (Gen. 3.17, 23) and the groaning of creation in Romans 8.19–23. It is supported by a literalistic reading of Isaiah 11.6–10. Most, however, understand this as *symbolic*. Bimson argues that for a lion to switch to a herbivorous diet would require 'a different digestive system, different teeth, and a different kind of jaw structure . . . in short, it would cease to be a lion in any meaningful sense'.[15] Even Aquinas argues, 'The nature of animals was not changed by man's sin.'[16] Moreover

[9] Cranfield, *Romans*, vol. 1, p. 414.

[10] Bimson, John J., 'Reconsidering a "Cosmic Fall"', *Science and Christian Belief* 18 (2006), pp. 63–81.

[11] Calvin, John, *Commentary on the Book of Genesis* (Edinburgh: Calvin Translation Society, 1847 [1554]), on Gen. 3.18–19.

[12] Milton, John, *Paradise Lost*, Book 10, lines 668–71 and 710–12.

[13] Bimson, 'Cosmic Fall', p. 66.

[14] Bruce, F. F., *The Epistle of Paul to the Romans* (London: Tyndale, 1963), p. 169.

[15] Bimson, 'Cosmic Fall', p. 69.

[16] Aquinas, Thomas, *Summa Theologiae* (60 vols, Lat. and Eng., Oxford: Blackfriars, 1963), I, qu. 96, art. 1.

many OT passages simply celebrate the goodness and wonder of creation (Pss. 104.24, 31; 145.16–17).

The greatest single problem of a 'cosmic fall' on the basis of humanity's sin is the state of creation during the long period of earth and the solar system prior to the creation of humankind. Even if we were to ignore, for sake of argument, some theories of biological and genetic evolution, what are we to say about the astral universe? Wright comments on Romans 8.19–21: 'The whole creation – sun, moon, sea, sky, birds, animals, plants – is longing for the time when God's people will be revealed as glorious human agents, set in authority over the world.'[17]

We cannot exempt the natural phenomena of geophysics, astrophysics, geology and meteorology from existing in their present form long before the creation and fall of humankind. Hence there is ambivalence about the term 'cosmic fall'. It does not primarily refer to a set of natural phenomena in themselves. But Cranfield expresses the issues well, together with Wright and Bimson. As we have already noted, he declares, 'The whole magnificent theatre of the universe . . . created for God's glory is cheated of its true fulfilment so long as man, the chief actor in the great drama of God's praise, fails to contribute his rational part.'[18] Again, to quote Wright, humankind was 'set in authority over the world'; now Paul points forward to what the new creation could be, 'true to the original purpose'.[19] Bimson writes, 'Fulfilment is made possible by the longed-for revealing of the children of God (Rom. 1:19). Then creation is liberated from its bondage to decay.'[20] Paul will offer a part-parallel in Colossians 1.20.

Undeniably there are *also other* elements behind the malfunction of the physical world. Niebuhr and Moltmann have traced how human selfishness and greed have further degraded and debased the physical world by the exploitation of earth's resources. Many today would include the use of fuels which can hasten climate change and global warming, with associated meteorological changes. In this sense, to speak of a cosmic fall is not 'wrong'. But in relation to Romans 8.19–21 a more subtle and measured approach is required, which few of the commentaries seem fully to address. Bimson's article is sophisticated and subtle. He holds a critical discussion with Andrew Linzey, Ruth Page and John Polkinghorne,

---

[17] Wright, 'Romans', *NIB*, vol. 10, p. 596.
[18] Cranfield, C. E. B., 'Some Observations on Romans 8:19–21' in Banks, Robert (ed.), *Reconciliation and Hope: New Testament Essays on Atonement and Eschatology Presented to L. L. Morris on His 60th Birthday* (Grand Rapids: Eerdmans, 1974), pp. 227 and 224–30.
[19] Wright, 'Romans', *NIB*, vol. 10, p. 596.
[20] Bimson, 'Cosmic Fall', p. 75.

commenting: 'God allows tectonic plates to slip and cause earthquakes, and bacteria to multiply and cause disease, because they are "free" to act in accordance with their nature.'[21] But there is also a cruciform pattern to what God 'allows': nature is advanced by apparent setbacks. For example, 'Supernova explosions, which destroy stars . . . are essential to the evolution of a galaxy toward a life-bearing phase.'[22] Thus 'cosmic fall' is an ambivalent notion. Sin has disrupted the physical universe, and we look forward to the new creation. But it does not demand pre-Adamic changes to creation.

In 8.23 Paul introduces the notion of 'the first fruits of the Spirit' (*tēn aparchēn tou pneumatos*). Hamilton made a special study of the term *first fruits* in 8.23, which carries forward the thought of 8.11 on the Holy Spirit and the resurrection of believers. The genitive 'of the Spirit' is one of apposition. Paul's point, in Hamilton's words, is:

> The gift of the Spirit in the present is to be understood as only the beginning of the harvest proper which will occur in the new creation of the future age . . . The centre of gravity lies in the future.[23]

Hamilton also compares Galatians 6.8 and 2 Corinthians 5.5, where *first fruits* are also linked with 'guarantee' (*arrabōn*) concerning the future. Danker confirms Hamilton's findings, arguing that the usual meaning is first fruits, although in Romans 8.23 the translation *birth certificate* 'also suits the context'.[24] What in some ways is a *partial* experience of the Holy Spirit in the present will become a *fuller* experience in the new creation, unhindered by any trace of sin, and is also authenticated, as if by a *birth certificate*. It is a pledge of the *fuller gift* yet to come.

Meanwhile Christian sons and daughters of God also 'groan inwardly' while they wait for 'adoption, the redemption of our bodies.' *We groan* underlines the intermediate tension of the present, our solidarity with all creation, and Luther's distinctive theme of *struggle*. We are already sons of God (8.14–16) but this has *yet to become manifest and public*. We have commented above on redemption as redemption *to*, redemption *by* and redemption *from*, as when Israel was redeemed *from* Egypt *by* God's holy arm *to* the promised land. The redemption 'of our bodies' will be the

---

[21] Polkinghorne, John, *Scientists as Theologians* (London: SPCK, 1996), pp. 48–9.

[22] Stoeger, W. R., 'Scientific Accounts of Ultimate Catastrophes in Our Life-bearing Universe' in Polkinghorne, John, and Welker, M. (eds), *The End of the World and the Ends of God* (Harrisburg, PA: Trinity Press International, 2000), p. 25.

[23] Hamilton, Neil Q., *The Holy Spirit and Eschatology in Paul* (Edinburgh: Oliver & Boyd, 1957; *SJT* Occasional Paper 6), p. 19.

[24] Danker, Frederick, *A Greek-English Lexicon of the New Testament and Other Early Christian Literature* (BDAG) (Chicago and London: University of Chicago Press, 3rd edn, 2000), p. 98.

final and ultimate stage of redemption from decay, sin, degeneration and corruption.

In verse 24 the future orientation becomes even clearer. *Hope* now becomes a dominant theme, and 'hope that is seen is not hope.' This is what Wittgenstein would have called 'a grammatical remark', namely one about the *logical grammar* of *hope*. 'Hope' is used here in the sense of what is hoped for. The Greek *elpizō* can translate any of four Hebrew words, including *betach* (*confidence*, Ps. 16.9) and *yāchal* (*to wait in hope*, Ps 31.24). In verse 24a *hope* may denote the human disposition, but in verse 24b it denotes what we hope for, or the object of hope. The first occurs in 1 Corinthians 13.13, the second in Hebrews 11.1. In apocalyptic thinking, hope first arises because of a perceived contradiction between the present and the future. The fulfilment of hope depends on God's promises and his faithfulness to fulfil them. In *Surprised by Hope*, Wright includes paradise, the *parousia* and the resurrection in this theme.[25] Dunn comments on 'we are saved', 'Paul can use the aorist because of the nature of Christian hope as firm confidence in God's purpose and power.'[26] He adds that Paul may also be warning us against 'enthusiastic' tendencies towards triumphalism about the Spirit's work in the present.

'Who hopes for what is seen?' (v. 24c) yields multiple MS readings. P[46], B, C, D, G, 33, Old Syriac, Clement and Origen read *elpizei*; ℵ*, A and Coptic read *hupomenei* (*Who hopes?* Or *Who waits?*). Metzger reports that the UBS Committee supports the former majority reading.[27] Moreover *ho gar blepei tis, ti kai elpizei* ('What someone sees, why does he also hope for it?') is supported by ℵ[2], A, C, K, 33, Syriac and Coptic, while 'Who hopes for what he sees?' is read by P[27], B* and others, and is followed by Nestle–Aland and Metzger. Jewett prefers the Nestle–Aland reading: 'Who hopes for what he sees?'[28] This does fit the context.

The Holy Spirit praying and the image of Christ (8.26–30)

Romans 8.26–27 expounds the work of the Holy Spirit. Paul declares, 'The Spirit helps us in our weakness; for we do not know how to pray as we ought'. The Holy Spirit prays *to* God the Father *through* the Son. In our 1987 Church of England Doctrine Commission Report we commented

---

[25] Wright, N. T., *Surprised by Hope* (London: SPCK, 2002).

[26] Dunn, *Romans 1—8*, p. 475.

[27] Metzger, Bruce, *A Textual Commentary on the Greek New Testament* (New York: UBS, 2nd edn, 1994), p. 457.

[28] Jewett, *Romans*, p. 505.

on 8.26: 'We are graciously caught up in a divine conversation, passing back and forth in and through the one who prays, "The Spirit himself bearing witness with our spirit" (Rom. 8:16).'[29] Prayer is 'participation in a divine dialogue . . . The whole creation . . . is taken up in this Trinitarian flow.'[30]

The Greek for 'helps us' (*sunantilambetai*) occurs in Josephus and the LXX, with only one occurrence in the NT. Deissmann suggested the colloquial 'lend a hand'.[31] Danker interprets the active form to mean *to take someone's part by assisting, come to the aid of*, or even *to be involved with*.[32] The prefix *sun* is simply intensive. Some have criticized 'Likewise' (v. 26 NRSV) as implying that God shares in the 'groaning'. Scholars as different as Käsemann and Macchia (the Pentecostal) believe that *sighings* would be more accurate here, and almost certainly refer to speaking in tongues. Käsemann calls it 'a matter of ecstatic cries . . . the participation of pneumatics . . . *glossolalia* [with] inexpressible sighs in the present passage'.[33] Macchia declares, 'In tongues we groan for a liberty in the Spirit that is not yet fulfilled (Rom. 8:26).'[34] This interpretation goes back to Origen and Chrysostom.[35]

The one problem with this suggestion is that Paul describes such prayer as 'intercession' (*huperentugchanei*), not 'praising'. Leenhardt rejects the notion that this verse alludes to ecstatic prayer.[36] Wright, surely with more accurate regard to context, interprets this as the corporate 'groaning of the church, in the midst of a groaning world'.[37] The Holy Spirit and the Church sigh at the calamitous state of the world, with its hunger, disease, wars and oppression, in ways which are too deep and too vast to be easily expressed in plain words. 'Too deep for words' (NRSV) translates *alalētos* (*unutterable*). Denney also suggests 'sighs that baffle words'.[38] The corporate sighing of the Church for the world fully explains why this is *intercession for others*. Paul appears to regard tongues in 1 Corinthians 14, while useful as uninhibited praise, as also merely 'building up the self', and as seldom inaudible. I once warmed to this identification, but now see several difficulties about it. I share Wright's view.

---

[29] Church of England Doctrine Commission, *We Believe in God* (London: Church House Publishing, 1987), p. 108.
[30] Doctrine Commission, *We Believe in God*, pp. 109 and 111.
[31] Deissmann, Adolf, *Light from the Ancient East* (London: Hodder & Stoughton, 1910), p. 87.
[32] Danker, BDAG, p. 89.
[33] Käsemann, Ernst, *Commentary on Romans* (London: SCM, 1980), pp. 240–1.
[34] Macchia, Frank D., *Baptized in the Spirit* (Grand Rapids: Zondervan, 2006), p. 281; and 'Sighs Too Deep for Words: Toward a Theology of Glossolalia', *JPT* (1992), pp. 47–73.
[35] Chrysostom, *Homilies on the Epistle to the Romans* (Eng., *NPNF*, ser. i, vol. 11, p. 447).
[36] Leenhardt, *Romans*, pp. 230–1, especially his footnotes on p. 231.
[37] Wright, 'Romans', *NIB*, vol. 10, p. 598.
[38] Denney, James, 'Romans', *Expositor's Greek Testament*, vol. 2 (Grand Rapids: Eerdmans, 1910), p. 651.

In verse 27 Paul stresses that it is *the Holy Spirit himself who prays, and inspires prayer, within us.* The Spirit searches our hearts, which, as Bultmann and Theissen emphasize, includes the confused jungle of our unconscious, as well as our deepest drives, emotions and inclinations to action.[39] This is exactly where we need the Spirit's ministrations. There is no barrier on God's side, for 'God . . . knows what is in the mind of the Spirit'. Once again the Trinitarian dimension is implied, because 'the *Spirit* intercedes . . . according to the will of *God*', through *Jesus Christ*, our Lord.

Some versions of the NT signal a fresh break in the argument at verse 28. The NRSV and NIV begin a new paragraph here. But Wright insists,

> Verse 28 does not represent a completely new thought . . . It is bound tightly to the sequence of argument . . . The train of thought is, 'God knows the mind of the Spirit'; *but* we know *that God works all things together for good* for those who love God.[40]

This brings us to a notorious crux in textual criticism. Perhaps surprisingly the NRSV reads 'All things work together for good . . .' together with the AV/KJB. This is the reading of ℵ, C, D, G and 33. But 'God' (*ho theos*) is added to the sentence by the earlier P[46], A, B and Origen, and is followed by NJB, REB and NIV. In the latter case 'work[s] together with' (*sunergei*) is understood intransitively with the indirect object 'all things'. A further complication is that P[46] reads *pan* (singular, *all*). Fitzmyer comments: 'In view of the fluctuation in the text tradition, it is not easy to be certain about which interpretation is better. Any one of them would suit the context.'[41] Dunn regards both readings as having good support, though he thinks the Alexandrian editor smoothed out the text by adding 'God', rather than 'all', as the subject.[42] Jewett cites Dodd's comment that 'all things' risks 'a natural tendency towards progress', which is *not* Paul's view.[43] Nygren, Byrne and Käsemann favour the AV/KJB and NRSV reading ('All things'), but Jewett, Cranfield and Wright advocate the second ('God'), which we support.[44]

---

[39] Theissen, Gerd, *Psychological Aspects of Pauline Theology* (Eng., Edinburgh: T & T Clark, 1987), pp. 57–114 and throughout.

[40] Wright, 'Romans', *NIB*, vol. 10, p. 600.

[41] Fitzmyer, *Romans*, p. 523.

[42] Dunn, *Romans 1—8*, p. 466.

[43] Jewett, *Romans*, p. 526; Dodd, C. H., *The Epistle of Paul to the Romans* (London: Hodder & Stoughton, 1932), p. 138.

[44] Jewett, *Romans*, p. 526; Wright, 'Romans', *NIB*, vol. 10, p. 600; Cranfield, *Romans*, vol. 1, pp. 424–9 in detail.

'For those who love God' becomes emphatic, because it is placed at the beginning of the verse in the Greek text. Paul more usually speaks of God's love to humans, but there is a significant OT background on *love for God*. This is commanded in Scripture, which is proof that the word denotes not an emotion but *an attitude* and *action*. Wittgenstein is superb at distinguishing qualities demanding or inviting an imperative from those which do not. He cites, ironically, the imperative, 'Laugh at this joke!' In the *Zettel* he comments, 'Love is not a feeling. Love is put to the test, pain is not.'[45] Wright comments, 'The heart of the argument for assurance is the unshakeable and sovereign love of God, and the certainty that love will win out in the end.'[46]

In verse 28c Paul adds, 'Those who are called according to his [God's] purpose.' 'Called' (*klētos*) takes up the language of Romans 1.1, 6: a called apostle, and believers 'called by Jesus Christ'. 'Purpose' may reflect Isaiah 46.10: 'My purpose shall stand'. God's purpose is the establishment of the new creation. *Purpose* (*prothesis*) may include *plan* or *scheme*, and applies to God. Paul declares that the existence of 'those who love God' does not depend on how well love is shown, but on *God's prior election, choice, or grace*. In the theology of Barth 'election' takes a prominent place, especially since Christ is elected, and Christians are thereby elected 'in Christ'. Barth comments on verse 28:

> The love of God is not a particular form of behaviour within the sphere of human competence . . . It is the power and significance which God can bestow . . . love toward God is a humiliation . . . Has anyone who has loved God even thought otherwise? . . . Love knows itself to be altogether the gift of God, altogether the calling which is grounded upon the purpose comprehended in God before all time.[47]

Verse 29 draws out the implications of this further: 'Those whom he foreknew he also predestined to be conformed to the image of his Son'. Foreknowledge (Greek *hous proegnō*) and 'predestination' or marking out beforehand (*proōrisen*) are not abstract concepts, as they sometimes are in popular debates. They denote being marked out beforehand to be conformed to the image of Christ. Discussion about destiny depends on *to what* we are destined. We noted in our discussion of reception history

---

[45] Wittgenstein, Ludwig, *Zettel* (Ger. and Eng., Oxford: Blackwell, 1967), sect. 504.

[46] Wright, 'Romans', *NIB*, vol. 10, p. 601.

[47] Barth, Karl, *The Epistle to the Romans* (Eng., Oxford: OUP, 1933), pp. 318, 320 and 322; see Barth, Karl, *Church Dogmatics* II.2 (Eng., vol. 4, Edinburgh: T & T Clark, 1957), ch. 7, sects 32–5, pp. 3–508.

above that Aquinas emphasized Paul's doctrine of predestination without compromise, because it was the fruit of purpose in Christ. Since Paul has underlined the inability of humankind without God's grace, the emphasis on God's destining us is unavoidable. Everything depends on grace, not on human choice, as Paul and Aquinas make clear. Fitzmyer writes: 'It is to be regarded as the divine plan of election conceived in eternity (cf. Eph. 1:4) and moving in time to its realization, which will become definitive only in eternity itself.'[48] *Predestined* refers to 'God's gratuitous election . . . Christians are destined to reproduce in themselves an image of Christ by a progressive share in his risen life.'[49]

Paul has earlier referred to adoption. If Christians are of the same family as Christ, with God as their Father, Christ is the *firstborn* (*prōtokos*). This implies Christ's pre-eminence and the Sonship from which Christians derive their sonship. We may compare Colossians 1.15, 18; Hebrews 1.6; and Revelation 1.5 with verse 29, 'conformed to the image of his Son'. We may recall *the image of God* in Genesis 1.26–27; 1 Corinthians 15.49; and the language of Philippians 3.21. In simple terms, 'Paul's thought is of believers becoming like Christ.'[50] 'Adam Christology' stands in the background, in which Jesus Christ is the last Adam, the representative of the new creation. The image of God is fully recovered in Christ.[51] Believers share this destiny.

In verse 30 Paul produces what Jewett calls 'a classic climax to provide the last steps in the symmetrical chain . . . The verb tense continues . . . with "predestined . . . called . . . set right . . . and glorified."'[52] The ultimate term of this climactic progression is *glorified*. One reason for this glory is being conformed to the image of Christ. This harmonizes with what Paul has told the Corinthians about *the resurrection*: 'it [the *sōma* (*body*)] is raised in *glory*' (1 Cor. 15.43). Although, strictly, the glory is future, the past (aorist) tenses emphasize that the divine decision has been taken, and only denote its working out, which has yet to be consummated. Paul uses all the terms of verses 29–30 *to provide assurance, a sense of security, and total reliance on God.* Whiteley comments, 'The "security" of the Christian is based upon the eternal purpose of God.'[53]

---

[48] Fitzmyer, *Romans*, p. 524.

[49] Fitzmyer, *Romans*, p. 525.

[50] Dunn, *Romans 1—8*, p. 483.

[51] Barrett, C. K., *From First Adam to Last: A Study in Pauline Theology* (London: Black, 1962), pp. 97–8 and 92–120.

[52] Jewett, *Romans*, p. 530.

[53] Whiteley, D. E. H., *The Theology of St. Paul* (Oxford: Blackwell, 1970) p. 94; and pp. 89–91 and 93–4.

The final affirmation: the triumph of God's love (8.31–39)

Paul's opening rhetorical question, 'What then are we to say about these things?' belongs to his diatribe style. After 8.28–30, Wright declares, 'What remains is to celebrate.'[54] Paul now uses the first-person plural to denote 'we Christians'. Verses 31b–39 constitute four rhetorical strophes consisting of verses 31b–32, 33–34, 35–37 and 38–39. All the major scholars, including Barrett, Käsemann, Fitzmyer and Jewett, stress the diatribe form here.

The first strophe (vv. 31b–32) provides the setting of the law-court as in Job 1—2 and Zechariah 3. With God 'on our side', Christians need fear no accuser or prosecutor. 'He who did not withhold his own Son' may perhaps allude to Genesis 22, where Abraham offered up Isaac, but this cannot be certain. The verb 'withhold' (*pheidomai*) is traditionally translated 'spare', which is the normal LXX meaning. 'Gave him up' (*charisetai*) means *to give, graciously, to give freely as a favour*. On Romans 8.32, Danker paraphrases 'who graciously bestows wonderful things from the world beyond'.[55] The Greek prepositions for 'for' and 'against' are *huper hēmōn* and *kath' hemōn*. The further question, 'How will he not with him freely give us everything?' is significant. God's love to Jesus Christ cannot be doubted. But Paul has said that we are 'in Christ'. Thus it is through, in and with Christ that all God's blessings are channelled. Since God has freely given up his own Son, it is inconceivable that he could be 'against' us! His gift of 'everything' reminds us of Paul's earlier statement, 'All things are yours' (1 Cor. 3.21–23).

Paul's next two verses, which begin, 'Who will bring any charge against God's elect?' (v. 33), are punctuated as questions in various ways. Punctuation marks are much *later than the original text*. The NRSV (RSV, NIV, REB) places question marks after 'elect' (v. 33) and 'condemn' (v. 34), and makes 33b and 34b statements. The NJB makes 34b into a question. Fitzmyer sees a reference to the Servant Songs in Isaiah 50.4–11, which portray God as Vindicator.[56] Indeed, *justification* includes the idea of vindication as well as 'putting right', both 'right with God' and 'right' in terms of justice. Of all inconceivable hypotheses, the least conceivable of all is that Christ could condemn us, when he died and was raised on our behalf. It is an assurance, then, that he is God's executive, i.e. 'at the right hand of God' (v. 34).

---

[54] Wright, 'Romans', *NIB*, vol. 10, p. 609.
[55] Danker, BDAG, p. 1078.
[56] Fitzmyer, *Romans*, p. 532.

Cullmann takes Christ's role as intercessor very seriously, although mainly with reference to Hebrews 7.25. He believes, 'Christ intercedes for us no longer simply in a collective sense . . . Now he intercedes in every moment for each individual.'[57] The OT background suggests *enthronement*. Both the Spirit (Rom. 8.20–27) and Christ (v. 34) intercede with God for the Christian. After 'Christ who was raised', ℵ*, A, C, 33, Coptic and Ethiopic insert 'from the dead', which most attribute to a copyist. P[46], ℵ[2], B, D and G retain the shorter reading, which is probably correct.

The third strophe (vv. 35–37) begins, 'Who will separate us from the love of Christ?' So great is the love of Christ for us that nothing can sever our link with him. *Separate* (Greek *chōrisei*) derives from *chōra* (*space*), implying that no one can 'put a distance between Christ's love and us'.[58] NRSV places two question marks at the end of verse 35a and verse 35b, which reflects the best MSS. More significant is the textual variation between 'Christ' and 'God'. C, D, F, G, 33, Syriac, Origen and Athanasius attest 'Christ'. 'God' appears in ℵ, Coptic-Sahidic and Hippolytus. Metzger accepts the reading followed by the NRSV as especially 'binding together verses 34 and 35'.[59]

Paul totally excludes any notion that 'hardship, or distress, or persecution, or famine, or nakedness, or peril, or sword' could put a distance between us and the love of Christ. Paul has literally experienced all these himself (Rom. 2.9; 1 Cor. 4.11, 12; 15.30; 2 Cor. 4.9; 12.10; 11.26–27; Gal. 5.11). Each of the identical Greek words applies to Paul's experience.[60] Similar lists are known in Stoic literature, and sometimes in Jewish literature. In verse 36 Paul quotes from Psalm 44.22 (43.23 LXX).[61]

In the fourth strophe Paul adds 'height' and 'depth' to his list. In verse 38 Whiteley and Dunn regard 'height' and 'depth' as almost certainly 'astronomical terms: *height* (*Gk. hupsōma*) denotes . . . the highest point in the heavens reached by the heavenly body . . . *bathos, depth*, is the opposite'.[62] Whiteley claims, 'For his [Paul's] readers . . . it was a matter of no small importance that Christ should be victorious over astrological forces.'[63] W. L. Knox includes present and future as the present and future position of heavenly bodies.[64] Yet the interpretation of these entities remains open

[57] Cullmann, Oscar, *The Christology of the New Testament* (London: SCM, 2nd edn, 1963), p. 102.
[58] Robertson, A. T., *Word Pictures in the New Testament, vol. 4: Romans* (New York: R. Smith, 1931, p. 379.
[59] Metzger, *Textual Commentary*, p. 458.
[60] Cranfield, *Romans*, vol. 1, p. 440.
[61] Dunn, *Romans 1—8*, p. 505.
[62] Dunn, *Romans 1—8*, p. 508.
[63] Whiteley, *Theology of St. Paul*, pp. 23–4.
[64] Knox, W. L., *St Paul and the Church of the Gentiles* (Cambridge: CUP, 1939), pp. 106–7.

and debated. Cranfield and Jewett do not exclude this view, but argue that it is more probable that the reference here is to spatial locations.[65] Yet Wright argues that after listing physical threats in verse 35, Paul now addresses 'the forces that might stand behind those physical threats'; he further comments, 'Presumably the "rulers" here are heavenly ones, corresponding to the "elements" of Gal. 4:3, 9 and Col. 2:8, 20, though perhaps their earthly counterparts are not ruled out.'[66]

The significance of 'principalities and powers' has long been debated, but the consensus is that these are super-terrestrial powers. Carr argued the opposite case, but his book has not met with general favour.[67] Caird wrote precisely to indicate powers 'behind' human institutions.[68] Jewett believes that even fallen or evil angels, who will eventually be brought to their knees (Phil. 2.10), constitute the primary threat that Paul has in mind.[69] Similarly Käsemann speaks of 'a universe detached from God'.[70] None of these powers or forces can separate us from God's love, which is triumphant. All the 'powers' are relativized before the love of the sovereign God, and the Lordship of Christ. *Christians are secure in God's love, and God alone is sovereign.*

---

[65] Cranfield, *Romans*, vol. 1, p. 443; Jewett, *Romans*, p. 554.

[66] Wright, 'Romans', *NIB*, vol. 10, p. 615.

[67] Carr, A. Wesley, *Angels and Principalities: The Background and Meaning* (Cambridge: CUP, 1981; SNTMS 42; repr. 2005).

[68] Caird, George B., *Principalities and Powers: A Study in Pauline Theology* (Oxford: OUP, 1956).

[69] Jewett, *Romans*, pp. 551–2.

[70] Käsemann, *Romans*, p. 251.

18

Israel's unbelief: filling a gap in Paul's argument (9.1–29)

Virtually every commentator agrees that following Romans 1—4 and then 5—8, chapters 9—11 begin a third main section of Paul's argument. Apart from that fact, Wright rightly comments, 'Everything about Romans 9—11 is controversial.'[1] The greatest problem concerns the role of the chapters in the epistle. Wright believes, with some justice, that these chapters 'present . . . a complex and integrated whole, which in turn is closely integrated into the warp and woof of the rest of the letter'. It builds, he adds, on the foundations laid in chapters 1—8 and prepares especially for the appeal in chapters 14 and 15. John Ziesler also recognizes the key place of 9—11, and against objections about the 'high incidence of OT quotation' replies that its argument requires this.[2]

Today this represents the consensus of contemporary commentators. Cranfield observes, 'Very many features of chapters 1—8 . . . are not understood in full depth until they are seen in the light of chapters 9—11.'[3] Fitzmyer, Dunn and Wright see these chapters as filling a perceived gap in Paul's argument in 1—8. It is all very well to speak of God's promises to Abraham and his faithfulness to his word, but the objection arises, 'Has God's word failed?' What about the counter-evidence of the unbelief of Israel in general?[4] Jewett personalizes the issue, questioning whether Paul as 'apostle to Gentiles' could be perceived as exhibiting 'anti-Jewish feelings'.[5] Like Wright, he is concerned that Gentile Christians in Rome should not share the 'anti-Jewish' attitudes of many Roman pagans. To quote Wright, it may seem as if 'a hole has been ripped in the story of God and Israel'.[6]

---

[1] Wright, N. T., 'Romans' in the *New Interpreter's Bible* (*NIB*) (Nashville: Abingdon, 2002), vol. 10, p. 620.

[2] Wright, 'Romans', *NIB*, vol. 10, p. 626, and Ziesler, John, *Paul's Letter to the Romans* (London: SCM, 1989 and 1990), p. 38.

[3] Cranfield, C. E. B., *A Critical and Exegetical Commentary on the Epistle to the Romans*, vol. 2 (Edinburgh: T & T Clark, 1979; ICC), p. 445.

[4] Dunn, James D. G., *Romans 9—16* (Dallas: Word, 1988; WBC 38), p. 518; Fitzmyer, Joseph A., *Romans: A New Translation with Introduction and Commentary* (New York: Doubleday, 1992; AB 33), pp. 539–42.

[5] Jewett, Robert, *Romans: A Commentary* (Minneapolis: Fortress, 2007; Hermeneia), p. 556.

[6] Wright, 'Romans', *NIB*, vol. 10, p. 622.

Many commentators until perhaps the late 1970s did not view Romans 9—11 in this way. It is notorious that Nygren devotes generally excellent comments to Romans 1—8 over about 350 pages, and then spends only 100 pages on the second half of this epistle. Dodd suggests that Romans 8 could naturally lead to 12.1–21, and that chapters 9—11

> can be read quite satisfactorily without reference to the rest of the epistle ... It has been suggested that the three chapters were originally a separate treatise which Paul had by him, and which he used for his present purpose. There is a good deal to be said for this view.[7]

Even the pietist exegete Bengel comments on chapter 9: 'This and the tenth and eleventh chapters are an appendix, as it were, on the exclusion of most of the Jews from Christianity.'[8] Calvin, however, takes account of Paul's positive concern for Jews.[9]

Recent commentators have been more diligent in seeking a contextual understanding of the text. Wright is critical of theologians who simply extract 'a doctrine of predestination' from chapter 9. He comments,

> [Paul's] heart-breaking grief in 9:1–3 shows that 'God's word cannot have failed', while his work among the Gentiles 'will bring Israel to faith at last' (11:14), and Paul's example demonstrates that Jews 'can still be saved (11:1–6) ... as part of the remnant'.[10]

Further, 'Gentile Christians should not despise non-Christian Jews or regard them as unsavable.'[11]

The tragic puzzle of Israel's unbelief (9.1–5)

Paul introduces the subject by telling of his terrible grief. This begins with a triple declaration: 'I am speaking the truth ... I am not lying ... my conscience confirms it by the Holy Spirit' (v. 1). He emphasizes this because he is aware of the seriousness of what is at issue in persuading Jewish and Gentile Christians of his positive attitude towards Jews. Cranfield comments, 'If the epistle did not present a serious answer to the question of the Jews, it certainly could not be that key to the true understanding

---

[7] Dodd, C. H., *The Epistle of Paul to the Romans* (London: Hodder & Stoughton, 1932), p. 148.

[8] Bengel, J. Albert, *Gnomon Novi Testamenti* (Lat., Stuttgart: Steinkopf, 1866; Eng., *New Testament Word Studies*; 2 vols, Grand Rapids: Kregel, 1971), vol. 2, p. 105.

[9] Calvin, John, *Calvin's Bible Commentaries: Romans* (London: Forgotten Books, 2007 [1847]), pp. 247–50.

[10] Wright, 'Romans', *NIB*, vol. 10, pp. 623 and 624.

[11] Wright, 'Romans', *NIB*, vol. 10, p. 626.

of the OT which Luther claimed that it was.'[12] His triple oath affirms that the apostle to the Gentiles is not 'anti-Jew', which is an important assurance in Rome. First, we recalled that many Jews would have poured back into the city with the death of Claudius and the end of his decree; second, Rome itself, in contrast to imperial Romans, tended to be suspicious of Jews. Riots in Palestine/Israel would not have reassured them.

Conscience was a key term in 1 Corinthians 8—10, which we have discussed at length above (on Rom. 2.15). Against Pierce's original claims, this is a positive, not a negative use of the term, as Thrall has argued. The Holy Spirit witnesses to a good conscience about Paul's motives.

Nevertheless Paul declares in verse 2 that he has 'great sorrow [Greek *lupē*] and unceasing anguish [*odunē*] in my heart' concerning his kinspeople the Jews. *Heart*, we observed, denoted the core of one's being, involving feeling, intellect, will and the unconscious. Verse 3 indicates how he is literally 'torn apart'. Ryder Smith gives a moving account of how Moses and Paul are 'torn apart' when their mediation on behalf of the people leads them to say, 'Forgive their sin – and if not, blot me out of your book', or 'I should wish that I myself were accursed [*anathema*] and cast off from Christ for the sake of my own people.' Smith comments in the first place, on Moses,

> *He was as a man that is torn in two.* His unity with the people was so vital that he was ready to die for them. Yet he could not forsake Jehovah with them. It is the tension between these two passions that is the hallmark of saviours . . . He was two men in one, and the two struggled with each other.[13]

Accursed in the LXX translates the Hebrew *cherem* (Deut. 7.26; Josh. 6.17; 7.12). NRSV translates *cherem* as 'the abhorrent thing' and 'devoted to destruction'. The six occurrences in the NT usually mean *cast off* or *accursed*.[14] How devastating such an explicit expression of Paul's attitude and utter grief would be! How many of us would dare to echo such incredible, self-forgetting words? Calvin comments, 'What is it to be separated from Christ but to be excluded from the hope of salvation?'[15]

Paul is utterly sincere when he agrees with contemporary Jews that 'the adoption, the glory, the covenants, the giving of the law, the worship, and the promises' (v. 4) all belong to Israel. So do 'the patriarchs', and in terms

---

[12] Cranfield, *Romans*, vol. 2, p. 446.

[13] Smith, C. Ryder, *The Bible Doctrine of Salvation* (London: Epworth, 1941), pp. 32–3 (his italics).

[14] Danker, Frederick, *A Greek-English Lexicon of the New Testament and Other Early Christian Literature* (BDAG) (Chicago and London: University of Chicago Press, 3rd edn, 2000), p. 63; Lohfink, N., 'cherem' in Botterweck, G. J., and Ringgren, H. (eds), *Theological Dictionary of the Old Testament* (*TDOT*) (15 vols, Grand Rapids: Eerdmans, 1974–), vol. 5, pp. 180–99.

[15] Calvin, *Commentary*, p. 248.

of physical and cultural descent 'the Messiah, who is over all, God blessed for ever. Amen' (v. 5). All these are genuine privileges and signs of God's favour. As Dunn observes, the shift from 'Jews' to 'Israel' is appropriate here for the people of God, and is 'a larger title, able to embrace all who inherit the promise to Abraham, Isaac, and Jacob . . . His [Paul's] thought is primarily of the covenant people to whom God will remain faithful.'[16]

'Adoption' is distinctive, linking Romans 8.15, 23 with Exodus 4.22 and Hosea 11.1. Dunn, again, comments: 'The gospel to Jew and Gentile is all of a piece with, wholly continuous from, that first divine . . . sheer grace.'[17] Adoption (*huiothesia*) reminds us of the allegory of Hagar and Sarah, in Galatians. 'Covenants' is probably plural because these were often renewed (Gen. 6.18; 9.9; 15.18; 17.2; Exod. 2.24). The singular is perhaps wrongly supported by P[46], B, F and G, as against ℵ, C, 33, Vulgate and Syriac. Metzger accords a 'B' grade to the plural reading as indicating that it is 'almost certain'.[18] In the case of *promises* P[46] reads the singular. All these privileges have been mentioned: the promise to Abraham, the law to Moses, fulfilment in Christ. If these now belong to those in Christ, we Gentile Christians should not belittle the status of these privileges for Israel.

These textual problems, however, pale into insignificance when compared with the notorious divergence in Romans 9.5. Sanday and Headlam write, 'The interpretation of Rom. 9:5 has probably been discussed at greater length than any other verse of the N.T.'[19] They provide a long note on different views of the text. In one respect the problem cannot be solved, because everything rests on punctuation, and the Greek text was not punctuated in Paul's day. In another respect, it could be deemed important, because some readings would make this perhaps the only place where Paul explicitly calls Christ 'God', as another writer expresses this in Hebrews 1.3 and 1.8. Because of the first point about punctuation, Sanday and Headlam rightly comment, 'The question is one of interpretation, not criticism.' They also comment, 'The older versions . . . seem to labour under the same obscurity as the original.'[20]

Generally three possibilities have been suggested. (i) The whole clause is referred to Christ after a comma, i.e. 'According to the flesh, the Messiah,

---

[16] Dunn, *Romans 9—16*, p. 533.

[17] Dunn, *Romans 9—16*, p. 533.

[18] Metzger, Bruce, *A Textual Commentary on the Greek New Testament* (New York: UBS, 2nd edn, 1994), p. 459.

[19] Sanday, William, and Headlam, Arthur C., *Critical and Exegetical Commentary on the Epistle to the Romans* (Edinburgh: T & T Clark, 1902; ICC), p. 233.

[20] Sanday and Headlam, *Romans*, p. 234.

who is over all, God blessed for ever'; (ii) a full stop (or period) is placed in the middle of the verse: 'According to the flesh, the Messiah, who is over all. God be blessed for ever'; (iii) a full stop is again placed in the middle of the sentence, i.e. 'According to the flesh the Messiah. God, who is over all, be blessed for ever'.

The first clearly ascribes deity to Jesus Christ, and was adopted by Irenaeus, Tertullian, Hippolytus, Novatian, Cyprian, Athanasius, Chrysostom and Augustine.[21] Some argue that the strongest evidence against the first view is that ℵ has no punctuation, and possibly A points in this direction. B has a colon after 'according to the flesh', and leaves no space in the following sentence. Origen finds ascribing 'God', rather than 'Son of God', to Christ in Pauline letters difficult. Erasmus was the first to say that no doctrine could be inferred from Romans 9.5, as there was no way of deciding certainly about the three interpretations. Among modern scholars, the uncharacteristic theme of ascribing deity explicitly to Christ in Paul meets with some doubt, but not always rejection.

The Greek text of *Deutsche Bibelgesellschaft* (1993 edn, by Aland) has 'Christ . . . the one who is God over all'. The second edition of Nestle–Kilpatrick (1958) anticipates this exactly. But the REB (1990) opts for (ii): 'Messiah. May God, supreme over all, be blessed for ever!' On the other hand NIV retains (i): 'Christ, who is God over all, for ever praised', and NJB has: 'Christ who is above all, God, blessed for ever'. The AV/KJV adopts (i). The NRSV follows (i), but perhaps less decisively and explicitly than the NIV and KJB.

Cranfield considers six possibilities rather than three, and offers complex arguments over nearly six pages, in the end comparing the main three. He concludes that in a broad sense (i) is the most likely, affirming 'Christ's lordship over all things . . . and secondly his divine nature'.[22] Dunn is sympathetic with (i), admitting its stylistic propriety and accordance with Paul's style in Romans 1.25; 2 Corinthians 11.31; Galatians 1.5. But in the end he understands a full stop before 'God over all', which is to be expected, and asserts, 'The Christology implied in (i) is without parallel in Paul.'[23] Dunn follows Käsemann, Kuss, Lietzmann, Barrett, Leenhardt, Wright and NEB. On the other hand Cranfield is joined by Bruce, Cullmann, Michel,

---

[21] Irenaeus, *Against Heresies*, 3.16.2 (Eng., *ANF*, vol. 1, p. 441); Tertullian, *Against Praxeas*, 13 (Eng., *ANF*, vol. 2, p. 608); Hippolytus, *Against Noetus*, 2 (Eng., *ANF*, vol. 5, p. 224); Novatian, *Treatise on the Trinity*, 30 (Eng., *ANF*, vol. 5, p. 642); Cyprian, *Treatises*, 12.6 (Eng., *ANF*, vol. 5, p. 518); *Four Discourses against the Arians*, 3.10 (Eng., *NPNF*, ser. ii, vol. 4, p. 311); and *Discourses*, 4.1 (*NPNF*, ser. ii, vol. 4, p. 433).

[22] Cranfield, *Romans*, vol. 2, p. 469.

[23] Dunn, *Romans 9—16*, p. 529.

Murray, Nygren, Fitzmyer and Jewett, who argue that doubts are in effect countered by Philippians 2.6.[24]

On the content of verses 4–5, we have not yet considered 'the giving of the law, the worship . . . the patriarchs, and . . . the Messiah'. 'The giving of the law' probably refers to God's giving the law to Moses, which is prized so highly by Israel and the Jews. 'The worship' would usually denote the sacrificial cultus and the Temple, the true worship of the one true God, in contrast to human devices of worship. The term probably also embraces the synagogue. 'The patriarchs' primarily refers to Abraham. But Paul reminds his readers that the ultimate privilege is to have nurtured the Jewish birth of Jesus the Messiah.

A final word should be added on 'promises'. Promises look forward to what has not yet occurred. When Hebrew 11.1 declares, 'Faith is the assurance of things . . . not seen', the words 'not seen' include not only the invisible realm but more especially what is *not yet taken place*. A promise is forward-looking, and invites or demands trust. The promise to Abraham in Romans 4 constitutes a classic example: God made a promise (4.13) and guarantee (4.16), and 'No distrust made him [Abraham] waver concerning the promise of God' (4.20). He placed himself entirely in God's hands. Through both promise and covenant an *entirely secure relationship is established*. Eichrodt writes that in the covenant 'Men know exactly where they stand; *an atmosphere of trust and security is created.*'[25]

In Christian theology Luther, Tyndale, Barth and Rahner, among others, have made much of *promise*. Tyndale even anticipated some basic aspects of speech-act theory by showing that many utterances in the Bible have the effect of *performing actions*.[26] Promise constitutes a paradigmatic model of this. In promise God *pledges himself to act* in certain ways. A promise is what Austin calls a 'commissive', with life-changing effects.[27]

God's promises in the history of Israel: his inscrutable ways (9.6–18)

Paul captures the theme in verse 6: 'It is not as though the word of God had failed. For not all Israelites truly belong to Israel'. 'Not as though'

---

[24] Jewett, *Romans*, pp. 555 and 567–8.

[25] Eichrodt, Walther, *Theology of the Old Testament*, vol. 1 (London: SCM, 1961), p. 38 (his italics).

[26] Tyndale, William, 'Pathway into the Holy Scriptures' in *Doctrinal Treatises* (Cambridge: Parkers Society, 1848), pp. 3–13.

[27] Thiselton, Anthony C., 'The Paradigm of Biblical Promise as Trustworthy, Temporal, Transformative Speech-acts' in Lundin, R., Walhout, C., and Thiselton, A. C. (eds), *The Promise of Hermeneutics* (Grand Rapids: Eerdmans, 1999), pp. 223–40.

(Greek *ouch hoion de hoti*) is an unusual idiom for the NT, for which English *is* has to be supplied. 'Failed' strictly means *came to nought*. Barrett heads this section 'God's Elective Purposes'.[28] He adds, 'Israel cannot be defined in terms of physical descent, or simply understood "on the human side".'[29] The promise of God, not the nation's blood and soil, define Israel. Nevertheless, in spite of this distinction, 'Paul is contriving to disinherit the majority of his fellow-Jews, to write a charter of Christian anti-semitism.'[30]

Paul makes a distinction in verse 7 between 'Abraham's children' and 'his true descendants'. While we should not dismiss the concept of Jews by race alone, this prepares us for Paul's redefinition of Israel as Jews who are in Christ. It recalls John the Baptist saying, 'Do not presume to say . . . "We have Abraham as our ancestor" . . . God is able from these stones to raise up children to Abraham' (Matt. 3.9). Moreover, Ishmael was born of Abraham and Hagar (Gen. 15.2). But only Isaac was born of the promise (Gen. 18.10; 21.12). The same theme occurs in Isaiah 41.8; Psalm 105.6; 2 Chronicles 20.7; and 3 Maccabees 6.13. In Paul it occurs elsewhere in Galatians 3.16, 19; and 2 Corinthians 11.22; as well as Romans 4.13, 16, 18; and 11.1. Hence Paul explains in verse 7, 'It is through Isaac that descendants shall be named after you', quoting Genesis 21.12 (LXX) verbatim. The NRSV 'descendants' masks the Greek word for *seed* which it translates. Barrett and Jewett regard *seed* as a key 'restricted' category, although Dunn calls it 'extensive' because it includes children of promise.[31]

Paul presses home the point in verse 8. He declares, 'It is not the children of the flesh who are the children of God, but the children of the promise are counted as descendants [Greek *sperma*].' Galatians 4.22, 30 suggest a parallel argument. Käsemann points out that the contrast between flesh (*sarx*) and promise (*epaggelia*) soon became replaced by that between flesh and Spirit. Paul then quotes an amalgam of LXX Genesis 18.10 and 18.14: 'About this time I will return and Sarah shall have a son.'[32] The supplementary text provides the key word 'son'. The passages confirm Israel's election as son.

The whole section 9.6–13 rehearses the OT narrative of Israel's call through Abraham (v. 7), Isaac (vv. 8–9), and Rebecca and Jacob (vv. 10–13). It will then move on to the exodus (vv. 14–18) and then, in Wright's words, 'to exile and, through it, to the fulfilment of God's worldwide promise to

---

[28] Barrett, C. K., *The Epistle to the Romans* (London: Black, 1957), p. 179.
[29] Barrett, *Romans*, p. 180.
[30] Cranfield, *Romans*, vol. 2, p. 473.
[31] Jewett, *Romans*, p. 576; Dunn, *Romans 9—16*, p. 540.
[32] Dunn, *Romans 9—16*, p. 541.

Abraham (vv. 19–24)'.[33] Scriptural proofs follow in verses 25–29. The birth of Isaac to Sarah was itself a providence of promise. The promise moves on to include Jacob and Rebecca (v. 10). In verse 11 we learn that all the vicissitudes of the Isaac–Rebecca–Jacob–Esau narratives are testimony 'that God's purpose of election might continue'. The same principle as that which characterized God's dealings with Abraham continues, namely 'not by works' but through faith or trust. It extends to Rebecca and Jacob. Hence Paul explicitly declares this in verse 12. No one could imagine that 'good works' characterized Jacob. But God's 'call' (Greek *ek tou kalountos*) found expression in 'The elder shall serve the younger.' The quotation comes from Genesis 15.23. The unfathomable nature of God's call finds further expression in 'I have loved Jacob; but I have hated Esau', a quotation from Malachi 1.2–3 (v. 13).

Wright comments on verse 13:

> It will not do to water this down by suggesting that 'hate' here really means 'loved somewhat less'; even that would be arbitrary, and would merit the question in v. 14 [i.e. is there injustice on God's part?] just the same.[34]

The context in Malachi considers the devastation suffered by Edom (Esau), and God's unmerited love to Israel. Admittedly many commentators try to soften verse 13: Barrett renders it 'God preferred Jacob'. But Wright's point is convincing. Indeed in verses 11–12 'works' or merit is excluded, because election was made even before the birth of each. Paul declares: 'Even before they had been born or had done anything good or bad . . . not by works but by his call'. Jewett endorses the point: it is best 'to allow the words from Malachi to stand as an extreme statement of Paul's basic point'.[35]

The questions beginning in verse 14 return to diatribe style: 'What then are we to say? Is there injustice on God's part?' Paul has used such questions in 3.5; 4.1; 6.1; 7.7; and 8.31. It is also a classic example of Greek *mē*, expecting the answer 'no'. Having viewed the history of Israel through Abraham, Isaac and Jacob, Paul turns to expound the inscrutable ways of *God*. It is unthinkable (Greek *mē genoito*) that God could harbour injustice. Everything in God has its unfathomable origin in God's election or decision, and his grace and love. Hence, 'He says to Moses, "I will have mercy on whom I have mercy, and I will have compassion on whom I have compassion"' (v. 15). Hence: 'It depends not on human will or

---

[33] Wright, 'Romans', *NIB*, vol. 10, p. 635.
[34] Wright, 'Romans', *NIB*, vol. 10, p. 637.
[35] Jewett, *Romans*, p. 580.

exertion, but on God who shows mercy' (v. 16). Humankind has no right to complain, for God is free to choose in accordance with nothing but his own will. The quotation from Exodus 33.19 agrees with the LXX precisely, but is also close to the Hebrew.

God is not 'free' in any *arbitrary* sense, but free to act in accordance with his loving character and promises. Cranfield and Dunn associate the oracular statement in Exodus 33.19 with God's self-revelation in Exodus 3.14, 'I will be what I will be.'[36] Dunn further notes that 33.19 is one of the most frequently cited texts in post-biblical Jewish literature. Paul does not reflect any independence from Jesus. This is exactly the application of the parable of the Labourers in the Vineyard: grace eclipses everything else (Matt. 20.1–16).

In 9.17–18 Paul reinforces the point from a different scene in the exodus narrative, namely that of Moses before Pharaoh in Exodus 9.16. God has both 'raised' Pharaoh up (v. 17) and 'harden[ed his] heart' (v. 18) entirely for God's purposes, which will be 'proclaimed in all the earth' (v. 17). These purposes are that 'He [God] has mercy on whomsoever he chooses' (v. 18). The same principle applies to Pharaoh's 'hardening' (v. 18). None of this is arbitrary. Even God's suspension of judgement has a purpose in the will of God. It is, as Wright argues, 'part of the means, not only of rescuing Israel from slavery, but of declaring God's name to the world'.[37] The point here is that, in Barrett's words, 'Pharaoh exists not to further his own ends, but God's'; Pharaoh had thought himself 'master of the situation in Egypt', but in fact has been urged to further Israel's history and God's glory.[38] The word *hardened* is used frequently in Exodus 7—14 (Exod. 8.15, 32; 9.34), and can mean *unyielding, stubborn*, and was originally a medical term for rough or hard skin. Ziesler comments, 'Just as the selection of Israel-within-Israel was for the divine purpose, so was Pharaoh, though on the negative side, as a foil for the power of God.'[39]

God's sovereign freedom and the remnant (9.19–29)

The heading is Ziesler's title for this section. Paul seeks to answer even more thoroughly the question, 'Is there injustice on God's part?' (v. 14), and proceeds to expound the well-known analogy of the potter and the clay (vv. 20–21). The question, 'Why does he still find fault?' (v. 19) looks

[36] Cranfield, *Romans*, vol. 2, p. 483; Dunn, *Romans 9—16*, p. 522.
[37] Wright, 'Romans', *NIB*, vol. 10, p. 639.
[38] Barrett, *Romans*, p. 186.
[39] Ziesler, *Romans*, p. 243.

as if the dialogue-partner in the diatribe is not yet satisfied. But most understand, 'You will say to me' or 'Will you say to me?' as the objector's question, and understand 'he finds fault' as meaning, 'Why does God still find fault?'[40] Cranfield insists that Paul is *not* here thinking 'of the ultimate destiny of the individual', as Calvin appears to have understood it. In 'Who can resist (*tis anthestēken*) his will?', the perfect active indicative verb can mean 'Who maintains a stand?' (with present force); or 'Who can manage to resist?' Leenhardt comments,

> If man presumes to dispute with God, he must at least try to share God's angle of vision, if he can . . . God's providential government must not be judged by the limited views of man. To help his readers adjust to this field of vision, Paul proposes that they should consider the parable of the potter.[41]

In verses 20–21 Paul introduces this parable. Hunter claims that the argument has reached an *impasse*, while Dodd calls it 'the weakest point in the whole epistle', because here 'A mechanical determinism annihilates morality. Of course the objector is right.'[42] Bruce simply comments, 'God is not answerable to man.'[43] Paul quotes the words directly from Isaiah 29.16 verbatim, and the analogy is found also in Isaiah 44.8; 45.8–10; Jeremiah 18.6; and Wisdom 12.12; 15.7. Paul would have been aware that he was citing a familiar OT analogy. We also discussed Paul's uses of analogy above, with particular reference to Gale's work on the subject. On verse 20 Fitzmyer imagines a moulded object saying to a potter, 'Why did you make me an unshapely pot, rather than a beautiful vase?' On verse 21 he comments, 'The freedom of the potter exemplifies God's sovereign freedom to choose Israel and destine it for fidelity to his covenant.'[44] Wright concludes, 'Israel has no right of appeal, no right to answer God back.' The reason why some commentators (mainly from the 1930s to the 1950s) regard Paul's argument as hopeless is that 'Post-Enlightenment thought . . . has not yet considered the seriousness of sin.'[45]

In verses 22–23 much depends on how we understand the word 'desiring' (NRSV) or 'willing' (Greek *thelōn*). Some understand it as causal, i.e. 'because God willed'. Others regard it as concessive, 'although God willed'. The NRSV 'desiring' and the NIV 'choosing' imply a causal construction. The NJB reads it as concessive. Leenhardt comments, 'God exercises a

---

[40] Fitzmyer, *Romans*, p. 568; Cranfield, *Romans*, vol. 2, p. 489.

[41] Leenhardt, Franz J., *The Epistle to the Romans* (London: Lutterworth, 1961), p. 255.

[42] Dodd, *Romans*, pp. 158–9.

[43] Bruce, F. F., *The Epistle of Paul to the Romans* (London: Tyndale, 1963), p. 195.

[44] Fitzmyer, *Romans*, p. 569.

[45] Wright, 'Romans', *NIB*, vol. 10, p. 641.

patience which has no parallel in the potter's craft.'[46] Repentance and salvation are 'the guiding plan of His providential action ... His patience tolerates "vessels of wrath", which, however, are ripe for destruction.'[47] In any case the construction of the sentence is left incomplete: no apodosis follows the protasis, and the reader is required to complete it.[48] In the end, Denney, Fitzmyer, Black, Leenhardt and Wright understand the participle as concessive. Jewett regards *thelōn* as 'purposive rather than ... causal or concessive'.[49] Yet, like most others, he adds: 'The predominance of mercy over wrath in Paul's elaboration of the metaphor of the potter ... is conveyed by the wording that God "endures with great patience ... those who deserve wrath."'[50]

In verses 23–29 Paul expounds his mercy to the world and to Israel. 'To make known the riches of his glory' suggests not simply the glory of his sovereign majesty, but also the glory of his compassion and love. In verses 24–26 Paul shows how God extends his mercy to the Gentiles, and in verses 27–29 introduces the concept of the 'remnant' of Israel. Unless verse 23 is understood as a new thought, 'to make known' is a purpose clause. 'He has prepared beforehand' (Greek *proētoimasen*) puts 'predestination' in its proper context as 'made ready' for glory. Our section on reception history demonstrates the importance of this passage for Aquinas and others.

Paul clarifies the scope of this corporate election and predestination by stating 'including ... not ... the Jews only but also ... the Gentiles', among those whom he has called (v. 24). In verses 25–26 he stresses that this was predicted in the OT, especially in Hosea 2.23 (2.25 in the LXX) and Hosea 2.1 (LXX; 1.10 Hebrew text). Jewett comments,

> There is a consensus that Paul intentionally altered the wording of Hos. 2:25, 'I will say' to *kalesō*, 'I will *call*', thus linking the citation directly to the divine calling of Jews and Gentiles in v. 24 and providing a connection with ... 'call' in Gen. 21:12.[51]

Stanley anticipates Jewett. He observes: 'The text of Hos. 2:25 ... has been so thoroughly adapted to suit its present application that few of its original words remain intact.'[52] It was originally a promise for mercy to Israel, but

---

[46] Leenhardt, *Romans*, p. 257.

[47] Leenhardt, *Romans*, p. 258.

[48] Dunn, *Romans 9—16*, p. 558.

[49] Jewett, *Romans*, p. 595.

[50] Jewett, *Romans*, p. 596.

[51] Jewett, *Romans*, p. 600.

[52] Stanley, Christopher D., *Paul and the Language of Scripture: Citation Technique in the Pauline Epistles and Contemporary Literature* (Cambridge: CUP, 1992; SNTSMS 74), p. 109.

'not my people', which once meant sinful Israel, means in Romans 9 the Gentiles. God takes those who have *no right to be called 'God's people' and, by pure grace and mercy, extends his renewed covenant to them as 'My people'*.

Interestingly 9.26 includes the word *there* (Greek *ekei*): '*there* they shall be called children of the living God.' Munck suggests that Paul had the vision that 'The Gentile nations are to gather in Jerusalem, where its Messianic kingdom is to be established.'[53] Hence, he argues, Paul is frequently concerned with the relation between the Gentiles (including their offering of collection) and Jerusalem.[54]

Paul rounds off the argument in 9.27–29 with two passages from Isaiah: 10.22–23 with 28.22. Isaiah 10.22 recalls God's promise to Abraham: 'Though your people of Israel were like the sand of the sea, only a remnant [*to hupoleimma*] of them will return.' Paul substitutes 'will be saved'. In Greek 'The Lord will execute his sentence on the earth quickly and decisively' is rendered by NEB as: 'The Lord's sentence . . . will be summary and final' (v. 28). Paul uses *suntelōn kai suntemnōn* from the LXX, while the use of perfect participles with *sun-* means *finishing it and cutting it short*. Isaiah 10.23 has been conflated with Isaiah 28.22b.

The second quotation in verse 29 comes from Isaiah 1.9 (LXX and Hebrew text). Isaiah 1.9 follows a prophecy of desolation for Israel, but concludes, 'If the LORD of hosts had not left us a few survivors, we would have been like Sodom, and become like Gomorrah' (v. 9). Paul quotes verse 9 in full exactly. It corroborates Isaiah 10.22. But what makes all the difference from pagan nations is *the remnant* in Isaiah 1.9 and Romans 9.29. As Cranfield comments, 'It is a miracle of grace . . . God's mercy spares a remnant.'[55]

Wright warns us that one problem for 'modern' readers today is that many instinctively rebel against any notion of sovereign power, in contrast to liberal democracy. But we may need to think again when we are speaking of God, whose power is all-wise, all-merciful, and motivated by nothing but grace and generosity. Even the history of Israel as a whole can take on a new meaning, as Paul seeks to show in chapter 9.[56]

---

[53] Munck, Johannes, *Paul and the Salvation of Mankind* (London: SCM, 1959), p. 306.
[54] Munck, *Paul*, pp. 247–309.
[55] Cranfield, *Romans*, vol. 2, p. 502.
[56] Wright, 'Romans', *NIB*, vol. 10, p. 644.

19

God's faithfulness and Israel's responsibility (9.30—10.21)

The stumbling of Israel (9.30–33)

'What then are we to say?' continues the diatribe style, which invites the continued involvement of the audience and readers. In 9.30–31 Paul depicts a huge irony. He explains that the Gentiles had *not* sought righteousness, but in the end attained it through *faith*, even if not through the law. By contrast, Israel *had* sought righteousness, but could *not* attain it, because they sought it through the *law*. Paul clarifies this in verse 32a: 'Why not? Because they did not strive for it on the basis of faith, but as if it were based on works.' The problem for Israel was that the Gentiles had never bothered about their relation with God, whereas Israel had done. *So, they ask, was this all for nothing?*

Fitzmyer writes, 'In chapter 9 Paul has so far considered the problem of Israel from the standpoint of God; now he begins to consider it from the standpoint of Israel.'[1] Ziesler rightly warns us that righteousness is 'a multi-faceted term . . . This is what historical Israel apart from the faithful remnant has missed, and what those Gentiles who have turned to Christ have found.'[2] Ziesler's comment does justice to verse 32, but misses the qualifying point of verse 33. It would be odd to say that everything depends on the right concept of '*faith*', rather than saying that everything depends on *Christ*, 'a rock that will make them fall' (v. 33). In popular media today, many say, 'My faith has saved me', when they really mean, '*Christ* has saved me.'

Cranfield explains:

> Rom. 9:30 – 10:13 has made the guilt of Israel abundantly clear: it is guilty because it had failed to obey its own law, that very law for which it has been so zealous. It was to faith in Christ that the law was all along leading.[3]

[1] Fitzmyer, Joseph A., *Romans: A New Translation with Introduction and Commentary* (New York: Doubleday, 1992; AB 33), p. 576.

[2] Ziesler, John, *Paul's Letter to the Romans* (London: SCM, 1989 and 1990), p. 250.

[3] Cranfield, C. E. B., *A Critical and Exegetical Commentary on the Epistle to the Romans*, vol. 2 (Edinburgh: T & T Clark, 1979; ICC), p. 505.

Jesus Christ is the inner meaning of the law. Cranfield adds that 'the Gentiles' (v. 30 AV/KJB; RV) or 'the pagans' (JB) are both incorrect, for Greek *ethnē* denotes *some* Gentiles, not all.[4] Fitzmyer also clarifies this: '[Israel's] pursuit of the good was not wrong, but the mode of doing so had become inadequate.'[5] Hence the contrast between faith and works surfaces once again, as in 3.20, 28. Paul will expound and explain this in 10.2. Some MSS ($\aleph^c$, D, 33) add the explanatory 'of the law' after 'works'. But P^{46}, $\aleph^*$, A, B and G rightly retain the shorter form.

Paul concludes verse 32 with 'They have stumbled over the stumbling-stone'. Jews, or many of them, found the gospel what Paul calls a *skandalon* (*snare*, or *stumbling block*), as in 1 Corinthians 1.25. The quotation in verse 33 is a mixture of Isaiah 28.16 and 8.14.[6] Stanley says that this conflation 'has provoked endless rounds of debate, and given rise to a number of important theories concerning early Christian use of the Bible'.[7] Paul himself undertook the conflation, which is not unlike 1 Peter 2.6–8 and Ephesians 2.20. The asyndeton of the Greek gives the words 'a special solemnity... Israel has failed to recognize Him who is the meaning and the goal of the law, and has rejected Him.'[8] The middle part of Isaiah 28.16 has been replaced by part of Isaiah 8.14. The same two Isaiah texts are combined in 1 Peter 2.6–8, which suggests that Paul's theme forms part of an early collection of testimonies or quotations from the earliest Church, as Rendel Harris, Dodd and Lindars have suggested.[9] At first sight *the stone* appears to be the law; hence the translation 'trusts in it'. But the ultimate reference is to *Christ*, as the main reading of NRSV, 'believes in him', rightly suggests. Wright urges that one reason for this rejection is the crucifixion of Jesus, as in 1 Corinthians 1.23 and Galatians 5.11. He concludes, 'The Messiah remains the key to what he [God] has done with Israel... Israel remains God's people according to the flesh.'[10]

---

[4] Cranfield, *Romans*, vol. 2, p. 506.

[5] Fitzmyer, *Romans*, p. 579.

[6] Dunn, James D. G., *Romans 9—16* (Dallas: Word, 1988; WBC 38), p. 583.

[7] Stanley, Christopher D., *Paul and the Language of Scripture: Citation Technique in the Pauline Epistles and Contemporary Literature* (Cambridge: CUP, 1992; SNTSMS 74), p. 120.

[8] Cranfield, *Romans*, vol. 2, p. 510.

[9] Harris, J. R., *Testimonies* (2 vols, Cambridge: CUP, 1916–20), vol. 1, pp. 18–19 and 26–7; Dodd, C. H., *According to the Scripture* (London: Nisbet, 1952), pp. 42–3; and Lindars, Barnabas, *New Testament Apologetic* (Philadelphia: Westminster, 1961); Cranfield, C. E. B., 'Romans 9:30—10:4', *Int* 34 (1980), pp. 70–4.

[10] Wright, N. T., 'Romans' in the *New Interpreter's Bible* (*NIB*) (Nashville: Abingdon, 2002), vol. 10, p. 651.

The new law as Christ, and as being new (10.1–13)

Paul again expresses his grief that Israel in general has failed to recognize God's purpose. He describes his hope for their salvation not only as his 'heart's desire' but also as his active prayer (v. 1). He testifies that the Jews have a genuine 'zeal' for God, even if it is 'without knowledge' (AV/KJB) or 'not enlightened' (NRSV). Bell regards zeal/jealousy (Greek *zēlos/parazēloun*) as the key to 9—11. He sees Romans 10.2 as entirely consonant with 10.19. He writes:

> Concerning the word play *zēlos/parazēloun* . . . Israel has a zeal for God (or a jealousy for God) . . . but not according to knowledge (10:2). Israel will not be saved through zeal based on ignorance, but through being provoked to jealousy.[11]

In Romans 10.2 this represents the 'zeal' of the pre-conversion of Paul; in 10.19 it is manifested in anger; in Romans 11.11, 14, as emulation. 'Jealousy is manifested in different ways in the two chapters.'[12] Thus the *zēlos* words build a 'double bridge': between Israel's failure to believe the gospel, and Israel's salvation; and between Israel's salvation and the salvation of the Gentiles.

Although Paul asserts the misunderstanding of the law on the part of Jews or wider 'Israel', this does not deny their 'zeal for God'. But this is not 'according to knowledge' (Greek *kat' epignōsin*). Both Bell (who has deep reservations about Sanders' 'New Perspective') and Dunn (who, with modifications, generally favours it) agree that the pre-conversion Paul knew this zeal from the inside. Dunn writes, 'He [Paul] too had taken the sword to protect Judaism's distinctive prerogatives.'[13] This becomes even clearer in verse 3 in the contrast between 'the righteousness that comes from God' and 'seeking to establish their own'. Sanders' view at this point might seem to require modifications, even if he has many insights also.

A much-discussed text is: 'For Christ is the end of the law' (v. 4, Greek *telos gar nomou Christos*). The term *end* (*telos*) used once to be understood in the sense of termination. Many who recently have rejected this interpretation include Jewett and Wright, who convincingly point out that Paul's statement is not context-free, but clearly follows all that precedes it. They therefore propose 'Christ is the *goal* of the law', which is equally

---

[11] Bell, Richard H., *Provoked to Jealousy: The Origin and Purpose of the Jealousy Motif in Romans 9—11* (Tübingen: Mohr, 1994; WUNT II.63), pp. 103–4.

[12] Bell, *Provoked to Jealousy*, p. 358 and pp. 5–43.

[13] Dunn, *Romans 9—16*, p. 587.

the meaning of *telos*.[14] It is *not*, they insist, a summary of some doctrine of freedom from the law, but takes up the different senses of *law* from the previous chapter. The NEB and JB perpetuated misunderstanding by translating respectively 'Christ ends the law', and, 'Now the Law has come to an end'. By contrast the NJB translates 'The Law has found its fulfilment in Christ'. In the past, for example, Bengel had commented: 'The law presses a man, till he flies to Christ . . . In Christ there is an end to the validity of the law.'[15]

Not all older commentators took this view. Danker includes in the range of meanings denoted by *telos*: (i) termination, completion, end; (ii) close, conclusion; (iii) goal, outcome; (iv) the last in a series, rest, remainder; and (v) a meaning irrelevant to this verse. He includes Romans 10.4 under (iii), although he writes: 'Christ is the goal and the termination of the law at the same time, somewhat in the sense of Gal. 3:24–25.'[16] Similarly Delling includes 'end, goal, perfection and climax, in its [the word's] *semantic range*'.[17] When the LXX speaks of 'until the end' (*eis telos*) it usually means reaching some intended goal or completion. When Plutarch says, 'Justice is the goal of the law', the meaning of *telos* is similar to that of 10.4.[18]

The context of chapters 9—10 suggests not the total abolition of the law, but that believing Jews and Christians should observe the law in a new way, i.e. 'So that there may be righteousness for everyone who believes' (10.4b). Faith plays a vital role; but not in the abstract. Faith is defined by that towards which it is directed, namely Christ. Wright sums up the point, citing numerous passages: 'In 10:4 Paul does not intend to declare the law's abrogation in favour of a different "system", but rather to announce that the Messiah is himself the climax of the long story of God and Israel.'[19]

Most of the Church Fathers tended to opt for either 'fulfilment' or 'goal', often comparing Matthew 5.17, 'Do not think that I have come to abolish the law . . . not to abolish but to fulfil.'[20] Augustine appears to have adopted ambiguous meanings, sometimes claiming the meaning *termination*, but rejecting *abolition* and defending *perfection*. Nicholas of Lyon and Aquinas understood it as 'perfection'. In recent times 'termination' has

[14] Jewett, Robert, *Romans: A Commentary* (Minneapolis: Fortress, 2007; Hermeneia), p. 619; Wright, 'Romans', *NIB*, vol. 10, p. 652.

[15] Bengel, J. Albert, *Gnomon Novi Testamenti* (Lat., Stuttgart: Steinkopf, 1866; Eng., *New Testament Word Studies* (2 vols, Grand Rapids: Kregel, 1971), vol. 2, p. 121.

[16] Danker, Frederick, *A Greek-English Lexicon of the New Testament and Other Early Christian Literature* (BDAG) (Chicago and London: University of Chicago Press, 3rd edn, 2000), pp. 998–9.

[17] Delling, Gerhard, '*telos etc.*' in Kittel, G., and Friedrich, G. (eds), *Theological Dictionary of the New Testament* (*TDNT*) (10 vols, Grand Rapids: Eerdmans, 1964–76), vol. 8 (1972), pp. 49–50.

[18] Plutarch, *Princ. Iner.*, 780C; also cited by Jewett, *Romans*, p. 619.

[19] Wright, 'Romans', *NIB*, vol. 10, p. 658.

[20] Cranfield, *Romans*, vol. 2, pp. 516–17.

been supported by Lietzmann, Sanday and Headlam, Dodd, Michel and Käsemann. On the other hand Leenhardt declares, 'Christ fulfils the underlying intention of the law and supersedes it.'[21] Cranfield goes much further: 'He [Christ] is the goal . . . Paul is concerned to show that Israel had misunderstood the law . . . Christ is the goal to which all along the law has been directed.'[22] Dunn (with Cranfield, Ziesler and Wright) quotes Badenas: 'Christ embodies the righteousness which the law promised.'[23] Denney among older commentators and Moule more recently see the law as continuing, but as ending *as a means of salvation*.

Romans 10.5–11 gives corroboration of this interpretation, and is 'a difficult but vital passage'.[24] Paul begins a new discussion of faith. The righteousness 'that comes from faith' (v. 6) leads to the experience that 'The word is near you' (v. 8). Edith Humphrey has made a special study of 10.6–8 within 9.30—10.21. She points out that too many commentators dismiss or bypass the imagery of 10.6–7 on the assumption that 'cosmic journeys' are metaphorical or impossible.[25] Certainly Paul makes a major allusion to Deuteronomy 30.11–14, as Hays stresses, although not to Deuteronomy 30 alone.[26] 'Do not say in your heart' reflects Deuteronomy 8.17 and 9.4. Moreover in Baruch 3.29–30 this introduction is followed by Baruch 4.1, 'Who has gone up into heaven and brought her [i.e. Wisdom or Torah] down?' Humphrey writes, quoting Hays and Suggs, 'Paul's filtered citation of Deuteronomy echoes these Wisdom traditions in which Wisdom is identified with Israel's Torah.'[27] She correctly argues that, according to Paul, the Torah and Divine Wisdom are no longer far away, but have come near and are open to all through Christ. She also appeals to indirect corroboration in *Targum Neofiti* and to Philo. In Christ the law is no longer an esoteric mystery. Paul's discussion in 2 Corinthians 3—4, especially 4.6, 'in the face of Jesus Christ', shows this.

---

[21] Leenhardt, Franz J., *The Epistle to the Romans* (London: Lutterworth, 1961), p. 266.

[22] Cranfield, *Romans*, vol. 2, p. 519.

[23] Dunn, *Romans 9—16*, p. 590; and Badenas, R., *Christ the End of the Law: Romans 10:4 in Pauline Perspective* (Sheffield: JSOT Press, 1985), p. 119; Ziesler, *Romans*, p. 258.

[24] Wright, 'Romans', *NIB*, vol. 10, p. 658.

[25] Humphrey, Edith M., 'Why Bring the Word Down? The Rhetoric of Demonstration and Disclosure in Romans 9:31—10:21' in Soderlund, Sven K., and Wright, N. T. (eds), *Romans and the People of God* (Grand Rapids: Eerdmans, 1999), pp. 131 and 129–48.

[26] Hays, Richard, *Echoes of Scripture in the Letters of Paul* (New Haven: Yale University Press, 1989), p. 29; Wright, N. T., *The Climax of the Covenant: Christ and the Law in Pauline Theology* (Edinburgh: T & T Clark; and Minneapolis: Fortress, 1991), pp. 193–216.

[27] Humphrey, 'Why Bring the Word Down?', p. 133; Hays, *Echoes*, p. 80; and Suggs, Jack, 'The Word Is Near You': Romans 10:6–10' in Farmer, W. R., Moule, C. F. D., and Niebuhr, R. R., *Christian History and Interpretation* (Cambridge: CUP, 1967), pp. 289–312.

Paul emphasizes, then, that God's command is *not* hidden away in heaven, as if people need to wonder, 'Who will go up to obtain it?' Nor, as in Baruch 3.35–36; 4.1, is it beyond the sea. For 'the sea', Paul substitutes 'the abyss', as in Psalm 107.26 (106.26 LXX). When he alludes to the law or Wisdom, Paul sees the figure of Christ, and in him the goal, intention and fulfilment of the law. In response to those who claim that Paul is 'stretching' Deuteronomy 30, Barrett points out that he is not proving doctrine by it, but using it rhetorically, to indicate a suggestive thought. Barrett comments, 'He is not using his quotation as a rigid proof . . . but as a rhetorical form.'[28] The counterpart, he says, of bringing Christ down from heaven is not crossing the sea, but bringing Christ up from the underworld, or the abode of the dead. This also is sheer impossibility since the resurrection has already happened. Cranfield goes even further: Paul's treatment of Deuteronomy 30.11–12, he says, is not 'merely arbitrary, like much of the exegesis of Qumran . . . There is a real inward justification for what Paul is doing here. It is not arbitrary typology, but true interpretation in depth.'[29]

At the beginning of these difficult verses, 'The righteousness that comes from faith' (*hē ek pisteōs dikaiosunē*) is actually personified as the speaker: it 'says'. There is no need to bring Christ 'down' from heaven; he has already come and been raised from the dead. In spite of those who, like Dunn, are not happy with a notion of the Incarnation in Paul (in spite of Phil. 2.6–11), it is arguable that it is implicit in these verses. Cranfield, however, appeals to 'the fact that the Son of God has now become incarnate' as shedding light on Paul's meaning.[30] Jewett follows Humphrey in stressing the importance of Baruch 3.29–30, Philo, *The Posterity of Cain*, 84–5, and *Targum Neofiti* 1, for Paul's use of Deuteronomy 30.12–14. In the end, he observes, 'From a rhetorical point of view, the version of this text cited by the imaginary character called Righteousness by Faith is more coherent and succinct than Deuteronomy.'[31]

The conclusion of verse 8 prepares the way for the pre-Pauline confession of verse 9. The word 'in your heart', which is 'the word of faith that we proclaim', turns out to be the common gospel shared by the whole apostolic Church before Paul. Neufeld and many others discuss this pre-Pauline confession of faith.[32] Paul states, in harmony with his predecessors,

---

[28] Barrett, C. K., *The Epistle to the Romans* (London: Black, 1957), p. 199.

[29] Cranfield, *Romans*, vol. 2, p. 524.

[30] Cranfield, *Romans*, vol. 2, p. 525.

[31] Jewett, *Romans*, p. 627.

[32] Neufeld, Vernon H., *The Earliest Christian Confessions* (Leiden: Brill, and Grand Rapids: Eerdmans, 1963), pp. 43, 62, 68 and throughout.

'If you confess [Greek *ean homologēsēis*] with your lips that Jesus is Lord and believe in your heart that God raised him from the dead, you will be saved' (v. 9). As long ago as 1940 Hunter included this among his 'Pre-Pauline Formulae' (together with Rom. 1.1–4; and Rom. 4.24), as distinct from pre-Pauline traditions (1 Cor. 11.23; 15.3–5). This, he insists, comes from the common Christian credo.[33] This preaching has two components: God raised Christ from the dead (cf. 1 Cor. 15.2), and Jesus is Lord (1 Cor. 12.3; Phil. 2.11). Other passages in Paul which refer to belief in the resurrection of Christ are Romans 4.24; 8.11; 2 Corinthians 4.14; and Galatians 1.1; in common with 1 Peter 1.21. *Homologeō* is the regular word for *confess*, as Cullmann, Carrington, Neufeld and others corroborate.[34]

Belief and public confession are inseparable, as Pelagius observed. Christ's resurrection is seen as the action of God, as we noted above with reference to Dahl. 'Saved' denotes here future eschatological salvation, but, as Scott has shown, Paul uses the term with all three tenses. It is decisive in the past (as when someone is 'saved' from a sinking ship); it is a continuous experience (as when a lifeboat takes the rescued person to the shore); and it is future expectation (as when he or she lands safely on *terra firma*).[35]

Meanwhile Neufeld writes, 'The confession of Jesus as the Christ was in the first instance a personal declaration of faith . . . [Then] the primitive confession served as the basic core of the proclamation (Rom. 10:9, II Cor. 4:5; Acts 5:42) . . .'[36] Increasingly it became a confession in the public world, and came 'to designate the Christian who has suffered persecution . . . for his faith'.[37] Dunn, Fitzmyer, Jewett and others broadly adopt this approach. Whether, however, as some have maintained, this is also a *baptismal* confession seems to go beyond explicit evidence.

In verses 10–11 the NRSV 'one believes' and 'one confesses' represents the *present passive* 'it is believed' (*pisteuetai*) and 'it is confessed'. In verse 11 Paul quotes from Isaiah 28.16 (LXX), which he did in Romans 9.35. But Paul adds 'all' who believe, which the NRSV translates negatively as 'no one' who believes in him (v. 11). In verse 10, Wright observes, 'The connection of righteousness with faith is clear.'[38] On the other hand, 'Christ

---

[33] Hunter, A. M., *Paul and His Predecessors* (London: SCM, 1940, 2nd edn, 1961), p. 28.

[34] Cullmann, Oscar, *The Earliest Christian Confessions* (London: Lutterworth, 1949); Carrington, Philip, *The Primitive Christian Catechism* (Cambridge: CUP, 1940); Neufeld, *Earliest Christian Confessions*, pp. 13–32 and 42–68.

[35] Scott, C. Anderson, *Christianity According to St. Paul* (Cambridge: CUP, 1927).

[36] Neufeld, *Earliest Christian Confessions*, pp. 144 and 145.

[37] Neufeld, *Earliest Christian Confessions*, p. 18.

[38] Wright, 'Romans', *NIB*, vol. 10, p. 664.

is Lord' may well be a baptismal confession. Wright approves of 'The one who believes in him will not be put to shame', and regards 'disappointed' as too weak.[39]

Paul returns to his major concern in verse 12: 'For there is no distinction between Jew and Greek; the same Lord is Lord of all and is generous to all who call on him.' Paul had argued in Romans 1—3 that *all alike* were in sin, and in Romans 4—8 that *all alike* were justified through Jesus Christ, and faith in him. This speaks directly to Paul's concern about mutual respect in the Church between Jewish Christians and Gentile Christians. *All* are responsible to Christ as Lord of all, and *all* belong primarily to him. Jewett adds, 'The honour/shame distinctions that divided the Greco-Roman world have been eliminated by Christ, [who is] "Lord of all".'[40]

Paul brings his argument to a climax in verse 13, with a traditional quotation from Joel 2.32 (LXX). The 'all' of Joel 2 underlines the universal scope of the promise. Elsewhere in the NT the passage features in Acts 2.16–21 on the Day of Pentecost. In Joel 2.28 God has promised to pour out his Spirit on 'all flesh'. 'Lord' (*kurios*) in Joel referred to God, but in Romans *kurios* refers to Jesus Christ. In Dunn's words,

> In the eschatological time introduced by Christ it is the universal openness of God's grace to *all* who believe which leaves Jew without advantage over Greek, since Gentiles can now share in what was previously a more exclusively Jewish covenant relationship.[41]

The citation of Joel 2.32, he continues, 'is a salvation-history point . . . He [Paul] is stressing the complete continuity between God's purpose through his covenant with Israel and the climax of that purpose in Christ.'[42]

Israel's failure to respond to the gospel (10.14–21)

Israel has not taken advantage, however, of its ready access to God and his word through Christ. Paul reaffirms, again in the form of a diatribe, that the gospel was offered to all in Christ. Paul anticipates four possible objections to this argument from his imaginary dialogue-partner: (i) people cannot believe unless the gospel has been preached to them by messengers who have been sent (vv. 14–15); (ii) the gospel has not been accepted by everyone (vv. 16–17); (iii) some may not have heard the gospel (v. 18);

---

[39] Wright, 'Romans', *NIB*, vol. 10, p. 665.
[40] Jewett, *Romans*, p. 632.
[41] Dunn, *Romans 9—16*, p. 610.
[42] Dunn, *Romans 9—16*, p. 617.

and (iv) Israel may still not have understood it (vv. 19–21).[43] The key lies in 11.13–14, where Paul celebrates his apostolic vocation to preach to the Gentiles to make Israel 'according to the flesh' jealous of the Gentile response.[44]

This could be expressed in another way. In general the Jews have not believed the gospel. If they have not called on his name, why is this? Is it because they have never heard the gospel? That would imply that no preacher has been sent! But a preacher has been sent, in accordance with Isaiah 52.7, 'How beautiful . . . are the feet of the messenger'. It is, rather, that they have not 'believed what we have heard' (Isa. 53.1).

Paul's first question arising from these four issues, 'How are they to call on one in whom they have not believed?', has traditionally been understood as arguing that the Jews have no excuse for their attitude; they are fully responsible for it. This interpretation has been taken by Chrysostom, Knox, Barrett, Munck and others.[45] At minimum, Paul says that they have had every opportunity to come to faith. Yet he concedes that these are necessary conditions: preaching, acceptance, hearing and understanding. However, Calvin understands Paul's emphasis to lie on his justification for preaching to the Gentiles.[46] The NRSV is correct to translate the verbs in the questions as deliberative subjunctive: 'How are they to call?' (Greek *pōs oun epi kalesōntai*). 'How are they to believe?' (Greek *pōs pisteusōmin*). 'How are they to hear?' (Greek *pōs akousōsin*). These are all aorist *subjunctives*.

The condition of requiring a preacher is strengthened by verse 15, in which Paul quotes from Isaiah 52.7. It is closer here to the Hebrew text than to the LXX. The preacher must be 'sent' (Greek *apostellō*) and this becomes *apostolos* (*apostle*) as the Catholic commentator Estius asserts.[47] Fitzmyer also comments, 'The preacher is spokesman for another, not . . . someone with his own message, authorized by himself . . . Paul uses the verb *apostellein*, alluding to the "apostolic" origin of the testimony of the Christian church.'[48] Preachers need to be 'sent'. This relates closely to Paul's call as apostle to the Gentiles.

In verse 16 Paul observes, 'But not all have obeyed the good news', and cites Isaiah 53.1 (LXX). 'Obeyed' translates *hupakouō*, which means both

---

[43] Fitzmyer, *Romans*, p. 595.

[44] Wright, 'Romans', *NIB*, vol. 10, p. 666; and Bell, *Provoked to Jealousy*, throughout.

[45] Munck, Johannes, *Paul and the Salvation of Mankind* (London: SCM, 1959), pp. 40 and 300; Barrett, *Romans*, pp. 203–6.

[46] Calvin, John, *Calvin's Bible Commentaries: Romans* (London: Forgotten Books, 2007 [1847]), pp. 294–6.

[47] Estius, William, *D. Pauli Epistolas Commentarii* (3 vols, Lat., Moguntiae: Francisci Kirchhemii, 1858), vol. 1, p. 236.

[48] Fitzmyer, *Romans*, pp. 596–7.

listen and *submit to.* Scripture confirms that many will not respond. The verse continues the thought of verse 15, but formulates a second objection to Paul's case: the gospel has not been accepted by everyone, as the prophets foretold.

In verse 17 faith begins with listening to the word of the gospel. This verse shows the importance of preaching, and (contrary to trends in some churches) preaching by those who are trained to articulate the gospel, especially that 'Jesus is Lord' (10.9). Fitzmyer understands *hupakoē pisteōs*, the obedience of faith, from Romans 1.5 (not v. 17), as 'the personal commitment of faith' which results from hearing the word of Christ.[49]

The question, 'Have they not heard?' (v. 18), strictly translates *mē ouk ēkousan*; but *mē* expects the answer 'no', so 'Did they fail to hear?' might well be better. 'Hear' picks up the word from verse 17 (Greek *ex akoēs*). Paul has used the triple conjunction Greek *menounge* in 9.20, where it meant 'On the contrary'; NRSV renders it 'Indeed they have'. Paul then quotes Psalm 19.4 (18.5 LXX) following the LXX word for word: 'Their voice has gone out to all the earth'. Dunn calls this 'a hyperbolic vision of the full eschatological sweep of the Gentile mission (1.8; 2 Cor. 2:14; 3:2; Col. 1:6, 23; I Thess. 1:8)'.[50] 'The ends of the world' are relevant to Paul's plans for a future mission to Spain, the end of the Mediterranean world.

Nevertheless in verse 19 Paul turns to Israel in the sense of Jews by race to whom the promise was made: 'Did Israel not understand?' He now turns to Deuteronomy 32.21 (LXX). Here comes the key term 'jealousy', rendering *parazēlōsō*. Bell devotes more than eight pages to *parazēloō* and this verse. It means especially 'provoke to jealous anger' here.[51] The parallel line is 'With a foolish nation I will make you angry' (v. 19). The Jews had worshipped 'no-gods', and God now shows favour to a 'no-people' (or NRSV 'not a nation'). In Bell's words, 'If a foolish nation has known the gospel, then Israel should have known.'[52] The same applies to 'understanding' the gospel. Israel has been given a spirit of stupor (11.8), and has stumbled over the stone of offence (9.33). Israel has not understood the gospel, as in 10.3, and 1 Corinthians 1.23. Bell considers seven possible interpretations of verse 19. He concludes that Israel becomes jealous of the Gentiles in anger, but must learn the right kind of jealousy.[53] In effect, Ziesler agrees, commenting:

---

[49] Fitzmyer, *Romans*, p. 598.
[50] Dunn, *Romans 9—16*, p. 624.
[51] Bell, *Provoked to Jealousy*, p. 96.
[52] Bell, *Provoked to Jealousy*, p. 98.
[53] Bell, *Provoked to Jealousy*, pp. 103–14.

Israel has been set aside in favour of another nation. This roughly corresponds to Rom. 9:14–29, though it is more negative . . . Isa. 65:1 in v. 20 . . . stresses not the rejection of Israel, but the gathering in of the Gentile nations.[54]

Verse 21 continues to follow the LXX text of Isaiah, except that Paul places 'All day long' before 'I have held out my hands to a disobedient . . . people.' These words underline the persistency of Israel's lack of response and of God's patience. As Bell notes, 'God's revealing himself to the Gentiles and not to Israel finds a parallel in Matt. 11:25–27; the inclusion of the Gentiles is not distinctive to Paul.'[55] Bell concludes, the emphasis of 10.14–21 is less on Israel's guilt than on the gospel's being for 'the whole world' (10.14–18), for the Gentiles as well as for the Jews. Deuteronomy 32.1–43 was important both for Paul and for other NT writers, as Bruce stresses. Paul uses Deuteronomy 32.5 in Philippians 2.15; and uses Deuteronomy 32.16–17 in 1 Corinthians 10.20, 22; while Deuteronomy 32.43 (LXX) occurs in Hebrews 1.6. In chapter 11 Paul will show how the response of the Gentiles provokes Israel, or the remnant of Israel, to turn to God through Christ.

---

[54] Ziesler, *Romans*, p. 267.
[55] Bell, *Provoked to Jealousy*, p. 105.

20

The salvation of 'all Israel' (11.1–36)

The principle of the remnant (11.1–10)

Wright introduces chapters 9—11 by warning us that many advocates of 'dispensational' theology, according to Scofield and others, regard Romans 11 as a critical text in predicting the eventual salvation of Jewry, perhaps following the institution of the Jewish state in 1947–8. Some also stress the tragedy of the Nazi Holocaust. Nevertheless, he warns us, we should not consider theological and political theory beforehand, and then careful exegesis. If Paul does say anything about 'ethnic Jews', salvation remains through faith in Jesus Christ.[1]

As Bell and Wright point out, Romans 10.19, 21 provoke the question with which Paul begins 11.1: 'Has God rejected his people?'[2] In the light of what he has said about God's purpose and promise, he replies to this question with an emphatic 'By no means!' (Greek *mē genoito*). He cites the example of himself, who remains a Jew in the purest sense: 'I myself am an Israelite, a descendant of Abraham, a member of the tribe of Benjamin.' God has not 'rejected' (Greek *mē apōsato, to push away, to repudiate*) his people (v. 2). Paul quotes Psalm 94.14, changing its future to an aorist, or punctiliar tense. P^{46} and G read 'the inheritance' instead of 'the people'. Metzger suggests that this is a Western assimilation to Psalm 94 (93 LXX).[3]

God has not abandoned his people Israel; Paul constitutes an example of this. Paul speaks from within 'Israel'.[4] He explicitly adds 'whom he foreknew', i.e. Israel was part of God's plan or purpose for the world. He then appeals to what Scripture said about Elijah (1 Kings 18.1–46). The prophet Elijah stood against worship of the *baalim* under Queen Jezebel, indeed against 450 prophets of 'Baal' on Mount Carmel. But in the midst

---

[1] Wright, N. T., 'Romans' in the *New Interpreter's Bible* (*NIB*) (Nashville: Abingdon, 2002), vol. 10, p. 673.

[2] Bell, Richard H., *Provoked to Jealousy: The Origin and Purpose of the Jealousy Motif in Romans 9—11* (Tübingen: Mohr, 1994; WUNT II.63), p. 107.

[3] Metzger, Bruce, *A Textual Commentary on the Greek New Testament* (New York: UBS, 2nd edn, 1994), p. 464.

[4] Dunn, James D. G., *Romans 9—16* (Dallas: Word, 1988; WBC 38), p. 635.

of Elijah's subsequent depression, God reassured him that he was not alone (v. 3); indeed 'Seven thousand men . . . have not bowed the knee to Ba'al' (1 Kings 19.18; Rom. 11.4). The practical relevance of this comes in 11.6: 'So too at the present time there is a *remnant, chosen by grace.*' This verse introduces the key term *remnant has been chosen* (Greek *leimma kat' eklogēn*).

Paul clinches the point by what Wittgenstein would have called a 'grammatical' remark, i.e. a comment on the internal *logic* of the *concept* of grace: 'If it is by grace, it is no longer on the basis of works, otherwise grace would no longer be grace' (v. 6). Barrett comments, 'Paul is here defining his terms . . . If you confuse such opposites as faith and works, then words will simply lose their meaning.'[5] I wrote 35 years ago:

> [This] provides a paradigm case of what grace amounts to. If grace does not exclude the notion of works, it can mean either nothing or everything . . . Paul is not giving information, but clarifying their *concept* of grace . . . He is making a grammatical remark.[6]

Paul begins his second diatribe in verse 7, with the question, 'What then?', which is a rhetorical question. Wright suggests that the second clause is also a question: 'What Israel sought, did it not obtain?' Paul then replies, 'Well, the elect obtained it – but the rest were hardened' (v. 7).[7] The reference to *being hardened* looks back to 9.14–24. It is part of Jewish theology, Wright adds, that if the time for repentance is delayed or extended, those who remain stubborn become hardened. Romans 9.17–18 alluded to the 'hardening' of Pharaoh. Jewett comments that Paul reiterates the argument of 9.30–33; Israel's failure is because of the misconception that 'righteousness' is based on works.[8] This is confirmed in verse 8, 'God gave them a sluggish spirit, eyes that would not see . . . down to this very day.' Paul links together parts of Deuteronomy 29.3; Isaiah 29.10; and Psalm 69.23–24.

In verse 9 Paul quotes Psalm 69.23–24 (68.23–24 LXX). *Snare, trap* and *stumbling-block* recall his argument about foolishness in 1 Corinthians 1.18–25. Ziesler points out that this theme is prominent also in the Gospels (Mark 3.5; 6.52; 8.17; John 12.40) and in 2 Corinthians 3.14.[9] In verse 10 Paul alludes to Deuteronomy 29.3 and Isaiah 29.10. He has cited the Law, the Prophets and the Writings.

---

[5] Barrett, C. K., *The Epistle to the Romans* (London: Black, 1957), p. 209.

[6] Thiselton, Anthony C., *The Two Horizons* (Exeter: Paternoster, and Grand Rapids: Eerdmans, 1980), p. 389.

[7] Wright, 'Romans', *NIB*, vol. 10, p. 676.

[8] Jewett, Robert, *Romans: A Commentary* (Minneapolis: Fortress, 2007; Hermeneia), p. 661.

[9] Ziesler, John, *Paul's Letter to the Romans* (London: SCM, 1989 and 1990), p. 271.

The redefinition of 'all Israel': rejection is not final (11.11–32)

NRSV 'Have they stumbled so as to fall?' is rendered more clearly by Wright: 'Granted that Israel according to the flesh has "stumbled", has that stumble meant a permanent "fall"? Certainly not, Paul replies.'[10] (1) The first stage of his three-stage reply is that Israel's temporary failure has been for the good of the Gentiles, and Israel will become jealous of this (11.11–16). (2) The second stage of the argument concerns 'branches broken off God's cultivated olive tree, while the Gentiles are like wild branches grafted in surprisingly' (11.17–24).[11] (3) The third stage is the mystery of God's dealings with Israel, and the redefined 'all Israel' (11.25–32). The eventual conclusion is a paean of praise (11.33–36).

(1) 'Salvation has come to the Gentiles' (NRSV). This has the purpose of making Israel jealous (v. 11, Greek *eis to parazēlōsai*). Knox calls this the turning point in the argument.[12] Israel reaches a state of sin or 'failure' (Greek *paraptōma*). Byrne observes that Greek *ptaiein* and *piptein* overlap in the sense of 'fall', although the second term is irreversible.[13] This fall leads to the salvation of the Gentiles; Israel is provoked to jealousy. Munck writes,

> What was Paul's conception of the way leading from the Jews' jealousy to their salvation? . . . As soon as the Jew can see and realize that the *Gentiles* are attaining what was promised to *Israel*, the possibility of jealousy exists.[14]

The early pre-Pauline view, Munck and Whiteley argue, was to see Israel as the 'rudder' that guided the Gentiles in. But in Paul's theology, Gentiles become the rudder to lead the Jews to salvation, as 'the true Israel'.[15]

In verse 12, as Wright and others observe, the NRSV 'defeat' and 'riches' as well as 'defeat' and 'full inclusion' reflect a deliberate contrast, except that NRSV may not be the most adequate translation. NRSV's 'defeat' (Greek *hēttēma*) may strictly mean *failure* (RSV) or *falling-off* (NEB), but here represents a 'cutting down of numbers' (Barrett) or 'diminution' (Wright), in contrast to 'full inclusion' (NRSV) or *fullness* (Greek *to plērōma*). In contrast to the persistent 'narrowing down' of Israel until it becomes the remnant, and ultimately turns to Christ (Rom. 5.12, 18), even so after the

---

[10] Wright, 'Romans', *NIB*, vol. 10, p. 679.

[11] Wright, 'Romans', *NIB*, vol. 10, p. 680.

[12] Knox, John, 'The Epistle to the Romans', *Interpreter's Bible* (*IB*) (Nashville: Abingdon, 1954), vol. 9, p. 568.

[13] Byrne, Brendan, *Romans* (Collegeville: Liturgical Press, 1996 and 2007; Sacra Pagina 6), p. 344.

[14] Munck, Johannes, *Paul and the Salvation of Mankind* (London: SCM, 1959), p. 45 (my italics).

[15] Whiteley, D. E. H., *The Theology of St. Paul* (Oxford: Blackwell, 1970), p. 87.

coming of Christ 'all Israel' swells into a 'fullness', i.e. *full strength*, or the *complete number of the faithful*. Bell comments, 'In 11:12 Paul . . . issues the *a fortiori* argument that if Israel's disobedience means riches for the world . . . how much more their fullness.'[16]

In verses 13–17 Paul directly addresses his Gentile readers. ('You' is emphatic.) Barrett offers us a helpful paraphrase of verse 13: 'The more I make of my Gentile mission, the more jealous will the Jews become, and this will lead in the end to what I desire – their salvation.'[17] In pastoral terms, Knox observes, Paul distances himself from any form of ministry which might involve contempt for the Jews.[18] 'Inasmuch then, as I am an apostle to the Gentiles' means: 'in his very capacity as apostle of the Gentiles . . . Paul was [not] turning his back upon the unbelieving Jews'.[19] Knox, Cranfield and Wright remind us of the pastoral situation in Rome, where Paul seeks to foster mutual respect between Jewish and Gentile Christians. Wright observes, 'This section . . . is an argument against Gentile arrogance.'[20]

Many commentators seem to ignore the tentative and modest words 'if perhaps', or 'if by any means' (Greek *ei pōs*). Paul leaves his degree of success and the precise means in the hands of God. He 'glorifies his ministry' only with extreme humility. NRSV's oversimple 'in order to' misses this point. Even Paul is uncertain about both the means and the time when this provoking to jealousy will have its redeeming effects. Jewett briefly notes this, and renders 'provoke to jealousy' as a subjunctive, i.e. 'might make zealous/jealous'.[21] Bell insists that the verb *parazēlōsō* is future indicative.[22] Robertson argues that grammatically both are equally possible.[23] Käsemann comments, 'Nowhere is the apostle's unbounded sense of mission more apparent'; any indefiniteness comes from 'diplomatic caution', perhaps in view of its being a joint mission with others.[24]

Paul looks forwards to 'the reconciliation of the world' (v. 15) by reason of Israel's initial rejection and subsequent acceptance of the gospel. It would be rash to argue for or against universalism on the basis of universal

---

[16] Bell, *Provoked to Jealousy*, p. 115.
[17] Barrett, *Romans*, p. 215.
[18] Knox, 'Romans', *IB*, vol. 9, p. 570.
[19] Cranfield, C. E. B., *A Critical and Exegetical Commentary on the Epistle to the Romans*, vol. 2 (Edinburgh: T & T Clark, 1979; ICC), p. 359.
[20] Wright, 'Romans', *NIB*, vol. 10, p. 681.
[21] Jewett, *Romans*, p. 679.
[22] Bell, *Provoked to Jealousy*, p. 116.
[23] Robertson, A. T., *Word Pictures in the New Testament*, vol. 4: *Romans* (New York: R. Smith, 1931), p. 395.
[24] Käsemann, Ernst, *Commentary on Romans* (London: SCM, 1980), p. 306.

reconciliation (v. 15) or on the basis of 'some of them' (v. 14). Some questions can be answered neither by Paul nor by us. Some understand 'life from the dead' as new life for dead Israel; others understand it as the general resurrection. Dunn insists that 'acceptance' means 'final acceptance', and that 'life from the dead' looks forwards to the resurrection as a consequence of reconciliation.[25]

The climax of Paul's first stage of the argument in chapter 11 has special importance, mainly because of the term *first fruits* (Greek *aparchē*) and also because of *root* and *branches* (v. 16). Whiteley regards 'participation' as a major theme here, but also somehow sees it as a rival term to 'substitution' for the benefits of Christ's atonement. In Romans 11.16 he speaks of 'the presupposition of the firstfruits' because 'If the first portion of dough is consecrated, so is the whole lump . . . The first portion actually accomplishes that [the sanctification] of the whole lump'.[26] Jewett also speaks here of 'the principle of extended holiness'.[27] But this is wholly complementary to substitution as one means among others of speaking of the atonement. Hamilton's perspective is more eschatological. *First fruits*, he says, suggests 'a complete bestowal in the future', as in Romans 8.11.[28] Wright explains, 'The whole is sanctified by the part: the lump by its first fruits, the branches by the root.'[29] This first image is drawn from Numbers 15.20, on the feast of Weeks. Part of the dough is offered to God, and the entire batch is then considered holy. The second image of the root and branches repeats the same point through a different metaphor. Bell, Käsemann and Michel regard the 'root' as denoting the patriarchs, although Origen and Theodore of Mopsuestia understood it as representing Christ.[30] Leenhardt, Fitzmyer and Wright regard it as representing the remnant.[31] Jewett regards Israel 'as the root and a Gentile believer as the Branch'.[32]

(2) The second stage of Paul's 'reply' concerns branches broken off from God's cultivated olive (failing Israel), while the Gentiles are like wild branches unexpectedly grafted into the tree (11.17–24). Ramsey showed that in the ancient world the grafting of a wild olive upon an old olive

---

[25] Dunn, *Romans 9—16*, pp. 657 and 658.

[26] Whiteley, *Theology of St. Paul*, p. 132.

[27] Jewett, *Romans*, p. 683.

[28] Hamilton, Neil Q., *The Holy Spirit and Eschatology in Paul* (Edinburgh: Oliver & Boyd, 1957; *SJT* Occasional Paper 6), p. 19.

[29] Wright, 'Romans', *NIB*, vol. 10, p. 683.

[30] Käsemann, *Romans*, p. 308; Bell, *Provoked to Jealousy*, p. 123.

[31] Fitzmyer, Joseph A., *Romans: A New Translation with Introduction and Commentary* (New York: Doubleday, 1992; AB 33), p. 614; Wright, 'Romans', *NIB*, vol. 10, p. 683.

[32] Jewett, *Romans*, p. 683.

tree was a familiar practice for invigorating the tree, just as Paul used the imagery.[33] Yet sometimes today it is said that grafting wild shoots onto cultivated stock is poor horticultural practice. Bell takes both of these arguments into account, and concludes: 'Paul was aware that the process he describes was contrary to the usual practice' (11.24, against nature), but that it nevertheless took place.[34] Ziesler and Jewett have brought up to date Ramsay's citation of horticultural practices. Like Bell, Jewett and Ziesler refer to Columella, a contemporary of Paul, who gives good evidence for the ancient practices.[35]

Whatever we make of verse 17, most commentators from Barrett to Jewett agree that '*Do not boast . . .*' (v. 18) is the heart of the matter. Jewish Christians or Jews should not boast in their possession of the law and covenant. But neither should Gentile Christians, who are grafted in, boast, because the health of the tree depends on the *root. Outsiders share in what the root provides.* Jews and Gentiles, Wright comments, cannot claim that the Messiah is theirs alone. The present middle imperative 'do not have the habit of glorying' (Greek *mē katakauchō*) suggests a *continuing* process. The verb appears only here in Paul, and Bultmann renders it, 'boast in triumphant comparison with others'.[36]

'You will say' (v. 19) expresses Gentile objections to Paul's argument. He is *even-handed* to both sides. He admits that branches were removed *to make room for the Gentiles.* 'That is true' (v. 20), Paul agrees, but you stand firm only through faith. The Greek offers a word-play between unbelief (*apistiā*) and faith (*pistei*). If faith is true God-given faith or trust, there is no room for arrogance. In verse 21 Paul reminds them that *faith is a moment-by-moment attitude towards God.* It involves awareness of God's sovereign will not to spare some, whether they be Jew or Gentile.

The grafting in and breaking off of branches must be seen as 'the kindness and the severity of God', with which no one should trifle (v. 22). The Gentiles should certainly not misconstrue God's purpose as if to imply 'God prefers the Gentiles, after all!' Everything comes down to whether God will 'spare' people; it does not relate to human phenomena. The Gentiles' 'surprise' at their inclusion should not blind them to their origin in Israel, the root to whom they are branches. Even Israel will be 'grafted in', if it

---

[33] Ramsay, William, *Paul and Other Studies* (New York: Armstrong, 1906), pp. 219–21.

[34] Bell, *Provoked to Jealousy*, p. 124.

[35] Jewett, *Romans*, pp. 684–6; Baxter, A. G., and Ziesler, John A., 'Paul and Arboriculture: Romans 11:17–24', *JSNT* 24 (1985), pp. 24–32; Ziesler, *Romans*, p. 279.

[36] Bultmann, Rudolf, '*kauchaomai*' in Kittel, G., and Friedrich, G. (eds), *Theological Dictionary of the New Testament* (*TDNT*) (10 vols, Grand Rapids: Eerdmans, 1964–76), vol. 3, p. 653.

does not persist in unbelief, for this is within God's power (v. 21). The key is 'God is able'.

Many debate the proper placing of 'contrary to nature' (v. 24). Ziesler rejects the NRSV punctuation, although Fitzmyer seems to echo it. In the light of his own research and Ramsay's comments, he insists, 'The grafting of wild olive shoots into a cultivated but ailing tree was a normal procedure.'[37] So what is 'contrary to nature' is not this, but the Gentiles 'belonging' to the root. It is 'contrary to nature' that those who were *not* God's people have *become* God's people.

(3) The third stage of Paul's sustained reply since verse 11 concerns the mystery of God's purpose for Israel, and the important *redefinition of 'all Israel'* (vv. 25–32). The central term in verse 25 is 'this mystery' (*to mustērion touto*). This is the first occurrence of 'mystery' in Romans. Paul used the word in 1 Corinthians 2.1, 7; 4.1; 13.2; 14.2; 15.51; and later in Romans 16.25. It primarily means 'something too profound to be discovered by human ingenuity'. Christ, as the content of the mystery, is beyond unaided human reasoning or discovery. In the Graeco-Roman and oriental mystery religions the term meant 'secret rite', but this is not at all the meaning in the NT. Danker distinguishes between the NT meaning as (a) *private counsel of God* (Matt. 13.11; Mark 4.11; Rom. 11.25; 1 Cor. 2.1; 4.1; Eph. 1.9; Col. 2.2); and (b) *that which transcends normal understanding* (Eph. 5.32; 2 Thess. 2.7).[38] The two meanings are not entirely different, since often, especially in Paul, it denotes what was once God's secret counsel, but is now revealed in Christ, even if it surpasses human understanding and discovery. It requires divine revelation. Fitzmyer helpfully comments: 'Paul thinks of three things: the partial insensibility of Israel, the manner of Israel's salvation; and the salvation . . . of all humanity.'[39] The Greek translates Aramaic *rāz* in Daniel 2.18, 19, 27, and in Qumran, *Pesher Habakkuk* (1QpHab 7.1–4, 13–14).

The NRSV smooths away Paul's introductory phrases, which are more literally: 'I would not have you ignorant' (1 Cor. 10.1; 2 Cor. 1.8; 1 Thess. 4.13). Paul asserts: 'A hardening has come on the part of Israel' (v. 25, Greek *pōrōsis apo morous*). But *apo merous* can mean *in part*, or also *for a while* (as in 15.24). Barrett, Wright and Cranfield find that the temporal meaning fits well 'until the full number of the Gentiles has come in'.[40] On

---

[37] Ziesler, *Romans*, p. 281.

[38] Danker, Frederick, *A Greek-English Lexicon of the New Testament and Other Early Christian Literature* (BDAG) (Chicago and London: University of Chicago Press, 3rd edn, 2000), pp. 661–2.

[39] Fitzmyer, *Romans*, p. 621.

[40] Wright, 'Romans', *NIB*, vol. 10, p. 688; Cranfield, *Romans*, vol. 2, p. 527.

the other hand, if the Gentiles are included in Christ as 'Israel', the phrase could still mean *the part of Israel* in the sense of the *Jewish* part. Bell comments, 'The *pōrōsis* [hardening] corresponds to the verb *pōroun* of 11:7, where Paul contrasts "the elect" with the rest.'[41]

We reach now the *redefinition of 'all Israel'* in verse 26. Bell calls its meaning 'a crucial question for the exegesis of the whole chapter'.[42] Cranfield and Bell (followed broadly by Ziesler) suggest four possible interpretations: (i) 'All Israel' denotes 'all the elect, both Jews and Gentiles'. This is advocated by Calvin, Jeremias and others.[43] (ii) 'All Israel' denotes 'the elect of the nation Israel', as advocated by Bengel.[44] (iii) It means 'the whole nation, including every single member', as Aquinas argued; (iv) It means 'Israel as a whole, but *not necessarily* including every individual member', as Käsemann, Cranfield, Dunn, Fitzmyer and others argue.[45] Cranfield firmly rejects (i), because 'Israel' cannot be understood in a different sense from Israel in verse 25, and in verses 11–32 as a whole. He regards (ii) as little better, concluding, 'The most likely interpretation is (iv)'.[46] This view is probably correct, namely the whole of the true Israel, although not in the sense of 'every single person'. 'All' can mean 'the whole' in Greek.

Paul quotes Isaiah 59.20–21a (LXX) almost exactly in verses 26b–27. The Hebrew text reads 'a Deliverer will come to Zion'; the LXX has already translated it as 'the Deliverer will come on behalf of Zion'. Paul chooses the LXX rendering, which would be more familiar to readers. This also confirms the view that 'all Israel will be saved' constitutes an eschatological event. The reference to 'my covenant with them' in verse 27 may recall Jeremiah 31.33 and Ezekiel 36.27, as well as Isaiah 59.21. This again stresses the continuity of God's purposes for the history of his people. 'When I take away their sins' probably also alludes to Isaiah 27.9.

Verses 28–32 sum up the argument of verses 11–27. Fitzmyer comments, 'Here he [Paul] contrasts Israel with the predominantly Gentile readers to whom he is writing.'[47] The temporary failure of ethnic Israel to respond to the gospel makes them 'enemies of God' in need of reconciliation (Rom. 5.10). But God can make providential use of this stage of history 'for your

---

[41] Bell, *Provoked to Jealousy*, p. 128.

[42] Bell, *Provoked to Jealousy*, p. 136.

[43] Calvin, John, *Calvin's Bible Commentaries: Romans* (London: Forgotten Books, 2007 [1847]), p. 255.

[44] Bengel, J. Albert, *Gnomon Novi Testamenti* (Lat., Stuttgart: Steinkopf, 1866), p. 602; Eng., *New Testament Word Studies* (2 vols, Grand Rapids: Kregel, 1971), vol. 2, p. 132.

[45] Bell, *Provoked to Jealousy*, pp. 136–8 (his italics); Barrett, *Romans*, pp. 123–4; Cranfield, *Romans*, vol. 2, p. 576; Dunn, *Romans 9—16*, p. 681.

[46] Cranfield, *Romans*, vol. 2, p. 577.

[47] Fitzmyer, *Romans*, p. 625.

[the Gentiles'] sake'. But as far as election is concerned, Israel remains beloved by God, first because of their ancestors, Abraham and the patriarchs (v. 28b); and second, because 'the gifts and the calling of God are irrevocable' (v. 29). 'Irrevocable' (Greek *ametamelia*) means *not to be regretted* (AV/KJB, 'without repentance').[48] Wright comments,

> Nor would it make any sense that in the last minute massive numbers of Jews alive at the time will suddenly arrive at Christian faith . . . God's salvation must be found where God has accomplished it, revealed it, and proclaimed it.[49]

He adds, God does have 'two tracks' to salvation. God has not 'written off' the Jews. He concludes (v. 29): 'There will always be ethnic Jews among the "true Jews" of 2.29.'[50]

NRSV 'They too may now receive mercy' (v. 31) obscures textual doubt about 'now'. *Now* is found in ℵ, B, D^q and Coptic, but P^{46}, A, D^b and G omit it. The UBS classifies it as 'C', i.e. difficult to decide.[51] In the past Gentiles were disobedient, and the Jews obedient, but this was reversed with the coming of Christ.

In verse 32 this becomes a universal or worldwide principle: 'God has imprisoned all in disobedience so that he may be merciful to all.' As Ziesler remarks, obedience and disobedience are not 'matters of ethics', but of 'being or not being God's people'.[52] Jewett concludes by commenting:

> With this climactic reference to God's mercy . . . the keynote for the third proof . . . Paul not only expresses the essence of the gospel, but also makes clear that *no* remnant or claims of cultural superiority, or . . . entitlement . . . can remain legitimate.[53]

Dunn declares,

> It is only to the disobedient that he [God] can show mercy . . . The history of Israel reveals the pattern of God's dealing with humankind . . . The double emphasis of 9.18–23 is thus shown to be not an embarrassing diversionary corollary, but actually the key to the whole . . . The ultimate purpose is one of mercy.[54]

---

[48] Danker, BDAG, p. 53.

[49] Wright, 'Romans', *NIB*, vol. 10, p. 692.

[50] Wright, 'Romans', *NIB*, vol. 10, p. 693.

[51] Metzger, *Textual Commentary*, p. 465.

[52] Ziesler, *Romans*, p. 288.

[53] Jewett, *Romans*, p. 711.

[54] Dunn, *Romans 9—16*, p. 696.

Concluding hymn of adoration (11.33–36)

Paul has drawn a contrast between human incomprehension and the unfathomable mystery of God's wisdom, sovereignty, purpose, mercy and love. As in 1 Corinthians 2.6–16, his theme is the inscrutable wisdom of God and its revelation through the Holy Spirit, but here in Romans it is a hymn of praise expressing wonder and adoration before the mystery of God's ways. As Cranfield observes, 'election' and divine purpose leave no hint of glory for *Paul*, let alone fatalism, but 'a hymn of wondering praise' about 'God's faithfulness' to his promises, and joy beyond all human imagining.[55] The Greek 'O the depths of the riches and wisdom and knowledge of God' begins *ō bathos ploutou kai sophias kai gnōseōs theou*. These things are 'unsearchable' (Greek *anexeraunēta*). The themes are God's profundity and immensity.

God's judgements reach beyond purely human criteria. 'Who has known the mind of the Lord?' (v. 34) is also quoted in 1 Corinthians 2.16, and fits the LXX of Isaiah 40.13. 'Who has given a gift to him?' (v. 35) sheds the spotlight on *God's pure sovereign grace*. Those who underplay the significance of Romans 9—11 would never be moved to hymn God's wisdom, grace, mercy and wonder in this way. God's treatment of Jews and Gentiles is no mere sociological problem, but reaches to the heart of God's inscrutable wisdom. Fitzmyer observes, 'There is no reason to think that Paul has borrowed this hymnic composition from some source.'[56] Just as 1 Corinthians 13 grows naturally out of his experience in Corinth, so this hymn tightly reproduces the wonder of Romans 9—11.

'For from him and through him and to him are all things' (v. 36) sums up the dynamic character of God as *source and goal of the universe*, as well as of Christ as Mediator. Cranfield believes that this doxology 'probably reflects Hellenistic Jewish borrowing from Stoic sources' (Sir. 43.27; Philo, *Spec. Leg.* 1.208).[57] Albert Schweitzer drew a contrast between a static Stoic world-view, and the 'dramatic world view characteristic of late Jewish eschatology', whereby Paul can assert that everything is *from, through* and *to* God.[58] (He rejects 'in God' as un-Pauline, which would admittedly raise problems about Acts 17.28.) Cranfield strongly distances this from Stoic 'pantheism'. Paul simply affirms, he says, that *God is Creator, Sustainer and Goal of all things*. Similarly Dunn, after citing parallels from Philo, Seneca

---

[55] Cranfield, *Romans*, vol. 2, p. 589.
[56] Fitzmyer, *Romans*, p. 633.
[57] Cranfield, *Romans*, vol. 2, p. 591.
[58] Schweitzer, Albert, *The Mysticism of Paul the Apostle* (London: Black, 1931), p. 11.

and Marcus Aurelius, declares that Paul's use of Stoic language 'does not, of course, indicate that Paul here becomes a spokesman for Stoic pantheism . . . The language had already been domesticated within Jewish monotheism.'[59] Colossians 1.16 offers a parallel. Jewett also offers examples of parallels in Philo, Marcus Aurelius and Seneca. Wright, however, regards Paul as standing in the tradition of the great psalmists. He expresses his grief and prayer, retells the story of Israel, and concludes with a paean of praise.[60]

Finally, Paul employs the kind of doxology that we find in Philippians 4.20: 'To our God and Father be glory for ever and ever.' It prepares for the climatic vision of 15.9–12, in which all nations join in the chorus of glorifying God.[61] 'Amen' is too often devalued today. It does not at all denote 'the end' of a prayer or service, but is a *solemn reaffirmation*, inviting congregational *response and active participation* in what has been prayed on behalf of them.

---

[59] Dunn, *Romans 9—16*, p. 702.
[60] Wright, 'Romans', *NIB*, vol. 10, p. 696.
[61] Jewett, *Romans*, p. 722.

21

The outworking of the Christian life: sacrifice and worship (12.1–21)

Romans 12.1—15.13 constitutes a new section after chapters 9—11, and aims to show how the Christian life works out in practical terms in the everyday world. Chapter 12 begins with *sacrifice* and worship, and leads on to *practical life in relation to other people*. Chapter 13.1–7 then concerns a Christian attitude *to civic authorities*, while 13.8–14 regards love as the fulfilling of the law. Chapter 14.1—15.13 addresses the relation between the 'weak' and the 'strong'.

'Therefore' shows that what follows is an inference from chapters 1—11. Bjerkelund has argued that 'I appeal' (Greek *parakalō*) is not merely rhetorical, but replicates a form drawn from diplomatic letters. It presupposes the request of either a friend or an authoritative official.[1] As one who is yet to visit Rome, Paul could use it especially as an apostle. 'To present' may be a technical term for the offering of a sacrifice. The word *bodies* denotes precisely what we observed in the comment of Käsemann, which we discussed under 1.24; 4.19; and 6.12. Käsemann called *body*

> that piece of the *world* which we ourselves are and for which we bear responsibility ... [in our] ability to communicate ... In the *bodily obedience of the Christian ... the lordship of Jesus finds visible expression.*[2]

Only in our *outward* and *public* life and conduct, he adds, does an allegiance to Christ as Lord become 'credible' as gospel message.

Hence the presentation of our bodies to God constitutes a holy and acceptable sacrifice and even 'spiritual' (NRSV; Greek *logikēn*) worship (*latreian*). The AV/KJB had 'reasonable service' for the last two words. As Cranfield observed, *latreia* denotes 'the *action* of worshipping, the continuous offering of our whole selves in all our concrete living ... our "logical" action of worshipping.'[3] Since 'spiritual' (Greek *pneumatikos*)

---

[1] Bjerkelund, Carl J., *Parakalō: Form, Funktion und Sinn der parakalō-Sätze* (Oslo: Universitetsforlaget, 1967), pp. 58–74 and 109–10.

[2] Käsemann, Ernst, 'Primitive Christian Apocalyptic', in *New Testament Questions of Today* (London: SCM, 1969), p. 135 (my italics).

[3] Cranfield, C. E. B., *A Critical and Exegetical Commentary on the Epistle to the Romans*, vol. 2 (Edinburgh: T & T Clark, 1979; ICC), p. 601.

usually means in Paul 'of the Holy Spirit', its use in the NRSV may perhaps be questioned. Cranfield discusses the term over some four pages, concluding that it is no simple matter to decide on Paul's exact meaning. It would be difficult to reconcile his use of *bodies* with inwardness. It is easier to understand it as 'rational', but not in the Stoic sense. He translates 'your *understanding* worship', i.e. with the comprehension of the mind.[4]

'Understanding' and 'rationality' simply show that all Paul's descriptive theology from Romans 1—11 to Romans 12—15 is integrally related together. Wright brings this out clearly. Paul's 'exhilaration' at the end of chapter 11, he says, leads inevitably to the exhortation that 'Christians, Jew and Gentile alike, now offer to the one true God the full and final sacrificial worship: Israel's worship is made complete.'[5] In these chapters, he adds, Paul often echoes the teaching of Jesus.

Because they constitute the 'new humanity' in Christ (Rom. 5.12–21), Christians should not be 'conformed to this world' (v. 2). Paul makes a studied contrast between *Be not conformed* (Greek *mē sunschēmatizesthe*) and *be transformed* (*metaporphousthe*) 'by the renewing of your minds'. Both are *present* tense, meaning 'Stop being conformed to the world', and 'Go on being transformed'. The first verb denotes being conformed to someone else's pattern. J. B. Phillips translates, 'Don't let the world around you squeeze you into its own mould.' The Greek for 'world' equally means 'this age'. Fitzmyer's translation 'to this present world' captures both senses. The world is passing, imperfect and doomed to pass away (1 Cor. 2.6; 7.31). The second verb denotes a 'profound transformation', which is 'not the Christian's own doing but the work of the Holy Spirit'; hence the passive form.[6]

Traditionally writers have drawn a distinction between verbs embodying Greek *schema* as denoting *outward appearance*, and *morphē* as denoting *real likeness*, but Barrett, Cranfield and others respond that 'there are too many examples of their being apparently treated as simply synonymous' for the distinction to be consistently maintained.[7] Nygren comments,

> It will not do for them [Christians] to live on in the old nature, just as if nothing had happened through Christ ... [The believer] has left the old *aeon* ... his mind must not remain in the old and be conformed to it.[8]

---

[4] Cranfield, *Romans*, vol. 2, pp. 595 and 602–5.
[5] Wright, N. T., 'Romans' in the *New Interpreter's Bible* (*NIB*) (Nashville: Abingdon, 2002), vol. 10, p. 700.
[6] Cranfield, *Romans*, vol. 2, p. 607.
[7] Cranfield, *Romans*, vol. 2, p. 607.
[8] Nygren, Anders, *Commentary on Romans* (London: SCM, 1952), p. 418.

Renewal of the *mind* is crucial for Christians, because pressures to conform to majority society are constant and repeated, and Christians must not let themselves be moulded by the world. Renewal of the mind (Greek *anakainōsis*) is vital. Harrisville has expounded its continuity and contrast with the old, and its dynamic power to crowd out the old as God's new creation.[9] 'Mind' (Greek *nous*) is more prominent in Paul than many realize, ultimately seeking 'the mind of Christ' (1 Corinthians 2.16). It includes intellectual capacities, but also much more: attitudes, mind-set and so on. We must be Christ's through and through, so that we may 'discern what is the will of God', as Christ did.

One last comment on verse 2 concerns punctuation. The Textus Receptus, AV/KJB and RV use no explanatory punctuation: 'to prove what is the good, and acceptable, and perfect, will of God'. But the RSV, NEB and Aland insert a comma, and NRSV, a dash: 'what is the will of God – what is good and acceptable', as defining the will of God. Either way sums up the transformed life of the Christian.

Romans 12.3–13 applies the previous two verses to Christian attitudes between fellow-believers. In Rome it was Paul's passion to inculcate mutual respect and tolerance between Jewish Christians and Gentile Christians. He looks for a humility that springs from sober judgement. It applies to the two groups in Rome to cultivate what Paul had urged in 1 Corinthians 12—14. On verse 3 Fitzmyer comments, 'However gifted Christians may be they are still members of the body of Christ, called to serve one another.'[10] They must use their gifts unselfishly. Paul warns against boasting in Romans 11.18, 20, 23; 1 Corinthians 4.8–13; 5.6; 13.2; and elsewhere. Jewett connects this with the self-perception of 'charismatic' Christians. He comments: 'The "will of God" . . . should determine the shape of one's self-image.'[11] It is noteworthy that Paul urges 'sober-mindedness' on the young congregation.

Paul appeals to the analogy of the body and *limbs* (v. 4) which, as Robinson urges, is a more accurate term than '*members*'.[12] Christians are not like 'members' of an automobile club, but limbs (Greek *melē*) of the body of Christ. Paul most famously used the analogy of the body and limbs in 1 Corinthians 12.12, 27. It was already a familiar analogy in the Graeco-Roman world, in which Mitchell and Collins trace it to

---

[9] Harrisville, R. A., 'The Concept of Newness in the New Testament', *JBL* 74 (1955), pp. 68–79.

[10] Fitzmyer, Joseph A., *Romans: A New Translation with Introduction and Commentary* (New York: Doubleday, 1992; AB 33), p. 645.

[11] Jewett, Robert, *Romans: A Commentary* (Minneapolis: Fortress, 2007; Hermeneia), pp. 739 and 741.

[12] Robinson, J. A. T., *The Body: A Study in Pauline Theology* (London: SCM, 1952; SBT 5), pp. 58 and 78–9.

a well-known political metaphor for harmony and co-operation.[13] It was used, for example, by Livy, who places it on the lips of Senator Menenius Agrippa to persuade plebeians on strike to return to work for the benefit of the state.[14] Plato also used it before Paul; Epictetus, Paul's approximate contemporary, uses it, and Plutarch after Paul.[15] Martin conclusively shows that Paul turned the Graeco-Roman model upside down. Paul does *not* say that plebeians should work for the good of senators, but that the gifted should work for the benefit of the whole body, including the less gifted.[16] As in 1 Corinthians 12.14–26, Paul explains, 'Not all the members have the same function'. This, as in 1 Corinthians, begins Paul's embryonic ecclesiology. Depending on views of authorship, this becomes developed in Ephesians and the Pastoral Epistles.

Verse 5 elucidates this, together with Christian unity with one another and with Christ: 'We, who are many, are *one body in Christ*, and individually we are members [limbs] one of another.' The English word 'individually' does not fully convey the Greek: *to kath' heis allēlōn melē*. Nor does the NIV *each member*. Wright suggests that it is 'almost "one by one" as though Paul were . . . pointing to each person . . . in turn'.[17] As in 1 Corinthians, Paul stresses that the body is *one*, even, Dunn insists, *in view of* its diversity.[18] Paul declares in 1 Corinthians 12.19: 'If all were a single member, where would the body be?'

In verses 6–8 Paul lists 'gifts that differ' in a way reminiscent of 1 Corinthians 12.27–30. Those gifts, which are identical in Romans 12.6–8 and 1 Corinthians 12.27–30, include prophecy, teaching and leadership. These may vindicate Jewett's claim that these are largely 'charismatic' gifts, although there is a similar list in Ephesians 4.11. On the other hand classical commentators, including Augustine, Aquinas, Luther, Calvin, Matthew Henry, Wesley and Bengel, *all understand 'prophecy' as the exposition of doctrine*. Aquinas, for example, claims that 'Prophetic knowledge pertains most of all to the intellect.'[19] He equates 'prophecy' in 1 Thessalonians

---

[13] Mitchell, Margaret M., *Paul and the Rhetoric of Reconciliation* (Tübingen: Mohr, 1992), pp. 68–83 and 157–64; Collins, R. F., *First Corinthians* (Collegeville: Glazier/Liturgical Press, 1999; Sacra Pagina 7), pp. 458–60.

[14] Livy, *Ab Urbe Condita*, 2.32.7–11.

[15] Plato, *Republic*, 5.470C–D and 2.370A–B; Epictetus, *Discourses*, 2.10.4–10.5; and Plutarch, *Moralia*, 478D.

[16] Martin, Dale B., *The Corinthian Body* (New Haven: Yale University Press, 1995), pp. 39–40, 38–63 and 94–103.

[17] Wright, 'Romans', *NIB*, vol. 10, p. 710.

[18] Dunn, James D. G., *Romans 9—16* (Dallas: Word, 1988; WBC 38), p. 725.

[19] Aquinas, Thomas, *Summa Theologiae* (60 vols, Lat. and Eng., Oxford: Blackfriars, 1963), I, qu. 173, art. 2.

5.19–20 with 'preaching' in the normal sense of the term.[20] In modern thought Hill, Müller and Gillespie offer sustained arguments for understanding 'prophecy' as 'applied pastoral preaching'.[21] Nevertheless Paul describes the gifts as *charismata* in verse 6. All require grace for each task. Exhortation (Greek *parakalōn*) is a function of prophecy in verse 8. The final three gifts, *giving, leading* and *showing compassion,* 'develop the idea . . . [that] givers should be generous' (v. 8).[22]

In 12.9–13 Paul focuses on *love* in the Christian life. NRSV 'genuine' may more accurately be rendered 'sincere' (v. 9, Greek *anupokritos*). Paul also has Greek participles where the NRSV uses imperatives: 'hate what is evil, hold fast to what is good'. Love (Greek *agapē*), as we noted, is not a feeling, or else it could not be commmanded. It is a *disposition* or mind-set, accompanied by *action*. It is possible for 'love' to be insincere, or merely a performance. 'Hating' what is evil is a strong word, which suggests shrinking away from what is evil, and turning one's back on it. Similarly 'hold fast to' what is good translates Greek *kollōmenoi* (from *kolla, glue*), which literally denotes sticking to it, as if with glue.

Technically NRSV adds 'mutual' in verse 10, but it is rightly implied by the word translated 'affection'. For the Greek *philostorgos* denotes the *family* affection, loving dearly or 'heartfelt love', which is *reciprocal* within a family.[23] This is qualified by Greek *philadelphia* (*tender love between brothers*), where (here) *brother* is used to denote *fellow-Christian*. Christians should 'lead the way' (Greek *proēgoumenoi*) in showing honour to one another. Danker gives this word the main meaning *go before and show the way*, although he admits that many versions choose *esteem more highly* (broadly NRSV).[24]

'Be ardent in spirit' (v. 11 NRSV) is a famous crux of interpretation. The AV/KJB translates this 'be fervent in spirit'; but the RSV rendered it, 'be aglow with the Spirit'. Centuries ago Augustine lamented the fact that 'spirit' and 'Spirit' could be confused or ambivalent. The Greek is simply *tō pneumati zeontes*, which in purely linguistic terms could denote either the human spirit or the Holy Spirit. But in practice Paul seldom

---

[20] Aquinas, *Summa*, I, qu. 173, art. 3, reply to obj. 4.

[21] Hill, David, *New Testament Prophecy* (London: Marshall, 1979), pp. 110–40 and 193–213; Müller, Ulrich B., *Prophetie und Predigt im Neuen Testament* (Gütersloh: Mohr, 1975), pp. 11–46 and throughout; and Gillespie, Thomas W., *The First Theologians* (Grand Rapids: Eerdmans, 1994), throughout.

[22] Wright, 'Romans', *NIB*, vol. 10, p. 711.

[23] Danker, Frederick, *A Greek-English Lexicon of the New Testament and Other Early Christian Literature* (BDAG) (Chicago and London: University of Chicago Press, 3rd edn, 2000), p. 1059.

[24] Danker, BDAG, p. 869; and Wright, 'Romans', *NIB*, vol. 10, p. 711.

uses *pneuma* to denote a psychological or inner state within human beings; it nearly always refers to the Holy Spirit, especially in the case of the adjective *pneumatikos* (*under the influence of the Holy Spirit*).[25] Cranfield writes, 'It is more natural to take *pneumati* to refer to the Holy Spirit (as do Origen, probably Chrysostom, Theophylact, and also Calvin and many modern scholars).'[26] This supports, rather than undermines, the plea for the Christian to be set on fire. Dunn favours this.[27] Fitzmyer is willing for either; Wright follows the NRSV interpretation. 'Do not lag in zeal', or 'do not be slothful', conveys the meaning of the NRSV.

The exhortation of verses 12–13 reminds us of 1 Thessalonians 5.12–22, where Paul also provides a series of short commands. The references to hope and to perseverance in suffering look back to Romans 5.3–5 and Romans 8.24–25, and to 8.17–18. Persistence in prayer comes in Philippians 4.6 and 1 Thessalonians 5.17. Christians must commune with God on every occasion. In verse 13 participating in, or sharing in (Greek *koinōnountes*) the needs of the saints anticipates Paul's specific exhortation to Gentile Christians to contribute to the collection for the needs of the church in Jerusalem. He has constantly urged that they are *one* people, who share in the honour or pain of different parts of the one body of Christ. In their local neighbourhood they are 'to extend hospitality to strangers' (Greek *tēn philoxenian diōkontes*). Hospitality was deeply rooted and well regarded in ancient society. In the OT Abraham was commended for showing hospitality (Gen. 18.1–6; Heb. 13.2; Philo, *De Abraham*, 107–114; Josephus, *Antiquities*, 1.196). Jewett speaks of 'the early Christian revitalization of the Graeco-Roman and Jewish ethics of hospitality'.[28] In the ancient Roman Empire travel was always fraught with danger, and welcoming and assisting strangers with provision and protection was especially needed in a strange city.

Commentators agree that the text of verses 14–21 probably comes from traditional pre-Pauline Christian material. Wright and Jewett call attention to the change in syntax and grammar, namely from a string of participles to a pair of imperatives, and then further participles.[29] 'Bless those who persecute you' can be found in Luke 6.18–35; Matthew 5.38–48; Acts 7.60; and 1 Corinthians 4.12. In verse 15 Paul returns to participles: 'Rejoice

[25] Thiselton, Anthony C., *The Holy Spirit: In Biblical Teaching, through the Centuries, and Today* (Grand Rapids: Eerdmans, and London: SPCK, 2013), pp. 76–8.

[26] Cranfield, *Romans*, vol. 2, pp. 633–4.

[27] Dunn, *Romans 9—16*, p. 742.

[28] Jewett, *Romans*, p. 765.

[29] Wright, 'Romans', *NIB*, vol. 10, p. 713; Jewett, *Romans*, pp. 765–6.

with those who rejoice, weep with those who weep.' It is unclear whether this still applies primarily within the Church or also in the wider world. Dunn suggests the latter, speaking of 'a sense of solidarity with the poor and oppressed'; Cranfield both agrees and suggests that Paul thinks 'more particularly of Christians'.[30] The injunction is reminiscent of 1 Corinthians 12.26, 'If one member suffers, all suffer together with it; if one member is honoured, all rejoice together with it.' Sometimes mutual commiseration is more difficult than mutual celebration.

'Live in harmony with one another' (v. 16) is strictly 'thinking the same things toward one another', as in 1 Corinthians 1.10 (Greek *to auto . . . phronountes*). Dunn renders 'Do not be haughty' as 'do not cherish proud thoughts'. This again strikes at the root of Jewish arrogance against Gentile Christians, and of Gentile arrogance against Jewish Christians. 'Associate with the lowly' calls to mind 1 Corinthians 9.22, 'To the weak, I became weak', and 10.32, 'Give no offence to Jews or to Greeks'. The injunction, 'Don't keep paying attention to people in high positions', could be very relevant to those in Rome. Barrett understands *tapeinois* to mean *those who do humble or menial tasks* in 'keep company with the humble.'[31]

'Do not repay anyone evil for evil' (v. 17) reflects Matthew 5.38–42 and Luke 6.29. Similarly 'take thought for what is noble in the sight of all' reflects Proverbs 3.4 (LXX). Barrett helpfully translates this: 'Plan to lead an honest life before all men.' The Greek word *kala* can mean *noble*, *honest* or *fine*, while 'before all' means *in the public life*. In verse 18, 'so far as it depends on you' explicates 'if it is possible'. Christians must do their best to live peaceably with all, i.e. never to be provocative. Paul adds, 'Never avenge yourselves' (v. 19). The reason is found in Deuteronomy 32.35, which Paul quotes: 'Vengeance is mine, and recompense'. This refers to *God's* exclusive right to redress the balance of justice; human vengeance takes from God what is *his* alone. In verse 20 Paul presses home the point: 'If your enemies are hungry, feed them; if they are thirsty, give them something to drink'. Paul directly quotes the LXX of Proverbs 25.21–22.

How this question is to be understood with its addition of 'heaping coals of fire on his head' is regarded as 'ancient' and 'tricky' by Dunn.[32] Augustine, Jerome and recently Cranfield regard it as a burning shame leading to repentance. Others interpret it simply to mean, 'Leave your enemy to God, but try to increase his guilt by your acts of kindness.' Ziesler

---

[30] Dunn, *Romans 9—16*, p. 746; Cranfield, *Romans*, vol. 2, p. 641.
[31] Barrett, C. K., *The Epistle to the Romans* (London: Black, 1957), p. 241.
[32] Dunn, *Romans 9—16*, p. 750.

and Dunn allude to an Egyptian ritual in which hot coal is placed on the head as both a punishment and a sign of repentance. But both admit that this is merely speculative, and requires us to assume that Paul knew of it.[33] Jewett helpfully calls this 'burning pangs of shame' felt by an adversary, 'moved by the generosity of the persecuted'.[34]

Wright comments, 'It is impossible to act in one's own case with sufficient impartiality, which is why . . . God reserves the sole right to judicial punishment . . . "Coals of fire" are almost certainly intended as the burning shame of remorse'.[35] The concluding verse (v. 21), 'Overcome evil with good', once again recalls the Sermon on the Mount. This truly is victory, for 'God will outlast and gain the victory over evil'.[36] It is the victory of the cross through sacrifice and vindication.

---

[33] Ziesler, John, *Paul's Letter to the Romans* (London: SCM, 1989 and 1990), p. 306; Dunn, *Romans 9—16*, p. 751.

[34] Jewett, *Romans*, p. 777.

[35] Wright, 'Romans', *NIB*, vol. 10, pp. 714 and 715.

[36] Dunn, *Romans 9—16*, p. 756.

22

Christian obligations (13.1–14)

Christian obedience to civil authorities (13.1–7)

Romans 13.1–7 may appear to introduce a new tone into Paul's argument, which in some ways it does. Nevertheless we shall see that discussion of God's 'righteousness' and governance of the world to produce 'order' continues the theme of earlier chapters, together with the Christian's duty to live out the practical implications of the new life. This now concerns its relation to *public* life. Romans 13.1–7 has been enormously influential. From the early Church Fathers until after the Reformation Paul's emphasis on submission to 'the governing authorities' (13.1) was generally viewed in positive terms. Paul explains: 'For there is no authority except from God . . . authorities . . . have been instituted by God' (v. 1) as 'God's servants' (v. 6).

Nevertheless in modern thought there have emerged more cautious expositions of Romans 13.1–7. The 'state' has been seen often to overstep its mark on many occasions. Naziism, totalitarianism and state suppression of religion have coloured the approach of a number of writers, notably Cullmann. He writes concerning Romans 13.1–7, 'Few sayings in the NT have suffered as much as this one'; it has been used 'as if . . . to abet the crimes of a totalitarian State'.[1] It appears, he adds, to contradict much of the teaching of Jesus. Paul has just been advocating love, not law. Schlier and Caird on principalities and powers and Yoder on Mennonite theology may suggest the same negative approach.[2] We have traced some of these differences in our section on reception history.

NRSV's 'governing authorities' for Greek *exousiais* is correct. O'Donovan writes that 'the State' is not the appropriate word in the ancient world for 'political community', which is 'the essential *esse* of human society', to provide order in place of anarchy and chaos.[3] Similarly Thielicke declared, 'The State is simply the institutionalized form of God's call to order . . .

---

[1] Cullmann, Oscar, *The State in the New Testament* (London: SCM, 1963), p. 46.

[2] Yoder, John, *The Politics of Jesus* (Grand Rapids: Eerdmans, 2nd edn, 1994), pp. 104–7; Schlier, Heinrich, *Principalities and Powers in the New Testament* (New York: Herder, 1961).

[3] O'Donovan, Oliver, *The Desire of Nations: Rediscovering the Roots of Political Theology* (Cambridge: CUP, 1996), p. 233.

a remedy required by our corrupted nature ... which puts a stop to the destruction of the fallen world.'[4] Emil Brunner also calls it a divine 'ordinance', reflecting 'preserving space', without which 'no communal life is conceivable'.[5] O'Donovan links Romans 13.1–7 with 'righteousness', i.e. 'To reward the just and punish the evil ... dividing right from wrong.'[6] The liberation theologian José P. Miranda also links it with righteousness and justification in Romans: the righteousness of God is revealed (Rom. 1.18—3.20) and is not merely a private affair only, but concerns public life.[7]

We noted under 'Reception history' the views of Augustine, Aquinas and Calvin. Calvin asserts the place of God's ordinance, and the need for Christian submission to it: 'Rulers are not a terror to good conduct, but to bad' (Rom. 13.3). We also noted a similar view of political institutions from Origin, Chrysostom, Lactantius, Basil and Augustine, and Aquinas.[8]

The church in Rome was especially conscious of imperial power and authority, as Käsemann comments.[9] Up to that time there had been no systematic persecution of Christians. Understandably a few scholars regard 13.1–7 as a non-Pauline interpolation, partly because of its lack of christological reference. These theorists, however, are predictable, including O'Neill and Schmithals; but there is no evidence for it. Paul urges submission (Greek *hupotassō*) to civil authorities, for they would have no authority (*exousia*) unless 'given by' God (Greek *hupo*). Paul's words apply to *legitimate* authorities. They are 'ordained' as such (Greek *tetagmenal eisin*). Hence Brunner calls their authority 'ordinances'. Calvin understood this passage to mean 'the Lord ... approves and is pleased with the function of magistrates', who rightly bear 'honourable titles' as representing God, whether they are magistrates, governors or kings. He writes, 'Rulers are the ministers of God', to prevent those who 'introduce anarchy'.[10] But Calvin also understood this passage as *not* defending excessive abuse of power.[11]

[4] Thielicke, Helmut, *Theological Ethics, vol. 2: Politics* (Grand Rapids: Eerdmans, 1979), p. 17.

[5] Brunner, Emil, *Natural Theology* (Eugene, OR: Wipf & Stock, 2002 [1948]), p. 29.

[6] O'Donovan, Oliver, *The Ways of Judgment* (Grand Rapids: Eerdmans, 2005), pp. 4 and 7.

[7] Miranda, José P., *Marx and the Bible: A Critique of the Philosophy of Oppression* (London: SCM, 1977), pp. 137 and 109–92.

[8] Origen, *Against Celsus*, 8.14 (Eng., *ANF*, vol. 4, p. 664); Chrysostom, *Homilies on the Epistle to the Romans*, Homily 23 (Eng., *NPNF*, ser. i, vol. 11, pp. 511–14); Lactantius, *Constitutions of the Holy Apostles*, 2.13 (Eng., *ANF*, vol. 7, p. 436); Basil, *Letter* 6.5 (Eng., *NPNF*, ser. ii, vol. 8, p. 314); Aquinas, Thomas, *Summa Theologiae* (60 vols, Lat. and Eng., Oxford: Blackfriars, 1963), I-II, qu. 90 and qu. 96, arts 4 and 5; II-II, qu. 65, art. 2.

[9] Käsemann, Ernst, *Commentary on Romans* (London: SCM, 1980), p. 350.

[10] Calvin, John, *Institutes of the Christian Religion*, ed. H. Beveridge (2 vols, London: Clark, 1957), 4.20.1–5.

[11] Calvin, *Institutes*, 4.20.5–7.

In Paul's life the authority of Rome had saved him from the arbitrary persecution of Jews, the attacks of bandits, and much else. That 'powers' could overstep the mark decreed by God is well illustrated by Schlier, Caird and Wink.[12] Wright points to the extravagant claims made by the burgeoning imperial cult, in contrast to which 'Romans 13 constitutes a severe demotion of arrogant and self-divinizing rulers.'[13] Nevertheless he remains squarely on the side of O'Donovan and others, as against Yoder. Romans 13.1–7, he says, is about running civic communities, in which authorities demand appropriate obedience for the welfare of society.

It is instructive to compare the varied attitudes to political authorities in Jewish literature of this era. The pro-Roman Josephus urges, 'No ruler attains his office except by the will of God' (*Jewish War*, 2.140). On the other hand Enoch 46.5 has an eschatological vision when God 'shall put down kings from their thrones because they do not extol him'. Yet again the Wisdom of Solomon declares, 'O kings . . . your dominion was given you from the Lord and sovereignty from the Most High' (Wis. 6.1, 3).

After considering the thrust of 13.1–7 as a whole, we need to examine particular words in specific verses. In verse 1 the NRSV rightly translates Greek *psuchē* as 'person'. The word may occasionally denote *soul*, but *life* or *person* is the usual meaning. Even in English *a hundred souls* often means *a hundred people*. 'Governing authorities' (NRSV) is appropriate for Greek *exousiais*, in spite of Carr's minority argument to the contrary.[14] The periphrastic perfect tense *tetagmenai eisin* means *stands ordained by God*.

In verse 2 NRSV 'resists' translates a word meaning *has taken his stand against*. 'What God has appointed' translates a very rare word, *diatagē*, which occurs later in the papyri. There it varies from *arrangement* to *testamentary disposition*.[15] In verse 3, Paul reverts to the diatribe style 'for a few lines' in the question 'Do you wish to have no fear of the authority?' – which would resonate with many of the readers.[16] NRSV 'Do what is good' accurately translates the Greek words, but 'live honestly' (NJB) and 'do right' (NEB, NIV) also capture the sense. In verse 4

[12] Schlier, *Principalities and Powers*; Caird, G. B., *Principalities and Powers: A Study in Pauline Theology* (Oxford: OUP, 1956); Wink, Walter, *Naming the Powers*, *Unmasking the Powers* and *Engaging the Powers* (3 vols, Augsburg: Fortress, 1984, 1986 and 1992).

[13] Wright, N. T., 'Romans' in the *New Interpreter's Bible* (*NIB*) (Nashville: Abingdon, 2002), vol. 10, p. 719.

[14] Carr, A. W., *Angels and Principalities* (Cambridge: CUP, 1981; SNTSMS 42).

[15] Moulton, James H., and Milligan, George, *The Vocabulary of the New Testament* (London: Hodder & Stoughton, 1952 [1930]), p. 155.

[16] Dunn, James D. G., *Romans 9—16* (Dallas: Word, 1988; WBC 38), p. 763.

Paul asserts that civil authorities are normally *God's servants* (*diakonos*), which outside ecclesiology is the regular term for an *official, functionary* or *servant*. The debate among ethicists is whether these authorities can cease to act as God's appointed servants if they step beyond legitimate boundaries.

Romans 13.5, Wright comments,

> leads Paul back to reiterate his initial command, now with extra reason: one must submit, both because the alternative is 'wrath' . . . and also because, recognizing the God-given role of authority, the educated Christian conscience ought to become disquieted if it finds itself resisting God's 'stewards'.[17]

As we noted under Romans 2.15, conscience usually operates *retrospectively* by inflicting discomfort after wrong action (as Pierce argued), and occasionally *prospectively* by indicating good actions ahead of their performance (as Thrall argued). In verse 6 it is probably prospective, since taxes must be paid 'for the same reason'.

In verses 6–7 Paul specifically considers the obligation to pay taxes (Greek *phorous*) to authorities who are 'God's ministers' (AV/KJB) or 'God's servants' (NRSV; Greek *leitourgoi theou*). Greek *phorous* originally meant *tribute*, as from a subject nation, but in Rome would broadly mean *taxes*. *Leitourgoi*, Denney comments, underlines the *official* character of the service by political agents.[18] In verse 7 Paul uses both Greek *phoron* and the more usual *telos* for taxes. The Christian must dutifully pay whatever is due to civil authorities. The modern world offers plenty of scope to apply this principle: employment law; taxation; driving on the roads; and paying one's bills on time, and so on.

Love, the law and the dawning of the new age (13.8–14)

The link with 13.1–7 is easy to understand: don't leave any obligation unfulfilled. Denney notes about 13.1–7, 'There is perhaps nothing in the passage which is not already given in our Lord's word, "Render to Caesar the things that are Caesar's and to God the things that are God's".'[19] Yet the same is true of love as the fulfilment of the law (v. 8, Greek *nomon peplērōken*). Wright sees Romans 2.17–29; 3.27–31; 8.1–8; and 10.5–11 in the background as showing how the Torah is fulfilled in love of one's

---

[17] Wright, 'Romans', *NIB*, vol. 10, p. 721.

[18] Denney, James, 'Romans', in *Expositor's Greek Testament* (*ExGrT*) (5 vols, Grand Rapids: Eerdmans, [1910]), vol. 2, p. 697.

[19] Denney, 'Romans', *ExGrT*, vol. 2, p. 695.

neighbour.[20] There is a verbal link with 13.1–7 in 'what is due' (Greek *ophelias*).

Verses 8b–10 show that loving others is not somehow a 'soft option' to obeying the law. It cannot be *less* than the law: but only *more*. In verse 9 Paul quotes from the Decalogue: Deuteronomy 5.17, 18, 19, and 21, in the sequence of the LXX. In verse 9 'Love your neighbour as yourself' comes originally from Leviticus 19.18, and then occurs in Matthew 5.43 (more loosely in Mark 12.31; Matt. 22.39; and Luke 10.27; as well as Gal. 5.14 and Jas. 2.8). In Leviticus 19.18 *neighbour* denotes a fellow-Israelite, but as most today urge, 'For Jesus the term had universal range', and this is equally true of Paul.[21] Cranfield quotes Pelagius as commenting on verse 10, 'To omit to do good is an actual wrong-doing.'[22] He also observes that the general commandment to love in no way implies that we can forget the Ten Commandments. Some churches today so uniformly use what they call 'the shortened form of the Ten Commandments' in the Holy Communion Service that some congregations never hear them read. Moule and Dunn urge that Paul's general comment about love 'fulfilling' the law in no way excuses an antinomian attitude on the part of Christians, as if to avoid or belittle the Torah and the Commandments.[23]

In verse 9 'are summed up' translates the rare Greek word *anakephalaioutai*. In addition to its use in Ephesians 1.10 the noun *anakephalaiōsis* is often used in Christian theology to denote the theme in Irenaeus that Jesus Christ 'summed up' or 'recapitulated' in himself the history of Israel and humanity to grant us a new beginning. 'This word' refers to the *logos* of divine revelation. 'You shall love your neighbour as yourself' excludes all egocentrism and narcissism, which is the root of human sinfulness and idolatry. We discussed the meaning of *love* (Greek *agapē*) under 12.9. The performance of these verses (13.8–10) builds up trust in the community.[24]

In 13.11–14 Paul urges zeal in the light of the approaching End and the dawning of the New Age. NRSV 'you know what time it is' translates Greek *eidotes ton kairon* (v. 11). Several books have been written on perceived differences between *kairos* and *chronos*, words for *time* in Greek. *Kairos*

---

[20] Wright, 'Romans', *NIB*, vol. 10, p. 724.

[21] Cranfield, C. E. B., *A Critical and Exegetical Commentary on the Epistle to the Romans*, vol. 2 (Edinburgh: T & T Clark, 1979; ICC), p. 677; Dunn, *Romans 9—16*, pp. 779–80.

[22] Cranfield, *Romans*, vol. 2, p. 678.

[23] Moule, C. F. D., 'Obligation in the Ethics of Paul' in *Essays in New Testament Interpretation* (Cambridge: CUP, 1982), pp. 261–77; and in Farmer, W. R., Moule, C. F. D., and Niebuhr, R. R., *Christian History and Interpretation: Studies Presented to John Knox* (Cambridge: CUP, 1967), pp. 389–406; and Dunn, *Romans 9—16*, p. 777.

[24] Dunn, *Romans 9—16*, p. 781.

was traditionally rendered the *critical moment* or *right time*; *chronos* was traditionally rendered *time-as-duration*.[25] Danker still maintains the traditional view. Cullmann argues that the biblical writings assume a linear view of time, which does justice to 'stages of redemptive history'. But *within this linear framework*, cyclical time allows for the great Jewish and Christian festivals round the year, and there are also special favourable times of opportunity. The study of narrative also allows for 'narrative-time', as against chronological time. This usually serves *a plot*. Paul regards the favourable or critical moment (v. 11, *kairos*) to be the 'hour' (Greek *hora*; NRSV 'moment') to wake from sleep. It is the dawn of the new age. Pannenberg also compares resurrection to waking from sleep. Jesus speaks of his 'hour' in John.

Some MSS read 'the hour *for you to wake from sleep*' (NRSV): P[46], אᶜ, D, G and 33. Most scholars reject this.[26] Greek *eidotes* (*knowing*) suggests a well-known truth. Some interpret the Greek of verse 11b to mean 'For salvation [in the future] is nearer *to us* now than when we became believers' (NRSV); others render it '*Our* salvation is nearer than when . . .' Barrett favours the first, since salvation is cosmic, and not simply 'ours'. Dunn, Cranfield and Ziesler follow Barrett, but Fitzmyer and Wright follow the second interpretation.[27] 'Night' is used in Paul of the condition of unbelievers *and* of Christians for whom the new age has dawned, but the old has not yet vanished. Some speak of Christians 'between the ages'. In Wright's words, 'That full day was yet to come . . . Christians . . . live in the interval between the early signs of dawn and the sunrise itself, and their behaviour must be appropriate for the day, not the night.'[28] Once again, Paul echoes the saying of Jesus (Mark 1.15).

In verse 12 Paul expands and applies the metaphor of night and day. He has used it in 2 Corinthians 6.14 and 1 Thessalonians 5.4–5; it occurs in the OT in Psalm 43.3; Isaiah 2.5; 9.2; 42.6; and Isaiah 60.1–5; and in the NT in Luke 16.8; John 1.4–9; 3.19–21; 8.12; and Acts 26.18. 'The night

---

[25] Barr, James, *Biblical Words for Time* (London: SCM, 1962); Marsh, John, *The Fullness of Time* (London: Nisbet, 1952); Cullmann, Oscar, *Christ and Time* (London: SCM, 1951); Danker, Frederick, *Greek-English Lexicon of the New Testament and Other Early Christian Literature* (BDAG) (Chicago and London: University of Chicago Press, 3rd edn, 2000), pp. 497–8 and 1092.

[26] Metzger, Bruce, *A Textual Commentary on the Greek New Testament* (New York: UBS, 2nd edn, 1994), p. 467.

[27] Dunn, *Romans 9—16*, p. 786; Fitzmyer, Joseph A., *Romans: A New Translation with Introduction and Commentary* (New York: Doubleday, 1992; AB 33), pp. 682–3; Cranfield, *Romans*, vol. 2, p. 681; Ziesler, John, *Paul's Letter to the Romans* (London: SCM, 1989 and 1990), pp. 315 and 319; Wright, 'Romans', *NIB*, vol. 10, p. 728.

[28] Wright, 'Romans', *NIB*, vol. 10, p. 727.

is far gone' (NRSV) has the sense of *well advanced* or *almost over* (Greek *proekopsen*). With Paul's vivid picture of daybreak, the further metaphor of *laying aside* (NRSV) or *casting off* (Greek *apotithēmi* and *apekduō*) night-clothes, and putting on what is respectable for the day, follows naturally. Another metaphor is suggested: Christians need 'the armour of light'. They must be prepared for battle. A. G. Hogg wrote of a realm of infinite forces, 'where the world exists only by sufferance . . . in which the world lies like a foolish, wilful dream in the solid truth of the day'.[29] Paul uses the metaphor of armour in Romans 6.13; 2 Corinthians 6.7; Ephesians 6.13–17; and 1 Thessalonians 5.8.

Paul expands the ethical and christological implications of the metaphors in verses 13–14. NRSV's 'Let us live honourably . . .' represents 'walk' (Greek *peripateō*) which Paul uses at least 30 times, since *walk* (*halakāh*, from *halak*) is the normal Hebrew–Jewish term for practical conduct. Cranfield suggests several possible interpretations: (i) alluding to the relative respect-ability of what people do in broad daylight, as opposed to 'the revelries and debaucheries of the night-time'; (ii) conduct as if the final Day were already here; (iii) the gradual dawning of the Coming Age; (iv) the Day as a metaphor for the state of enlightenment, in contrast to paganism. In the end he prefers (iii), especially since *day* must be used consistently with the previous verses.[30] As in Romans 1.18–32, Wright argues that Paul targets 'abuse of the body, one's own and often that of others . . . wild parties, drinking-bouts, sexual immorality and licentiousness . . . They belong with the old age.'[31] They may be compared with 'the works of the flesh' in Galatians 5.19. Carrington and Selwyn relate this conduct to common pre-Pauline catechesis.

Lest Wright's language seem extravagant, he is simply translating the Greek words which Paul chooses. Greek *euschēmenōs* means *honestly* or, in context, *decently*. Greek *kōmois* (plural) means *revellings*, and *methais*, 'drunkenness' (NRSV). Greek *koitais* (NRSV 'debauchery') means *sexual promiscuity*. NRSV 'licentiousness' is an adequate translation of Greek *aselgeias*. As in 1 Corinthians 3.3 Paul explains 'jealousy and strife' as being 'of the flesh'. Ziesler distances these vices from the situation in Rome: 'We cannot deduce from this verse that they [Roman Christians] were greatly given to drunkenness.'[32] On the other hand, Jewett cites evidence for the

---

[29] Hogg, A. G., *Redemption from This World* (Edinburgh: T & T Clark, 1924), p. 26.

[30] Cranfield, *Romans*, vol. 2, pp. 686–7.

[31] Wright, 'Romans', *NIB*, vol. 10, p. 729.

[32] Ziesler, *Romans*, p. 320.

persistence of some of these vices at Roman dinner parties, including drinking bouts, and even the promotion of 'strife'.[33]

'Put on the Lord Jesus Christ' (v. 14, Greek *endusasthe*) denotes an act, rather than a process. This verse became a key factor in the conversion of Augustine, as he recounts in his *Confessions*.[34] He wrote,

> I suddenly heard the voice of a boy or a girl . . . chanting . . . 'pick it up and read it' . . . I read the paragraph on which my eyes first fell: 'Not in rioting and drunkenness . . . but put on the Lord Jesus Christ, and make no provision for the flesh . . .'

To *put on* Christ is connected with baptism in Galatians 3.27. The metaphor *put on* also implies being '*clothed in Christ*'. 'To put on the Lord Jesus Christ means here to embrace again and again, in faith and confidence, in grateful loyalty and obedience, Him to Whom we already belong.'[35] This makes no provision for human nature in its fallenness. 'Make provision', Jewett observes, is found in legal, administrative and business contexts.[36]

[33] Jewett, Robert, *Romans: A Commentary* (Minneapolis: Fortress, 2007), pp. 826–7; and Winter, Bruce, 'Roman Law and Society in Romans 12—16' in P. Oakes (ed.), *Rome in the Bible and Early Church* (Grand Rapids: Baker, 2002), pp. 67–102, esp. 86.

[34] Augustine, *Confessions*, 8.12.29; Eng., Augustine, *Confessions and Enchiridion*, ed. A. C. Outler (Philadelphia: Westminster, 1955; LCC 7), p. 176.

[35] Cranfield, *Romans*, vol. 2, p. 688.

[36] Jewett, *Romans*, p. 828.

23

Mutual welcome and respect: 'the strong' and 'the weak' (14.1—15.13)

Christian liberty and the challenge to each group (14.1–12)

Paul's subject concerns 'those who are weak in faith'. They are not to be despised or frowned upon as second-class Christians, but welcomed (v. 1). But *who are these 'weak'*? Paul has only recently written 1 Corinthians, in which the *weak* and the *strong* constituted two distinct groups. Perhaps 'weak' was the term chosen by 'the strong' to characterize them as 'others'. As in 1 Corinthians, Paul seeks to empathize with each group, but in the end calls for *mutual respect and tolerance*. Barrett defines the weak in Romans as those who only half grasp that people are justified and reconciled to God 'not by vegetarianism, sabbatarianism, or teetotalism, but by faith alone – or, better – by God's own free electing grace'.[1]

More accurately, in 1 Corinthians those who have a 'weak' conscience are those who have insufficient *self-awareness and confidence*. They suffer from a lack of knowledge in relation both to self-image and to other Christians, and are thereby insecure.[2] Horsley and Gardner show how the meanings relate together.[3] In some contexts in Paul 'the weak' may also denote people of *low social standing* while 'the strong' may also mean those with social power, influence, political status and wealth.

Which is the dominant meaning, however, in Romans 14? The two meanings are not mutually exclusive. In Romans the term tends to denote Jewish Christians who are only partially free from the law, and attempt to retain some of the practices to which Barrett refers. Knox and Manson see the church in Rome as reflecting the situation in Corinth, denoting primarily those who are immature in Christian character and

---

[1] Barrett, C. K., *The Epistle to the Romans* (London: Black, 1957), p. 256.

[2] Thiselton, Anthony C., *The First Epistle to the Corinthians: A Commentary on the Greek Text* (Grand Rapids: Eerdmans, and Carlisle: Paternoster, 2000; NIGTC), pp. 643–58; Gooch, Peter D., '"Conscience" in 1 Corinthians 8 and 10', *NTS* 33 (1987), pp. 244–54; and Gooch, P. D., *Pastoral Knowledge: Philosophical Studies in Paul* (Notre Dame: University of Notre Dame Press, 1987), pp. 102–23.

[3] Horsley, R. A., 'Consciousness and Freedom among the Corinthians: 1 Corinthians 8—10', *CBQ* 40 (1978), pp. 574–89; Gardner, Paul D., *The Gifts of God and the Authentication of a Christian* (Lanham, MD: University Press of America, 1994).

experience.[4] In verse 2 Paul explicitly alludes to eating 'only vegetables', and comments, 'Those who eat must not despise those who abstain, and those who abstain must not pass judgement on those who eat' (v. 3). Verses 5–6 refer to the observance of particular holy days. Habitual meat-eaters may incidentally be among the wealthier group, since meat was expensive. Dunn concludes that some of God's people were 'visibly drawn in the daily lifestyle expressed in diet and festivals'.[5] Cranfield carefully considers six possible interpretations, concluding, with Barrett, that the weak showed 'literal obedience of [to] the ceremonial part of the law'.[6]

Wright comments,

> The best reading of the problem, I think, is that the discussions Paul knows to exist within the Roman church have at least a strong element about them of the Jew/Gentile tension that has been underneath so much of the letter.[7]

But, he adds, the equation is not one to one, for Paul himself is both a Jew and one of the strong. Jewett agrees: the 'powerful' imposed the name 'the weak', especially by appealing to their religious scruples.[8]

In verse 1 the opposite to welcoming the weak is 'quarrelling over opinions'. As in Corinth, the differences between Christian groups can become an excuse for polemic and mutual criticism. Also, as in 1 Corinthians, Paul describes the approaches of each group, not least to show that he understands the reasons for their controversy (v. 2). The key is that each group 'must not despise' (Greek *exoutheneitō*, *regard as 'nothings'*) the other (v. 3). This is two-sided or mutual. Paul adds, '*God* has welcomed them. Who are you to pass judgement on servants of another?' (vv. 3b, 4a). Every believer belongs to the Lord. If God welcomes them, who are we to do anything different? It is 'before their own lord that they stand or fall' (v. 4). 'And they will be upheld' (v. 4c, Greek *stathēsetai*), *made to stand*. In verse 5 Paul resumes his description of each group's attitudes. This time he places the emphasis not on diet, but on the observance of holy days.

Paul admits that each group may reach their conclusions through honourable motives: those 'who eat, eat in honour of the Lord . . . while those who abstain, abstain in honour of the Lord' (v. 6). Both groups give

---

[4] Knox, John, 'The Epistle to the Romans', in *Interpreter's Bible* (*IB*) (Nashville: Abingdon, 1954), vol. 9, pp. 612–16.

[5] Dunn, James D. G., *Romans 9—16* (Dallas: Word, 1988; WBC 38), p. 797.

[6] Cranfield, C. E. B., *A Critical and Exegetical Commentary on the Epistle to the Romans*, vol. 2 (Edinburgh: T & T Clark, 1979; ICC), p. 694 and pp. 690–6.

[7] Wright, N. T., 'Romans', in the *New Interpreter's Bible* (*NIB*) (Nashville: Abingdon, 2002), vol. 10, p. 731.

[8] Jewett, Robert, *Romans: A Commentary* (Minneapolis: Fortress, 2007; Hermeneia), p. 834.

thanks to God in their respective actions. Thus Paul fully understands each side, and sympathizes with their motives. This is almost exactly a replay of 1 Corinthians 10.23–33. Paul urges the strong, 'Eat whatever is sold in the meat market . . . For "the earth is the Lord's and everything in it"' (1 Cor. 10.25). Nevertheless there may be a situation in Corinth when out of consideration for another Christian, 'Do not eat it' (1 Cor. 10.29). Similarly in Rome, 'You must not pass judgment [on the others]' (Rom. 14.3). This finds a parallel in 1 Corinthians 4.3–5, 'It is the Lord who judges me. Therefore do not pronounce judgement'. In both epistles he calls for mutual respect.

Paul has also warned the Galatians: 'You are observing special days, and months, and seasons, and years' (Gal. 4.10–11). Later he repeats to the church in Colossae: 'Do not let anyone condemn you in matters of food and drink or of observing festivals, new moons, or sabbaths' (Col. 2.16–17). Romans 14.5b establishes a key criterion: 'Let all be fully convinced in their own minds.' Dunn comments, 'From this we may deduce that . . . many Jewish Christians (and Gentile Christians influenced by Jewish tradition) regarded the continued observance of the special feast days of Judaism (particularly the Sabbath) as of continuing importance.'[9] After all, the Sabbath was an identity-marker for Judaism and part of the Decalogue. In verse 5 'one day to be better' (NRSV) is rendered 'more sacred' in NIV and 'holier' in NJB, although no Greek word corresponds with this.

Paul then applies the principle in the light of the heart of the gospel (14.7–9). *Christians belong to the Lord: 'Whether we live or whether we die, we are the Lord's'* (v. 8). Bultmann writes on this passage and Christian freedom:

> He [the Christian] no longer bears the care for himself . . . but lets *this care go, yielding himself entirely to the grace of God; he recognizes himself to be the property of God* (or of the Lord) and lives for Him.[10]

Bultmann compares this with 1 Corinthians 6.19, 'You are not your own . . . you were bought with a price', and also Galatians 2.20. He also cites 1 Corinthians 3.21–23, 'All things are yours . . .' To accept Christ as Lord means to *belong to him, in trust and obedience* while he, for his part, will *care for those who belong to him.* This is why Paul rejoices to call himself 'Christ's slave' (Rom. 1.1). Moreover Christians *corporately* belong to the Lord: 'We do not live to ourselves' (v. 7). *To sin against a fellow-Christian is also to damage the Lord's property.*

---

[9] Dunn, *Romans 9—16*, p. 805.
[10] Bultmann, Rudolf, *Theology of the New Testament*, vol. 1 (London: SCM, 1952), p. 331 (my italics).

If all Christians must give an account of themselves to their Lord, Paul poses the rhetorical question: 'Why do you pass judgement on your brother or sister?' (v. 10). In 'Why do you despise your brother or sister?', *despise* means, as we noted, 'to show by one's attitude' that the entity concerned is a 'nothing', or 'has no merit or worth'.[11] 'We will all stand beneath the judgement seat [Greek *bēma*] of God' (v. 10) reflects 2 Corinthians 5.10. In verse 11 Paul cites Isaiah 45.23 (LXX), simply inverting 'every tongue' and 'shall give praise' (Greek *exomologēsetai*). The verb also means 'to confess' in parallel with Philippians 2.10–11. In verse 12 Paul explicates this further: 'Each of us will be accountable to God' (NRSV). The Greek is 'give account', and ℵ, A, C, D and 33 include 'to God'. But Metzger regards this as questionable, since it is easy to see why copyists should have added the word.[12]

Christian love and generosity of attitude (14.13–23)

Although Paul was even-handed in verses 1–12, the general impression is that in theological terms the 'weak' tended to compromise Christian freedom in Christ. But freedom cut both ways: the strong were free to ignore secondary rules and regulations; the weak were free to observe them; as long as both were 'fully convinced' (v. 5) in their minds about their appropriate conduct. Paul now turns from freedom to love. The attitude of love should be generous. Indeed in 1982 Jewett published a work based largely on Romans 14.13—15.7.[13]

Mutual criticism between the groups seems in fact to have been the case (v. 13). For the present *subjunctive* 'let us therefore no longer pass judgement on one another' (Greek *mēketi krinōmen*) implies strictly, 'Let us no longer have the habit of criticizing . . .', as Barrett and Robertson suggest.[14] Also, as in 1 Corinthians, Paul urges that we must 'resolve instead never to put a stumbling-block or hindrance in the way of another' (v. 13). What situation in modern life could find a use for a 'stumbling-block'? The use is metaphorical: *proskomma* may mean 'a cause for offence'.[15] In literal

---

[11] Danker, Frederick, *A Greek-English Lexicon of the New Testament and Other Early Christian Literature* (BDAG) (Chicago and London: University of Chicago Press, 3rd edn, 2000), p. 352; Robertson, A. T., *Word Pictures in the New Testament, vol. 4: Romans* (New York: R. Smith, 1931), p. 412.

[12] Metzger, Bruce, *A Textual Commentary on the Greek New Testament* (New York: UBS, 2nd edn, 1994), p. 469.

[13] Jewett, Robert, *Christian Tolerance: Paul's Message to the Modern Church* (Louisville: Westminster/John Knox, 1982; Biblical Perspectives on Modern Issues).

[14] Robertson, *Word Pictures*, vol. 4, p. 414; Barrett, *Romans*, p. 262.

[15] Danker, BDAG, p. 882.

terms the modern equivalent might be a *trip-wire*. The NRSV is perhaps weaker than it should be. The word *proskomma* (*cause of stumbling*) occurs in the NT only in Paul and in 1 Peter: Romans 9.32, 33; 14.13, 20; 1 Corinthians 8.9; 1 Peter 2.8. But *skandalon* (*snare*) occurs in Matthew 13.41; 16.23; 18.6–7; Romans 9.33, 11.9; 14.13; 1 Corinthians 1.23; Galatians 5.11). The verb *skandalizō* occurs some 25 times in the Synoptic Gospels. In 1 Peter 2.8 there is an allusion to the early Christian tradition of the 'stone that makes them stumble'.

Matthew 18. 6–7 refers to putting 'a stumbling-block before one of these little ones who believe in me'. Dodd regards the whole discussion in Paul as turning on 'the exegesis and application of . . . traditional sayings of Jesus'.[16] The verses reflect such sayings as 'Judge not that you be not judged' (Matt. 7.1). Further, Dodd comments about Paul's view of diet, that it simply reflects the words of Jesus, 'There is nothing outside a person that by going in can defile' (Mark 7.18, and broadly Mark 7.14–23). Dodd calls this link 'perhaps the most interesting and illuminating' of passages from early Jesus tradition.[17] Paul clinches this in verse 14: 'In the Lord Jesus . . . nothing is unclean in itself', only if it is *thought* to be unclean. The word *koinos* (v. 14) is used in the sense of 'ritually unclean' as in Mark 7.15a, because it comes into contact with anything and everything.[18]

In verses 15–17 Paul exposes the irony of conduct intended to please God, but which has the opposite effect of 'injuring' (v. 15) a brother or sister. Hence he exclaims, 'Do not let what you eat cause the ruin [strong word] of one for whom Christ died.'[19] 'Injure' translates *lupeitai* which often means 'is grieved', but may also mean *embarrass* or *harm*, implying either that the injured people may find eating a strain for their *own* faith, *or* a needless anxiety for the other group. Dunn translates 'deeply upset', or 'outraged'.[20] We discussed *agapē* (*love*) under 12.9. Once again, 1 Corinthians offers several parallels, for example, 'So by your knowledge the weak man is destroyed, the brother for whom Christ died' (1 Cor. 8.11); and 'if food is a cause of my brother's falling, I will never eat meat, lest I cause my brother to fall.'[21] Similar themes occur in 1 Corinthians 10.23–33.

The situation could, if unchecked, become a vicious circle (v. 16): the strong congratulate themselves on their emancipation and freedom;

---

[16] Dodd, C. H., *Gospel and Law* (Cambridge: CUP, 1951), pp. 49–51.

[17] Dodd, *Gospel and Law*, pp. 49–51.

[18] Cranfield, *Romans*, vol. 2, p. 713.

[19] Danker, BDAG, pp. 115–16.

[20] Dunn, *Romans 9—16*, p. 820.

[21] Francis, Fred O., and Sampley, J. P., *Pauline Parallels* (Philadelphia: Fortress, 2nd edn, 1984), p. 64.

the weak detect in the others a sense of pride which seems to confirm the importance of their holding the line. Hence in verse 17 Paul reiterates that God's kingdom can bring only 'righteousness and peace and joy in the Holy Spirit'. Love and peace must put an end to such a spiral of mutual recrimination. Fitzmyer observes, 'The essence of the kingdom does not consist in freedom from such things as dietary regulation, but in the freedom of the Christian to react to the prompting of the Holy Spirit.'[22] Paul rarely uses *kingdom*, but does so only on occasion (1 Cor. 4.20; 6.9). It could be misunderstood as a political term. The parallels with 1 Corinthians go beyond 1 Corinthians 8—10; for example the 'All things are lawful for me' controversy in 1 Corinthians 6.12–20, and probably disdain for 'the body' in 1 Corinthians 5.1–13. In 1 Corinthians 6.13 Paul speaks of food and the digestive system (Greek *koilia*), in contrast to God and the Lord.

Anyone who serves God in the way which Paul has indicated is both 'acceptable to God' and 'has human approval' (v. 18 NRSV). As Käsemann argues, Paul's 'in this' (Greek *en toutō*) links verse 18 closely with the previous argument.[23] In verse 19, 'Let us then pursue [Greek *diōkōmen*] what makes for peace' (NRSV) is a controversial MS reading. It is found in C, D and 33, but the indicative mood, *diōkomen* (*we pursue*) is found in ℵ, A and B. In the end the UBS Committee chaired by Metzger marginally preferred the subjunctive, in spite of earlier and wider support for the indicative.[24] In addition to striving for peace, which is the main issue, Paul equally urges 'mutual upbuilding' (Greek *ta tēs oikodomēs tēs eis allēlous*; in word-for-word terms, *the things of building up for one another*). *Building up* (Greek *oikodomeō*) yet again features regularly in 1 Corinthians (verb in 1 Cor. 8.1, 10; 10.23; 14.4, 17; noun in 1 Cor. 3.9; 14.3, 5, 12, 26). Margaret Mitchell devotes some 12 pages to discussing Paul's use of the building metaphor for concord and reconciliation.[25]

In verse 20 Paul substantially repeats his exhortation in verses 14–15. But as in 1 Corinthians, having asserted the right of the strong to freedom to eat, he adds a condition in verse 21: as long as it does not cause your brother or sister to stumble. The Western text appears to expand the verse (adding *skandalizetai to proskoptei*) which was absorbed by ℵ[c], B, D, and G and 33.[26] Paul urges that it is no use doing the right thing for the wrong

---

[22] Fitzmyer, Joseph A., *Romans: A New Translation with Introduction and Commentary* (New York: Doubleday, 1992; AB 33), p. 697.

[23] Käsemann, Ernst, *Commentary on Romans* (London: SCM, 1980), p. 361.

[24] Metzger, *Textual Commentary*, p. 469.

[25] Mitchell, Margaret M., *Paul and the Rhetoric of Reconciliation* (Tubingen: Mohr, 1992), pp. 99–111.

[26] Metzger, *Textual Commentary*, p. 469.

reason or with a damaging effect, which is an important pastoral and ethical principle. In verse 21 he states the positive corollary: it is right to abstain if to do otherwise would cause another to stumble.

In the final section of the chapter (vv. 22–23) Paul argues that all genuinely right actions must proceed from full conviction and be fully consonant with the Christian faith. The sentence 'Whatever does not proceed from faith is sin' (v. 23) has given rise to numerous theological and ethical controversies. As Cranfield, Ziesler and other commentators insist, it should not be abstracted from its context, and simply be interpreted as if it were a universal or context-free maxim.[27] In verse 22 the clause 'the faith that you have' can be understood either as a statement or as a question, provided that 'which' (Greek *hēn*) is included. The inclusion of 'which' is supported by ℵ, A, B and C, but otherwise most later MSS omit it. The UBS Committee under Metzger saw the case as balanced.[28]

The allusion to faith recalls 14.1–2. What is important is our decision 'before God' (v. 22). Happy are the people, says Paul, who have no reason later to condemn themselves 'because of what they approve' (Greek *dokomazei*). With that proviso, the matter lies between the Christian and God. At the beginning of verse 22, both Wright and Robertson call attention to Paul's direct use of *su*, which they both translate as 'You there!'[29] 'Approve' includes testing and approving.

In verse 23 'Whatever does not proceed from faith' depends for its meaning on its implied contrast. Virtually all commentators agree that it should not be interpreted out of context. (i) Augustine interpreted it in contrast to *unbelief* among pagans. Hence, he thought, it refers to pagan 'works' performed before justification by grace through faith, in effect invoking the universality of sin in the Jewish and Gentile world without Christ, as in Romans 1.18—3.20. Thus, before citing Romans 14.23, he comments, 'Nor can a man do any good thing, unless he is aided by . . . the grace of God through Jesus Christ our Lord.'[30] Today most commentators reject this as a context-free interpretation. (ii) Others understand it as meaning that all actions done contrary to conscience are sin. Thus Thomas Aquinas declares in his *Summa Theologiae*,

---

[27] Ziesler, John, *Paul's Letter to the Romans* (London: SCM, 1989 and 1990), p. 355; Cranfield, *Romans*, vol. 2, pp. 728–32.

[28] Metzger, *Textual Commentary*, pp. 469–70.

[29] Robertson, *Word Pictures*, vol. 4, p. 416.

[30] Augustine, *Against Julianus* in *Against Two Letters of the Pelagians*, 1.7 (Eng., *NPNF*, ser. i, vol. 5, p. 379); cf. 3.14 (Eng., *NPNF*, ser. i, vol. 5, p. 409); and five other references.

When the will is at variance with erring reason, it is against the conscience . . . for it is written (Romans 14:23), 'All that is not of faith', – i.e. that is against conscience – 'is sin'. Therefore the will is evil when it is at variance with erring reason.[31]

This tends also to be too generalizing. (iii) Cranfield argues that we need to interpret *faith* as Paul uses it in 14.1, 22, and 23a, which suggests that 'one's faith (in the basic NT sense . . .) allows one to do a particular thing . . . It means *one's confidence that* one's Christian faith *allows one* to do something.'[32]

Wright confirms this point by pointing out that in Romans the faith of Abraham is the paradigm case of faith, which stressed *trust and confidence*, and excludes wavering or doubt.[33] We must add the proviso that what faith *is* depends on to whom or to what it is directed, and here in Paul it is directly related to Christ. Dunn dissents from Cranfield, arguing for its general status. But in the end he also regards it as 'creaturely dependence, which is man's proper attitude and response to God'.[34] But Jewett declares,

Dunn is among the few commentators who take the maxim at face value, contending that whatever is not an expression of dependence and trust in God . . . is marked by that fatal flaw of human presumption and/or self-indulgence.[35]

Jewett insists, however, on relating it to welcoming the weak as well as the strong, and therefore Paul cannot be calling 'half-heartedness' sin. Indeed he describes as ironic the interpretation of Augustine, which had the very opposite effect from that intended by Paul. The verse should be seen as part of 'Paul's extraordinary defence of Christian tolerance'. It must be admitted that there is some force in Jewett's argument.

There are also other possible contrasts to *faith* in this verse. One may be fearful of the opinions of others, although Paul has stressed the need to take this into account. However, it could be fear of those who normally belong to the same group. *Faith* could also stand in contrast to sheer desire or pleasure. It is clear, however, that any decision must be 'before God', and must encourage peace and upbuilding.

The final problem posed by the transition between chapters 14 and 15 is that of MS readings. The doxology 'Now to him who is able to strengthen

---

[31] Aquinas, Thomas, *Summa Theologiae* (60 vols, Lat. and Eng., Oxford: Blackfriars, 1963), I-II, qu. 19, art. 5.

[32] Cranfield, *Romans*, vol. 2, p. 729 (his italics).

[33] Wright, 'Romans', *NIB*, vol. 10, p. 742.

[34] Dunn, *Romans 9—16*, p. 829.

[35] Jewett, *Romans*, p. 872.

you . . . be glory for evermore through Christ Jesus' usually today comes as 16.25–27. The NRSV contains a marginal note at the end of 14.23 to the effect that some ancient authorities add here 16.25–27. Some witnesses include it both here and at 16.25–27. P[46] places it at the end of chapter 15. A and 33 include it both here and *also* after 16.23. F joins 14.23 immediately with 15.1. P[61], ℵ, B, C, D and Old Syriac place it at the end of chapter 16.[36]

The UBS Committee under Metzger concluded that the responsibility for ending Romans at chapter 14 probably lay with Marcion or his followers in the second century. It also considered that the more serious disruption would be whether Paul himself produced two letters: a shorter form of the epistle ending at 15.33, and a longer version to Rome ending at 16.27. In spite of anxieties about the Pauline authorship of the last two chapters caused by the diversity of the placing of the doxologies, the Committee remained convinced that the most probable solution is that the whole epistle is Pauline up to the end of chapter 16. We have discussed this in Chapter 5 under 'The integrity of the epistle', including Manson's theory that Paul wrote two versions of the letter.

Christ our model and example, and the need for mutual welcome (15.1–13)

Christ remains the key model for how the 'strong' should bear with the failings (real or supposed) or the weak. In 15.1 Paul uses Greek *dunatoi* to denote those who are capable, competent and in this sense powerful. The NRSV 'put up with' is one of two possible translations of *bastazō* which can mean either *to carry, to sustain a burden* or *to endure, to put up with*.[37] One point of note is that Paul identifies himself with the 'strong' by his use of the word *we*. Christ 'did not please himself' (v. 3), as in Philippians 1.1–5 and 2 Corinthians 8.9. In verse 2 Paul stated the matter positively: 'Each of us must please our neighbour' and (again) *build* him or her up. *Neighbour* probably recalls Leviticus 19.18, as cited in Romans 13.9–10 and Galatians 5.14.

In verse 3 Paul quotes the LXX of Psalm 69.19 (68.10 LXX) exactly, which is a lament by upright sufferers for their suffering and reproaches. The key point is that, in Cranfield's words, 'The second person singular pronoun (*you*, Gk. *se*) refers to God; the reproaches levelled against God have fallen upon this righteous sufferer', i.e. Paul's christological

---

[36] Metzger, *Textual Commentary*, pp. 470–2 and 476–7.
[37] Danker, BDAG, p. 171.

interpretation.[38] In verse 4 Paul makes his well-known declaration: 'Whatever was written in former days was written for our instruction'. It closely repeats what Paul asserted in 1 Corinthians 9.10: 'Does he not speak entirely for our sake? It was indeed written for our sake'. It also reflects Romans 4.23, 24: 'The words "it was reckoned to him" were written not for his [Abraham's] sake alone, but for ours also.' James W. Aageson, for example, wrote on Paul's transformative and christological interpretation of Scripture through a book bearing a similar title, namely *Written Also for Our Sake: Paul and the Art of Biblical Interpretation*.[39] Aageson comments: 'Time has not rendered the Scripture obsolete. It still functions as a voice for the instruction and edification of the community.'[40] He especially focuses on the relevance of Scripture to Paul's mission to the Gentiles, and also that 'for Israel, Christ has become a stumbling block'.[41] He adds, 'The Bible provides a line of continuity from one generation to the next.'[42] Scripture speaks especially of 'Israel the Rootstock of the Church'.

The phrase 'by steadfastness and by the encouragement of the scriptures' anticipates the Book of Common Prayer's Collect for the Second Sunday in Advent (Bible Sunday) 'that by patience and comfort of Thy Holy Word' we may study the Scriptures. Paul's reference to hope echoes Romans 1—5. Again Paul urges mutual support. In verses 5 and 6 Paul formulates a doxology to the God who is faithful and steadfast, who has spoken through the Scriptures of God's single purpose for the Church and the world. 'Together' emphasizes the oneness and unity of Jewish and Gentile Christians as in 'live in harmony with one another' (v. 5).

The second half of the present sub-section (15.7–13) begins with the pivotal verse stressed by Jewett, 'Welcome one another, therefore, just as Christ has welcomed you' (v. 7). *Welcome* (Greek *proslambanesthe*), according to Danker, may take on five possible meanings. But he rightly accords his fourth in this context: *to extend a welcome,* or *receive into one's home or circle of acquaintance.* This occurs in Romans 14.1 and 15.7a, and of God's or Christ's *accepting a believer* in 14.3 and 15.7b. Dunn and Wright also render it *welcome.* Manson suggested 'Take to your heart'.[43] Jewett

---

[38] Cranfield, *Romans*, vol. 2, p. 773; similarly Fitzmyer, *Romans*, pp. 702–3.

[39] Aageson, James W., *Written Also for Our Sake: Paul and the Art of Biblical Interpretation* (Louisville: Westminster/John Knox, 1993), pp. 49 (on Rom. 4.23–24 and 1 Cor. 9.9–10) and 50 (on Rom. 15.4), and elsewhere.

[40] Aageson, *Written Also for Our Sake*, p. 50.

[41] Aageson, *Written Also for Our Sake*, p. 63.

[42] Aageson, *Written Also for Our Sake*, p. 67.

[43] Manson, T. W., 'St Paul's Letter to the Romans – and Others' in Donfried Karl P. (ed.), *The Romans Debate* (Grand Rapids: Baker Academic, 2nd edn, 1991), pp. 1–15.

complains that too many commentators reduce Paul's word 'to vague sentiments of "mutual acceptance"'.[44] Dunn, Murray and Stuhlmacher speak of 'mutual acceptance'.[45] On the other hand Michel and Black regard the common meal as the primary context for welcoming others into one's particular society or 'home' in the Christian family sense.[46] The 'strong' must regard the 'weak' as genuine brothers and sisters, for whom no difference or barrier exists. This must include the most intimate congregational meetings. Jewett continues: 'If all of the groups in Rome participate in the extension of hospitality to outsiders, it will serve "to put an end to the hostile competition, and to admit the basic legitimacy of the other side".'[47]

After the key injunction in 15.7a the whole of 15.7b–13 becomes an extended doxology or paean of praise. Wright shows how it gathers up God's purposes through Christ in all Paul's previous chapters. Wright concludes, 'It is not that he [God] has done things for Jews, and another for Gentiles; God has designed mercy for all (11:28–32), but . . . the purpose for Israel always had the Gentiles in mind.'[48] Hence in verses 8–9 Paul points out that in this respect Jesus Christ became 'a servant of the circumcised' (the Jews) to confirm the promises made to Israel 'that the Gentiles might glorify God for his mercy.' In other words, the pastoral concern of Jewish Christians for Gentile Christians, and of Gentile Christians for Jewish Christians, must reflect God's concern in grace for the well-being of all.[49] Thus 15.7b–13 becomes a quasi-liturgical expression of praise and thanksgiving for *God's faithfulness* throughout history.

Hence Paul stresses God's grace 'that he might confirm the promises given to the patriarchs' (v. 8; e.g. 4.16) and receive glory from the Gentiles also (v. 9). Käsemann calls the acceptance of the Gentiles 'an eschatological miracle'. Paul then quotes the LXX of Psalm 18.49 (Ps. 17.50 LXX), which in turn reflects 2 Samuel 22.50. In verse 10 he then quotes the OT again, this time from Deuteronomy 32.43. In this passage, as Dunn observes, the Hebrew text emphasized 'a strong promise of God's covenant faithfulness to his people', while the Greek LXX 'allows not only a much more universal perspective, but the crucial reading *meta tou laou autou*' (i.e. *with* his people).[50]

---

44 Jewett, *Romans*, p. 888.
45 E.g. Dunn, *Romans 9—16*, p. 845.
46 E.g. Black, Matthew, *Romans* (London: Oliphants, 1973; NCB), p. 200.
47 Jewett, *Christian Tolerance*, p. 29, and Jewett, *Romans*, p. 888.
48 Wright, 'Romans', *NIB*, vol. 10, p. 747.
49 Ziesler, *Romans*, p. 336, expresses this also.
50 Dunn, *Romans 9—16*, p. 849.

This is more sympathetic with the Gentiles, which is more appropriate in a Diaspora context, as is a regular feature of the LXX.

The catena of quotations continues. In verse 11 Paul cites Psalm 117.1 (Ps. 116.1 LXX); 'Praise the Lord, all you Gentiles' (Greek *panta ta ethnē*), where the Greek is close to the Hebrew. In verse 12 he cites Isaiah 11.10, 'The root of Jesse shall come [which relates to Israel], the one who rises to rule the Gentiles [which relates to the Gentiles]'. Isaiah may refer to the Davidic dynasty, which is to be a rallying point for Gentiles.[51] On the basis of these passages quoted in verses 9–12 and his previous arguments in this epistle, Paul reaches a climax in verse 13 in the benediction: 'May the God of hope fill you with all joy and peace in believing . . . by the power of the Holy Spirit.' Again, Paul emphasizes *God and his faithfulness*, while *believing* reflects Romans 4 (on Abraham's faith), and *joy*, *peace* and *hope* reflect the work of the *Holy Spirit* in Romans 5.1–5.

The phrase 'the God of hope' may, as Cranfield and Dunn suggest, mean either that God is the source of hope or that he is the object of hope.[52] Indeed Paul prays that the readers may abound or overflow (Greek *perisseuein*) in hope. Practical Christian attitudes, such as joy, peace and hope, flow from theological truth about the faithfulness of God, which has been expounded in the epistle.

---

[51] Fitzmyer, *Romans*, pp. 896–7.
[52] Cranfield, *Romans*, vol. 2, p. 747; Dunn, *Romans 9—16*, p. 851.

24

Paul's travel plans and the coming missionary task (15.14—16.2)

Paul's missionary practice (15.14–21)

In Romans 15.14–21 a central theme finds expression in verse 20: 'I make it my ambition to proclaim the good news, not where Christ has already been named, so that I do not build on someone else's foundation'. This reflects two things which have already been said in 1 Corinthians: primarily in 1 Corinthians 3.10–15: 'Like a skilled master builder I laid a foundation, and someone else is building on it'; and secondarily 1 Corinthians 2.1–5: 'I did not come proclaiming the mystery of God to you in lofty words ... I decided to know nothing among you except Jesus Christ, and him crucified.' Barrett explains that this was not simply to avoid rivalry, but to cover as wide an area as possible. In Rome the situation was different, because the Christian faith had already become firmly established there. Hence here Paul needs to explain how his missionary strategy involves Rome, and in due course to emphasize how the church there features in his plans to reach Spain.

Paul does not doubt that the faith has already been founded and planted in Rome authentically (vv. 14–16). He is 'confident about you', recognizing that the church in Rome is 'full of goodness, filled with all knowledge, and able to instruct one another' (v. 14). It is not because of any spiritual deficiency on the believers' part that he has written to introduce himself, even if there remain relatively minor points of which he needs to remind them (v. 15). Even then, his main concern remains that of being 'a minister [Greek *leitourgon*] of Christ Jesus to the Gentiles, in the priestly service [Greek *hierourgounta*] of the gospel of God'.

The Greek words *leitourgon* and *hierourgounta* may seem unexpected in this context, but belong together with the meaning *to offer a sacrifice* (as in Philo and Josephus). Paul is referring specifically to offering the *sacrifice of his life*, as in Romans 12.1 and Philippians 2.17. Here it may apply also to the offering of the Gentiles. In this sense the NRSV 'priestly' may be a technically correct translation of the Greek. But it could nevertheless be misleading, if it is understood to denote sacerdotal priesthood

248

in the NT. Cranfield translates it *serve with the holy service*.[1] Denney and Robertson make this point very emphatically.[2] 'The offering of the Gentiles' (v. 16) gives point to the sacrificial language used earlier. Munck comments on this phrase,

> The object of this service is that the Gentiles' offering may be acceptable, being sanctified by the Holy Spirit. It is ... [t]he offering that Paul as the priest of Jesus Christ has brought to God, having kindled their faith by the preaching of the gospel.[3]

Munck devotes some seven pages to discussing the role of 15.14–21 in Paul's missionary strategy. It looks back to Romans 9—11 in achieving 'the fullness of the Gentiles'. Paul 'has not addressed a church lacking strength and maturity, but it is his apostleship to the Gentiles that justifies him in his exhortations'.[4] Paul has written in response to the special grace which God has given him. In verse 17 he goes on to speak of the glory arising from this apostleship. He explains to the church in Rome that 'for the time being he has finished his task only in the East' (v. 19).[5] Otherwise he seeks to preach only where Christ's name has not been heard. But at the time of writing 'The Gentiles' offering is still a future event which will crown Paul's work among the Gentiles.'[6] Paul explains that he would not dare to speak in this way, were it not *Christ's* work through him (v. 18).[7]

In what sense has Paul 'completed' God's work in the east? Paul declares, 'From Jerusalem and as far around as Illyricum I have fully proclaimed the good news of Christ' (v. 19). His concern in Romans 9—11 was for 'all Israel'. Here it is the full number of the Gentiles. Wright observes, 'This is in fact one of the longest discussions Paul gives anywhere of how he conceives his apostolic work, and why he has made the decisions he has.'[8] A shorter comparable discussion occurs in 2 Corinthians. Dunn anticipates Wright's comment: 'Paul gives an overview of his missionary

---

[1] Cranfield, C. E. B., *A Critical and Exegetical Commentary on the Epistle to the Romans*, vol. 2 (Edinburgh: T & T Clark, 1979; ICC), p. 756.

[2] Robertson, A. T., *Word Pictures in the New Testament, vol. 4: Romans* (New York: R. Smith, 1931), p. 20; Denney, James, 'Romans', in *Expositor's Greek Testament* (*ExGrT*) (5 vols, Grand Rapids: Eerdmans, [1910]), vol. 2, p. 712.

[3] Munck, Johannes, *Paul and the Salvation of Mankind* (London: SCM, 1959), p. 50.

[4] Munck, *Paul*, p. 49.

[5] Munck, *Paul*, p. 51.

[6] Munck, *Paul*, pp. 51–4.

[7] Barrett, C. K., *The Epistle to the Romans* (London: Black, 1957), p. 276.

[8] Wright, N. T., 'Romans' in the *New Interpreter's Bible* (*NIB*) (Nashville: Abingdon, 2002), vol. 10, p. 752.

work . . . It is a sweeping vision of missionary strategy in a single stroke of the brush.'[9] Paul rounds off this part of his argument by biblical quotation in verse 21 from Isaiah 52.15 (LXX). This relates to the Servant's commission to the Gentiles: 'Those who have never heard of him shall understand.'

Paul's travel plans (15.22–33)

Paul opens his travel plans by referring to the necessary delay in his eagerness to arrive in Rome, probably because of his busyness in 'completing his mission'. The Greek translation *often* (Greek *ta polla*) is either adverbial (NRSV) or an internal accusative (i.e. things keep cropping up in my work). There is also a difference of textual reading: P[46], B, D, F and G read *pollakis* (*many times* or *often*); but ℵ, A and C read *ta polla*, which is adopted by most commentators. The verb *being hindered* is imperfect, and strictly means *kept being hindered*. Fitzmyer explains Paul's concern, 'for place after place in that Eastern area preoccupied him so that he could not come to Rome, no matter how often he thought of doing so'.[10]

In verse 23 'with no further place for me in these regions' may convey the impression that Paul has grossly overestimated the extent of his outreach, even to the point of self-congratulation. Wright observes, 'This sounds extraordinary, given the tiny number of Christians we must envisage compared with the population in general.'[11] But, following Dunn and Fitzmyer, he replies that as a church-planter and missionary strategist he was concerned here with representative communities.

Paul makes a major claim in verse 24. He hopes to come to Rome 'when I go to Spain.' Indeed he hopes not only 'to see you on my journey', but also 'to be *sent on* by you, once I have enjoyed your company for a little while' (v. 24). It would be a *mistake* simply to think of Rome as a *stopping place* on the way from the east to Spain. Jewett is entirely convincing in claiming that the special expertise of many Roman Christians was in speaking Latin, rather than only Greek, together with their knowledge of the Roman administrative system of provincial government. This would suggest that *they, rather than Paul alone*, had the necessary gifts for spearheading mission in Spain. In language, Spain was totally different from the eastern provinces. Paul wanted to establish a common theology and

---

[9] Dunn, James D. G., *Romans 9—16* (Dallas: Word, 1988; WBC 38), pp. 868–9.

[10] Fitzmyer, Joseph A., *Romans: A New Translation with Introduction and Commentary* (New York: Doubleday, 1992; AB 33), p. 716.

[11] Wright, 'Romans', *NIB*, vol. 10, p. 755.

common vision with the Christians in Rome, so that in due course *they* (perhaps with him) would be the heart of the mission to Spain.[12]

Jewett also regards the Jewish population of Spain as sparse, in contrast to the claims of Cranfield and Käsemann. These rely, he insists, on outdated information.[13] Moreover Latin was spoken in the major cities, while many people spoke only their own language in rural areas. Roman senators were also appointed as proconsuls of praetorian rank in the government of Spain, much of which had been a senatorial province since the time of Augustus. Jewett examines Spain region by region.[14] When we reach 16.2, we shall note that Jewett considers Phoebe to be 'an upper-class benefactor', who will present Paul's letter to Rome, and in due course superintend the mission to Rome.[15] In verse 24 some manuscripts add 'I will come to you'; but P[46], $\aleph$*, A, B, C and D omit it.

Meanwhile in verse 25 Paul explains: 'At present, however, I am going to Jerusalem in a ministry to the saints'. He further explains in verse 26 that Macedonia (mainly the churches of Philippi and Thessalonica) and Achaea (Corinth) 'have been pleased to share their resources with the poor among the saints at Jerusalem'. It was vital to Paul's apostleship to promote the oneness of Jews and Gentiles in Christ, by appealing for a collection from the Hellenistic Church for Jerusalem. His word for *collection* is Greek *koinonia* (*what we share in common*), as in verse 26 and 2 Corinthians 8.4. *What is common* is *not only* financial, but *nothing less than this*. In 2 Corinthians 8.4 the church was 'begging us earnestly for the privilege of sharing in this ministry to the saints'.

In verses 25–27 Paul further explains that he is going to Jerusalem with the collection from the churches in Macedonia and Achaea, confirming, as we have noted, that they were pleased to do this. In retrospect we know that it would have been a matter of years, not weeks, before he had eventually arrived in Rome. Acts 20 recounts how Paul sailed from Philippi to Miletus and Ephesus. He was then recommissioned by the church in Ephesus. He sailed to Tyre, and came to Caesarea, having forebodings from the churches about his fate in Jerusalem. Paul declares that he was ready 'not only to be bound but even to die in Jerusalem' (Acts 21.13), and arrived there at first to be welcomed by the Christians (21.17–26).

---

[12] Jewett, Robert, *Romans: A Commentary* (Minneapolis: Fortress, 2007; Hermeneia), pp. 14–80 and 83–9.

[13] Jewett, *Romans*, p. 74; Bowers, W. P., 'Jewish Communities in Spain in the Time of Paul the Apostle', *JTS* 26 (1975), pp. 395–402.

[14] Jewett, *Romans*, pp. 77–9.

[15] Jewett, *Romans*, pp. 89–91.

But then Jews from Asia stirred up the crowd, and 'all the city was aroused'. They seized Paul and tried to kill him (21.30–31). Paul was rescued by a Roman tribune and soldiers, who arrested him (perhaps in protective custody; 21.32–36). Acts 22—24 recounts Paul's speeches, his examinations by Festus and Felix, and his appeal to Caesar. Acts 25—28 recounts his subsequent long journey to Rome.

The collection was far more than an attempt to alleviate poverty in Jerusalem. It was part of an act of *mutual solidarity* between Jewish and Gentile Christians. The raising of funds among the Gentile churches symbolized this recognition of Jewish Christians *as part of their one family*; the acceptance of the gift equally symbolized Jewish recognition that Gentile Christians were also *part of that single family*. Munck rightly comments, 'Paul's journeys and their objects are a part of his theology.'[16] Paul regarded both Jerusalem and Rome, he argues, as having distinct roles in the history of salvation. Among the contributing churches he traces Galatia and Corinth (1 Cor. 16.1), Corinth and Macedonia (2 Cor. 8.1), Berea, Thessalonica, perhaps Derbe (Acts 20.4–5), and Antioch (Acts 11.29). Wright strongly emphasizes this. He declares, 'Paul's coming with the collection would thus be a new vision of the long prophesied pilgrimage of the nations to Zion.'[17] The collection was not the payment of legal levy imposed by Jerusalem on its daughter churches.

Verse 27b refers back to Romans 9—14, namely that the Gentiles have *shared in* the Jews' spiritual things; therefore they could reciprocate by *sharing* material things. The NRSV 'have delivered to them what has been collected' does not strictly correspond with Paul's Greek. He actually wrote, 'And have sealed to them [Greek *sphragisamenos*, from *sphragizō*, *to seal*] their fruit'. NJB reads 'have given this harvest into their possession'. Paul uses a mixed metaphor which cannot readily be translated into English. But the meaning is clear: Paul wants to deliver the money safe and sound, and therefore uses the word *seal*. Fitzmyer explains, 'When the tenant farmer delivered the harvested fruit or produce to the owner, the sacks were marked with the farmer's seal as an identification of its source.'[18]

Paul repeats his intention to visit Rome, and thence Spain (v. 29), when he has completed his prior task. This will be 'in the fullness of the blessing of Christ', as rightly in NRSV. P46, ℵ*, A, B, C, D, Old Latin and Coptic

---

[16] Munck, *Paul*, p. 284.
[17] Wright, 'Romans', *NIB*, vol. 10, p. 756; also McKnight, S., *A Light to the Gentiles* (Minneapolis: Fortress, 1991), pp. 47–8; Nickel, Keith F., *The Collection: A Study of Paul's Strategy* (London: SCM, 1966), pp. 1–143.
[18] Fitzmyer, *Romans*, p. 723; and Wright, 'Romans', *NIB*, vol. 10, p. 757.

retain *fullness*, while ℵ^c and 33 omit it. *Fullness* may mean *what is brought to completion*, although it may simply mean *abounding* or *pure* blessing.

At verse 30 Cranfield suggests that Paul begins, as it were, a new paragraph. 'I appeal' (NRSV) may indeed mean *appeal* (Greek *parakaleō*), but may *equally* mean *to ask, to request* or even *to exhort*. We referred above to Bjerkelund's book on this word, where he claims that it can denote a request coming from an official person, here probably as *apostle to the Gentiles*. The substance of the appeal is 'to join me in earnest prayer . . . on my behalf' (v. 30), for rescue from the plans of unbelieving Jews in Judaea. As we have seen from Acts, several churches probably had intelligence about plots against Paul in Judaea. The NRSV loosely renders the substance of the appeal or request: 'Join me in earnest prayer'. The NEB and REB are much closer to Paul's Greek when they translate it as 'be my allies in the fight', and the NIV, 'join me in my struggle'. The Greek is *sunagōnisasthai*, a compound infinitive, with *sun-* (*with*) coupled with *agōn* (*struggle* or *contest*). The word occurs only here in the NT. But it is important for the spiritual notion of struggling in prayer, or for struggling before God together with a partner. Pfitzner has written an entire book on this word in Paul. He draws a clear distinction between Jewish and Greek attitudes to athletes, and shows that Paul draws sparingly on the popular notion in the Graeco-Roman world.[19] Jesus Christ suffered struggle and agony in prayer (Matt. 26.42; Luke 22.44).

Paul asks the readers to pray with him that he may be 'rescued' or 'snatched out' of the hands of the unbelievers who plot against him. He also prays that the gift of the Gentile churches will be acceptable to Jewish Christians in Jerusalem. He faces a difficult and dangerous time, but also looks forward to his visit to Rome and Spain. He faces the dangers with courage, but looks forward to Rome as a break and refreshment from these stresses. In verse 33 he prays that the God of peace may be with the church in Rome. Some manuscripts, as we have noted, place the blessing at this point, which otherwise occurs at the end of chapter 16.

The special commendation of Phoebe (16.1–2)

Phoebe forms part of Paul's missionary plan, as Jewett has convincingly argued. In effect, this is a short letter of recommendation for Phoebe, who was deacon or minister (Greek *diakonos*) of the church at Cenchreae.

---

[19] Pfitzner, Victor C., *Paul and the Agōn Motif: Traditional Athletic Imagery in the Pauline Literature* (Leiden: Brill, 1967).

Cenchreae was one of the two seaports of Corinth. One port, Lechaeum, faced west for trade with Italy and Rome, while the other, Cenchreae, faced east for trade with Ephesus, Asia Minor and further afield. Corinth was an enormously busy commercial seaport, which was largely dependent on trade or business for its prosperity and influence. As I have argued elsewhere, Corinth was a prosperous, bustling, international centre of trade and industry.[20] The distance between the two ports was less than 6 miles. It stood on the narrow isthmus between northern and southern Greece. Many preferred to use the two port facilities available at Corinth, rather than sail around Cape Malea, the southern tip of Greece. Ships could often be transported between the two ports on rollers, or by means of porters or slaves, who would carry the cargoes across the narrow isthmus. Corinth would collect port fees and oversee a thriving trade and income.

Corinth also made a vast income from tourism, business and manufacturing. The Isthmian Games were nearby, second in importance only to the Olympic Games. Many flocked to Corinth for new opportunities of employment. The city needed dockers, porters, secretaries, accountants, guides, bodyguards, blacksmiths, carpenters, cooks, housekeepers, literate and menial slaves, and hoteliers. It boasted an entrepreneurial culture, with a dynamic drive for success and upward mobility. It was far more dynamic than sleepy Athens, which relied on its past, while Corinth had become a well-ordered Roman colony. Prisca and Aquila saw Corinth as a prime location for their trade, namely leather goods and tent-making, when many Jews were expelled from Rome.

Phoebe's port town of Cenchreae would have shared in this enormous prosperity and success. Jewett argues convincingly that the word correctly translated 'benefactor' (16.2 NRSV; Greek *prostatis*) is 'a technical term for an upper-class benefactor'.[21] Hence, Paul explains, 'she has been a benefactor of many and of myself as well' (16.2). She would therefore, Jewett argues, have been a person of some means, able to undertake business journeys with an entourage of some size. Byrne numbers her among the 'wealthy women . . . who acted as patrons for others'.[22] Thus, Jewett argues, when Paul asks the church in Rome to help her 'in whatever she may require from you', it is inconceivable that such a wealthy woman would

---

[20] Thiselton, Anthony C., *1 Corinthians: A Shorter Exegetical and Pastoral Commentary* (Grand Rapids: Eerdmans, 2006), pp. 1–14; and Thiselton, Anthony C., *The First Epistle to the Corinthians: A Commentary on the Greek Text* (Grand Rapids: Eerdmans, and Carlisle, Paternoster, 2000; NIGTC), pp. 1–22.

[21] Jewett, *Romans*, p. 89.

[22] Byrne, Brendan, *Romans* (Collegeville: Liturgical Press, 1996 and 2007; Sacra Pagina 6), pp. 447–8.

need help for her business or her food or housing, but *only for the work of the gospel*. The need is for her missionary patronage. She would be the one to spearhead the outreach to Spain, as well as in all probability reading out Paul's letter to the church or churches in Rome. If she were the reader, Paul might have felt that it would embarrass her to give her too glowing an account of her leadership as *diakonos* and benefactor in Cenchreae.

On the details of 16.1–2, some manuscripts omit *our* sister, but ℵ, B, C, D and 33 retain it, and this seems correct. 'I commend' (Greek *sunistēmi*) is also correct. The church at Cenchreae may well have been based in Phoebe's house, on analogy with a church at Anaploga in the suburbs of Corinth. Wiseman has excavated sites at Anaploga, where a large villa shows every sign of holding Christian meetings of worship.[23] The Greek *diakonos* was once regarded as the title of a subordinate role, but nowadays (especially since the research of Collins) is regarded as denoting either *leader* or *deputy*. To *welcome Phoebe in the Lord* is the phrase also used of welcoming the beloved Epaphroditus (Phil. 2.29) with suitable honour. In Jewett's words, 'Phoebe should be welcomed with honours suitable to her position . . . as a congregational leader . . . and her role in the missionary project envisioned.'[24]

---

[23] Wiseman, James, 'Corinth and Rome' in *ANRW*, p. 528; Murphy-O'Connor, Jerome, *St Paul's Corinth* (Wilmington: Glazier, 1983), pp. 153–61; Thiselton, *First Epistle to the Corinthians*, pp. 860–1.
[24] Jewett, *Romans*, p. 945.

25

Final greetings, final appeal and doxology (16.3–27)

The greetings (16.3–16)

Greetings occur in more than one of Paul's letters, but Wright helpfully asks why Paul includes some 25 names here, whereas 'there is a remarkable absence of named greetings' in Paul's other epistles.[1] Paul does mention Stephanas, Fortunatus and Archaicus in 1 Corinthians 16.15–18, but they had come to visit him, and Stephanas was his first convert in Achaea. Otherwise greetings are usually minimal, except perhaps for two names in Colossians 4.15, 17, which is another church which Paul had not yet visited. Where he knew the church well, as every pastor knows, the selection of named people leads one into a very sensitive area, for one cannot name everyone, and those who are omitted may feel slighted. Further, not only was the church in Rome unknown, but Paul may well be selecting representatives from several house-churches as congregations in Rome. Finally, he knew many of them already from meeting them in other locations in the empire, where social mobility was great.

In 16.3–5 Prisca and Aquila are known from Acts 18.2, 26; and 1 Corinthians 16.19; and later the names occur in 1 Timothy 4.19. These were Paul's hosts and co-workers for 18 months in Corinth; they shared the same trade; and were among the closest of Paul's friends. Apart from them, and possibly Epaenetus, Mary, Andronicus and Junia, there seems to be inadequate evidence for Ollrog's argument that Paul has ordered his list in the sequence of closeness to the people named.[2] Aquila was a Jew who came originally from Pontus, and Aquila and Prisca had moved from Rome to Corinth, when Claudius expelled many of the Jews from Rome in AD 49 (Acts 18.2). Some MSS read the diminutive form *Priscilla*. Paul adds that they 'risked their necks' for his life. Bruce comments that Priscilla would never have risked her life for Paul, had the 'popular mythology of

[1] Wright, N. T., 'Romans' in the *New Interpreter's Bible* (*NIB*) (Nashville: Abingdon, 2002), vol. 10, p. 761.

[2] Ollrog, W.-H., *Paulus und seine Mitarbeiter* (Neukirchen: Neukirchener Verlag, 1979).

his alleged misogyny' been true![3] The couple again hosted a house-church in Rome (1 Cor. 16.19).

Epaenetus (v. 5), Paul notes, was his first convert in Asia, while Mary has worked very hard in God's work at Rome (v. 6). We know nothing else about them. The earliest MS evidence is evenly divided between Greek *Marian* (Mary) in A, B, C and Coptic, and *Mariam*, the Hebrew name, in P[46], D, F and G. Most writers accept the equal possibility of both. The Graeco-Roman name 'Mary' may have been derived from the masculine name Marius. In verse 7 Paul greets Andronicus and Junia, who are described as Paul's relatives. They were in prison with Paul, 'prominent among the apostles', and had become Christian converts even before Paul. But Cranfield argues, 'By (Gk.) *suggeneis* Paul almost certainly means fellow-countrymen and not relations.'[4] NRSV and NIV imply relatives.

Junia is now unanimously recognized as a *woman's* name, in contrast to the masculine *Junias*. Traditionally this has been debated. But Eldon Epp, who is a distinguished and excellent textual critic, recently published *Junia: The First Woman Apostle*, which has proved decisive in the debate.[5] Epp traces textual history, exegesis, lexical forms and the name *Junia* in early Christian writers. He examines, for example, the so-called neutral text of Westcott and Hort, other major manuscripts and even the sixteenth-century Textus Receptus, to show that although many traditional sources read *Junias*, the modern view is decisively that Paul referred to *Junia*. He concludes, 'There was an apostle, *Junia*. For me this conclusion is indispensable.'[6] *Junias* is largely restricted to the era between the thirteenth century and about 1998. Probably Andronicus and Junia were husband and wife, or possibly brother and sister. They are 'prominent among the apostles' (NRSV; Greek *episēmoi*, *notable*). Wright and Jewett, writing in the twenty-first century, confirm this point.

Ampliatus, Urbanus, Stachys, Apelles and the family of Aristobulus are the next to be mentioned (vv. 8–10). According to Jewett, *Ampliatus* was coined as a slave name with the meaning *ample*. He might have been a slave or a freedman and is Paul's 'beloved in the Lord'. Urbanus (v. 9) is also known personally to Paul as a co-worker. As we noted earlier, it is important not to regard Paul as a lone, solitary or freelance missionary, but as one surrounded by co-workers, who had been commissioned by

---

[3] Bruce, F. F., *Paul: Apostle of the Free Spirit* (Exeter: Paternoster, 1977), p. 457.

[4] Cranfield, C. E. B., *A Critical and Exegetical Commentary on the Epistle to the Romans*, vol. 2 (Edinburgh: T & T Clark, 1979; ICC), p. 788.

[5] Epp, Eldon Jay, *Junia: The First Woman Apostle* (Minneapolis: Fortress, 2005).

[6] Epp, *Junia*, p. 80.

the church of Antioch, and worked in a team. Urbanus' name is Latin, and occurs in many Roman inscriptions. Stachys is also personally known to Paul, and is called 'my beloved'. His is a less common Greek name. In verse 10 Paul mentions Apelles, whose name Lightfoot identified as that of someone belonging to the imperial household.[7] 'Approved in Christ' (Greek *dokimos*) has the sense of having been tested and proved to be genuine. If Paul does not know Apelles personally, he knows his reputation as a genuine, sincere and fully committed Christian. The last name in verses 8–10 appears in the phrase 'those of Aristobulus'. The NRSV inserts 'family of Aristobulus', in place of the Greek definite article (Greek *tous ek tōn Aristobulou*). There is a similar construction in 1 Corinthians 1.11: 'those of Chloe'. The definite article, then, may refer to the family of Aristobulus, or to his slaves, or to his business employees or partners. Any identification of Aristobulus remains purely speculative.

In verses 11–16 Paul names 14 further people. Herodion is called Paul's 'relative' (NRSV), but the Greek term *suggenē* may, as we have observed, mean *relative, kinsman* or *compatriot*. Narcissus was a well-known name in Rome. Jewett and Wright inform us that a certain Narcissus was a freedman who rose to great heights under Claudius, only to become the victim of jealousy, and be forced to commit suicide after the death of Claudius. But we cannot tell whether this name denotes the same man. Once again the Greek 'the of Narcissus ones' (*tous ek tōn Narkissou*) is indeterminate, denoting either slaves or family, but Jewett and Wright stress that this group may well have been the congregation that met in the house of Narcissus.[8] Cranfield suggests that they were 'a distinct group within the Imperial household'.[9]

Tryphaena and Tryphosa (v. 12) may have been sisters, and hence the similarity of their names. They are called workers or hard workers (Greek *kopiōsas*) in the Lord. Persis is beloved (perhaps '*the* beloved' suggests widespread affection in the church), and has laboured in the Lord. Dunn and Jewett comment, '*Persis* seems to have been a popular name for female slaves.'[10] *Rufus* (v. 13) is a Latin name, again often the name of a freedman or a slave. It was a nickname, denoting 'Red-head'. He may well have been the Rufus to whom Mark 15.21 alludes, namely the son of Simon Cyrene,

---

[7] Lightfoot, J. B., 'Excursus on "Caesar's Household"' in *Saint Paul's Epistle to the Philippians* (New York: Macmillan), p. 174 and pp. 171–8.

[8] Wright, 'Romans', *NIB*, vol. 10, p. 763; Jewett, Robert, *Romans: A Commentary* (Minneapolis: Fortress, 2007; Hermeneia), p. 967.

[9] Cranfield, *Romans*, vol. 2, p. 793.

[10] Dunn, James D. G., *Romans 9—16* (Dallas: Word, 1988; WBC 38), p. 897; Jewett, *Romans*, p. 968.

who carried the cross. Dunn, Jewett, Cranfield and others think that this connection is probable, but Fitzmyer is more doubtful.[11] Paul describes the mother of Rufus as 'a mother to me also'. Jewett suggests that this may mean that she provided hospitality and even patronage for Paul; but it may have denoted something much more personal than this.

In verses 14–15 about seven names follow, including 'the brothers and sisters who are with them'. These are a mixture of Greek and Latin names. In the list as a whole, 19 names are Greek; eight are Latin; and one or two are Hebrew or Jewish.

Wright points out, 'To the modern Western eye, the most striking feature in the list of greetings is that nearly half the people named are women. Some of them are taking leading roles in the church.'[12] A second feature is that many represent the diversity of small congregations spread out over the vast city, being co-workers or friends of Paul, and being socially mobile. Patrons and hosts were becoming increasingly recognized; others could be more vulnerable. Estimates of the size of the church vary greatly, but the believers may well have numbered between 40 and 100 in all, which would allow for ready friendships and personal knowledge of each other.

Many commentators regard the formula in verse 16, 'with a holy kiss', as a regular greeting among Christians (1 Cor. 16.20; 2 Cor. 13.12; 1 Thess. 5.26). Here it constitutes a deliberate expression of Christian family intimacy after the long list of names. According to convention, the kiss was a sign of family relationships.[13] This family 'extension' seems distinctive to *Christian congregations*. It built strong relationships among diverse ethnic groups and all ages, and shows the extent of family fellow-feeling among Christians in the pagan and Jewish world of the day. 'Holy' guards against abuses of this practice. Murray suggests, 'Paul characterizes the kiss as "holy", and thus distinguishes it from all that is erotic or sensual.'[14] Ziesler asks when it became 'a regular part of Christian worship': if this was so, why does Paul command it? It certainly became a regular practice, he says, in later years.[15] 'All the churches of Christ greet you' expresses the bond between Christian churches throughout the empire. Theologically the churches constituted one undivided body in Christ.

---

[11] Cranfield, *Romans*, vol. 2, pp. 793–4; Dunn, *Romans 9—16*, p. 897; Käsemann, Ernst, *Commentary on Romans* (London: SCM, 1980), p. 414; Fitzmyer, Joseph A., *Romans: A New Translation with Introduction and Commentary* (New York: Doubleday, 1992; AB 33), p. 741.

[12] Wright, 'Romans', *NIB*, vol. 10, p. 763.

[13] Stählin, Gustav, 'phileō' in Kittel, G., and Friedrich, G. (eds), *Theological Dictionary of the New Testament* (*TDNT*) (10 vols, Grand Rapids: Eerdmans, 1964–76), vol. 9 (1974), p. 119 and pp. 119–27.

[14] Murray, John, *The Epistle to the Romans* (Grand Rapids: Eerdmans, 1997), p. 232.

[15] Ziesler, John, *Paul's Letter to the Romans* (London: SCM, 1989 and 1990), p. 353.

A last appeal and final greetings (16.17–23)

As in 1 Corinthians and elsewhere, Paul's final appeal concerns 'those who cause dissensions [Greek *dichostasias*, i.e. *cleavages* or *splits*, like *schismata* in 1 Cor. 1.10] and offences' (Greek *skandala*, i.e. *things that trip people up*). Paul appeals to them to be on the lookout for these causes of splits. To judge from 1 Corinthians 1.10 these divisions were probably initiated by differences of personality, which became transformed into rivalries and power-play. In Corinth these were caused by ranking people's favourite leaders. There is always a lurking danger, even today, that cliques or even house groups can lead eventually to splits based on ambition for power and control. Even the pagan Greek writer Aristophanes warned his readers that jealousy or power-seeking could set 'little word traps and double-talk' to make another group seem inferior.[16]

Jewett and Byrne regard verses 17–20 as an anonymous interpolation into Romans 16. Jewett argues that 'look out for' (Greek *skopeite*) is strongly negative, and more provocative than would usually be the case in authentic Pauline epistles, while Byrne claims that these verses undermine Paul's earlier call for tolerance. The language is admittedly drawn from political rhetoric, but Margaret Mitchell and others have shown how Paul regularly uses such language in 1 Corinthians 1.10–13.[17] Jewett also finds the phrase *in opposition to the teaching* (v. 17) rare and un-Pauline. But these points hardly seem to warrant excluding the passage from the chapter, especially in the light of parallels in 1 Corinthians which we cite.[18] The passage in 1 Corinthians 5.1–5 suggests a further parallel, and does not undermine the call for mutual respect between the strong and the weak made in that epistle.

Paul confirms that these splits and snares have come about for no good reason (v. 18). Those who promote them serve only themselves. As Dunn observes, this may refer to failing Christians or alternatively to outsiders.[19] Their use of 'smooth talk and flattery' and of deceiving the simpleminded reminds us, once again, of 1 Corinthians 2.1–5, and 3.18–21. Two excellent studies of pride and rhetoric at Corinth have been provided by Stephen Pogoloff and Andrew Clarke.[20]

---

[16] Aristophanes, *Acharnenses*, 687.

[17] Mitchell, Margaret M., *Paul and the Rhetoric of Reconciliation* (Tübingen: Mohr, 1992).

[18] Jewett, *Romans*, pp. 988–96; and Byrne, Brendan, *Romans* (Collegeville: Liturgical Press, 1996 and 2007; Sacra Pagina 6), p. 456.

[19] Dunn, *Romans 9—16*, p. 903.

[20] Pogoloff, Stephen, *Logos and Sophia: The Rhetorical Situation in 1 Corinthians* (Atlanta: Scholars Press, 1992; SBLDS 134); Clarke, Andrew, *Secular and Christian Leadership in Corinth* (Leiden: Brill, 1993).

In verse 19 Paul wants their model obedience and goodness to be supplemented by wisdom and shrewdness about possible evil influences. Goodness and guilelessness is not quite enough. He writes, 'I rejoice over you' (NRSV), which seems to place the stress on the church, as in ℵ*, A, B and C. But some Western texts, including P⁴⁶, D*, F and G, change the order of words. Cranfield remarks, 'The Roman Christians had a reputation to live up to.'[21] The clause 'will shortly crush' (Greek *suntripsei, the future*) constitutes a promise, but some MSS (including A) make it *suntripsai*, which would render it a prayer-wish. This supposed improvement is unlikely to be original. Many read 'the grace' here in verse 20, and omit it in verse 24. Metzger's Committee argues that 'The grace of our Lord Jesus be with you' is the shorter and original form, as read by P⁴⁶, ℵ and B.[22]

Additional greetings come in verses 21–23. Those named *send* greetings; they are *not recipients* of them. It is predictable that Timothy, as one of Paul's co-workers, should wish to send greetings. Dunn states, 'Timothy is the person who is most frequently mentioned elsewhere in Paul's letters (1 Cor. 4:17; 16:10; 2 Cor. 1:19; Phil. 2:19; 1 Thess. 3:2, 6).'[23] Lucius is unlikely to be the Lucius of Acts 13.1, but some identify him with Luke, the author of Luke–Acts. *Sosipater* is a common name, and may be one of the delegates travelling with Paul. Jason could be Paul's host from Thessalonica (Acts 17.5–7). But none of these suggestions can be certain.

Tertius (v. 22) is Paul's secretary, who actually wrote the letter, probably at Paul's dictation. He may have been secretary to Paul's probable host Gaius. We cannot generalize about the varied roles of secretaries, except that secretaries were often used in the first century in Greece. Gaius (v. 23), who is Paul's host, was baptized by Paul as one of his first converts. He probably was a leading figure in the church. Erastus was city treasurer, and one of Paul's helpers (Acts 19.22). He was probably the benefactor whose pavement-inscription can still be seen just outside the archaeological boundaries of ancient Corinth. *Quartus* was a common name among slaves and freedmen.

Final doxology (16.25–27)

Some MSS, including Origen, place the doxology after 14.23. This is understandable if Marcion's version of Romans extended only to Romans 14.

---

[21] Cranfield, *Romans*, vol. 2, p. 802.

[22] Metzger, Bruce, *A Textual Commentary on the Greek New Testament* (New York: UBS, 2nd edn, 1994), p. 476.

[23] Dunn, *Romans 9—16*, pp. 908–9.

The doxology is retained at this point by P⁶¹, ℵ, B, C, D, Old Latin, Old Syriac, Coptic (Sahidic and Bohairic) and Clement. Hence the UBS Committee chaired by Metzger retained it, although the Committee admitted that this decision was difficult.[24] As it stands, the doxology is similar to that which later occurs in Ephesians 3.20–21. Its emphasis on God remains characteristic of Romans, and divine sovereignty has been apparent in Romans 8.28 and 9.17. The NRSV 'strengthen' accurately means *to make stable, to establish* or *to be firm*.[25] It is natural to pray for the consolidation of the church. The word is often used by second-century apologists and the early Fathers. 'My gospel' is distinctively Pauline (Rom. 2.16; 2 Cor. 4.3; 1 Thess. 1.5). The phrase 'the revelation of the mystery' was used in *1 Enoch* 49.2, although in *1 Enoch* and Qumran the secret is usually still hidden. In Paul, however, the mystery has become an open one. It was 'kept secret' for long ages, but is now disclosed (v. 26a). Again, this coheres well with 1 Corinthians (1 Cor. 2.1, 7; 4.1; 14.2; 15.51–52); as well as with Romans 11.25.

In verse 26 Paul underlines that the prophetic writings are part of 'the Bible of the Church' for the Gentiles. This merely formalizes his regular approach to Isaiah and other biblical writings throughout the epistle. In Cranfield's words, 'It involves recognizing . . . a contrast between the mystery of past hiddenness and its having been made manifest in the present through the prophetic writings.'[26] The obedience of faith has been a much-discussed phrase. We commented on it in Romans 1.5, of which this may be a conscious reflection.[27]

Finally, Paul ascribes glory for ever 'to the only wise God' through Jesus Christ (v. 27). This is clearly a monotheistic expression of faith. It in no way compromises any later formulation of the Holy Trinity, for in the latter confession God is still *One*. As Gregory of Nyssa and Gregory of Nazianzus later argued, numerical meaning is irrelevant to the intention of this formulation. God is the *one God*, to whom the worship of his people is directed. The reference to 'one God' also underlines the continuity of Israel and the Church, or of Christian Jews and Christian Gentiles. It totally excludes Marcion's claim in the second century for a discontinuity

---

[24] Metzger, *Textual Commentary*, pp. 436–7.
[25] Danker, Frederick, *A Greek-English Lexicon of the New Testament and Other Early Christian Literature* (BDAG) (Chicago and London: University of Chicago Press, 3rd edn, 2000), p. 945.
[26] Cranfield, *Romans*, vol. 2, p. 811.
[27] Garlington, Don, *Faith, Obedience, and Perseverance: Aspects of Paul's Letter to the Romans* (Eugene, OR: Wipf & Stock, 2009; reprinted from Tübingen: Mohr, 1994; WUNT 791), pp. 10–31 and 144–63.

and disruption between the two Testaments, let alone for two distinct 'Gods'. God is not only wise, but *uniquely so*; not only powerful and loving but *uniquely so* (1 Cor. 1.24, 30). Paul sets the model for prayer and worship: prayer is *to* the Father, *through* the Son, and in the light of Romans 8.26, *by* the urging of the Holy Spirit. 'Amen' means 'May it be so'. It is not equivalent simply to 'The End', but is a liturgical *participation*, which has been carried over from Jewish worship.

Bibliography

Aageson, James W., *Written Also for Our Sake: Paul and the Art of Biblical Interpretation* (Louisville: Westminster/John Knox Press, 1993).

Ambrose, *Letters* (Eng., *NPNF*, ser. ii, vol. 10, pp. 411–73).

Apuleius, *The Golden Ass* (London: Penguin, 1999).

Aquinas, Thomas, *Summa Theologiae* (60 vols, Lat. and Eng., Oxford: Blackfriars, 1963).

Aquinas, Thomas, *Super epistolas S. Pauli Lectura* (Turin: Marietti, 1953); Eng., *Aquinas Study Bible: St. Thomas Aquinas on Romans*, online at <http// consolamnipublications/about-cp>.

Aristotle, *De Mundo* (Gk and Eng., Harvard, MA: Harvard University Press, 1939; LCL).

Athanasius, *Letters* (Eng., *NPNF*, ser. ii, vol. 4, pp. 554–81).

Atkinson, James, *Luther and the Birth of Protestantism* (Atlanta: John Knox Press, 1981).

Augustine, *Against Two Letters of the Pelagians* (Eng., *NPNF*, ser. i, vol. 5).

Augustine, *Confessions*, ed. H. Chadwick (Eng., Oxford: Oxford University Press, 1992).

Augustine, *Confessions and Enchiridion*, ed. A. C. Outler (Philadelphia: Westminster Press, 1955; LCC 7).

Augustine, *Disputation against Fortunatus* (Eng., *NPNF*, ser. i, vol. 4, pp. 113–24).

Augustine, *The Letter of Petilian the Donatist* (Eng., *NPNF*, ser. i, vol. 4, pp. 519–628).

Augustine, *On Marriage and Concupiscence* (Eng., *NPNF*, ser. i, vol. 5, pp. 260–308).

Augustine, *On the Merits and Remission of Sins* and *On the Baptism of Infants* (Eng., *NPNF*, ser. i, vol. 5, pp. 12–78).

Augustine, *On the Spirit and the Letter* (Eng., *NPNF*, ser. i, vol. 5, pp. 80–115).

Austin, J. L., *How to Do Things with Words* (Oxford: Clarendon Press, 1962).

Badenas, R., *Christ the End of the Law: Romans 10:4 in Pauline Perspective* (Sheffield: JSOT Press, 1985).

Bailey, D. S., *Homosexuality and the Western Tradition* (New York: Longmans Green, 1955).

Baillie, Donald M., *God Was in Christ* (London: Faber & Faber, 1948).

Baird, J. A., *Audience Criticism and the Historical Jesus* (Philadelphia: Westminster Press, 1969).

Barr, James, *Biblical Words for Time* (London: SCM, 1962).

Barr, James, *The Semantics of Biblical Language* (Oxford: Oxford University Press, 1961).

Barrett, C. K., *The Epistle to the Romans* (London: Black, 1957).

Barrett, C. K., *From First Adam to Last: A Study in Pauline Theology* (London: Black, 1962).

Bartchy, S. S., *Mallon Chrēsai: First-Century Slavery* (Missoula: Scholars Press, 1973).

Barth, Karl, *Church Dogmatics* (Eng., 14 vols, Edinburgh: T & T Clark, 1957).

Barth, Karl, *The Epistle to the Romans* (Eng., Oxford: Oxford University Press, 1933).

Basil, *Letters* (Eng., *NPNF*, ser. ii, vol. 8).

Baxter, A. G., and Ziesler, John A., 'Paul and Arboriculture: Romans 11:17–24', *JSNT* 24 (1985), pp. 24–32.

Bell, Richard H., *Provoked to Jealousy: The Origin and Purpose of the Jealousy Motif in Romans 9—11* (Tübingen: Mohr, 1994; WUNT II.63).

Bengel, J. Albert, *Gnomon Novi Testamenti* (Lat., Stuttgart: Steinkopf, 1866); Eng., *New Testament Word Studies* (2 vols, Grand Rapids: Kregel, 1971).

Best, Ernest, 'Paul's Apostolic Authority', *JSNT* 27 (1986), pp. 3–25.

Betz, H. D., *Galatians* (Philadelphia: Fortress Press, 1979; Hermeneia).

Bimson, John J., 'Reconsidering a "Cosmic Fall"', *Science and Christian Belief* 18 (2006), pp. 63–81.

Bjerkelund, Carl J., *Parakalō: Form, Funktion und Sinn der parakalō-Sätze* (Oslo: Universitetsforlaget, 1967).

Black, Matthew, *Romans* (London: Oliphants, 1973; NCB).

Blackwell, Ben C., and others (eds), *Reading Romans in Context: Paul and Second Temple Judaism* (Grand Rapids: Zondervan, 2015).

Boguslawski, Steven, 'Thomas Aquinas' in Greenman, Jeffrey P., and Larsen, Timothy (eds), *Reading Romans through the Centuries*, pp. 81–99.

Boswell, J., *Christianity, Social Tolerance and Homosexuality* (Chicago: University of Chicago Press, 1980).

Boswell, J., *Same-Sex Unions in Pre-Modern Europe* (New York: Villard Books, 1994).

Bovon, François, 'Introduction' to *Exegesis: Problems of Method* (Pittsburgh: Pickwick, 1956).

Bowers, W. P., 'Jewish Communities in Spain in the Time of Paul the Apostle', *JTS* 26 (1975), pp. 395–402.

Bradshaw, Timothy (ed.), *The Way Forward?* (London: Hodder & Stoughton, 1997).

Bray, Gerald, 'Ambrosiaster' in Greenman and Larsen(eds), *Reading Romans through the Centuries*, pp. 21–38.

Bray, Gerald (ed.), *Romans: Ancient Christian Commentary on Scripture*, vol. 6 (Downers Grove, IL: InterVarsity Press, 1998).

Brown, F., Driver, S. R., and Briggs, C. A., *Hebrew and English Lexicon of the Old Testament* (Lafayette, IN: Associated Publishers, 1980).

Bruce, F. F., *The Epistle of Paul to the Romans* (London: Tyndale Press, 1963).

Bruce, F. F., *Paul: Apostle of the Free Spirit* (Exeter: Paternoster Press, 1977).

Brunner, Emil, *Natural Theology* (Eugene, OR: Wipf & Stock, 2002 [1948]).

Bultmann, Rudolf, 'kauchaomai' in Kittel and Friedrich (eds), *TDNT*, vol. 3 (Grand Rapids: Eerdmans, 1965), p. 653.

Bultmann, Rudolf, 'New Testament and Mythology' in Bartsch, Hans-Werner (ed.), *Kerygma and Myth* (Eng., London: SPCK, 1953).

Bultmann, Rudolf, 'The Problem of Hermeneutics' in *Essays Philosophical and Theological* (London: SCM, 1955), pp. 251–2.

Bultmann, Rudolf, 'Reply to Critics' in Kegley, Charles W. (ed.), *The Theology of Rudolf Bultmann* (London: SCM, 1966), pp. 257–87.

Bultmann, Rudolf, *Der Stil der paulinischen Predigt und die kynisch-stoische Diatribe* (Göttingen: Vandenhoeck & Ruprecht, 1910; FRLANT 13).

Bultmann, Rudolf, *Theology of the New Testament*, vol. 1 (London: SCM, 1952).

Byrne, Brendan, SJ, *Romans* (Collegeville: Liturgical Press, 1996 and 2007; Sacra Pagina 6).

Caird, George, B., *Principalities and Powers: A Study in Pauline Theology* (Oxford: Oxford University Press, 1956).

Calvin, John, *Calvin's Bible Commentaries: Romans* (London: Forgotten Books, 2007 [1847]).

Calvin, John, *Commentary on the Book of Genesis* (Edinburgh: Calvin Translation Society, 1847 [1554]).

Calvin, John, *Institutes of the Christian Religion*, ed. H. Beveridge (2 vols, London: James Clarke & Co., 1957).

Carr, A. W., *Angels and Principalities: The Background and Meaning* (Cambridge: Cambridge University Press, 1981; SNTSMS 42; repr. 2005).

Carrington, Philip, *The Primitive Christian Catechism* (Cambridge: Cambridge University Press, 1940).

Chrysostom, *Homilies on the Epistle to the Romans* (Eng., NPNF, ser. i, vol. 11; repr. Grand Rapids: Eerdmans, 1975).

Church of England Doctrine Commission, *We Believe in God* (London: Church House Publishing, 1987).

Church Report, *Some Issues in Human Sexuality: A Guide to the Debate* (London: Church House Publishing, 2003).

Cicero, *Tusculan Disputations* (e-book, Project Gutenberg, 2005).

Clarke, Andrew, *Secular and Christian Leadership in Corinth* (Leiden: Brill, 1993).

Clines, D. J. A., 'The Image of God in Man', *Tyndale Bulletin* 19 (1968), pp. 53–103.

Clough, David L., *On Animals* (London and New York: Bloomsbury, 2012).

Coakley, Sarah, *God, Sexuality, and the Self* (Cambridge: Cambridge University Press, 2013).

Collins, R. F., *First Corinthians* (Collegeville: Glazier/Liturgical Press, 1999; Sacra Pagina 7).

Combes, I. A. H., *The Metaphor of Slavery in the Writings of the Early Church* (Sheffield: Sheffield Academic Press, 1997; JSNTSS 156).

Conzelmann, Hans, '*charis*' in TDNT, vol. 9, pp. 372–402.

Coolman, Holly Taylor, 'Romans 9—11' in Levering, Matthew, and Dauphinais, Michael (eds), *Reading Romans with St. Thomas Aquinas* (Washington, DC: The Catholic University of America, 2012), pp. 101–12.

Crafton, J. A., *The Agency of the Apostle* (Sheffield: Sheffield University Press, 1991).

Cranfield, C. E. B., *A Critical and Exegetical Commentary on the Epistle to the Romans* (2 vols, Edinburgh: T & T Clark, 1975 and 1979; ICC).

Cranfield, C. E. B., 'Romans 9:30—10:4', *Interpretation* 34 (1980), pp. 70–4.

Cranfield, C. E. B., 'Some Observations on Romans 8:19–21' in Banks, Robert (ed.), *Reconciliation and Hope: New Testament Essays on Atonement and Eschatology Presented to L. L. Morris on His 60th Birthday* (Grand Rapids: Eerdmans, 1974), pp. 224–30.

Cullmann, Oscar, *Baptism in the New Testament* (London: SCM, 1950).

Cullmann, Oscar, *Christ and Time* (London: SCM, 1951).

Cullmann, Oscar, *The Christology of the New Testament* (London: SCM, 2nd edn, 1963).

Cullmann, Oscar, *The Earliest Christian Confessions* (London: Lutterworth Press, 1949).

Cullmann, Oscar, *The State in the New Testament* (London: SCM, 1963).

Cyprian, *Treatises*, 12.6 (Eng., *ANF*, vol. 5).

Dahl, M. E., *The Resurrection of the Body* (London: SCM, 1962).

Danker, Frederick, *A Greek-English Lexicon of the New Testament and Other Early Christian Literature* (Chicago and London: University of Chicago Press, 3rd edn, 2000; abbreviated as BDAG).

Davies, W. D., *Paul and Rabbinic Judaism* (London: SPCK, 2nd edn, 1955 [1948]).

Deissmann, Adolf, *Light from the Ancient East* (London: Hodder & Stoughton, 1910).

Deissmann, Adolf, *St Paul: A Study of Religious and Social History* (Ger., 1911; Eng., London: Hodder & Stoughton, 1926).

Delling, Gerhard, '*telos etc.*' in Kittel and Friedrich (eds), *TDNT*, vol. 8 (1972), pp. 49–50.

Demson, David, 'John Calvin' in Greenman and Larsen (eds), *Reading Romans through the Centuries*, pp. 137–48.

Denney, James, *The Death of Christ* (London: Hodder & Stoughton, 1950).

Denney, James, 'Romans' in *Expositor's Greek Testament* (5 vols, Grand Rapids: Eerdmans, [1910]), vol. 2, pp. 645–6.

Dobschütz, E. von, *Der Apostel Paulus* (Halle: Waisenhaus, 1926).

Dodd, C. H., *According to the Scripture* (London: Nisbet, 1952).

Dodd, C. H., *The Apostolic Preaching and Its Developments* (London: Hodder & Stoughton, 1936).

Dodd, C. H., *The Epistle of Paul to the Romans* (London: Hodder & Stoughton, 1932).

Dodd, C. H., *Gospel and Law* (Cambridge: Cambridge University Press, 1951).

Donfried, Karl P., 'Introduction' to Donfried, Karl P. (ed.), *The Romans Debate* (Grand Rapids: Baker Academic, 2nd edn, 1991).

Dunn, J. D. G., *Baptism in the Holy Spirit* (London: SCM, 1970).

Dunn, J. D. G., 'The Formal and Theological Coherence of Romans' in Donfried, Karl P. (ed.), *The Romans Debate* (Grand Rapids: Baker Academic, 2nd edn, 1991), pp. 245–50.

Dunn, J. D. G., 'The New Perspective on Paul: Paul and the Law' in Donfried (ed.), *The Romans Debate*, pp. 299–308.

Dunn, J. D. G., *Paul and the Mosaic Law* (Tübingen: Mohr, 1998; WUNT 89).

Dunn, J. D. G., *Romans 1—8* and *Romans 9—16* (Dallas: Word Books, 1988; WBC 38).

Dunn, J. D. G., *The Theology of Paul the Apostle* (Edinburgh: T & T Clark, 1998).

Eckstein, H.-J., *Der Begriff Syneidesis bei Paulus* (Tübingen: Mohr, 1983).

Edwards, Mark, *John* (Oxford: Blackwell, 1988).

Eichrodt, Walther, *Theology of the Old Testament*, vol. 1 (London: SCM, 1961).

Engels, Donald, *Roman Corinth* (Chicago: University of Chicago Press, 1990).

Epictetus, *Discourses* (2 vols, Harvard and London: Heinemann, 1925; LCL).

Epp, Eldon Jay, *Junia: The First Woman Apostle* (Minneapolis: Fortress Press, 2005).

Estius, William, *D. Pauli Epistolas Commentarii* (3 vols, Lat., Moguntiae: Francisci Kirchhemii, 1858).

Eusebius, *Ecclesiastical History* (Eng., *NPNF*, ser. ii, vol. 1, pp. 1–403).

Evans, Gillian R., *The Language and Logic of the Bible: The Road to the Reformation* (Cambridge: Cambridge University Press, 1991).

Evans, Robert, *Reception History, Tradition, and Biblical Interpretation: Gadamer and Jauss in Current Practice* (London: Bloomsbury/T & T Clark, 2014).

Fee, Gordon, *God's Empowering Presence: The Holy Spirit in the Letters of Paul* (Peabody: Hendrickson, 1994; and Milton Keynes: Paternoster Press, 1995).

Filson, Floyd V., *The New Testament against Its Environment* (London: SCM, 1950).

Fish, Stanley, *Doing What Comes Naturally* (Oxford: Clarendon Press, 1989).

Fish, Stanley, *Is There a Text in This Class? The Authority of Interpretative Communities* (Cambridge, MA: Harvard University Press, 1980).

Fitzmyer, Joseph A., *Romans: A New Translation with Introduction and Commentary* (New York: Doubleday, 1992; AB 33).

Francis, F. O., and Sampley, J. P., *Pauline Parallels* (Minneapolis: Fortress Press, 2nd edn, 1984).

Gadamer, Hans-Georg, *Truth and Method* (London: Sheed & Ward, 2nd edn, 1989).

Gagnon, R., *The Bible and Homosexual Practice* (Nashville: Abingdon Press, 2001).

Gale, Herbert, M., *The Use of Analogy in the Letters of Paul* (Philadelphia: Westminster Press, 1964).

Gardner, Paul D., *The Gifts of God and the Authentication of a Christian* (Lanham, MD: University Press of America, 1994).

Garlington, Don, *Faith, Obedience, and Perseverance: Aspects of Paul's Letter to the Romans* (Eugene, OR: Wipf & Stock, 2009; reprinted from Tübingen: Mohr, 1994; WUNT 79).

George, Timothy, 'Martin Luther' in Greenman and Larsen (eds), *Reading Romans through the Centuries*, pp. 101–19.

Gillespie, Thomas W., *The First Theologians* (Grand Rapids: Eerdmans, 1994).

Godet, F. L., *Commentary on St. Paul's Epistle to the Romans* (New York: Funk & Wagnalls, 1883).

Gooch, Peter D., '"Conscience" in 1 Corinthians 8 and 10', *NTS* 33 (1987), pp. 244–54.

Gooch, Peter D., *Dangerous Food: 1 Corinthians 8—10 in Its Context* (Waterloo, ON: Wilfred Laurier University Press, 1993).

Gooch, Peter D., *Pastoral Knowledge: Philosophical Studies in Paul* (Notre Dame: University of Notre Dame Press, 1987).

Goppelt, L., *Typos* (Grand Rapids: Eerdmans, 1982).

Greenman, Jeffrey P., and Larsen, Timothy (eds), *Reading Romans through the Centuries* (Grand Rapids: Brazos Press, 2005).

Gutiérrez, Gustavo, *A Theology of Liberation* (Eng., New York: Orbis, 1973).

Hall, Christopher A., 'John Chrysostom' in Greenman and Larsen (eds), *Reading Romans through the Centuries*, pp. 47–57.

Hamilton, Neil Q., *The Holy Spirit and Eschatology in Paul* (Edinburgh: Oliver & Boyd, 1957; *SJT* Occasional Paper 6).

Hanson, A. T., *The Paradox of the Cross in the Thought of St. Paul* (Sheffield: Sheffield Academic Press, 1987).

Hanson, R. P. C., *Allegory and Event* (London: SCM, 1959).

Harris, J. R., 'St. Paul's Use of Testimonies in the Epistle to the Romans', *Expositor* 8.17 (1919), pp. 401–14.

Harris, J. R., *Testimonies* (2 vols, Cambridge: Cambridge University Press, 1916–20).

Harrisville, R. A., 'The Concept of Newness in the New Testament', *JBL* 74 (1955), pp. 69–79.

Harrisville, R. A., *The Concept of Newness in the New Testament* (Minneapolis: Augsburg, 1960).

Harvey, Richard, *Mapping Messianic Jewish Theology* (Milton Keynes and Colorado Springs: Paternoster Press, 2009).

Hatch, Edwin, and Redpath, Henry A., *A Concordance to the Septuagint* (2 vols, Athens: Beneficial Book Publishers, 1977; abbreviated as Hatch-Redpath).

Hays, Richard, *Echoes of Scripture in the Letters of Paul* (New Haven: Yale University Press, 1989).

Heidegger, Martin, *Being and Time* (Oxford: Blackwell, 1973 [1962]).

Hepburn, R. W., 'Demythologizing and the Problem of Validity' in Flew, A., and MacIntyre, A. (eds), *New Essays in Philosophical Theology* (London: SCM, 1955).

Hester, James D., *Paul's Concept of Inheritance: A Contribution to the Understanding of Heilsgeschichte* (Edinburgh: Oliver & Boyd, 1968; *SJT* Occasional Paper 14).

Hill, David, *Greek Words and Hebrew Meanings* (Cambridge: Cambridge University Press, 1967; SNTSMS 5).

Hill, David, *New Testament Prophecy* (London: Marshall, 1979).

Hippolytus, *Against Noetus*, 2 (Eng., ANF, vol. 5).

Hofius, O., 'Sühne und Versöhnung: Zum paulinischen Verständnis des Kreuzestodes Jesu' in Maas, E. (ed.), *Versuche, das Leiden und Sterben Jesu zu verstehen* (Munich: Schnell & Steiner, 1983), pp. 25–46.

Hogg, A. G., *Redemption from This World* (Edinburgh: T & T Clark, 1924).

Holland, Tom, *Contours of Pauline Theology* (Fearn: Mentor, 2004).

Holland, Tom, *Romans: The Divine Marriage* (Eugene, OR: Pickwick, 2011).

Holmberg, Bengt, *Paul and Power* (Lund: Gleerup, 1978).

Holub, Robert C., *Reception Theory* (London and New York: Methuen, 1984).

Horsley, R. A., 'Consciousness and Freedom among the Corinthians: 1 Corinthians 8—10', *CBQ* 40 (1978), pp. 574–89.

Hübner, H., *Law in Paul's Thought* (Edinburgh: T & T Clark, 1984).

Humphrey, Edith M., 'Why Bring the Word Down? The Rhetoric of Demonstration and Disclosure in Romans 9:31—10:21' in Soderlund, Sven K., and Wright, N. T. (eds), *Romans and the People of God* (Grand Rapids: Eerdmans, 1999), pp. 129–48.

Hunter, A. M., *Paul and His Predecessors* (London: SCM, 1940; 2nd edn, 1961).

Hurst, L. D., and Wright, N. T. (eds), *The Glory of Christ in the New Testament* (Oxford: Oxford University Press, 1987).

Irenaeus, *Against Heresies* (Eng., *ANF*, vol. 1).

Iser, Wolfgang, *The Act of Reading: A Theory of Aesthetic Response* (Baltimore and London: Johns Hopkins University Press, 1978).

Jauss, Hans Robert, 'Question and Answer: Forms of Dialogic Understanding', *Theory and History of Literature* 68 (1989), pp. 51–94.

Jauss, Hans Robert, *Toward an Aesthetic of Reception* (Minneapolis: University of Minnesota Press, 1982).

Jeffers, James S., 'Jewish and Christian Families in First-Century Rome' in Donfried, K. P., and Richardson, P., *Judaism and Christianity in First-Century Rome* (Grand Rapids: Eerdmans, 1998), pp. 128–50.

Jeremias, Joachim, 'Abba' in *The Central Message of the New Testament* (Eng., London: SCM, 1965), pp. 9–30.

Jervis, L. Ann, *The Purpose of Romans* (Sheffield: JSOT Press, 1991; JSNTSup 55).

Jewett, Robert, *Christian Tolerance: Paul's Message to the Modern Church* (Louisville: Westminster/John Knox Press, 1982; Biblical Perspectives on Modern Issues).

Jewett, Robert, *Paul's Anthropological Terms* (Leiden: Brill, 1971).

Jewett, Robert, *Romans: A Commentary* (Minneapolis: Fortress Press, 2007; Hermeneia).

Johnson, Alan F., *Romans* (2 vols, Chicago: Moody Press, 1974 and 1985).

Jones, O. R., *The Concept of Holiness* (London: Allen & Unwin, and New York: Macmillan, 1961).

Josephus, *Jewish War* (e-book, Project Gutenberg, 2009).

Judge, Edwin A., 'The Conflict of Educational Aims in New Testament Thought', *JCE* 9 (1966), pp. 32–45.

Judge, Edwin, A., 'St Paul and Classical Society', JAC 15 (1972).

Judge, Edwin A., 'The Social Identity of the First Christians: A Question of Method in Religious History', *JRH* 11.2 (1980), pp. 201–17.

Judge, Edwin A., *The Social Pattern of the Christian Groups in the First Century* (London: Tyndale Press, 1960).

Jüngel, Eberhard, *God as the Mystery of the World* (Edinburgh: T & T Clark, 1983).

Kamlah, R., *Die Form der katalogischen Paränese im der Neuen Testament* (Tübingen: Mohr, 1964; WUNT 7).

Käsemann, Ernst, *Commentary on Romans* (London: SCM, 1980).

Käsemann, Ernst, 'Primitive Christian Apocalyptic' in *New Testament Questions of Today* (London: SCM, 1969).

Kevan, Ernest F., *The Grace of Law: A Study in Puritan Theology* (Grand Rapids: Baker, 2003 [1965]).

Kim, Seyoon, *Paul and the New Perspective* (Grand Rapids: Eerdmans, 2002).

Knox, John, 'The Epistle to the Romans', *Interpreter's Bible* (*IB*) (Nashville: Abingdon Press, 1954), vol. 9, pp. 353–668.

Knox, W. L., *St Paul and the Church of the Gentiles* (Cambridge: Cambridge University Press, 1939).

Knox, W. L. *Some Hellenistic Elements in Primitive Christianity* (London: Oxford University Press and British Academy, 1944).

Kümmel, Werner G., *Introduction to the New Testament* (London: SCM, 1966).

Kuss, Otto, *Der Römerbrief übersetzt und erklärt* (3 vols, Regensburg: Pustet, 1957–78).

Lactantius, *Constitutions of the Holy Apostles* (Eng., *ANF*, vol. 7, pp. 385–508).

Lampe, G. W. H., *The Seal of the Spirit* (New York and London: Longmans Green, 1951).

Lampe, Peter, *Die stadtrömischen Christen in den ersten beiden Jahrhunderten* (Tübingen: Mohr, 1987; WUNT II.18); Eng., *From Paul to Valentinus: Christians at Rome in the First Two Centuries* (Minneapolis: Fortress Press, 2003).

Leenhardt, Franz J., *The Epistle to the Romans* (London: Lutterworth Press, 1961).

Lendon, J. E., *Empire of Honour: The Art of Government in the Roman World* (Oxford: Clarendon Press, 1997).

Leon, H. J. *The Jews of Ancient Rome* (Peabody: Hendrickson, 1995).

Levenson, Jon Douglas, *Creation and the Persistence of Evil* (Princeton: Princeton University Press, 1994).

Levison, J. R., *Portraits of Adam in Early Judaism: From Sirach to 2 Baruch* (Sheffield: JSOT Press, 1998).

Levy, I. C., Krey, P. D. W., and Ryan, T., *The Bible in Medieval Tradition: The Letter to the Romans* (Grand Rapids: Eerdmans, 2013).

Lewis, C. S., *The Problem of Pain* (London: Bles, 1940).

Lieu, Judith, *Marcion and the Making of Heretics* (Cambridge: Cambridge University Press, 2015).

Lightfoot, J. B., 'Excursus on "Caesar's Household"' in *Saint Paul's Epistle to the Philippians* (New York: Macmillan, 3rd edn, 1878, repr. 1903), pp. 171–8.

Lindars, Barnabas, *New Testament Apologetic* (Philadelphia: Westminster Press, 1961).

Livy, *Ab Urbe Condita* (Lat. and Eng., Cambridge: Loeb Classical Library, 1919 and repr.).

Lohfink, N., *'cherem'* in Botterweck, G. J., and Ringgren, H. (eds), *Theological Dictionary of the Old Testament* (*TDOT*) (15 vols, Grand Rapids: Eerdmans, 1974–), vol. 5, pp. 180–99.

Lossky, Vladimir, *The Image and Likeness of God* (London: Mowbray, 1974).

Lubac, Henri de, *Medieval Exegesis, vol. 1: The Four Senses of Scripture* (Grand Rapids: Eerdmans, 2000).

Luther, Martin, *Commentary on Romans* (Grand Rapids: Kregel, 1954; reprinted 1976).

Luther, Martin, *Luther: Lectures on Romans* (Philadelphia: Westminster Press, 1956; LCC).

Luther, Martin, *Luther's Works* (55 vols, St Louis and Philadelphia: Concordia and Fortress Press, 1955–2015).

Luther, Martin, *Martin Luthers Werke*, Weimar edition (57 vols, Weimar, 1883–1929 [1527]), vol. 24. (Cf. Eng., *Luther's Works*, American edition (55 vols, St Louis and Philadelphia: Concordia and Fortress Press, 1955–2015.)

Luther, Martin, *Preface to the Epistle to the Romans* (Nashville: Discipleship Resources, 1977).

Luz, Ulrich, *Studies in Matthew* (Grand Rapids: Eerdmans, 2005).

Macchia, Frank D., *Baptized in the Spirit* (Grand Rapids: Zondervan, 2006).

Macchia, Frank D., 'Sighs Too Deep for Words: Toward a Theology of Glossolalia', *JPT* (1992), pp. 47–73.

McGrath, Alister E., *Iustitia Dei: A History of the Christian Doctrine of Justification* (2 vols, Cambridge: Cambridge University Press, 1986).

McKnight, S., *A Light to the Gentiles* (Minneapolis: Fortress Press, 1991).

McLaughlin, Ryan Patrick, *Christian Theology and the Status of Animals* (New York: Macmillan/Palgrave, 2014).

Macquarrie, John, *An Existentialist Theology: A Comparison of Heidegger and Bultmann* (London: SCM, 1955).

Macquarrie, John, *The Scope of Demythologizing: Bultmann and His Critics* (London: SCM, 1960).

Malina, B. J., *The New Testament World: Insights from Cultural Anthropology* (Atlanta: John Knox Press, 1981).

Manson, T.W., 'St Paul's Letter to the Romans – and Others' in Donfried, Karl P. (ed.), *The Romans Debate* (Grand Rapids: Baker Academic, 2nd edn, 1991), pp. 3–15.

Marcel, Pierre C., *The Biblical Doctrine of Infant Baptism* (London: James Clarke & Co., 1953).

Marsh, John, *The Fullness of Time* (London: Nisbet, 1952).

Martin, Dale B., *The Corinthian Body* (New Haven: Yale University Press, 1995).

Martin, Dale B., *Slavery as Salvation* (New Haven: Yale University Press, 1990).

Martin, Ralph P., *Reconciliation: A Study of Paul's Theology* (London: Marshall, and Atlanta: John Knox Press, 1981).

Meeks, Wayne A., *The Writings of St Paul* (New York: Norton, 1972).

Bibliography

Metzger, Bruce, *A Textual Commentary on the Greek New Testament* (New York: United Bible Societies, 2nd edn, 1994).

Michel, O., *Der Brief an die Römer* (Göttingen: Vandenhoeck & Ruprecht, 4th edn, 1966).

Migne, J.-P. (ed.), Patrologia Graeca (abbreviated as Migne, PG).

Migne, J.-P. (ed.), Patrologia Latina (abbreviated as Migne, PL).

Milton, John, *Paradise Lost* (London: Penguin, 2000).

Minear, Paul, *The Obedience of Faith: The Purposes of Paul in the Epistle to the Romans* (London: SCM, 1971; SBT).

Miranda, José Porfirio, *Marx and the Bible: A Critique of the Philosophy of Oppression* (Maryknoll, NY: Orbis, 1974, and London: SCM, 1977).

Mitchell, Margaret M., *Paul and the Rhetoric of Reconciliation* (Tübingen: Mohr, 1992).

Moberly, R. W. L., *The Theology of the Book of Genesis* (Cambridge: Cambridge University Press, 2009).

Moltmann, Jürgen, *The Coming of God* (London: SCM, 1996).

Moltmann, Jürgen, *God in Creation* (London: SCM, 1985).

Moltmann, Jürgen, *The Trinity and the Kingdom of God* (London: SCM, 1981).

Moo, Douglas J., *The Epistle to the Romans* (Grand Rapids: Eerdmans, 1996; NICNT).

Moores, John D., *Wrestling with Rationality in Paul: Romans 1—8 in a New Perspective* (Cambridge: Cambridge University Press, 1995; SNTSMS 82).

Morgan, Robert, *Romans* (Sheffield: Sheffield Academic Press, 1995).

Morris, Leon, *The Apostolic Preaching of the Cross* (London: Tyndale Press, 1955).

Morris, Leon, 'The Theme of Romans' in Gasque, W. Ward, and Martin, Ralph P. (eds), *Apostolic History and the Gospel: Presented to F. F. Bruce* (Exeter: Paternoster Press, 1970), pp. 249–63.

Moule, C. F. D., 'The Judgment Theme in the Sacraments' in Davies, W. D., and Daube, E. (eds), *The Background to the New Testament and Its Eschatology: In Honour of C. H. Dodd* (Cambridge: Cambridge University Press, 1956).

Moule, C. F. D., 'Obligation in the Ethics of Paul' in *Essays in New Testament Interpretation* (Cambridge: Cambridge University Press, 1982), pp. 261–77; and in Farmer, W. R., Moule, C. F. D., and Niebuhr, R. R., *Christian History and Interpretation: Studies Presented to John Knox* (Cambridge: Cambridge University Press, 1967), pp. 389–406.

Moulton, James H., and Milligan, George, *The Vocabulary of the Greek Testament* (London: Hodder & Stoughton, 1952 [1930]).

Moxon, R. A., *The Doctrine of Sin* (London: Allen & Unwin, 1922).

Müller, Ulrich B., *Prophetie und Predigt im Neuen Testament* (Gütersloh: Mohr, 1975).

Munck, Johannes, *Paul and the Salvation of Mankind* (London: SCM, 1959).

Murphy-O'Connor, Jerome, *Paul: A Critical Life* (Oxford: Oxford University Press, 1997).

Murphy-O'Connor, Jerome, *St. Paul's Corinth* (Wilmington: Glazier, 1983).

Murray, John, *The Epistle to the Romans* (Grand Rapids: Eerdmans, 1997).

Neufeld, Vernon H., *The Earliest Christian Confessions* (Leiden: Brill, and Grand Rapids: Eerdmans, 1963).

Nickel, Keith F., *The Collection: A Study of Paul's Strategy* (London: SCM, 1966).

Nida, E. A., 'The Implications of Contemporary Linguistics for Biblical Scholarship', *JBL* 91 (1972), pp. 73–89.

Niebuhr, Reinhold, *The Nature and Destiny of Man* (2 vols, London: Nisbet, 1941).

Novatian, *Treatise on the Trinity* (Eng., *ANF*, vol. 5).

Nygren, Anders, *Agapē and Eros* (London: SPCK, 1957 [1932]).

Nygren, Anders, *Commentary on Romans* (London: SCM, 1952).

O'Brien, Peter T., *Introductory Thanksgiving to the Letters of Paul* (Leiden: Brill, 1977; NovTSup 49).

O'Donovan, Oliver, *The Desire of Nations: Rediscovering the Roots of Political Theology* (Cambridge: Cambridge University Press, 1996).

O'Donovan, Oliver, *The Ways of Judgment* (Grand Rapids: Eerdmans, 2005).

Ollrog, W.-H., *Paulus und seine Mitarbeiter* (Neukirchen: Neukirchener Verlag, 1979).

Origen, *Against Celsus* (Eng., *ANF*, vol. 4, pp. 395–669).

Origen, *De Principiis* (Eng., *ANF*, vol. 4, pp. 239–584).

Pannenberg, Wolfhart, *Basic Questions in Theology*, vol. 2 (London: SCM, 1971).

Pannenberg, Wolfhart, *Systematic Theology* (3 vols, Edinburgh: T & T Clark, and Grand Rapids: Eerdmans, 1991–8).

Parker, T. H. L., *Calvin's New Testament Commentaries* (Louisville: Westminster/ John Knox Press, 1993).

Parris, David P., *Reception Theory and Biblical Hermeneutics* (Eugene, OR: Pickwick, 2009).

Patte, Daniel, *Paul's Faith and the Power of the Gospel: A Structural Introduction to the Pauline Letters* (Philadelphia: Fortress Press, 1983).

Pfitzner, Victor C., *Paul and the Agōn Motif: Traditional Athletic Imagery in the Pauline Literature* (Leiden: Brill, 1967).

Philo, *Works*, ed. F. H. Colson and G. H. Whitaker (Gk and Eng., 10 vols, Cambridge, MA: Harvard University Press, 1929; Loeb Library).

Pierce, C. A., *Conscience in the New Testament* (London: SCM, 1955).

Plato, *Republic* (New Haven: Yale University Press, 2005).

Plato, *Timaeus* (Cambridge, MA: Hackett, 2000).

Plutarch, *Moralia* (London: Bell, 1898).

Pogoloff, Stephen, *Logos and Sophia: The Rhetorical Situation in 1 Corinthians* (Atlanta: Scholars Press, 1992; SBLDS 134).

Polkinghorne, John, *Scientists as Theologians* (London: SPCK, 1996).

Rad, Gerhard von, *Old Testament Theology*, vol. 1 (Edinburgh: Oliver & Boyd, 1962).

Räisänen, Heikki, *Jesus, Paul, and the Torah* (Sheffield: Sheffield Academic Press, 1992).

Räisänen, Heikki, *Paul and the Law* (Tübingen: Mohr, 1983; WUNT 29).

Ramsay, William, *Paul and Other Studies* (New York: Armstrong, 1906).

Ramsey, Ian T., *Models for Divine Activity* (London: SCM, 1973).

Ramsey, Ian T., *Religious Language: An Empirical Placing of Theological Phrases* (London: SCM, 1957).

Richardson, Alan, *Introduction to the Theology of the New Testament* (London: SCM, 1958).

Robertson, A. T., *Word Pictures in the New Testament, vol. 4: Romans* (New York: R. Smith, 1931).

Robinson, J. A. T, *The Body: A Study in Pauline Theology* (London: SCM, 1952; SBT 5).

Robinson, J. A. T., *The Human Face of God* (London: SCM, 1973).

Robinson, J. A. T., *Wrestling with Romans* (London: SCM, 1979).

Robinson, J. M., 'Hermeneutic since Barth' in Robinson, J. M., and Cobb, J. B. (eds), *New Frontiers in Theology, vol. 2: The New Hermeneutic* (New York: Harper & Row, 1964).

Rowland, Christopher, and Kovacs, Judith, *Revelation* (Oxford: Blackwell, 2004).

Rush, Ormond, *The Reception of Doctrine* (Rome: Pontifical Gregorian University, 1996).

Sanday, William, and Headlam, Arthur C., *Critical and Exegetical Commentary on the Epistle to the Romans* (Edinburgh: T & T Clark, 1902; ICC).

Sanders, E. P., *Jesus and Judaism* (London: SCM, 1985).

Sanders, E. P., *Paul and Palestinian Judaism* (London: SCM, 1977).

Sanders, E. P., *Paul, the Law, and the Jewish People* (Philadelphia: Fortress Press, 1983).

Schlier, Heinrich, *Principalities and Powers in the New Testament* (New York: Herder, 1961).

Schnackenburg, Rudolf, *Baptism in the Thought of St. Paul* (Oxford: Blackwell, 1964).

Schoeps, H. J., *Paul: A Theology of the Apostle in the Light of Jewish History* (London: Lutterworth Press, 1961).

Schubert, Paul, *Form and Function of the Pauline Thanksgivings* (Berlin: Töpelmann, 1939).

Schweitzer, Albert, *The Mysticism of Paul the Apostle* (London: Black, 1931).

Scott, C. Anderson, *Christianity According to St. Paul* (Cambridge: Cambridge University Press, 1927).

Scroggs, Robin, *The Last Adam* (Oxford: Blackwell, 1966).

Scroggs, Robin, *The New Testament and Homosexuality* (Philadelphia: Fortress Press, 1983).

Seder Olam Rabbah, *Seder Olam: A Rabbinic View of Biblical Chronology* (London: Jason Aroson, 1998).

Selwyn, E. G., *The First Epistle of St Peter* (London: Macmillan, 1947).

Siker, Jeffrey S., *Homosexuality in the Church: Both Sides of the Debate* (Louisville: John Knox Press, 1994).

Smith, C. Ryder, *The Bible Doctrine of Salvation* (London: Epworth Press, 1941).

Speiser, E. A., *Genesis* (New York: Doubleday, 1964).

Spicq, C., *Agapē in the New Testament* (3 vols, London: Herder, 1963).

Stählin, G. (with O. Grether), 'orgē, opgizomai' in Kittel and Friedrich (eds), *TDNT*, vol. 5, pp. 382–447.

Stählin, G., 'phileō' in Kittel and Friedrich (eds), *TDNT*, vol. 9 (1974), pp. 119–27.

Stanley, Christopher D., *Paul and the Language of Scripture: Citation Technique in the Pauline Epistles and Contemporary Literature* (Cambridge: Cambridge University Press, 1992; SNTSMS 74).

Stauffer, E., '*agape*' in Kittel and Friedrich (eds), *TDNT*, vol. 1, pp. 94–5.

Stendahl, Krister, 'The Apostle Paul and the Introspective Conscience of the West', Paper to the American Psychological Association in September 1961, in *HTR* 56 (1963), pp. 199–215; reprinted in Stendahl, *Paul among the Jews and Gentiles* (London: SCM, 1976).

Stoeger, W. R., 'Scientific Accounts of Ultimate Catastrophes in Our Life-bearing Universe' in Polkinghorne, John, and Welker, M. (eds), *The End of the World and the Ends of God* (Harrisburg, PA: Trinity Press International, 2000).

Stowers, Stanley K., *The Diatribe and Paul's Letter to the Romans* (Chico: Scholars Press, 1981; SBLDS 57).

Strack, Hermann L., and Billerbeck, Paul, *Kommentar zum Neuen Testament aus Talmud und Midrasch* (3 vols, Munich: Beck, 1969).

Straub, Werner, *Die Bildersprache des Apostels Paulus* (Tübingen: Mohr, 1937).

Sturrock, John (ed.), *Structuralism and Since: From Lévi-Strauss to Derrida* (Oxford: Oxford University Press, 1979).

Suggs, Jack, '"The Word Is Near You": Romans 10:6–10' in Farmer, W. R., Moule, C. F. D., and Niebuhr, R. R., *Christian History and Interpretation* (Cambridge: Cambridge University Press, 1967), pp. 289–312.

Tacitus, *Annals* (Lat., London: Methuen, 1939).

Tannehill, Robert C., *Dying and Rising with Christ: A Study in Pauline Theology* (Berlin: Töpelmann, 1967; BZNW 32).

Tertullian, *Against Praxeas*, 13 (Eng., ANF, vol. 2).

Tertullian, *The Resurrection of the Flesh* (Eng., ANF, vol. 3).

Theissen, Gerd, *Psychological Aspects of Pauline Theology* (Eng., Edinburgh: T & T Clark, 1987).

Theissen, Gerd, *The Social Setting of Pauline Christianity: Essays on Corinth* (Philadelphia: Fortress Press, 1982).

Thielicke, Helmut, *Theological Ethics, vol. 2: Politics* (Grand Rapids: Eerdmans, 1979).

Thielman, F., *Paul and the Law: A Contextual Approach* (Downers Grove, IL: InterVarsity Press, 1994).

Thiselton, Anthony C., *1 and 2 Thessalonians through the Centuries* (Oxford: Wiley-Blackwell, 2011).

Thiselton, Anthony C., *1 Corinthians: A Shorter Exegetical and Pastoral Commentary* (Grand Rapids: Eerdmans, 2006).

Thiselton, Anthony C., *The First Epistle to the Corinthians: A Commentary on the Greek Text* (Grand Rapids: Eerdmans, and Carlisle: Paternoster Press, 2000; NIGTC).

Thiselton, Anthony C., *Hermeneutics* (Grand Rapids: Eerdmans, 2009).

Thiselton, Anthony C., *The Holy Spirit: In Biblical Teaching, through the Centuries, and Today* (Grand Rapids: Eerdmans, and London: SPCK, 2013).

Thiselton, Anthony C., *The Living Paul: An Introduction* (London: SPCK, 2009).

Thiselton, Anthony C., 'The Paradigm of Biblical Promise as Trustworthy, Temporal, Transformative Speech-acts' in Lundin, R., Walhout, C., and Thiselton, A. C. (eds), *The Promise of Hermeneutics* (Grand Rapids: Eerdmans, 1999), pp. 223–40.

Thiselton, Anthony C., 'Reception Theory, Jauss and the Formative Power of Scripture', *SJT* 65 (2012), pp. 289–308.

Thiselton, Anthony C., *Systematic Theology* (Grand Rapids: Eerdmans, and London: SPCK, 2015).

Thiselton, Anthony C., *The Two Horizons* (Exeter: Paternoster Press, and Grand Rapids: Eerdmans, 1980).

Thornton, Lionel S., *The Common Life in the Body of Christ* (London: Dacre Press, 3rd edn, 1950).

Thrall, Margaret, 'The Pauline Use of *Suneidēsis*' *NTS* 14 (1967), pp. 118–25.

Tyconius, *Book of Rules* (Eng., Notre Dame: University of Notre Dame Press, 1988).

Tyndale, William, 'Pathway into the Holy Scriptures' in *Doctrinal Treatises* (Cambridge: Parkers Society, 1848).

Unnik, W. C. van, *Tarsus or Jerusalem* (London: Epworth Press, 1962).

Vanstone, W. H., *The Stature of Waiting* (New York: Morehouse Publishing, 1982 and 2006; and London: DLT, 2004).

Vidu, Adonis, *Atonement, Law and Justice* (Grand Rapids: Baker Academic, 2014).

Vögtle, A., *Die Tugend- und Lasterkataloge im Neuen Testament* (Münster: Aschendorff, 1936).

Volf, Miroslav, *Free of Charge* (Grand Rapids: Zondervan, 2005).

Vriezen, T. C., *Outline of Old Testament Theology* (Oxford: Blackwell, 1962).

Wagner, Günther, *Pauline Baptism and the Pagan Mysteries: The Problem of the Pauline Doctrine of Baptism in Romans VI:1–11, in the Light of Its Religio-Historical 'Parallels'* (Edinburgh: Oliver & Boyd, 1967).

Watson, Duane F., and Hauser, Alan J., *Rhetorical Criticism and the Bible* (Leiden: Brill, 1994; BI 4).

Watson, Francis, *Paul, Judaism, and the Gentiles* (Cambridge: Cambridge University Press, 1986; SNTSMS 56).

Webster, John, *Holiness* (London: SCM, and Grand Rapids: Eerdmans, 2003).

Weiss, Johannes, *Earliest Christianity* (2 vols, New York: Harper, 1959 [1937]).

Welborn, L. L., *Paul, the Fool of Christ: A Study of 1 Corinthians 1—4 in the Comic Philosophical Tradition* (London and New York: T & T Clark International/Continuum, 2005).

Welborn, L. L., *Politics and Rhetoric in the Corinthian Epistles* (Macon, GA: Mercer University Press, 1997).

Wenham, Gordon J., *Genesis 1—15* (Waco: Nelson/Word, 1987).

Wennberg, Robert N., *God, Humans, and Animals* (Grand Rapids: Eerdmans, 2003).

Wesley, John, *The Works of John Wesley* (Jackson edition, 14 vols, 3rd edn, 1831; reprinted by the Wesleyan Conference Office, London, 1872).

Whiteley, D. E. H., *The Theology of St. Paul* (Oxford: Blackwell, 1970).

Bibliography

Wibbing, S., *Die Tugend- und Lasterkataloge im Neuen Testament und ihre Traditionsgeschichte* (Berlin: Töpelmann, 1959; BZNW 25).

Wiedemann, T. E. J., *Greek and Roman Slavery* (London: Groom Helm, 1981).

Wiedemann, T. E. J., *Slavery: Greece and Rome* (Oxford: Oxford University Press, 1997).

Wikenhauser, Alfred, *Pauline Mysticism* (New York: Herder, 1961).

Wilckens, Ulrich, *Der Brief an die Römer* (3 vols, Zurich: Benzinger, 1978–82; EKKNT).

Williams, G. H. (ed.), *Spiritual and Anabaptist Writers* (London: SCM, 1957; LCC 25).

Wimsatt, W. K., and Beardsley, M., 'The Intentional Fallacy' in Wimsatt, William K., *The Verbal Icon: Studies in the Meaning of Poetry* (New York: Noonday Press, 1966 [1954]).

Wink, Walther, *Naming the Powers, Unmasking the Powers* and *Engaging the Powers* (3 vols, Augsburg: Fortress Press, 1984, 1986 and 1992).

Winter, Bruce, 'Roman Law and Society in Romans 12—16' in P. Oakes (ed.), *Rome in the Bible and Early Church* (Grand Rapids: Baker, 2002), pp. 67–102.

Wiseman, James, 'Corinth and Rome' in *ANRW*, p. 528.

Wittgenstein, Ludwig, *Zettel* (Ger. and Eng., Oxford: Blackwell, 1967).

Wolff, Hans W. *Anthropology of the Old Testament* (London: SCM, 1974).

Wright, David F., 'Homosexuality', *EQ* 61 (1989), pp. 291–300.

Wright, N. T., *The Climax of the Covenant: Christ and the Law in Pauline Theology* (Edinburgh: T & T Clark; and Minneapolis: Fortress Press, 1991).

Wright, N. T., *The Messiah and the People of God* (Oxford: Oxford University Press, 1980).

Wright, N. T., 'The New Inheritance According to Paul', *The Bible Review* 14.3 (1998).

Wright, N. T., *Paul and the Faithfulness of God* (London: SPCK, 2013).

Wright, N. T., *Paul: Fresh Perspectives* (London: SPCK, 2005).

Wright, N. T., 'Romans' in the *New Interpreter's Bible* (*NIB*) (Nashville: Abingdon Press, 2002), vol. 10, pp. 393–770.

Wright, N. T., *Surprised by Hope* (London: SPCK, 2002).

Wright, Tom, *What St. Paul Really Said* (Oxford: Lion, 1997).

Wuellner, W., 'Paul's Rhetoric of Argumentation in Romans' in Donfried, Karl P. (ed.), *The Romans Debate* (Grand Rapids: Baker Academic, 2nd edn, 1991), pp. 128–46.

Yinger, Kent L., *Paul, Judaism, and Judgment According to Deeds* (Cambridge: Cambridge University Press, 1999; SNTSMS 105).

Yoder, John, *The Politics of Jesus* (Grand Rapids: Eerdmans, 2nd edn, 1994).

Young, N. H., '*hilaskesthai*' and Related Words in the New Testament', *EQ* 55 (1983), pp. 169–76.

Ziesler, John, *The Meaning of Righteousness in Paul* (Cambridge: Cambridge University Press, 1972).

Ziesler, John, *Paul's Letter to the Romans* (London: SCM, 1989 and 1990).

Zizioulas, John, *Being as Communion: Studies in Personhood and the Church* (New York: St Vladimir's Seminary Press, 1985).

Zwiep, Arie W., *Christ, the Spirit, and the Community of God* (Tübingen: Mohr, 2010; WUNT II.293).

Index of biblical and patristic references

Index of modern authors

Index of modern authors

Index of modern authors

Index of subjects

Printed and bound by CPI Group (UK) Ltd, Croydon, CR0 4YY

13/04/2025

14656472-0005